SOME DREAMS DIE
UTAH'S GHOST TOWNS AND LOST TREASURES

BY GEORGE A. THOMPSON

Dream Garden Press
Great Salt Lake City

For Mom and Dad
They Are The Real Treasure!

———————————

DREAM GARDEN PRESS
1982

Front cover photograph: Grafton, Utah by DENNIS HAYNES

Back cover: Wolfe Cabin, Arches National Park by JOHN TELFORD

CONTENTS

Introduction

Ghost Town! What exciting images are conjured up when those words are heard. One pictures deserted streets with wind-blown tumbleweeds rolling aimlessly between rows of empty buildings, weathered cabins sagging wearily in the shadow of long silent mills, crumbling adobe walls, rotting wooden sidewalks, and chill winds whistling mournfully among nameless graves. Old-timers may recall sawdust floored saloons, gold coins clinking across faro tables and great foamy mugs of 5¢ beer.

But few ghost towns of today resemble that portrayal. Often little is left but broken foundations, piles of rubble, and everywhere bits and pieces of sun-purpled glass, the amethysts of the desert. What could be found today might be unrecoverable tomorrow, because the towns change from day to day. Many old settlements have vanished as if by the wave of a magician's wand, leaving only memories to prove they existed.

As fragile as memories are the stories of the people who lived in the deserted towns. There are many tales of hard working farmers who, after losing their savings in bank failures, forever after hid their money in post-hole banks, secret caches hidden under loose fenceposts. Upon their unexpected deaths the locations of their caches were lost, and today's treasure tale was born.

Outlaws, and Utah had its share, often buried loot from bank robberies and train holdups, and were then killed by pursuing posses, or sent to prison for life thus leaving their buried hoardes for today's treasure hunter. Even more intriguing are the stories of lost gold placers in distant desert places and silver ledges hidden among high snow covered peaks. There always seem to be enough facts to prove they exist, but not enough to locate them. Many lost mine stories originated in the days when Spanish miners explored the deserts and mountains of Utah. Contrary to what some historians maintain, Spanish history in Utah precedes the Dominguez-Escalante expeditions of 1776 by more than one hundred years.

Most treasure tales and lost mine stories are substantially true. Grandpa did bury his money somewhere out behind the barn and Uncle Al did have a mine somewhere. The older members of the family can remember Grandpa getting gold coins from his cache to pay the mortgage, and others saw the shiny silver ore Uncle Al dug at his mine. But after Grandpa died, no one knew where his cache was located, and Uncle Al never got around to telling anyone where his mine was before an outlaw killed him. Those kinds of stories have become today's treasure tales.

Many of today's ghost towns were prosperous mining camps, boom towns built upon silver and gold. But they might as well have been built upon sand, for they bloomed briefly, then faded and died. Sometimes they were deserted overnight when the miners left to answer the siren call of rich strikes elsewhere. More often they died when their veins pinched out, or when underground water flooded their shafts. Today their tired old buildings lean drunkenly against each other for support. Lone coyotes watch from dens on pock-marked mountainsides above, waiting for the miners' return, but in vain. The miner is gone forever, and the few fragile remnants of the town he built are disappearing as well.

The Mormons settled many of the places that have since become ghost towns. From the founding of Salt Lake City in 1847 until the mining boom of the 1870's, there was hardly a town in Utah that was not founded by the Saints. Crop failures caused by droughts, frosts in high mountain valleys, and floods along the river bottoms were three of the plagues visited upon the Saints.

A number of settlements had to be abandoned during the Walker and Blackhawk wars. It was during those troubled days that many pioneer forts were built to protect the citizenry. Small villages often grew up around those forts, but usually lasted only as long as they were needed. When the Indian troubles ended, they were often abandoned. Time and the seasons have done their work so well that at many of them there is hardly an "X" to mark their spots.

The building of the trans-continental railroad spawned a whole new kind of town in Utah. At irregular intervals along the railroad's right of way, depending upon the terrain the track layers encountered, as well as the availability of water and timber, hastily erected tent towns would spring up. Some disappeared and were forgotten as soon as the railhead moved on, while others grew into substantial cities, with schools, churches, well built homes and fine business buildings.

Forgotten way stations from the days of the Overland Stage and the Pony Express, still dot the quiet places of Utah's desert country. From the rocky canyons of the Deep Creek Range in the west, eastward across the glaring white salt deserts to the Wasatch Mountains, there winds a long line of lonely stage stations and Pony Express stops. Historical markers have been placed at some of them, but at others only crumbling rock walls remain. No one alive today can remember when stage coaches and pony riders followed those lonely trails stopping at places like Needle Rock, Dixie, and Traveler's Rest. It has been a long time since station keepers met dusty coaches as they rolled to a stop, or waved greetings to an express rider as he raced by. These places are the ghost towns of today, and are excellent locations for treasure hunters and relic seekers. Some look as if their occupants have been away for only a short time, while others have returned to their primordial state. No matter its size or how long its life, each should be remembered, if only as a place where people lived and died.

Utah's ghost towns are found from the vermillion cliffs and canyonlands of Dixie and San Juan in the south to the gray salt deserts and snow-capped peaks of the West Desert and the Wasatch in the north. Many can be reached in the family auto, but some require the ghost-towner to get out and hike, anywhere from a few minutes to a few miles, and several are beyond the end of any easy trail.

In the following pages those boom and bust has-been towns come to life once more, with stories of the characters who lived in them and the wild times they enjoyed. Included in these stories are hundreds of clues to finding lost treasure. Some lead only to a few coins hidden by a hermit, while others point the way to the riches of King Midas. There are stories of outlaw caches, and mines that filled the coffers of Spain with gold. So come along with me as we travel, once more, those Utah Ghost Town Trails.

Preface

Ghost-towners, relic hunters, prospectors and others who follow the back trails of Utah often rely on maps which are a century or more old. Although they are of great value in locating long forgotten settlements and lost sites, they do present a problem. All too often they use place names which are unknown today, and which careful research fails to identify. Often they are places that no longer exist; sometimes they are the cities and towns of today, identified by names which are no longer used. Some present-day communities have been known by three or four different names, and other widely separated towns have shared the same name. To spare the reader needless hours of research, a list of cities and towns whose names have been changed appears in Appendix #1.

A list of extinct counties has also been included, in Appendix #2, for those students of Utah history confused by references to counties which no longer exist. During the first two decades after the Utah Territory was settled, three of its counties were ceded to Nevada and one to Wyoming, while six others were absorbed by the counties which adjoined them. The names of three more were changed several years after they were established. The settlements described in this book lie within the present borders of Utah. To aid the reader in research, and to help him find the places he is looking for, these counties are listed by their original names and locations, as well as by their present designations.

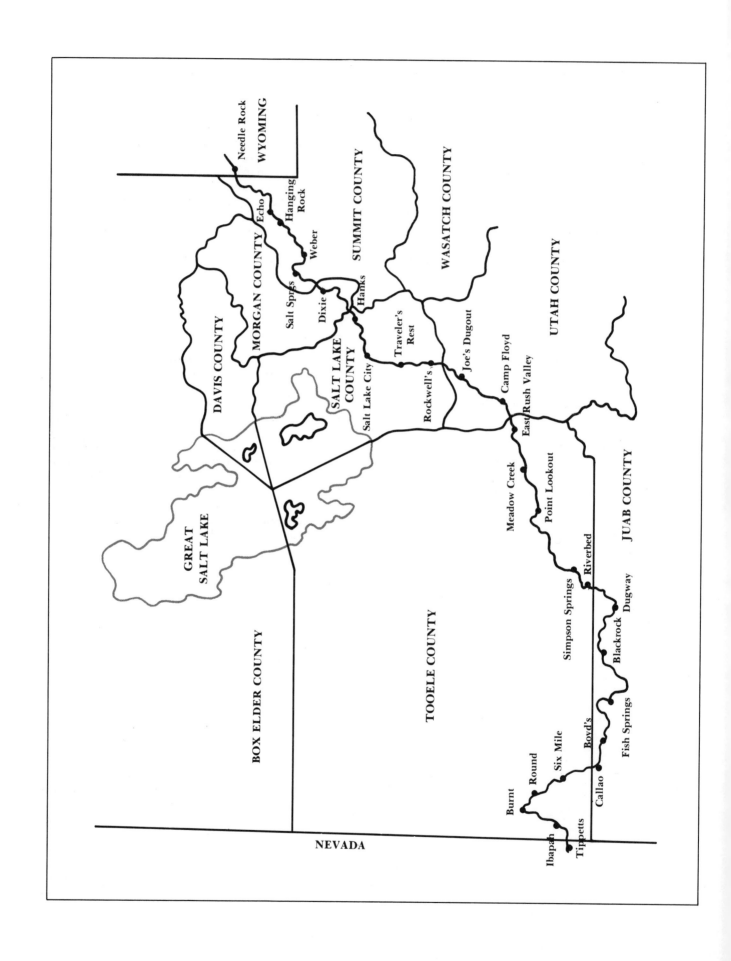

CHAPTER ONE

ALONG THE OVERLAND TRAIL

To follow the trail of the Overland Stage through Utah today is to follow the trail of pony tracks made more than a century ago. No sooner were the Mormon Pioneers settled in the valley of the Great Salt Lake than problems of communication and mail delivery began. At first, the settlers were more interested in keeping in touch with their friends in the east than they were with people farther west. As early as 1850 a mail contract was awarded to Col. Samuel Woodson to carry the mail from Independence, Missouri to Salt Lake City. Under Woodson's contract, mail delivery was slow and uncertain, and after several years of poor service, his contract was cancelled. In 1854 the firm of Magraw & Hockaday was awarded a contract, but it was terminated before their service began.

In 1856 a little known mail service was started by the Mormon Church. Named the Brigham Young Express & Carrying Company, but almost always called the "Y-X Company", it was a fore-runner of both the Overland Stage and the Pony Express. The Y-X Company was planned as, "A swift pony express to carry the mail" and would establish, "A coach line for passengers." Way stations, which were actually settlements with farms and business buildings, were established at regular intervals from Salt Lake City to Independence, Missouri. Most of them were later used by the Overland Stage and the Pony Express. With the outbreak of the Utah War in August, 1858, the Y-X Company's contract was cancelled, making the tremendous outlay of labor and financial backing by the Mormon Church a complete loss.

Later in 1858 a contract was granted to the firm of Hockaday & Leggett. That company improved the stations already established by the Y-X Company and outfitted them with supplies, livestock and express riders, but went bankrupt before it could begin service. It was purchased lock, stock and barrel by the firm of Russell, Majors & Waddell, the company which was to become famous for its short lived Pony Express.

Mail service from Salt Lake City to the west coast began as early as May, 1851 when Absalom Woodward and Major George Chorpenning began operations. Major Chorpenning was the famous trail blazer who had pioneered the Chorpenning Trail, the route used by the Overland Stage, Pony Express and Overland Telegraph Company. Although Woodward & Chorpenning were unable to maintain their service on a regular basis (Woodward was killed by Indians only a few months later), the firm continued to carry the mail, under great hardship, until May, 1860 when it was succeeded by Russell, Majors & Waddell. Their famed Pony Express stretched all the way from Independence to Sacramento and carried the mail until October, 1861 when the Overland Telegraph made the service obsolete.

Nearly all of Russell, Majors & Waddell's Pony Express stations were used by the Overland Stage Company. The stations were set up alternately as mail stations or express stations. Mail stations were operated by an agent and five or six employees, while express stations had only a company agent and a relief rider. Riders were paid $50 a month and agents $85; most other employees received $35. All of the pony riders were young, weighed 125 to 135 pounds and were armed with a revolver and bowie knife. The combined weight of their saddle and other gear was about 14 pounds, and the mail pouch never exceeded 20 pounds.

Although its service has been greatly glorified, the Pony Express was a financial disaster for its owners. When the service was initiated, postage cost the user $5 an ounce. When the company lost $60,000 per month at that price, it was dropped to $2.50 in hopes that business would improve. The volume of mail did increase, but the company still lost money. Eventually the price of postage was cut to $1 an ounce, but profits still eluded the owners. In March, 1862, Russell, Majors & Waddell went into bankruptcy with debts of more than a million dollars. The firm was taken over by the Holloday Stage Company, its largest creditor.

Ben Holloday, known as the "Stagecoach King," changed his company's name to the Overland Stage and built it into the west's largest transportation company. It was operated by Holloday until November, 1866 when the line was purchased by Wells Fargo & Company. Wells Fargo continued Holloday's far flung stage empire until 1869 when the rails of the Central and Union Pacific Railroads met at Promontory, Utah.

From the 1850's Salt Lake City was the central point along the overland route. Much of the history and romance of the Overland Trail occurred at those seldom remembered stations strung out across the deserts and mountains of Utah. Today those ghost stations, often little more than crumbling adobe walls and broken foundations, still evoke those exciting days when daring pony riders and shotgun guards rode the rutted tracks of the Overland Trail. Every one of them has a treasure tale to tell, if you only take the time to listen.

NEEDLE ROCK STATION
&
THE CACHE CAVE TREASURE

The easternmost Overland Stage station in Utah was Needle Rock, in Summit County near the Utah-Wyoming border. It was named for the Needle Rocks, a prominent landmark used as a guide by all early pioneers. Captain Albert Tracy, an officer with Johnston's Army during the Utah War, wrote in his journal, "Very

An old livery barn at Castle Rock Station, Echo Canyon.

Hanging Rock Station, also called Bromley's Station, lay below Echo Station in Echo Canyon.

peculiar rocks are the Needles, strange massive obelisks, paired in twins, projecting themselves high into the sky." The station was a regular stop, where teams were changed and meals and lodging could be had. But few travelers chose to stay any longer than necessary for the food was of the plainest kind, and the summers were hot on the barren plains and winter winds blew cold from the treeless hills.

From Needle Rock Station, the trail passed through open sage covered flats, down a grassy draw not far from the Cache Cave, which was just off the trail to the north. The cave had been the home of Indians long before the coming of white men, and was used later by mountain men, explorers and travelers. During the Utah War, Mormon military leaders used it as their headquarters while Mormon militiamen, under the leadership of Lot Smith, burned Fort Bridger and Fort Supply and barricaded Echo Canyon against the approach of Johnston's Army. The cave contains the names of more than 150 trappers, explorers and pioneers, some dating back to 1820. From Cache Cave the trail continued down a grassy canyon to Echo Station.

Cache Cave is exactly what its name suggests, a cave where caches were made. Mountain men cached furs there, and later it became a cache for outlaw loot, hidden there by the infamous Ike Potter Gang. Few today have heard of Ike Potter and his gang of cutthroats, but they terrorized small settlements throughout northern Utah during the 1860's. Allied with army

deserters from Camp Floyd and renegade Indians, Potter's gang waylaid lone travelers, ambushed wagon trains and attacked isolated settlements. They hid out at Cache Cave and it was common knowledge that Potter holed his loot somewhere there. His Indian followers received only horses and livestock; Potter kept all the money, gold and other valuables. Since he and his men weren't welcome anywhere, they had little chance to spend their ill-gotten gains.

In July, 1867, a letter written by Potter went astray. From it, residents of nearby Coalville learned that Potter and his cut-throats were planning to attack their town. It if hadn't been that the wrong man received Potter's note, the history of Coalville might be a lot different. As it was, the settlers were able to arm themselves. When the attack came in the afternoon of July 28th, 1867, the gang was met by armed settlers and Sheriff J.C. Roundy, backed by 13 deputies. Potter and his two lieutenants were taken by surpirse and arrested, while the rest were driven from town.

R.H. "Ike" Potter, Charley Wilson and John Walker were held at the town's rock schoolhouse. About midnight a group of armed men entered and marched the prisoners single file to the edge of town, where Potter was killed instantly by a shotgun blast. Wilson and Walker attempted to escape. Wilson was caught and killed alongside the Weber River. Walker escaped but had been shot at such close range by the mob's shotguns that his shirt was on fire! He was captured several days later in the mountains near Fort Douglas, where his throat was cut and his body left for the wolves.

With Potter, Wilson and Walker dead, there was no one who knew where Potter had cached the gang's loot. No doubt it included everything from rifles and pistols to wedding rings and gold coins, perhaps even rare Mormon coins which were in use then. Who knows what may be hidden at or near Cache Cave? If it was valuable when the Potter gang hid it, it's more valuable now!

ECHO STATION

Echo Station was located in Summit County on what was then called Red Fork Creek, later changed to Egan's Creek, and now known as Echo Canyon Creek. The station was often called Red Fork Station during the days of the Overland Stage, and in later years Castle Rock Station, a name it retained after it became a gasoline stop for automobiles. It was finally closed when the highway in Echo Canyon was rerouted. It was a crude place when first built. One early traveler described it as, "A mere structure of slabs to keep the wolves away."

High on the vertical cliffs above Echo Station Mormon minutemen led by Bishop Joseph Murdock built rock wall fortifications to stop the advance of Johnston's Army. Pine poles were cut square and blackened with stove black, and when seen from the canyon below, looked exactly like cannon barrels. 500 men with whatever weapons they could find stood guard behind those fortifications. Over the years many valuable relics have been found where those defenses were built. Only recently a treasure hunter discovered a rare muzzle-loading rifle under a cedar tree where it had been left and forgotten long ago. Who knows what else might be found?

Echo Station was also a main supply station for the Overland Telegraph Company when its lines were being strung down Echo Canyon. Countless thousands of insulators and miles of copper wire were stored there. Some of those supplies are still being dug up today. Meals and lodging were available to travelers. From Echo Station the trail continued down past Hanging Rock, also called Bromley's Station. Usually only up canyon stages stopped there. Hanging Rock boasted a fine spring, a welcome change from the muddy water of Red Fork Creek. From Hanging Rock, the road continued down to Weber Station.

WEBER STATION
&
THE MAIL ROBBER'S CACHE

Weber Station was located at the mouth of Echo Canyon in Summit County, alongside the Weber River, about 2 miles southeast of present-day Echo City. Weber Station was an important stop, since the trail forked there, with Kimball's Stage Line and

Weber Station on the Overland Trail. The mail robber's cache is buried not far from here.

Gilmer & Saulsbury's stages following the Weber River upstream to Fort Hoyt, Wanship, Rock Fort, Snyder's Station and over Parley's Canyon summit to Mountain Dell and Salt Lake City.

In time Weber Station gave birth to Echo City, built on the line of the Utah Eastern Railroad to Park City. When the Union Pacific built its line down Echo Canyon, Weber Station was absorbed by the original Echo City, not present-day Echo City. There were so many outlaws preying on Weber Station that the notorious Jack Slade had to be called in to thin them out.

From Weber Station the stage road followed the Weber River downstream to Salt Spring Creek, the site of present-day Henefer, where a brief stop could be made to rest the horses before climbing over a ridge and dropping into Thomas Canyon. The trail continued over Hogback Summit, a bare, windswept, sage covered ridge where the pioneers of 1847 got their first glimpse of the rugged mountains ahead. The road then followed Dixie Hollow Creek to its junction with Bauchmin's Creek, later renamed East Canyon Creek, where the next stop was made at Dixie Station.

Stagecoach robberies were almost daily fare along the road through Echo Canyon, thus when Wells Fargo purchased the line from Russell, Majors & Waddell in 1866 they soon asked for help from Washington. Before then, all a robber had to do was ride a few miles across the territorial line into Wyoming where he was beyond a posse's jurisdiction. President Andrew Johnson appointed John W. Clampitt as a special investigator, with jurisdiction on both sides of the line.

Weber Station had been plagued by mail thefts. Often at night, during the confusion of changing teams, two brigands would slip up to the coach, steal several sacks of mail, and carry them off. It happened so many times that there was no doubt someone at the station was in cahoots with the robbers, but no clues could be found in the hills around the station.

Not long after Inspector Clampitt arrived in Utah a wagon coming down Echo Canyon broke a wheel between Hanging Rock and Weber Station. The two men climbed a side canyon to locate a piece of hardwood to repair the broken wheel. About an hour's hike from the road they spotted smoke and went to investigate. To their surprise they came upon two men asleep by a campfire, which had been built from stacks of letters and mail sacks!

The two robbers were captured and taken to Hanging Rock Station where a telegram was sent to Inspector Clampitt at Salt Lake City. With two Salt Lake City policemen, Calmpitt rode to Hanging Rock Station where the two outlaws were placed under arrest. Their camp was searched, but no trace of the large amount of loot taken from the Wells Fargo stages could be found, and no amount of prodding could induce the robbers to tell where it was cached.

Both men were given long prison sentences. One tried to escape from a work gang building roads and

was shot and killed by a single rifle shot fired by a guard. The other served his sentence, and on the very day he was released stole a buckboard wagon and team and started for Echo Canyon. A posse was quickly formed and caught the thief at Parley's Park. He was taken back to Salt Lake City where he was sentenced to life imprisonment. He never got another chance to recover his loot, for he died in prison.

In his reminiscences John W. Clampitt didn't state exactly where the outlaw camp was located other than that it was about an hour's hike from the stage road between Hanging Rock and Weber stations, well hidden by large rocks. Unfortunately, there are an awful lot of rocks in the canyons between those stations. Since no one ever found the mail robber's cache, it must still be there. Starting on the mountainside above Weber Station and hiking towards Hanging Rock should be a good place to begin, especially for someone with a good metal-detector and a lot of time.

DIXIE STATION
&
SPANISH MINE, OR SINKHOLE?

Dixie Station, also known to early travelers as Carson House, was just over the top of Hogback Summit, a half mile inside Morgan County. Its site can be found in a small grove of stunted cottonwood and aspen trees, just west of the Mormon Pioneer Trail. It was easy to attack and hard to defend, but the Indians were usually not troublesome along that part of the trail. Overnight lodging could be had, but the station was a crude affair, and its meals were of the worst kind.

Even though its accommodations were poor, passengers who knew the trail ahead were often reluctant to leave. After Dixie Station the trail followed the rocky bed of Bauchmin's Creek and crossed it 13 times in 8 miles! The road then turned up an even narrower and rockier side stream which it followed to the summit of Big Mountain Pass. From the summit, crossed by the Donner Party in 1846 and the Mormons in 1847, the trail wound steeply down the west slope to Hanks Station, five miles below the pass and the last stop before Salt Lake City.

In the oak brush covered hills about 2 miles west of the stage road south of Dixie Station, there is a controversial hole in the mountain. Some say that it is a sinkhole, but others insist it is an old Mexican mine. They swear there is a cache of silver bars hidden somewhere inside! It is deep, and air rising from it indicates that another opening lower on the mountain must exist.

Lorin Mortenson homesteaded nearby on Taylor's Creek and recalled that livestock would sometimes fall into the bottomless hole. He helped cover it with logs in 1915, but before that, helped lower his Uncle Martin into the pit for "three lariat lengths", about 120 feet, without touching bottom. When they covered the hole a crowbar was dropped and could be heard ringing as it bounced from side to side in the shaft, "for what seemed like a long, long time."

The old shaft is open again now; the logs used to cover it back in 1915 have long since rotted away. Several years ago one of a group of college students from a geology class was lowered into the hole 250 feet, and discovered that the shaft has a number of side drifts with air currents coming from them.

Is it a sinkhole or a shaft? I'll let you decide, but remember, sinkholes occur in limestone in areas with a high water level. The strange hole on the mountain near Dixie Station is in sandstone, in an area drier than a parson's sermon!

HANKS STATION

Hanks Station was located on Mountain Dell Creek in Salt Lake County in the deep vale between Big and Little Mountains. The station's official name was Big Canyon Creek Station, but was almost always known as Hanks Station for its operator, Ephraim K. Hanks, who, with Bill Hickman and Porter Rockwell, was a leader of the infamous Sons Of Dan, or Danites, also known to gentiles as The Avenging Angels. Like Hickman and Rockwell, his name brought terror to the hearts of many for the mysterious killings attributed to the Avenging Angels were legion and many travelers breathed easier when his station was left behind. Needless to say, few stayed there overnight!

Not everyone believed that Hanks was as bad as he was portrayed. When the noted British writer, Sir Richard Burton, stopped at his station, he described him, "As a middle sized, fair haired, good looking man, not at all what I had thought the 'Terrible Ephe' would look like!"

From Hanks Station, the trail climbed over Little Mountain Pass and dropped steeply into Big Canyon, later renamed Emigration Canyon, and followed it to the place where only a few years earlier Brigham Young had said, "It is enough, this is the place!" From there it was only a few miles to Salt Lake City, and the end of the trail for many.

GREAT SALT LAKE CITY
&
COLONEL CONNOR'S CANNON

Clean hotels, well stocked shops and a chance to rest were welcomed by all travelers who reached Great Salt Lake City safely. The City Of The Saints always had the name "Great" before it on maps of the day, and was the only real city between the east and the Pacific coast. Today, a tall granite monument located at 147 South Main Street stands in memory of the Overland Stage drivers and the Pony Express riders of yesteryear. For those headed for the Comstock Lode in Nevada or the gold fields of California, the worst part of the trail was still ahead, for they faced what was then called "The Great American Desert!"

From Great Salt Lake City the road turned south past Parley's Canyon Creek, Mill Creek and Big Cottonwood Creek to Traveler's Rest, a small station where passengers could rest a few minutes while the horses were watered. The trail then continued south past Little Cottonwood Creek and Willow Creek to the next stop, which was Rockwell's Station.

There is a unique, and very valuable historical treasure hidden on the east bench of Salt Lake City, close by the stage road near Fort Douglas. It's not likely anyone will find it despite its being quite large. As a matter of fact, it's a cannon!

When Camp Floyd was abandoned by General Johnston's army most of its supplies were sold at a great loss. All of the munitions were hauled away by the departing army, except a splendid little brass cannon with a shiny bell atop it. When the army left to join the Civil War forces, General Johnston's cannon was taken to Fort Douglas and presented to the fort's commander, Col. Patrick Conner.

Col. Connor had the magnificent little cannon mounted in a special place near the fort's parade ground. It was fired only on very special occasions, and its little brass bell was rung to call the troops to military ceremonies. At that time there was a great deal of antagonism between Col. Connor's troops and young Mormon youths, and insults were frequently exchanged between them. One day a group of taunting youths told the soldiers that they could steal the cannon without being caught. They carried out their boast sooner than the soldiers expected.

A few nights later several Mormon boys crept silently by a lone sentry walking his post. As the guard neared the end of his patrol, the youths tied a rope to the cannon. While one held the bell quiet, the others pulled it from its mount and wheeled it off into the darkness.

Col. Connor was furious! He issued threats against Brigham Young and conducted a city-wide search. Meanwhile, the cannon was hidden under a haystack within sight of the fort! When the enormity of their prank dawned on them, the boys solved the problem by rolling the cannon to the edge of a shallow well and pushing it in. They were helped by a friend who was a freighter enroute to Leeds, a small town in southern Utah near St. George. Before the cannon was pushed over the brink, the freighter removed the brass bell knowing it would be a welcome addition to the tower of a new church being built in Leeds.

While Col. Connor fumed over his cannon, its bell hung in the church steeple at Leeds, calling the faithful to worship. Years later, when Leeds was nearly a ghost town, the bell came into the possession of W.H. Kesler, then owner of historic Cove Fort. Kesler hung it in a place of honor at the entrance to the fort where visitors can see it today.

But it will be a little more difficult to see the cannon. You will have to find a century old well, not far from the old stage road, in sight of Fort Douglas. Then you'll have to get permission to dig, and that may not be easy, for it's probably under someone's patio!

ROCKWELL'S STATION

Rockwell's Station, 12 miles south of Traveler's Rest in Salt Lake County, was first known as Utah Brewery because of a brewery built near the Point Of The Mountain, which separates Great Salt Lake and Utah valleys. The brewery was built at a cost of $17,000, in an area where wild hops abounded and grains were plentiful, but the business failed. The property was taken over by Porter Rockwell, co-chief of the infamous Danites, and became a station for the Overland Stage.

Unlike Hanks Station, also operated by a Danite chief, Rockwell's Station was looked forward to by travelers because Rockwell was a fine host, jovial and good natured, whose tales of early day adventures kept his listeners spellbound for hours. Perhaps the fact that he operated a still and sold "Valley Tan" whisky had some bearing on his popularity! Sir Richard Burton, the famed British author, visited Rockwell's Station on his way west, and was warned by Rockwell to "Watch out for white Indians", which he said "were the very worst kind!" He also told Burton that the trail ahead "Was about as fit for travel as Hell is for a powder magazine!"

It was common knowledge that Rockwell had killed many men, sometimes estimated at 100, and had a reputation of always getting his man. But to those with whom he had no quarrel, he was accommodating and always ready to share a jug. Those who had cause to fear him, though, remembered the words of a popular poem about him:

Have you heard of Porter Rockwell,
The Mormon triggerite?
They say he hunts for horse thieves,
When the moon is shining bright.
So if you steal a Mormon horse
I'll tell you what to do,
Get the drop on Porter Rockwell,
Or he'll get the drop on you!

From Rockwell's Station the road crossed the River Jordan, turned west at what was called the Old Indian Fort and climbed Ash Hollow to Joe's Dugout.

JOE'S DUGOUT STATION

Joe's Dugout was a crude place, named for its operator, Joe Dorton, also known as "Stropshire" Joe. Dorton earned his nickname from the coyote hole dugout he lived in. There was no water near his station, so Dorton decided to dig a well. For some reason he dug on top of a small hill instead of in a low spot where water would be closer to the surface. He dug more than 200' without finding a single drop.

An early traveler named W.G. Marshall stopped at Joe's Dugout where he inspected the well and met Porter Rockwell. In a book Marshall gave his impression of the Mormon Triggerite. "Rockwell was superstitious and believed that Dorton's well was inhabited by witches, ghosts and all sorts of evil spirits, all of which delighted in causing him misery whenever he passed by. One time he drove 30 horses past the well and every one of them became sick. Rockwell took his knife and cut each one on its tail, put a drop of blood from each one on a blade of dry straw and burned it, which he claimed cured their sickness immediately. He was very ignorant, and could neither read nor write. He died guilty of assassinating more than one hundred victims with his own hand."

Meals and lodging were not available at Joe's Dugout, although Rockwell's Valley Tan whiskey could be purchased for one dollar a bottle. Sir Richard Burton recalled that "a good brew of lager beer", could also be found there. But the stage tarried no longer than necessary for it was an easy ten miles down grade through Cedar Valley to Camp Floyd.

Officers' quarters at Camp Floyd, about 1859.

CAMP FLOYD

Camp Floyd in Utah County was established in 1858 as part of the agreement which ended the Utah War. It soon was the largest army camp in the country. Just across the creek was Dobietown, called Frogtown by some. It was said that the combined population of the camp and that hell-hole of saloons exceeded 7,000. Murder occurred daily at Dobietown and one newspaper correspondent reported, "The revolver and the bowie knife had nightly work to do there!" Camp Floyd was named in honor of John B. Floyd, Secretary of War in the Buchanan administration. When it was discovered that Floyd was a Confederate sympathizer, the name was changed to Camp Crittenden.

The Overland Stage began service to Camp Floyd in 1859 and the Pony Express the following year. Other than Salt Lake City, Camp Floyd's stores were the best stocked in Utah. At the camp sugar cost 65¢ a pound, calico cloth 45¢ a yard, candles were 33¢ each and nails sold for $5 a pound. The leading firm at that time was Gilbert & Livingston's General Store. But you can bet the wild and wooly dens at Dobietown got more travelers' money than the General Store did!

Camp Floyd and Dobietown were precisely the types of places that produced post-hole caches and buried valuables, since criminals, soldiers, and camp followers are seldom society's most responsible elements. From there the road continued west over Five Mile Pass and through sage covered foothills to East Rush Valley Station.

EAST RUSH VALLEY STATION

From Five Mile Pass it was an easy trip to East Rush Valley Station, also known as East Rush or The Pass, 12 miles from Camp Floyd. It was located on a dusty, cheerless, windswept flat, far from the nearest water. To the northeast, snow-capped Lewiston Peak looked down on the remote desert outpost, while the East Tintic Mountains guarded it on the southeast. To the west lay open desert.

When it was first established, East Rush Valley Station was an essential stop, and it was only through necessity that anyone would live at such a cheerless spot. Originally, the stage road turned northwest, crossed Rush Valley to Johnson's Pass, then known as Reynold's Pass, and went down its west slope into Skull Valley. Not long after it was built, the route was changed to follow a shorter and easier trail across sand dunes to Meadow Creek and Lookout Pass. During its short life it managed to serve as a rest stop before facing the dusty sand dunes ahead.

Because it was the least known and used station, it should be doubly attractive to relic hunters today. Who knows how many passengers made hurried trips out into the sagebrush behind the station, or how many whiskey flasks were thrown away after the last drop was drained?

MEADOW CREEK

Meadow Creek Station, the next stop west of East Rush Valley, was better known to travelers as Faust's Station, for its operator, Dr. Henry J. Faust, who was a distinct alternative to the typical rough and foul-mouthed station keeper. Dr. Faust was a well mannered, educated man who enjoyed discussing Shakespeare with his guests, and was a physician as well. When the famed Horace Greeley stayed overnight at Meadow Creek, Dr. Faust hid all the candles and lanterns so he would have to spend the night in conversation instead of writing as he had planned to do! A small creek made Faust's Station an oasis of green in barren Rush Valley.

Dr. Faust first came to Meadow Creek as an express rider and stayed to become its owner. In later years, after the Overland Stage was just a memory, he remained at the station and became a rancher. A small cemetery is located in the low foothills to the east, where several "tough nuts" killed in gunfights and a few "unknowns" are buried. Some of the original log cabins still stand along Meadow Creek, but are on private land. From Meadow Creek the old trail crossed a dry sage covered flat to the edge of the foothills and then climbed a cedar choked canyon to Lookout Pass, where the next stop was made.

The dog cemetery at Point Lookout Station, where "Aunt Libby" Rockwell buried her pets, complete with tombstones!

POINT LOOKOUT STATION

It is 8 miles from Meadow Creek to Point Lookout Station, located in Lookout Pass in Tooele County. No doubt, many travelers thought the station and pass were named for the fine views of Rush Valley to the east and Skull Valley to the west. But that is incorrect; it was named after Indians attacked a stagecoach there and express riders were warned to "Look out for Indians!" Point Lookout Station was also known as Rockwell's Station, named for its operators, "Uncle Horace" and "Aunt Libby" Rockwell. Although they were kin to Porter Rockwell, their station was too far west to be confused with Porter Rockwell's stop south of Salt Lake City.

Alvin Anderson operated a store where travelers could purchase supplies, and "Aunt Libby's" home cooked meals were a welcome change from the bacon and beans most stations served. Emigrants could also purchase water from "Uncle Horace's" fine spring, at 5¢ a bucket or 20¢ per team. Everyone who passed that way stopped to look at the strange little cemetery on the hillside across the canyon, where emigrants who died along the way, employees killed by Indians and "Aunt Libby's" pet dogs were buried side by side. It wasn't hard to tell which graves the dogs were buried in; they were the only ones with headstones! That strange little cemetery is still an object of interest to travelers.

Since Point Lookout was a popular stop where passengers could shop and spend the night, it's safe to assume there are many lost coins and relics there. Thus, it should be a good place to use a metal detector. From Point Lookout, the trail wound down a steep canyon into Skull Valley, and across that desolate wasteland to Simpson's Springs.

SIMPSON SPRINGS STATION

Known as Simpson Springs to gentiles, and Egan's Springs to Mormons, this Tooele County station was one of the main stops on the stage road through Skull Valley and the West Desert. Alvin Anderson, who operated a store at Point Lookout, also ran one at Simpson Springs. D.E. "Wood Leg" Davis was the station's first telegraph operator. Water from the fresh springs there was carried by all travelers leaving the station. Captain J.H. Simpson discovered the springs when he was surveying a railroad route in 1858, and Captain Howard Egan made them his base of operations while exploring the West Desert. Simpson Springs looked like a Frederick Remington painting. It consisted of a fort-like stone structure designed for defense against Indian attacks, because Porter Rockwell's "white Indians" were as troublesome as real Indians were, and many outlaw bands preyed on stagecoaches crossing the desert wastes of Skull Valley.

Today Simpson Springs is an ideal place to camp while crossing the desert, boasting shade trees and picnic tables. A tiny swimming hole was built during CCC and WPA days, and recently a reconstruction of the station has been completed. From Simpson Springs the road dropped down a rolling sand covered slope across an ancient riverbed to Riverbed Station.

RIVERBED STATION
&
LOST STAGECOACH HOLDUP GOLD

Located almost atop the Juab-Tooele county line, on the sun-baked desert floor, Riverbed Station was a desolate place. It is said that the wide, dry riverbed once connected the Great Salt Lake and Sevier Lake. That made no difference to travelers on the Overland Trail who would have welcomed a river; Skull Valley is a thirsty land, and there is no river at Riverbed, and there aren't any beds either!

Only the crudest kind of shelter greeted the visitor to Riverbed, and neither food nor lodging was available. A deep well provided water that most people thought was undrinkable. But the station did serve a useful purpose. In both directions the road climbed uphill through deep sand and stages going either way needed to rest and water their teams. Because of its isolated, defenseless location, Riverbed Station was frequently the scene of stagecoach holdups.

During a holdup, a lone bandit took the strongbox and $40,000. At least $10,000 in gold is still buried not far from the station just waiting for you to find it!

The highwayman fooled the stage driver and shotgun guard by means of a clever ruse. He laid face down in the sand amid the sparse greasewood brush by the side of the road. When the driver saw him he stopped the coach, convinced he'd come upon another Indian victim. But when the shotgun guard climbed down and rolled the "body" over, he found himself looking into the business end of a cocked six-shooter!

The bandit took the strongbox and the two men's weapons, and waved them on. Looking back, they saw him lead a horse from a sandy wash, load him with the heavy gold and hike off into the desert south of the station. Porter Rockwell was notified and was soon on the outlaw's trail. Several days later he found his camp on Cherry Creek at the south end of the Cedar Mountains. Rockwell watched the camp until he saw the outlaw dig up three bars of gold bullion. Convinced that was all of the loot, Rockwell made the arrest and took the bandit to Point Lookout Station. There he locked him in a root cellar while he slept. The bandit escaped, but Rockwell was immediately on his trail again. This time Rockwell killed him, so there would be no more escapes.

When the Danite surrendered the $30,000 he had seen the bandit carry to his camp from out in the cedars, he assumed that was all of the gold. He soon learned that had he waited a few more minutes, the bandit would have dug up another $10,000. Rockwell returned to the outlaw camp but couldn't find the rest of the gold in the drifting sand and cedars. No doubt $10,000 in gold is still buried in a shallow hole at the south end of the Cedar Mountains. All you have to do is find it!

DUGWAY STATION
&
THE INDIAN AMBUSH CACHE

Like Riverbed, Dugway Station in Juab County offered the most primitive accommodations for travelers. One visitor described it as a dugout in the ground, roofed with cedar logs and operated by two half-drunk boys! He added that the station had no table or chairs, and that tin plates of greasy stew were eaten while standing. Some early travelers referred to the station as the Express Station, for a reason now unknown. There wasn't feed for livestock or water for passengers. Three wells had been dug, one of them 120', without striking water. But a station was a necessity there, at the foot of the Dugway Range, where teams had to be rested before starting the steep climb to Dugway Pass.

On November 1st, 1851, Captain Absalom Woodward, who then had the mail contract between California and Utah, left Sacramento, bound for Salt Lake City. With him were four California gold miners, John

Hawthorne, Harry Benson, John Hamilton and a man named Kennedy. All had struck it rich in the gold fields and were returning to their homes in the east and were traveling together for mutual protection with Woodward as their guide. They had little trouble with Indians until they reached a Gosiute village near present-day Ibapah.

After they made camp, two of the Californians dragged an Indian maiden into the brush and violated her. When Capt. Woodward learned what had happened, he hurriedly got the party together and started across the Great Salt Desert before the Indian men returned to camp from their daily hunting trip. They had been gone only a few hours when Chief Antelope Jake and his warriors returned.

Chief Antelope Jake was outraged when he learned what had happened, and immediately planned his revenge. Since he knew his bows and arrows were no match for the white men's rifles, he by-passed Capt. Woodward's party far to the south and set up an ambush at Dugway Pass. As Capt. Woodward's party filed through the narrow pass, the Gosiute braves rained arrows down on them. They died before a shot could be fired.

Every item of clothing was stripped from the men's bodies, which were then rolled down a steep ravine and horribly mutilated. The clothing, pack saddles, mail sacks and bags of yellow nuggets were dumped into deep crevices near the pass. Only the pack animals and firearms were taken back to Ibapah.

Capt. Woodword's fate remained a mystery until May, 1852 when a mail carrier followed the wrong gulch from Dugway Pass and discovered the grisly, coyote-strewn remains of Woodward and the California miners. They were buried where they were found.

The identity of the four men killed with Capt. Woodward remained a mystery for fifty years until an Indian told the story of that day at Dugway Pass. Not until then did anyone learn of the bags of yellow rocks that had been dumped into crevices near the pass. During the past few years scraps of leather, rusted buckles and bits of pack saddles have been found in packrat's nests, but no one has found the California gold.

Drifting sand fills some crevices, while changing winds uncover others. Perhaps some day a stray wind will uncover the right crevice and reveal the lost gold of Dugway Pass. Maybe you'll be there when it happens!

BLACKROCK STATION
&
THE LOST CRYSTAL CAVE

When the stagecoach topped Dugway Pass, both team and passengers needed a breather before going on. This was especially true when the travelers had to hike behind the heavily laden coach, or worse yet, had to push it through deep sand. From the pass they could look out on the desert to the west. In the distance a black volcanic cone rose above the wasteland. In the shadow of that landmark was their next stop, Blackrock Station, but also called Rock House Station, for the black volcanic stone cabin located there.

Blackrock Station had nothing to offer the traveler except a short rest while the teams were changed, for water was at a premium, and meals and lodging were unheard of. Few stayed longer than necessary though the trail ahead was hard.

The desolate Thomas Range, southeast of Blackrock Station, is world-famous for its high quality topaz gemstones. Rockhounds from all over climb its rugged rhyolite peaks in search of gems, but almost always search the south end of the range. Charles Bishop, one of California's leading crystallographers, often collected crystals there, but believed that higher grade gems could be found at the untouched north end.

Bishop made several trips along the Pony Express trail from Vernon, south of Tooele, to the Thomas Range and each time found high quality gems. But, as time passed, he longed to try his luck on the north end. Then in 1965, the 75 year old man hiked alone into the rough rhyolite peaks. All day he searched, most of the time in a cold, driving rain. Nearly exhausted, he started the long hike back to his truck, parked south of Blackrock Station. In his own words Bishop later said, "I was thinking I would never make it out of the mountains, when suddenly my feet broke through a thin crust and I went crashing down into a deep hole."

When the dust settled, Bishop couldn't believe his eyes, for he was inside a giant geode, a cave-like cavity in the rock completely lined with glistening topaz crystals! Every one was perfectly formed and stunning in color. Bishop took all he could carry, and with great effort climbed out of the treasure cave.

Bishop returned to his truck and made the long drive back to California, but the difficult hike in the cold rain was too much for the old man, and he died shortly afterwards. Bishop described the fabulous gem cave to his friends, and had many of the beautiful gems to prove his story, but knowing that the cave is at the north end of the Thomas Range has been little help in locating it. Many have searched for Bishop's lost topaz cave, but none have found it. The north end of the Thomas Range is a big piece of country!

FISH SPRINGS STATION

Fish Springs Station in Juab County was a main stop in the West Desert route, and one looked forward to by pony express riders, stage drivers and passengers. After Blackrock Station, the trail passed by many deep pools of water that were stagnant, foul smelling and surrounded by black mud and tules. But at Fish Springs there were great pools of clean water. Some were boiling hot while others were ice cold and had fish swimming in them. It was those pools that gave the station its name, and the black, desolate Fish Springs Mountains as well.

30 years later and 15 miles farther west a mining camp would be born, and it too would be named Fish Springs. Many of the pools near the station were just the right temperature for swimming and washing off dust and grime acquired during the previous hundred miles or more. Water barrels were filled from the pools, because it was a dry journey to the next stop, around the north end of the Fish Springs Range, at Boyd's Station.

BOYD'S STATION

Boyd's Station, also known as Halfway Station, was located where the Overland Trail dipped into Juab County, at the point the Simpson and Egan trails separated. The Simpson Trail turned south and was used by miners headed for the silver strikes then being made in southern Nevada. The Egan Trail continued west, and was the route followed by the Overland Stage, and those headed for the Comstock Lode and the California gold fields. Traveling companions often parted company at Boyd's Station.

Although small, Boyd's Station was solid, built of mortared stone and had rifle portholes for defense against raiding Indians. Its ruins are now protected by a fence. Because it was a main fork in the overland trails, it is a good bet for relic hunters today. After leaving Boyd's Station, travelers bound west looked forward to the next stop at Willow Springs.

WILLOW SPRINGS STATION

Willow Springs was more often called Callao, named by an old prospector for a mining camp in Peru. It was an oasis in the desert where weary travelers were greeted by springs of fresh water, giant cottonwood trees and fields of green grass. Good overnight lodging and hot meals were available, the best since "Aunt Libby" Rockwell's. A number of ranchers and prospectors called Willow Springs home, thus the passenger who stayed overnight could often become acquainted with people other than employees of the stage company.

Indians were particularly troublesome at Willow Springs and on the trail west. They often raided the stage companies' herds, and more than a few were made into what old-timers call "good Indians." For many years a row of graves where "good Indians" were buried could be seen just south of the station.

Today several families live at Willow Springs, and continue to call it Callao. You'll be welcome, for visitors are few, but don't expect any services; the nearest gas station is more than a hundred miles away! After the oasis at Willow Springs, passengers were reluctant to face the desert trail to the next stop at Round Station.

ROUND STATION

From Willow Springs, the trail turned north into Tooele County. After six bone-jarring miles it reached Six Mile Springs, also called Mountain Springs, where

Passengers had only a few minutes to rest when the stage stopped at Round Station.

the coaches often stopped before continuing to Round Station. In one old guide book, Six Mile Springs is called Lost Springs, and is described as being "A water sink below the bench land, tufted with cottonwoods, willows and grass. To the east is Granite Rock, and through the gap ahead can be seen Round Station, six miles away across a salt flat." Round Station was sometimes called Reading Springs and was located at the mouth of Deep Creek Canyon, later renamed Overland Canyon.

Round Station was a circular, fort-like rock enclosure built in 1858 as a place where travelers could defend themselves against Indians. With no agent, it offered nothing but spring water and the protection of its walls. Many times Overland Stages raced bands of Gosiute Indians for its protective retreat. Unless that danger was present, only a brief stop would be made to rest tired horses and take on fresh water before entering narrow Deep Creek Canyon, a common place for Indian ambushes.

BURNT STATION

Established in 1859 and first known as Canyon Station, Burnt Station was at the head of Deep Creek Canyon in Tooele County, where the canyon walls were wide enough for a station house and livestock corrals to be built. It was burned twice in Indian raids, in 1861 and 1864. No two of the three buildings were in exactly the same place. Its last incarnation was christened Burnt Station. Because it sat in the depths of a narrow, twisting canyon, it was favored for Indian attacks, and at least two soldiers and five station agents and travelers were killed there. The stage driver never knew until he rounded the bend below the station whether he would be greeted by a relief driver or by a smouldering pile of ashes and the war-whoops of waiting Indians.

The ruins of three different stations can still be found and represent a possible bonanza for coin hun-

The price of gas is still 27¢ at Ibapah, but the pump's dry! -Deseret News-

ters and relic seekers. Also, don't overlook the possibility of post-hole caches, for none of the people who died there expected to, and their rainy-day caches may still be there somewhere.

The facilities were not good at Burnt Station, although plain meals and rough lodging could be had. Because of its reputation, few stayed there overnight. Above Burnt Station, the canyon widens onto Clifton Flats, where a few years later the wild mining camp of Clifton would spring to life. From the head of Deep Creek Canyon the trail crossed the Clifton Flats and followed the western edge of the Deep Creek Mountains to Ibapah Station, not far from the Nevada border.

IBAPAH STATION

Its name, an Indian word meaning "the clay colored water," Ibapah was the western-most station in Utah, in Tooele County near the Nevada border. Known at times as Deep Creek Station, it was located in the midst of the ancient hunting grounds of the Gosiute Indians, something that caused no end of trouble over the years. The station was operated by a man named Snyder. The creek it was built on was called Deep Creek because it ran in the bottom of a deep wash. On March 22nd, 1863, stage driver Henry Harper was killed by Indians just west of the station. Judge Mott, a passenger, climbed into the driver's seat, grabbed the reins from Harper's dying grasp, and brought the stage safely into Ibapah Station.

Because of good soil and ample water, a small farming community grew up near the station and in later years, when the gold mines at nearby Clifton were working, boasted 3 stores and 4 saloons. The farm community was established in 1859 by a group of settlers from Grantsville, led by Wilford Hudson. They had a lot of trouble with the Indians, and the settlement had to be abandoned from 1860 to 1862. Years later, when the Gosiute Reservation was designated, the settlers' land reverted to Indian control. Those long abandoned homesteads may be of interest to today's treasure hunter.

From Ibapah Station the Overland Trail turned west toward Tippett's Station just across the Nevada border, then continued to Antelope Station and points west. It was a long hard road from Needle Rock on the Wyoming border to Ibapah Station, but that's what was expected along the Overland Trail.

FORT HOYT STATION

As already described, Weber Station, the third along the Overland Trail, served as the junction between the Overland Stage, the local Gilmer & Saulsbury Line and Kimball's Stage Line, both of which followed the Weber River to Fort Hoyt in Summit County.

Fort Hoyt, also known as Fort Union, is near the present-day town of Hoytsville and was named for Samuel Hoyt, an early settler who built a grist mill there. The mill was built in 1862 and the fort in 1866, the latter because of Indian troubles during the Blackhawk War. 25 cabins were built at the fort, which was located 300' southwest of the historical marker on US-189.

Samuel Hoyt became quite wealthy and built a beautiful stone house which was lavishly decorated with imported marble statues and other costly furnishings. His old home, still beautiful, has been designated a state historical site. Fort Hoyt was a regular stop on both stage lines, where good accommodations could be had before continuing to Wanship Station.

WANSHIP STATION

Wanship Station was located where Silver Creek flows into the Weber River in Summit County. It was built in 1861 by Aaron Daniels, about a half mile north of present-day Wanship City. Daniels was something of a character. An early Mormon convert, he participated in explorations from Utah Valley to Fort Bridger. The town of Daniels and Daniels' Canyon in Heber Valley are named for him. At 63 years of age he married an Indian Girl, a survivor of the Bear River Massacre. He was interested in prospecting and was an occasional partner of Caleb Rhoades and Pick Murdock in the Lost Rhoades Mine and other old Spanish mines.

Wanship Station was first used by Gilmer & Saulsbury, one of the west's largest and best known stage lines. In 1869 the Kimball Stage Line began stopping at Daniel's station enroute from Echo City to Park City. The old station was in continuous use until the motor car replaced the horse, when it became a private home. It was torn down in 1912, but an historic marker on the abandoned highway between Wanship and Hoytsville marks its site.

ROCK FORT STATION

After leaving Wanship Station the road followed the Weber River upstream through Summit County to Rock Fort, a tiny farming community now covered by Rockport Lake. Old foundations and sidewalks can be seen when the lake is at low level, and should be a good place for today's detector equipped treasure hunter to spend some time. The settlement was first called Crandall and later Enoch City.

When the Blackhawk War threatened, settlers built an 8′ rock wall around the entire town, after which it became known as Rock Fort. When the Indian troubles ended, the wall was torn down and used to build houses and farm buildings. With its fort-like wall gone, the town's name was changed again to Rockport.

Today, all that is left is a little cemetery on a windswept ridge above the lake. You have to look close to see it, for sagebrush is fast reclaiming it. Its old tombstones are near the mouth of Three Mile Canyon, which the road followed to Parley's Park and Snyder's Station.

SNYDER'S STATION

Although it was called Snyder's Station by the companies having agents and livery stables there, it was better known as Kimball's Station, in honor of its long time operator, William H. Kimball. Its official name came from Samuel Snyder who operated a sawmill nearby as early as 1853. Snyder's Station was a regular stop for both the Kimball and the Gilmer & Saulsbury lines. Many prospectors stopped there to inspect the mountains to the south. William Kimball was a genial host, and many passengers looked forward to visiting him. He built a fine hotel, one of the best along the entire line, and it can still be seen today.

The station was a busy place after silver was discovered in 1869, and a branch of the Kimball Line carried miners to the diggings at Park City. A newspaper article in the New York *Herald* on June 17th, 1872 directed nationwide attention to Snyder's Station: "A body of mineral, said to be the greatest ever discovered, has recently been located in the Wasatch Mountains about 7 miles south of Kimball's (Snyder's) Stage Station near Parley's Park. The ledge is 30′ wide with 1,000 ounces of silver to the ton, and is valued at more than $5,000,000!" For years Snyder's Station was a favored destination of new prospectors arriving from the east, and is still worth visiting.

MOUNTAIN DELL STATION

From Snyder's Station the road climbed steeply to Altus, the small rest stop at the head of Parley's Canyon, where teams and passengers rested a few minutes before starting down the steep west slope. In earlier days the pass had been known as Golden Pass. The road down Parley's Canyon passed Morrell's Half Way House, where J. Dudler's Saloon and Pace & Archibald's General Store were located. Other forgotten places along the road to Salt Lake City included Felt's Resort, Pharaoh's Glen, Old Arm Chair and Roper.

Few coaches stopped at those roadhouses, but it was different going up. Where the canyon begins to widen out, just above Mountain Dell Revervoir, the stage station known as Mountain Dell was located. In 1858, Ephraim K. Hanks and Augustus P. Hardy built a hotel there. Later, it was sold to Leonard Hardy, and many called the station Hardy's Place after that. The hotel at Mountain Dell should not be confused with Hanks' Station on the Overland Trail, which was in another canyon five miles north.

A small section of land near the creek was cultivated, several sawmills were erected, and a few settlers moved in. By 1867 a ward of the Mormon Church was established. A little town began growing up near the station with a log meeting house being replaced by a fine stone building. But further growth was impeded when Salt Lake City acquired water rights in the canyon and eventually dried up the town. In addition, restrictions were placed on livestock and farming to protect the watershed. By the turn of the century its mountain canyon site was nearly deserted. Later, the rails of the Utah Central replaced the stage road, only to be abandoned in their turn for the automobile.

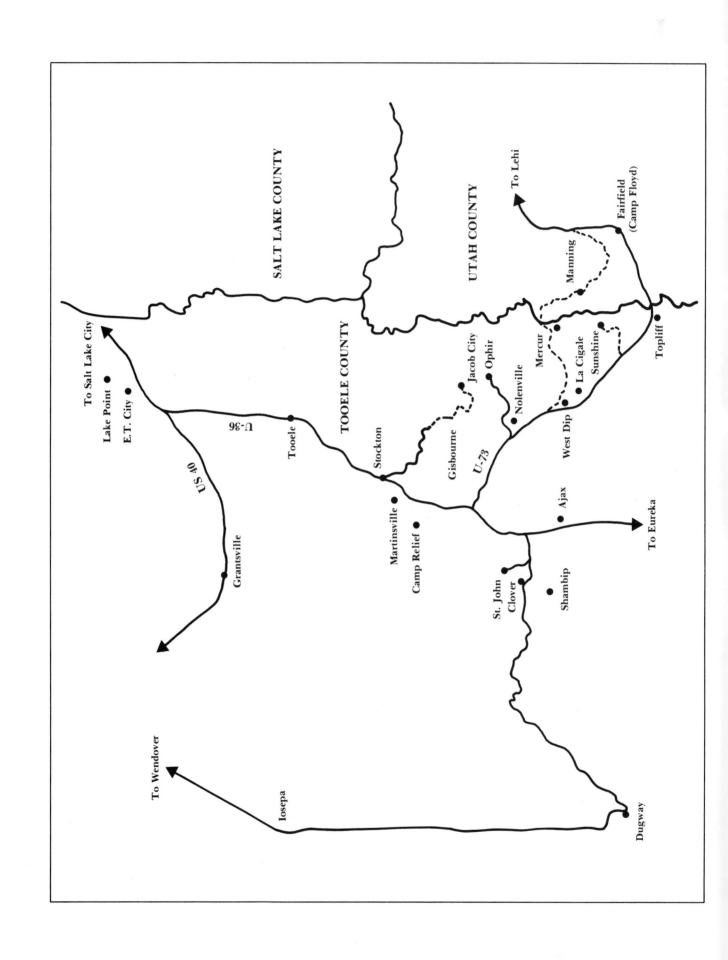

CHAPTER TWO

IN THE RUSH VALLEY DISTRICT

The first white men to explore the valley west of the Oquirrh Range were Spanish miners. They named the valley for the large number of "Tulares", or bulrushes, that grew on the shore of a shallow snow water lake. When Mormon settlers came to the valley, they called it "Tule" Valley for the Spanish "tulare", and named the fresh water lake at its northern end Lake Shambip. Over the years the settlers' "Tule" was gradually corrupted to "Tooele". During the early 1860's soldier-prospectors from Patrick E. Connor's California Volunteers discovered gold and silver in the Oquirrhs. The name changing went full circle when they renamed it Rush Valley for the bulrushes which had originally inspired the name Tulare. They also changed Lake Shambip to Rush Lake. Their mining claims were registered in the Rush Valley Mining District.

By 1865, two years after the Rush Valley District was organized, more than 400 mining claims had been located, and a wild camp named Jacob City was booming near the head of Dry Canyon. Col. Connor built the district's first smelter at Martinsville. Overnight, fabulous camps like Ophir, where $1,000,000 in silver was dug from a shallow hole, and Mercur, where whiskey was cheaper than water, exploded into being.

Not all of Rush Valley's towns were mining camps, however. Ajax was a strange town that was built underground, and Iosepa was a community of Hawaiians in the middle of Skull Valley. There was even a town named for a cricket! There were a lot of strange places in Rush Valley that today are interesting for those who follow the treasure trail. Ancient stamp mills and rusting gold pans may be junk to one man, but they are treasures to another. There are century-old whiskey bottles worth hundreds of dollars, and relics to gladden the heart of any antique collector.

JACOB CITY

Jacob City, one of Utah's earliest mining camps, was built near the head of Dry Canyon in Tooele County, southeast of present-day Stockton. It was reached by means of a steep, winding road which passed Gisbourne, another early camp. A few claims were being worked in Dry Canyon as early as 1863, and the townsite was established soon after that. In 1870 a newspaper reporter described Jacob City as "A stringtown along the bottom of a steep and narrow canyon, where houses are built leaning against the mountainside to keep them from falling into the canyon below." Capt. John Codman, a noted traveler and writer of that period, said of Jacob City, "Its buildings were hanging like a collection of crows' nests to the side of the mountain. The camp cannot be approached on wagon wheels and even sure footed horses are doubtful of their foothold on its streets, which are paved with boulders and drained by a creek in torrent!"

But five years later another visitor reported that Jacob City boasted, "Two stores, two first-class eating houses, two meat markets and other businesses as well, but all were out-numbered by saloons!" Most of its buildings were made of logs, but its grand hotel was built of "finished redwood". Col. Patrick Connor, "Father of Utah Mining", built the Great Basin Mill at Jacob City, while other mine owners erected the Jacob Mill at Martinsville.

Jacob City was the largest producer of precious metals in the district for a time, but as its mines became worked out, other discoveries were made in the Oquirrhs that lured away its miners and lulled Jacob City into a sleep from which it never awakened. When they moved to richer camps, the miners left many treasures for today's relic hunter. One of my favorites is a cobalt blue Hutchinson's Stopper "pop" bottle, embossed with the name "T. Parson's, Salt Lake City" which was found near an old cabin there.

GISBOURNE

Located high on the rugged face of the Oquirrhs south of Stockton in Tooele County was a mining camp named Gisbourne, often called Gibson. The road to it was originally built by Mack Gisbourne to reach his Queen Of The Hills Mine. When later strikes were made Gisbourne turned it into a toll road, and soon recovered the $23,000 it cost to build. On both sides of a windswept ridge below Gisbourne's mine, two rows of

crude cabins grew into the camp of Gisbourne.

When Capt. John Codman visited there in 1870, he described Mack Gisbourne as "Half owner of the Mono Mine, a property that earns him $30,000 each month. We met him at Jacob City, clothed in a shabby suit that could not have cost over $20 and smoking a cigar made in Cuba. For a man with a fortune, he looks more like a man in debt for his last meal!"

There were many prosperous businesses at Gisbourne, including a stock brokerage firm. For a few years the little camp was a busy place, but eventually faded before the brighter lights of Jacob City and Ophir. Today, Mack Gisbourne's toll road still passes by his Queen Of The Hills Mine. Where it crosses a windy ridge, several old cabins, caved in from the weight of years, can be seen in the brush below. Those frame skeletons are the ghostly remains of Gisbourne.

MARTINSVILLE
&
CAMP RELIEF

One of Tooele County's first settlements was located 3 miles south of Stockton, just west of U-36, near where an historical marker now stands. It was a stringtown that grew up along the now dried-up Rush Lake. The town's official name was Martinsville, so called because the town resembled their nest communities where each nest leans against its neighbor. Houses at Martinsville were built against one another so they wouldn't fall down! Most people familiar with Martinsville know it as Slagtown, for the great piles of slag left over from its smelting days.

By 1870 several large mills and smelters were in operation at Martinsville, reducing the rich silver ore being hauled from Jacob City and Gisbourne. Among

Camp Relief was established in 1853, but hardly a trace remained when Martinsville was built nearby in 1868. -Utah Historical Society-

them were the Chicago and Godbe smelters, both described as modern, up-to-date plants. The Waterman Smelter was located near town at the edge of Rush Lake. Apparently it was smaller than the others, and had only two furnaces, each 9' high and only a 28 ton per day capacity,

Martinsville was a lively place while it lasted, one visitor recalling that it had 8 business buildings, 6 of which were saloons! Southeast of the marker on U-36, a grove of trees can be seen by the railroad tracks. In those trees are the foundations of an old mill, that are about that's left of Martinsville.

Martinsville was built near the site of an even earlier settlement. In 1854, army troops under the command of Col. E.J. Steptoe, established Camp Relief at the edge of Rush Lake. On what later became the Denton Ranch, quarters for 85 dragoons and 136 teamsters were built, as well as billets for Col. Steptoe and his officers. Several large barns and stables were also built. While the camp was a busy place the firm of Bracken & Young was the post sutler. But by the time silver was discovered in the Oquirrhs and Martinsville was born, Camp Relief was only a memory. Its site should be a treasure hunter's bonanza today for the troops must have lost and thrown away many things. Why not give it a try?

SHAMBIP

The town of Shambip was in Tooele County, 3 miles southwest of St. John and 1 mile from the tiny settlement of Clover. In 1856 it was known as Johnson's Settlement, but later its name was changed to Shambip, an Indian word meaning "bulrush." It was the county seat of Shambip County, which was absorbed by Tooele, Juab and Utah counties in 1862.

By 1859, the county seat boasted enough population to warrant building a schoolhouse. Among her residents was Bill Hickman, the Danite Chief of Utah, who owned a ranch nearby. A stockade was built to protect residents against marauding Indians, but its creek bottom location proved to be a poor one for defense. In 1868 it was torn down and used to build a schoolhouse at St. John.

Clover Creek provided a minimum of irrigation water for the parched acres at Shambip. Thus, the town grew slowly. Both the county and the county seat lagged far behind their neighbors. Six years after it had been created by the territorial legislature, Shambip County was dis-incorporated.

Ruinous floods were common along Clover Creek. In 1878, a major one destroyed crops and drowned three friendly Indians who had been camped nearby. Mormon Church authorities advised the settlers to move to higher ground. Although they were reluctant to do so, in time they left their homes and moved to St. John and Clover. Sagebrush now covers the site of Shambip, and the tiny cemetery at the edge of the cedared foothills.

Not everything was on the level at old Ophir!

OPHIR

From Tooele go south 14 miles on U-36 to its junction with U-73, then turn southeast 5 miles to Ophir Canyon. The mining camp of Ophir, named for the fabled mines of King Solomon, is located 3 miles up canyon. The first claims were found in the late 1860's by Col. Connor's troops, and within a few weeks the town of Ophir was born. $1,000,000 in nearly pure silver was dug from a shallow pit at the Kearsage Mine in a few weeks, and by 1900 the camp's production had exceeded $13,000,000. Besides the Kearsage, the Velocipede, Shamrock, Miner's Delight and Wild Delirium mines all turned out a steady stream of silver bullion.

Senator W.A. Clark of Montana owned mining properties at Ophir, and built a short line railroad from the canyon to the rails of the San Pedro, Los Angeles & Salt Lake Railroad in Rush Valley. Ore from Ophir's mines was shipped to Godbe's Smelter and the Walker Brothers Pioneer Mill at Martinsville. More than 2,500 mining claims had been staked at Ophir by 1871, with some boasting values of 20,000 ounces of silver to the ton! That same year Ophir's population reached 1,200. But its life proved shorter than many camps along the Oquirrhs, for although its ore veins were rich, they were shallow. Except for a few big producers like the Ophir Hill Mine, they were soon worked out.

Ophir never really became a ghost town, because a few people have continued to call it home, though they've often numbered less than a dozen. With the recent rise in silver prices it might hear the sound of honky-tonk pianos and the roar of mine machinery again. But even if it never does, it is a pleasant place to visit. Its long closed buildings and empty houses are interesting subjects for shutter-bugs, since Ophir looks much like it did when Col. Connor's troops dug for silver more than a century ago.

NOWLENVILLE

The little hamlet called Nowlenville, often shown on old maps as Knollenville, was located south and west of the mouth of Ophir Canyon. Settled in 1869 as a farm community, Nowlenville got caught up in the boom at nearby Ophir and supplied the camp with farm and dairy produce. Although a small place, it had several stores and a Mormon Church, something unusual in Tooele County at that time. Most of the towns of Rush Valley were mining camps, and strongholds of the anti-Mormon Liberal Party. It's probably safe to say that the Liberal Party wasn't always exactly fair. In one election its candidate received 3,000 votes, more than twice the registered voters in the county!

Although Nowlenville started out as a farm community, there wasn't sufficient land or water to support the town it had become by the time Ophir collapsed. Thus, when the mining camp became a ghost town, Nowlenville folded also. People who lived in Nowlenville, many of whom had worked at Ophir, moved to greener pastures, while farmers suddenly had no market. Ophir's demise caused the death of Nowlenville, and by 1893 only three families remained. Today, there remains one small farm. It could be a good place to hunt for relics, though. More than 100 years of spring floods have washed much of Ophir down canyon to Nowlenville.

Bill Hickman lost his life trying to find Brigham Young's cursed gold!

LAKE POINT
&
BRIGHAM YOUNG'S CURSED MINE

Lake Point lay at the north end of the Oquirrh Mountains, 13 miles northeast of Tooele and approximately 1 mile from the present water level of the Great Salt Lake. When first settled in 1854, it was an outgrowth of E.T. City, a tiny settlement named for Ezra Taft Benson, a Mormon Church leader. Lake Point really began to grow when Dr. Jeter Clinton built a resort there. E.T. City wasn't faring well, anyway, for farmers there found the area's soil too salty and alakaline. But what really caused them to move to Lake Point was the advent of steamships on the Great Salt Lake. Mine owners discovered that ore could be shipped cheaply across the lake to Corinne, where mills and smelters were located. Almost overnight Lake Point became Utah's first seaport.

Silver ore was hauled by wagon to Lake Point and loaded onto steamships which carried it 80 miles north across the inland sea. The "City of Corinne" and the "Kate Connor" were large steam powered freighters, while the "Pioneer", "Rosy Brown" and "Pluribathah" were smaller ships. The "Kate Connor" which was owned by Col. Connor, could carry 300 passengers. Meanwhile business was so good at Dr. Clinton's resort that he built the Clinton Hotel, where he catered to as many as 50,000 guests per year.

A steam powered tractor hauls ore from Nowlenville to the San Pedro, Los Angeles & Salt Lake Railroad.

Among the early businesses at Lake Point were Shield's General Merchandise, Maxwell's Dry Goods, the Richville Flour Mill and the Utah Wool Company. In August, 1873, the rails of the Salt Lake, Pioche & Sevier Valley Railroad were laid into town. The railroad didn't prove to be a boon to the economy, however, for it brought higher, rather than lower, freight rates. Shipping ore by wagon had always been expensive, so mine owners began building mills closer to their mines, putting Lake Point's mainstay on the skids. The long piers that stretched out into the lake began to decay and its once proud ships came to an even more inglorious end.

The huge "City of Corinne" was renamed the "Garfield" with hopes of making it an excursion ship. But it burned near Black Rock, leaving only a charred skeleton to settle into the sand. The "Kate Connor" was sold to a livestock company which used it to haul sheep and cattle to the lake's islands. Lake Point was dead, and E.T. City was already only a memory. The lakeshore reverted to grasslands and cattle could be seen grazing where buildings once stood. Today the ruins of several stone buildings can be seen far from the lakeshore, where the lake's receding water has left them. They are the remains of the old woolen mills and all that is left of Lake Point, Utah's seaport.

During the 1860's, John Croslin, a convert to the Mormon Church, was hunting stray sheep in a canyon above Rowberry's Sawmill, which was located at Twin Springs, southwest of Lake Point, when he came upon a ledge of quartz rock heavily criss-crossed with wire gold. In deference to Brigham Young's admonition against mining, Croslin didn't tell anyone where the ledge was and went directly to the Mormon leader. Young told Croslin that he wanted no gold mines anywhere near Salt Lake City: "If you Elders want to go gold mining, go and be damned. I would not give a picayune to keep you from damnation!" He added that a curse would befall Croslin or anyone who developed the golden ledge. Croslin returned to Lake Point, knowing full well the value of the ledge, but fearing the prophet's warning.

People at Rowberry's Sawmill and around Lake Point knew of his find, and thus he was hard-pressed for information. He was true to his promise not to work the golden ledge, but did admit that he knew where it was. Croslin once said that he could stand in the doorway of Rowberry's sawmill and look into the canyon where the ledge was hidden. When friends began to ridicule him, he answered, "You may think the gold is not there, but I have seen it every time I pass that place. I have seen it while following my sheep, and when looking for timber. It is still there!"

A few years later, when his brother-in-law began selling pieces of raw gold around Lake Point and Tooele, it was thought that Croslin had revealed the lost ledge to him. Then one day the other man's body was found at the edge of the foothills. Some said he must have been killed by Indians, but there wasn't a mark on his body. Croslin claimed it was Brigham Young's curse!

It wasn't long before Coslin himself was killed in a mill accident. After he died two youths, said to be his nephews, claimed to have a map he'd made. They may indeed have found the mine for they got into a fight, perhaps over the division of the gold, and one killed the other. The killer was banished from Utah with a warning never to return. Was it the curse?

Suddenly, Bill Hickman appeared and persuaded Croslin's widow to help him find the gold ledge. Federal marshals, who were on Hickman's trail for murder, forced him to flee for his life. He was pursued to Wyoming where he died or was killed, depending on who tells the story. Mrs. Croslin became an outcast because of her association with him. Still more of the curse?

Until Brigham Young died in 1877, no one dared search for the lost Croslin Ledge, and as far as I know, no one has looked for it since. But if you decide to look for it, be careful, for terrible things happen to those who look for Brigham Young's cursed mine!

AJAX

From Tooele drive south 24 miles on U-36 to Ajax, now little more than a depression on the east side of the road. That depression contains what people throughout Rush Valley called the "Big Store", an unusual emporium built by William Ajax in 1870. Ajax's store was 80' wide and 100' long, built entirely underground, 20' beneath the desert floor! The huge hole was dug entirely by hand by Ajax. When completed it contained more than $150,000 worth of goods necessary for the mining camps of Rush Valley. At first, the settlement which grew up around Ajax's store was called Puckerville, though a post office was granted it under the name Centre. But as it blossomed into a regular town, people called it Ajax.

A modern hotel was built, above ground, providing first class meals and lodging. In addition, the roads and trails to other towns and mines met at Ajax. There were corrals for 100 horses, 300 cattle and 6,000 sheep. But Ajax and its unusual underground store depended upon the mines of Rush Valley, so when camps began to fade, the "Big Store" had no customers and was forced to close. Most of its surface buildings were hauled to other places, but the big underground store couldn't be moved.

It was thought the curious underground store would last forever, but one cold night, a hobo hiking along the SP, LA & SL Railroad took shelter in it and built a fire to keep warm. The desert dry timbers caught fire immediately. In minutes the entire structure was in flames, leaving only the large depression on the desert floor to mark its site.

Here and there relic hunters have dug shallow holes near a spring that still flows from a rusty pipe into an old barrel nearly rotted away with age. Sagebrush has claimed most of Ajax now, but a few reminders of its heyday can still be found. Who knows what else lays waiting in the ruins of the "Big Store"?

MERCUR

Go south from Tooele on U-36 to its junction with U-73, continue southeast for 5 miles to where a dirt road turns east, and follow it 8 miles to Mercur, one of Utah's most famous mining camps. The Sparrow Hawk Mine, discovered during the early 1860's, was probably the first claim staked at Mercur and started a mad rush to the new district. In 3 months a wild camp of 1,200 miners had exploded into being in the shadow of Lewiston Peak. The new camp of Lewiston's future did not look bright however, for its placer gold was shallow. They also found large veins of gold bearing quartz, but knew nothing about mining it. It turned out that the ore was complex and not easily milled by processes then known.

For years they worked on a method of milling the unusual mercury bearing gold ore they called mercur. Their persistence paid; during the 1890's the McArthur-Forrest process of milling was developed. Better known as the cyanide process, it breathed new life into the old camp. Almost overnight Lewiston boomed again, but this time it was called Mercur, after the "mercur" ore.

Mercur grew until its population topped 6,000 and it had every kind of business lining its streets. The vices were well known in Mercur, where there were more murderers than preachers. On Statehood Day, January 4th, 1896, just when its future looked brightest and its citizens were preparing for a gala celebration, the entire city burned to the ground! But its mines were too rich to let die; like the phoenix, Mercur rose from the ashes, bigger and richer than ever. New buildings sprang up everywhere. As proof of her permanence, the Salt Lake & Mercur Railroad was built from Camp Floyd to the flourishing town. By 1902 its population had reached 12,000. Life was cheap at Mercur, if nothing else was. Whiskey was cheaper than water, which was sold door to door for a dollar a bucket. Sugar cost $1 a pound and canned goods $2.50 each!

Mercur's mines and mills never stopped producing a steady stream of gold bars. The Golden Gate Mine alone produced $20,000,000! Then, on June 26th, 1902, a tiny tongue of flame in a back room of the Preble Hotel burst into an inferno, and Mercur burned a second time. Before the ashes cooled, a great cloudburst struck, and sent flash floods down the burned slopes that wiped away what little was left.

It didn't take long for Mercur to be deserted, and its mine shafts to cave in. For years the only people who visited there were relic hunters; every mountain thunderstorm exposed more remnants of its past to view. But modern prospectors have returned to Mercur. When fire and flood destroyed the town the gold remained. The Getty Oil Company now owns many of the old claims and is planning to reopen the camp a third time. It was a wild camp as Lewiston, and a boomtown as Mercur. Who knows what it will be this time?

WEST DIP & LA CIGALE

West Dip, or West Mercur as it was sometimes called, was located north of U-73, 1 mile south of the mouth of Mercur Canyon on the west slope of the Oquirrh Range. Like its twin, the little camp of La Cigale located a half mile south, West Dip had several promising mines, but their veins proved to be shallow. Nevertheless, as long as Mercur's ore held out, West Dip's future was secure because many miners preferred it to the high elevation of Mercur.

Even its role as a rest stop depended on Mercur's mines. Freighters and travelers often stopped to rest their teams there. But Mercur's future wasn't bright. After she burned and was deserted, West Dip was abandoned as well. Today black mine dumps mark its site, and caved cellars and buried trash piles are favored places for relic hunters as they search for bits and pieces of its past.

La Cigale, French for cricket, was also settled during the 1890's. There was a Cricket Mine at La Cigale, but whether the camp was named for the mine or for the large number of Mormon crickets found there is unknown. Like West Dip, its mines were not rich enough to support it without Mercur, and it died the same death. On the mountain front beyond its black waste dumps there stands an ancient looking stone wall. It is nearly the same color as the mountain itself, and hard to see. Only desert amethysts, sun-purpled bottles from yesterday, remain to prove that people once lived on those barren slopes.

MANNING
&
DEAD SOLDIER'S GOLD

Manning was also built on Mercur's fortunes but on the opposite side of the Oquirrhs, in Utah County. Its site can be reached on a dirt road that leaves U-73 just east of Camp Floyd. During the 1890's the gold camp of Mercur enjoyed a resurrection, thinks to the development of the cyanide process of ore treatment. One of the first companies at Mercur to use the process was the Mercur Gold Mining and Milling Company. Its leading promoter was L.S. Manning, whose name was given to Manning Canyon and later to the town of Manning. Since the cyanide process consumed large quantities of water which Mercur had little of, the company built its mill in Manning Canyon, where there was plenty of it.

Mercur, Utah's famous gold camp on June 26th. 1902.
-Utah Historical Society-

The next day, 2½ hours after the fire. -Utah Historical Society-

Manning grew up around the new mill, with the usual assortment of frame houses, false front buildings and honky-tonk piano saloons. Because the mill worked around the clock, a railroad was soon needed between it and Mercur. The only feasible route proved to be through Manning Canyon. The standard gauge Salt Lake & Mercur Railroad was built up its formidable slopes by J.G. Jacobs, and was completed on January 21st, 1895. Passenger service started the following June. Although it was only six miles up Manning Canyon, rails had to be laid for twelve in order to overcome the steep grades in the canyon. The grade was so tortuous, as it twisted and turned its way up canyon, that the engine was often alongside the caboose. It was claimed there wasn't a straight rail on the entire line!

Manning depended upon Mercur, and Mercur died when it burned to the ground in 1902. With its life blood dried up, Manning quickly died also. It wasn't

long before the rails of the SL & M were salvaged for scrap and its buildings claimed by the deep snows of winter. Little remains of Manning today but piles of stone where buildings once stood, and a great tailings pond where one of the west's first cyanide mills was built. Time has been cruel to Manning; but there is a lost mine close by which could bring it to life again if ever found.

Col. Connor allowed his soldiers stationed at Fort Douglas to prospect the nearby mountains. Col. Connor believed that the discovery of minerals near Salt Lake City would attract an influx of gentiles into Utah, and help dilute the Mormon population. He was also concerned that his troops not be "engaged in eating the bread of idleness."

In December, 1862, several troopers were prospecting in the Oquirrh Mountains. One of the soldiers, Pvt. James W. Baldwin, Co. A, 2nd Cavalry, climbed higher than the others and discovered a place where wire gold could be broken loose from a rose colored quartz ledge. Baldwin took as much of the wire gold as he could pry loose with his knife and, before starting down the mountain to his comrades, cut a large letter "B" in the bark of a huge pine tree.

Col. Connor pronounced the ore to be richer than any he had seen in California. The prospector-soldiers had intended to return immediately to Baldwin's ledge, but had found their fellows at the fort preparing to leave camp. On January 22nd, 1863 Col. Connor and his California Volunteers made a forced march north to the Bear River, where they surprised the Bannock Indians in their winter camp. One of the worst massacres of western history occurred, with nearly all the Indians, including women and children, being slaughtered. The massacre at Bear River has been a shameful blot on Utah history ever since.

During the massacre more than 300 Indians and 20 soldiers were killed. Among them was Pvt. James Bald-

Manning on the Salt Lake & Mercur Railroad. Your search for the Dead Soldier's Gold starts here! -Utah Historical Society-

win, killed on the morning of January 29th, 1863. His companions later searched for his ledge, but they found no trace of his wire gold.

Somewhere high in the Oquirrhs, probably not far from Manning, there may still be an old pine tree standing with a large letter "B" carved in its bark. If you find it, you should have no trouble finding Baldwin's lost ledge.

SUNSHINE & TOPLIFF

The little Tooele County mining camp with the cheery name of Sunshine was located in Sunshine Canyon, near the south end of the Oquirrh Range. It boasted several good mines, including the Sunshine Mine, for which the town was named. Other early properties included the Malvern and the Red Cloud. Owners of the latter boasted that they were sinking a shaft on a 26' wide vein of pay dirt. Owners of another early mine, the Overland, built a 100 ton mill on their property. A visiting reporter called the Old Fred Mine, "A splendid property!"

Today the magnificent 26' vein at the Red Cloud Mine and the Overland Mill are only memories, while the Old Fred isn't considered splendid anymore. Sunshine never achieved much fame of its own, sitting as it did in the shadow of nearby Mercur. It faded almost as quickly as it blossomed.

An almost impassable road climbs up Sunshine Canyon from U-73, and leaves the highway 8 miles southwest of Camp Floyd. A better road leaves the Manning to Mercur road near its summit, on the Manning side of the range. Whichever is taken, the huge mine dumps nearby leave no doubt where the townsite was. Much of the town has long vanished, but its dumps and shafts will last until the millennium. Relic hunters can still find mementos of Sunshine's past if they look in the right place. The last time I visited the old town, I found a pair of leg irons hanging from a cedar tree. I wonder what story they could tell?

From Sunshine's perch on the south end of the Oquirrhs, you can look south across ten miles of desert to the north end of the East Tintic Range, where another small camp lived out its brief life. Topliff was a camp whose economy was based on quarrying limestone rock used as flux in smelters. It was a solid town for awhile, and had several fine stone buildings, the empty shells of which still stand. To get to Topliff, go 6 miles west from Fairfield, then turn south 6 miles. If you hike among its ruins watch out for rattlesnakes, for they're thick as fleas on a dog's back! There are relics to be found at Topliff, if you don't get nervous easily. I found a beautiful purple beer mug there, and with a detector old coins and trade tokens can be found. Just be sure the buzz you hear comes from your detector, and not from a rattler!

IOSEPA

Iosepa was settled in 1889 in Skull Valley, near the site of what was called the old Quincy Ranch, 15 miles south of Timpie Springs in Tooele County, by Hawaiian converts to the Mormon Church. Its name is the Hawaiian spelling of Joseph, the name give to the town in honor of Joseph F. Smith, a Mormon Church leader who had once been a missionary in Hawaii. The

Only rattlesnakes call Topliff home now, so watch your step!

Even ghosts are lonely at old Iosepa in Skull Valley. -Deseret News-

townsite consisted of 1,280 acres, purchased at a cost of $40,000. There were soon well built stores, homes, a schoolhouse, a church and even an underground water system. Although the town was well planned, the Hawaiians were not adapted to the harsh desert climate of Skull Valley which was so unlike their island homeland, and they suffered terribly.

In an effort to fulfill Brigham Young's prophecy, "That the desert shall blossom as the rose", 300 fruit trees, 300 walnut trees, 100 ornamentals and numerous shrubs, including plenty of roses, were planted at Iosepa. But it wasn't part of nature's plan that roses grow in Skull Valley. And then, to add to their problems, during the 1890's leprosy made its dread appearance in the community! A pest house was built on a barren sun-baked flat away from the town. A flag was raised by the unfortunates confined there when food or water was needed. It wasn't until one man and two women had died at Iosepa that it was admitted that the islanders couldn't survive there. The experiment was given up in 1916 and the Mormon Church paid for Iosepa's citizens to return to Hawaii. There probably wasn't a dry eye in the town.

Atop a low benchland one half mile east of Timpie Springs road, fire hydrants and rows of stumps of trees planted by the Hawaiians can still be seen in the sagebrush where there once were streets. About a mile farther east is the most forlorn little cemetery in Utah; its tombstones bear legends written in strange looking Hawaiian characters. They mark the final resting places of the island settlers who died in Skull Valley's strange town of Iosepa.

Born in Hawaii, died at Iosepa. It was a hard life.
-Utah Historical Society-

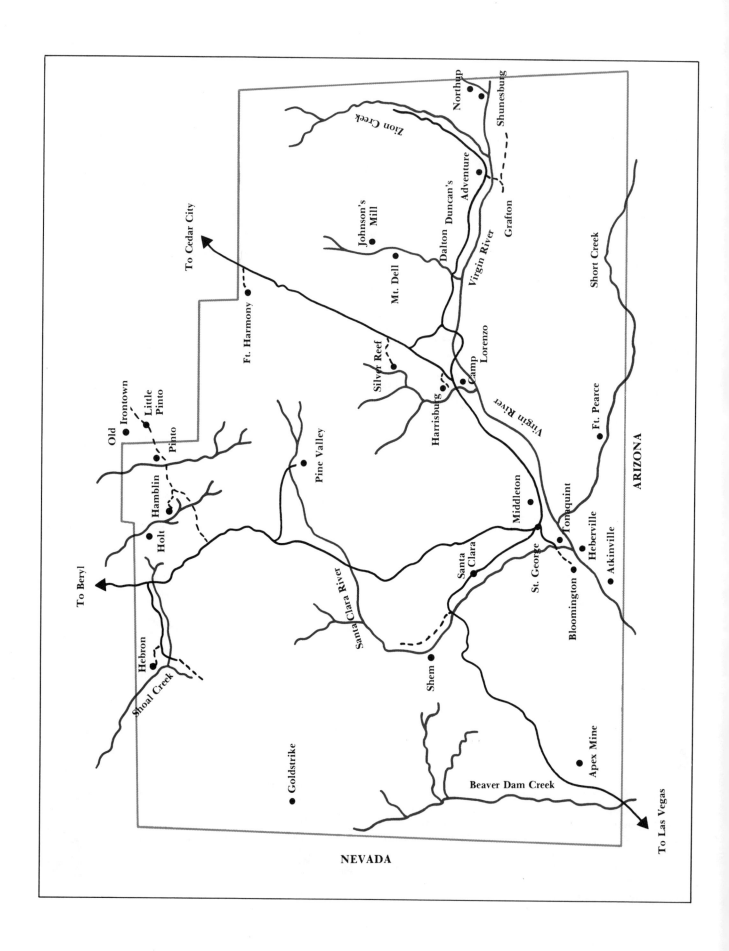

The Wells Fargo Bank at Silver Reef, as solid as the day it was built.

CHAPTER THREE

AWAY DOWN SOUTH IN DIXIE

Washington County is Utah's Dixie. To the Mormon settlers who first made their homes along the Virgin River, it must have seemed like the old south, for crops like cotton and sorghum could easily be grown, and fruit trees thrived wherever water could be brought to its vermillion soil. It was water that made Dixie blossom, and it was water that caused many of its towns to die. Sometimes there wasn't enough to save sunparched crops, but often there was so much that farms were flooded. One settler at Bloomington claimed there was little water to begin with, and what there was had to be made to run uphill. Another at Grafton complained he had so much that his barn was washed away!

Settlements along the Santa Clara and other streams suffered the same fate as those along the Virgin. Canals and flumes built at great labor were washed away, and stream beds were eroded so deeply that precious water couldn't be obtained from them. Many towns not abandoned because of drought or flood were deserted during the Blackhawk Indian War. Still others faded into oblivion with the failure of the United Order, a Mormon Church sponsored cooperative scheme of the 1870's.

Not all of Dixie's ghost towns were farm settlements. Included in their number are several once prosperous mining camps. Silver Reef was a unique camp. Although the best trained geologists of the day claimed that silver couldn't be found in sandstone, more than $8,000,000 worth of the white metal was dug from the red cliffs before that wild and wooly camp gained ghost town status. Shem and Hebron were unusual in that they were Mormon mining camps. Shem died when the Apex mine failed.

The story of Hebron's demise is less certain. The gentile version has it destroyed during a great earthquake in 1902. Mormons claim it was shaken to the ground by an act of providence because of its wickedness. But both agree that it was as wicked as Sodom!

Where earthquakes didn't lay waste to the land, and floods didn't wash it away, and the desert sun and winds hadn't yet burned it black, time took its toll. Dixie's ghost towns were hard won places in a harsh land, and today are favorite places for treasure hunters. It's a poor town in Dixie that doesn't have at least one treasure or lost mine tale to tell. But even if you don't find the pot at the end of the rainbow, it is the rainbow itself, and the red cliffs and snow-capped peaks that are the real treasures of Dixie.

SILVER REEF

There are two versions of how the fabulous mining camp of Silver Reef, 1½ miles northwest of Leeds, came into being. One claims that a grindstone made by Alma Angel of Leeds was broken while being transported to a mine at Pioche, Nevada, and as a joke a piece of it was taken to "Metaliferous Murphy", an assayer who had a reputation of finding high ore values in any rock tested. But even the miners who were used to Murphy's exaggerated reports were amazed when he reported that the pieces of grindstone assayed 200 ounces of silver to the ton! The other version has a visitor to Leeds astounded to see drops of melted silver oozing from a hot mantle stone over his host's blazing fireplace. Whichever story is true, the sandstone containing the high grade silver was traced to a ridge, or reef as such ridges are called in that area, where the wild one-of-a-kind boom town of Silver Reef would soon explode on the desert floor.

John Kemple is credited with the discovery of silver at the reef in 1869. He named his claim the Shauntie for Shauntie Town in Beaver County. But his claim went undeveloped. He couldn't find anyone willing to finance him, since geologists and engineers all agreed that silver couldn't be found in sandstone. Seven years later, in August, 1875, William Barbee, prospecting for the Walker Brothers of Salt Lake City, found an outcrop of silver ore near Kemple's earlier find, at a place where a wagon wheel had broken off the edge of the ledge. Barbee staked the Tecumseh claim on what he called Bonanza Flats, and made a shipment of $500

to the ton ore to the Walker Brothers mill at Salt Lake City. He staked out a townsite he named Bonanza City, and in less than a month it had become a boom town. Then Hyrum Jacobs came along, a peddler from Pioche who wanted to open a store, but refused to pay Barbee's price for a business lot. Jacobs went a mile beyond Bonanza City and set up the Silver Reef Store. Some newly arrived miners built their cabins near him, and Silver Reef was born.

During the next three months, 275 mining claims were registered. Silver Reef grew so fast it literally swallowed Barbee's Bonanza City. By the following spring it was a rough and ready town of 2,000 miners and boasted fine hotels, 1 bank, 9 stores, 6 saloons, several restaurants, a hospital, 2 dancehalls, a brass band, all of the popular lodges of the day, 2 newspapers, a Chinatown and 3 cemeteries whose populations grew almost as fast as the town's did.

Today its most noticeable landmark is a tall shaft of polished granite surrounded by a beautiful ornamental metal fence woven in the form of living shrubbery. Beneath the red soil lies the body of Henry Clark, Silver Reef's most notorious gambler. Clark was a dandy who dressed like a Mississippi river boat gambler and made a fortune in the gambling halls of Silver Reef. According to legend, he killed several men who accused him of cheating. One night Clark's luck was so good he couldn't seem to lose. He broke the bank at the faro table and had nearly bankrupted the roulette dealer when the owner ordered him to leave, implying that he was cheating. Clark went for his gun, but his luck had run out. The saloon owner beat him to

A quiet street at Silver Reef in 1885.

The grave of Henry Clark, gambler. He was a little too slow on the draw!

the draw and ended his winning streak for good! Henry Clark cached several fortunes at Silver Reef, but was a loner who told no one where they were hidden. No one has found any of his gold yet.

The leaders among the 37 mining companies at Silver Reef included the Barbee & Walker, Stormont, and Leeds and Christie. Some of the smaller properties were the Gisborn, Stormy King, Silver Plume, Lulu and Last Chance. Giant stamp mills roared day and night pounding out a never ending stream of silver, which was cast into 25 pound bars valued at $500 each. Hay sold for $50 a ton and Dixie wine was $2 a gallon. For awhile everyone was rich. In 1876 the Leeds claim was sold for $76,000 and produced that much silver for its new owner in less than a month! High concentrations of silver were found in logs of petrified wood which were common throughout the area. One reportedly yielded 17,000 ounces of the white metal!

By 1880 Wells Fargo had shipped more than $8,000,000 worth of bullion from Silver Reef's mines, but the boom was almost over. That year a union organizer named Tom Forrest killed Mike Corbis, a popular mine foreman. He was jailed at St. George for his protection from angry miners at Silver Reef. On the day of their friend's funeral the miners went to St. George and dragged Forrest from his jail cell. He was hung without a trial from a tree in front of George Cottom's house. After watching the hanging, Cottom, an old Mormon who didn't like anything about Silver Reef, said he had watched that tree grow for twenty years, but that that was the first time it had ever borne fruit!

The price of silver had been skidding, and dropped from $1.20 an ounce to only 65¢, forcing mine owners to cut wages from $4 to $2 a day. The newly unionized miners went on strike and the mines were closed. Water soon flooded the idle shafts. Almost as quickly as it had bloomed, Silver Reef died. Some of its buildings were moved to Leeds. Others were destroyed by fires and vandals. Many were torn down in hopes of quick riches when a cache of gold coins was found behind a secret wall panel in a saloon. A few more caches and post-hole banks were found, but the big casino, Henry Clark's gold, has not been found.

Today only the Wells Fargo Bank, several homes, the ruins of dozens of others and three old cemeteries remain at Silver Reef, the only place in the world where silver was found in sandstone.

HARRISBURG & ITS NAUGHTY NEIGHBORS

In 1859, Moses Harris led a small band of Mormon settlers to where Quail Creek joins the Virgin River, 7 miles southwest of Leeds. Although farmers there depended upon the meager flow of Quail and Cottonwood creeks, the settlement grew rapidly, and had a population of 200 by 1866. A church was built and there was a school attended by 60 students. At first the new town was called Cottonwood, but during a visit Brigham Young suggested it be named in honor of Harris.

Harrisburg became a favorite stopping place for wagon trains bound for California, and the fame of its vineyards and orchard was carried west by them. The town's population peaked in 1869. That year a plague

Harrisburg is a scene right out of old Mexico.

of grasshoppers destroyed its crops. The following year a long drought began that dried Cottonwood Creek to a trickle. Farms dried up under the hot Dixie sun and once green fields were abandoned. Every passing year saw more people leave. By 1890 Harrisburg had only 14 residents, and by 1910 there were none! Today the ruins of old stone houses, miles of hand built stone fence and a forgotten little cemetery are all that remain.

By the side of the Virgin River, a mile southeast of Harrisburg, the remains of a two-story rock house mark the site of Camp Lorenzo, a short lived Cotton Mission settlement also known as Brigham City. Between Camp Lorenzo and St. George several other small towns flourished temporarily. At Washington, a crumbling but much photographed old cotton mill still stands by the Virgin where it was built more than a century ago. Near it was Morristown, located in the "Washington Field". Between Morristown and St. George was Middleton, another small but promising community that, like the delicate Sego Lily, bloomed only briefly.

Middleton's most exciting day came in 1878. Ben Pollack had been warned that a band of "notorious horse thieves" were going to steal several prize mares from his corrals at Middleton. Pollack, with Sheriff A.P. Hardy and two deputies, was hidden near his corral that night when three men approached in the darkness. Sheriff Hardy yelled "Throw up your hands!" Gunfire erupted, and when the shooting was over, two rustlers lay on the ground seriously wounded. The third escaped into the darkness.

The wounded men turned out to be outlaws who were wanted at Pioche. Several days later two men who claimed to be law officers from that rough mining camp arrived at Middleton and took custody of the injured men. Sheriff Hardy turned over the two horse thieves and watched them ride out of town. The next day the bodies of both men were found by the side of the trail, still wearing leg-irons and shot through the head. The two "law men" were never seen again. It wasn't healthy to be a horse thief in Dixie!

GRAFTON

The ghost town of Grafton, probably the most photographed in the west, was first settled as Wheeler, in 1859, by Nathan Tenny and others on the south bank of the Virgin River just south of present-day Rockville. The new town had hardly begun to grow before the record floods of 1861 destroyed much of it. But the settlers' sense of humor wasn't daunted, even in the face of disaster. During the worst of the flood a baby girl was born. At her christening she was named Marvelous Flood!

When the flood waters subsided, they moved to New Grafton, 2 miles upstream. The new town thrived and soon claimed a church house, school, post office, several substantial store buildings and what old accounts refer to as an "Ethiopian Band"! Martin Slack and Jabez Woodward were the town's school teachers and James Ballard served as Bishop of the Mormon

The schoolhouse at Grafton. You may have seen Butch Cassidy and the Sundance Kid here! -Utah Historical Society-

No flowers decorate graves in the old Grafton cemetery.

Church. R.W. Reeves operated a general store and Alonzo Russell was the town blacksmith.

Grafton, named for a city in Massachusetts, became the first county seat of Kane County in 1864, before Washington County was created from its western territory. It grew rapidly until 1866 when the outbreak of the Blackhawk War forced its residents to flee to nearby forts for protection. It was while Grafton was deserted that a great storm, remembered as the 40 days and 40 nights of rain, greatly damaged the town and even washed a heavy grain mill away. Further flooding along the Virgin River finally forced its people to seek a less hazardous place to live.

By 1900 only 120 people remained, and they were soon gone. Today its old schoolhouse, picturesque church, and lonely cemetery in the shadow of the red sandstone cliffs are all that remain of the little town whose future once seemed so bright. But though it is abandoned, Grafton has been seen by millions, for it was featured in the movie classic, *Butch Cassidy And The Sundance Kid,* starring Robert Redford and Paul Newman. Could a ghost town ask for more fame than that?

HAMBLIN
&
SPANISH MINE NEAR MOUNTAIN MEADOWS

Hamblin was a small community located on Meadow Valley Creek near the east end of the Mountain Meadows, in what is now the Dixie National Forest. Although it was small, its name was destined to be known throughout the land. Hamblin was settled in

1856 by a small band of Mormons led by famed explorer and trail blazer Jacob Hamblin. Its growth wasn't rapid. During its early years it consisted of only a few dozen cabins and a half finished fort. Though the fort wasn't completed before the Blackhawk War ended, it did offer some protection to the settlers. All of the town's houses were built along one street, the east end of which was closed off by the church and schoolhouse. The Hamblin Co-Op Store at the opposite end of the street created a fort-like appearance.

The lush, green Mountain Meadows with its cold, sparkling streams had long been a favorite resting place for weary travelers along the Old Spanish Trail. In September, 1857, a wagon train of 138 men, women and children from Missouri and Arkansas known as the Fancher Party were camped there. The events leading up to the tragedy are well enough known that they need not be repeated. It is enough to say that after a three day seige, a band of crazed renegade Mormons and savage Indians disarmed the party. Then in cold blood they shot, knifed and clubbed 121 of the party to death. They spared only 17 children of such tender years that it was thought they would be too young to remember the awful slaughter.

The children were taken to Hamblin until they could be given to Mormon families to raise. But the dreadful massacre couldn't be kept a secret. Soon the names Mountain Meadows and Hamblin were known across the land. Jacob Hamblin, for whom the town was named, had always been a peace-maker with the Indians and a friend to travelers throughout Dixie. He was completely unaware of the tragedy until after it had occurred.

Nature seemed almost ashamed of the awful thing that had happened there. The cold springs which had watered the meadows since time began stopped flowing. The once green oasis dried up and became a desert. Sagebrush grew head high where only grass had been, as if trying to hide forever the horrible scar made by 121 nameless graves.

Hamblin tried to survive, in spite of its shame, but never outlived her disgrace. For some time new settlers continued to arrive, the pioneer Canfield family among them. The townsite was surveyed, but its days were numbered. Irrigation water came from Meadow Valley Creek, but a series of floods through the 1890's cut deeper into its already deep wash until water could no longer be raised from it onto the fields. People began leaving. It wasn't long before Hamblin was a deserted village. Like the Mountain Meadows, it became a place to be avoided, haunted forever by the ghosts of 121 murdered victims. Today, a rough dirt road leaves U-18 and winds its way through the foothills to the old Hamblin cemetery, all that remains of the town started by Jacob Hamblin.

Hamblin is the place to start your search for the Lost Hornblende Mine. The July, 1941 issue of the Utah State *Historical Quarterly* reported the following, in an article on Spanish mines in Utah: "Spanish priests, traders and soldiers of fortune traveled the Old Spanish Trail every year, and there is evidence that they prospected for minerals. After the Mormons began settlement in 1851, they found many old prospect holes in the mountains."

George and Fred Ashdown, early settlers of Cedar City, discovered one old mine tunnel high above the vermillion colored cliffs not far from the Mountain Meadows. It had been dug to a depth of 200' and looked as though it had been worked for a very long time. The Ashdowns dug out its badly caved portal and found many old Spanish tools. Those made of brass were still intact, but those of iron began to crumble as soon as the outside air touched them.

The Ashdowns were sawmill operators and thus had little interest in the ancient mine. But they did remove several pieces of heavy black rock which they later gave to a prospector named Ben Evans. Several years later in January, 1868, Evans wandered into Austin, Nevada, and had them assayed. The ore caused such a sensation at Austin that the Reese River *Reveille* reported, "The unusual black hornblende ore brought in from the Mountain Meadows country by Ben Evans is very rich in galena and silver. Evans claims that it came from a mine worked by the Spanish many years ago. That the Spanish formerly worked mines in that region is beyond doubt. Several of their shafts have been discovered there, and since low grade ores would have been of no interest to them, they sought only formations in which the precious metals such as native silver could be found." When Evans returned to Cedar City he found that the Ashdowns had moved on. No

one else knew where the old mine was located.

The lost hornblende mine would probably have been forgotten had not an elderly gentleman of Spanish descent arrived at St. George during the 1920's. He had an ancient looking map which his father had given him. The old man stayed with a rancher, but spent most of his time riding alone in the wild country around the Mountain Meadows, between the Bull Valley and Pine Valley mountains. The old Spaniard seemed very perplexed that he couldn't find what he was looking for.

Finally he could ride no more. He thanked the rancher for his generosity, but before leaving gave him the old map he had brought with him. He said he might return one day, but that if he didn't, perhaps the rancher could solve the riddle of the map, and locate a lost silver mine his ancestors had worked. He explained that he was old and had no one else to give the map to. It was written in Spanish with all sorts of strange markings on it, and showed mountain ranges and streams unknown to the rancher. Its distances were marked in leagues and varas. It appeared to be torn from a larger map, which, if it had been intact, might have made the riddle easier to solve.

The Spaniard told the rancher that the mine was in an outcrop of black hornblende rock most prospectors would ignore. He gave him a piece of the rock which had been his father's. It was heavily streaked with pure horn silver. The rancher spent little time searching for the mine, and no one knows what became of the old map. Most of the Mountain Meadows country is black volcanic rock, so a ledge of black hornblende would be pretty hard to find. And remember, the old man said it was in the place you would least expect it to be!

HOLT
&
ITS SECRET SILVER MINE

Four miles down Meadow Valley Creek below Hamblin, stood Holt, a town that in the early days rivaled Hamblin as the area's most prosperous community. Unlike Hamblin, which was located on a wide benchland above the creek, Holt was built along the creek bottom, on the Old Spanish Trail. It was settled by James Holt and his followers in 1874, and soon grew into a thriving mountain village. Alternate periods of drought and floods were destined to be Holt's lot, for when farmers at Hamblin didn't take all the water, flash floods would come racing down the canyon, covering Holt's fields with red silt.

Though its residents tried mightily to make Holt prosper, they couldn't win against the unpredictable river. One by one they left Holt to fend for itself. It couldn't even do a good job of that. Little remains today except outlines where cabins and houses once stood, and a sign marking the canyon bottom as part of the Old Spanish Trail. But Holt's treasure wasn't in its red-soil farms, but in its red rock hills, for somewhere close by is the Lost Holt Mine, a prize really worth looking for.

A story still told in Dixie claims that James Holt was searching for stray cattle in the cedar foothills near the edge of the Mountain Meadows north of Holt when he came upon an outcropping of "pretty red rock". Holt was interested in prospecting so he took several pieces of the rock, noting well the place he found them, and later had them assayed. His "pretty red rock" was full of gold!

In spite of Brigham Young's warning against mining, Holt was determined to develop his find. As he was preparing to take his sons to the outcrop the next morning he saw an old man with a long white beard riding an ancient mule approaching his farm. The stranger came to the door and asked for food. Although Holt was annoyed at the delay, he invited the old man into his home. No sooner was he seated than he said that he knew of Holt's discovery of the golden ledge. Then in a deep commanding voice, which Holt never forgot, he warned: "Forget what you have found, or that you ever saw it, or it will be the ruin of you and your family!"

Wondering at the old man's strange warning, Holt left for just a moment to see to the preparation of his food. When he stepped back into the room he was amazed to see that the old man was gone! He ran to the door and saw that his mule was gone also. To add to the mystery, there were no tracks of either man nor mule in the deep dust of the roadway!

Convinced that the mysterious stranger was one of the Three Nephites of Mormon legend, Holt never went near the ledge again, nor would he discuss it with his family and friends. The legend of the Three Nephites is well known to devout Mormons. They always appear as old men. Their appearance is sudden and supernatural. They warn the faithful of impending calamities, and then mysteriously disappear. Woe to any who fail to heed their warning.

Holt's gold discovery was well known to everyone at the Holt settlement. Nearly everyone there saw the ore, and after his death, his sons displayed the fabulously rich samples from the golden ledge. So if you just happen to be hiking the hills around old Holt, keep an eye open for an outcropping of "pretty red rock". But be sure to watch for an old white-bearded man riding an ancient mule. If he stops to talk to you, you'd better listen closely to what he has to say!

ADVENTURE

In the fall of 1860, Phillip Klingensmith led a wagon train of settlers from Iron County to the Virgin River, which they followed upstream 2 miles beyond Grafton to a place where irrigation water could be diverted onto the sandy river bottoms. As was customary among Mormons, ditches were dug and the red sandy soil broken by the plow before such luxuries as houses and barns were thought of. Before the first frosts of winter came, a small town with the romantic name of Adventure had been established. Among its first citizens were Orson Pratt, an early Mormon leader, and Dr. Scipio A. Kenner, then a well known physician and journalist in Utah.

In a few years Adventure was a substantial community, and the furthermost settlement up the Virgin River. Well built homes and farm buildings were erected. The new town never developed a business district, however, and depended instead upon the stores at nearby Grafton. Adventure might have survived if only more tillable land had been available. But most of its farmable ground was located along the river bottom, and when the disastrous floods of the early 1860's came, much of it washed away.

The settlers attempted to rebuild but it was hopeless. Before long most had moved upstream to settle Rockville, where the fields were higher and more land was available. Rockville's growth was matched by Adventure's decline.

PINTO & LITTLE PINTO

In 1856 Rufus Walker led a band of Mormon pioneers, including the families of Samuel Atwood, Richard Robinson, Amos Thatcher, David Tullis, Prime Coleman and others, to a green mountain meadow 6 miles east of Hamblin. There, they started a town called Pinto, named for the surrounding multi-colored hills. The site was on the Old Spanish Trail. Several stores and shops were built, including the Pinto Co-Op, and by 1859 a church had been erected. In 1866 that first small churchhouse was replaced by a new rock building. The historical marker at Pinto is built of stones from that building.

By 1871 Pinto had grown into a thriving community of solid, well built homes, many two stories high and built of finished stone. Several of those homes are in good repair and are occasionally used by their owners. But Pinto's growth was limited. Except for the green meadow land, there was little to attract new settlers. As the children grew up, many left for more promising places. As the years passed the original settlers took their places one by one in the little cemetery on the hillside above town. Many of the dates on those tombstones are from the early 1860's. At the turn of the century a new settlement named Newcastle was started not far to the north where more arable land was available. It wasn't long until Pinto was deserted. The Mormon Church discontinued its ward there in 1916, and by 1930 only two families remained. Neither of them were Mormons.

Six miles northeast of Pinto, three miles across the Iron County line, are the remains of Little Pinto, another settlement from the same period, which was even smaller than Pinto. Little Pinto was a suburb of Irontown, but it never grew beyond a village of half a dozen houses. It is shown on some maps as Page's Ranch. Today one of Little Pinto's ancient looking stone houses is still in use, just as solid as the day it was built so long ago. If you want to see how houses were built in the good old days, be sure to visit Pinto or Little Pinto. You won't be satisfied with modern houses anymore.

SHEM & CONGER
&
ZCMI'S LOST GOLD

In 1884, William Webb was cutting cordwood in the West Mountains, when he discovered an outcropping of high grade copper ore. Webb called his find the Apex. Little work was done on it until 1890 when the pioneer firm of Woolley, Lund & Judd at St. George obtained the property. Its new owners soon made the Apex Mine one of the state's leading copper producers. Other rich copper discoveries included the Mammoth, Morning Star, Mountain Chief and Black Warrior mines. The Black Warrior Mine had been operating as early as the 1870's, when its owner, W.B. Pace, erected a smelter on the Santa Clara River at what was called "the old Conger farm." A small smelter camp which grew up there was known as Conger. For several years both the Black Warrior and the Conger smelter operated satisfactorily, producing a good grade of silver-lead bullion in addition to the copper. But shipping the bullion 400 miles to the railroad put Pace deeply into debt and his property fell into receivership. The closing of his smelter marked the end of the settlement at Conger.

During its early days, ore from the Apex Mine was shipped to a smelter located "near the West Springs at the point of Red Hill". In 1898, a new smelter was built on the Santa Clara River between Gunlock and the Shivwits Indian Reservation, not far from where the Black Warrior smelter at Conger had been. An all Mormon town named Shem grew up around the new smelter, which was quite unusual in view of the church's opposition to mining. For a reason not now remembered, some old maps show the town as Jackson instead of Shem. Solid stone walls and the ruins of a rock dam can still be found 1½ miles along the Gunlock road, north of abandoned US-89. Beehive shaped charcoal kilns were built at Spring Hollow and Poor Hollow, at the foot of the Pine Valley Mountains, to produce charcoal for the smelter.

For the next ten years, while the Apex and other mines were working, Shem prospered, but gradually the veins worked out and the mines began to close. The Apex Mine was reopened years later, but by then Shem was only a memory. Today hardly a trace remains of the old camp. Nevertheless, Shem lasted ten years. That's a pretty good lifespan for a Washington County town!

The Apex Mine and the mills at Shem helped make Woolley, Lund & Judd southern Utah's richest merchandising firm, and it was the fortune mining made for them that gave birth to an intriguing treasure tale. Somewhere west of Shem, sixty pounds of gold

The church bell doesn't ring at Pinto anymore, and if it did no one would hear it.

The crew of the Apex Mine. The ore was hauled to the smelter at Shem.

lays in an unknown desert wash. In 1869 Frank Woolley was murdered by Indians, and $20,000 in gold coin he was carrying with him was thrown into a nameless gulch. It's still there today.

Woolley, Lund & Judd was the St. George branch of the Mormon owned ZCMI store chain. They dealt in farm produce, livestock and mining equipment throughout southern Utah and Nevada. It also marketed cotton in California which was grown at the Dixie Cotton Mission. For the convenience of their customers in Nevada and southern California, much of the firm's business was conducted through a bank at the Mormon settlement of San Bernadino, California.

In May, 1969 Frank Woolley made one of his regular business trips to San Bernadino to balance his firm's accounts. He withdrew $20,000 in gold coins from his account, and prepared to leave for Utah with an eastbound wagon train. But Woolley was delayed by business problems and the freight outfit left without him after he assured them he would catch up along the trail.

Woolley wrapped two bundles of gold coins in rawhide and concealed them in two five gallon water barrels, which he loaded onto his pack horse. He left San Bernadino several days after the freight train and crossed Cajon Pass and passed by Dunlop's Ranch before starting across the Mojave Desert. That was the last time he was seen alive.

When Woolley, Lund & Judd's freighters arrived at St. George, they were surprised to learn that Frank Woolley wasn't already there. They thought he had taken a shortcut and passed them somewhere along the

trail. The next mail brought a bank receipt showing that Woolley had received $20,000 in gold at San Bernadino. A search party learned that Woolley had passed by Dunlop's Ranch several weeks earlier. They found where he had camped at Resting's Springs and followed his trail eastward to where tracks of a band of Paiutes began following him.

Not far from the Muddy River settlements, they found where his horse and pack animal had been taken by the Indians. Empty cartridge cases were found and in a draw the remains of Woolley's body, stripped of all clothing, his bones scattered by coyotes. The Indian's trail was marked by items of Woolley's thrown away or lost, but became lost in the wilds of the Beaver Dam Wash country.

A few months later renegade Paiutes were seen around St. George, wearing Woolley's clothing and for several years travelers reported finding pieces of harness, pack saddles and camp equipment far off the trail. Later, Woolley's canteen and bedroll were found in a deep wash. But no trace was ever found of the two five gallon water kegs.

It's unlikely that the Paiutes kept Woolley's water kegs. The pack saddles needed to carry them had been thrown away, and the Indians never carried water with them, since they knew the secret water holes of the desert. It is certain that Woolley's property was discarded bit by bit as the Indians traveled eastward. So somewhere west of Shem, along a shortcut on the old Mormon Trail, sixty pounds of shiny gold eagles remain where they were thrown into a nameless gulch. They were worth $20,000, in 1869, they're probably worth more than a million dollars now!

This tunnel at Goldstrike looks like it was dug by giants.

GOLDSTRIKE

There are only two roads to Goldstrike. One's impassable and the other's impossible.

No one today can recall who first discovered gold in the Bull Valley Mountains, and mining records of the old camp are almost non-existent. A Utah Mining Association pamphlet states only that, "Gold was found during the early days at Goldstrike, but its veins played out and the mining rush subsided." Not much of an epitaph for a camp's entire life story!

A half mile west of the Gunlock road on abandoned US-89, a narrow dirt track leads north. A faded sign warns that you are entering the Shivwits Indian Reservation. 11 miles north an old log building once used as a stage station can be seen by the road. At the bottom of a steep down grade 19 miles from the highway, the East Fork of Beaver Dam Wash comes from a deep, dark canyon to the right. But don't be fooled by the name, for you're about as far from a beaver as you'll ever get! A jeep trail follows the usually dry East Fork upstream, but soon loses itself in deep sand.

A two mile hike up canyon reveals an old house and an ancient looking barn. After another mile several large tunnels dug into the sold rock cliffs can be seen, driven in almost at the water level of the intermittent creek. There are no waste dumps, the rock apparently having been washed away by spring floods. Several miles farther upstream there is a livable frame house and a sheet iron garage or shed, in the canyon below what was once the Hamburg Mine. But there's an easier way to get to the Hamburg Mine than hiking up the East Fork.

Five miles northeast of Gunlock, a steep, rocky road turns up Cove Canyon. A BLM sign proclaims it to be the Goldstrike Road, but it offers no distances or clues how to get there. Beyond Maple Ridge, 13 miles from the Gunlock road, a four-wheel-drive trail turns to the left, and drops steeply into the head of East Fork Canyon. It is about 5 miles to the old frame house in the canyon below the Hamburg Mine. Now, it may only be coincidence, but this is exactly the same section of the Old Spanish Trail followed by Peg-Leg Smith in 1828, and only a stone's throw from where he made the rich silver strike remembered now as the Lost Peg-Leg Mine!

Head high desert sage hides the rock ruins of some buildings, while bits and pieces of logs and boards burned black and twisted by the desert sun lay where they fell nearly a century ago. There are pieces of purple glass and rusting relics of yesteryear, but be careful where you put your hands, for there are rattlesnakes there too! The Hamburg and Bull Valley mines were among the camp's best producers, but the cost of hauling freight into camp and hauling ore out, when gold was only $16 an ounce, wasn't very attractive for investors, so Goldstrike didn't last long.

An old and seldom seen Park Service Atlas of Washington County reports, "Gold was mined long ago in the Goldstrike District, where miners found high grade ore. An amalgamation stamp mill was built, creating the mining camp of Goldstrike. Free gold was found in fractured limestone and in prophyry, but it was so highly altered that miners didn't always recognize it."

The stamp mill at Goldstrike hasn't turned a wheel for a long, long time now.

For the desert ghost-towner who likes to rough it, modern metal detectors and other techniques unknown at the time might make taking a closer look at that "highly altered" ore worth it. Remember, gold isn't $16 an ounce anymore, it's $400!

HEBERVILLE

Heberville really had its ups and downs! It was first settled in 1858 on the Virgin River one mile below its confluence with the Santa Clara River, 5 miles south of St. George. Heberville was part of the "cotton mission", an early day effort to make southern Utah a cotton producing area. But the "mission" was never very successful, for the cotton cost as much as $4 a pound to produce. Nevertheless, Heberville prospered, for its farms produced an abundance of crops and the town had several other businesses. During the Civil War, when prices soared due to scarcity, Heberville shipped 74,000 pounds to the east and 11,000 pounds to California.

The "cotton mission" came to an unplanned end at Heberville when disastrous floods destroyed a large part of the town and frustrated efforts to rebuild. Brigham Young visited the area in 1870. By then the Saints had about given up. He directed that they change the town's name to "Price City," perhaps to help their luck.

Under its new name, homes and businesses were rebuilt, and farms were cultivated again, but not to grow cotton. Instead, 700 fruit trees were planted. Price City might have prospered where Heberville had failed if the curse of the United Order of Enoch hadn't been inflicted on it. Under the United Order, settlers were required to place all of their worldly goods into a cooperative pool. Everyone would share equally in the fruits of their labors. But it soon became apparent that some were sharing more equally than others! When the United Order failed, discouraged Saints began leaving Price City, and it wasn't long until the red dust of Utah's Dixie covered its streets.

BLOOMINGTON

Bloomington was a twin of Heberville, located on the other side of the Virgin River. It was settled 12 years later. It was a busy place, boasting several prosperous businesses. It even had a newspaper, The Union Village *Echo*, published from 1881 to 1887 by Joseph Carpenter. Its masthead proclaimed, "Industry makes the desert blossom, while idleness leads to ruin!"

In 1875, the United Order was established at Bloomington, but for some reason now forgotten, it was called "The St. James Company." No matter what it was called, the results were the same as at other places where the socialist scheme was tried. Small farms and privately owned businesses had worked well at Bloomington, but the awkward and ungainly workings of the United Order, with its communal dining rooms and central crop storehouses proved unworkable.

Many became discouraged when others who worked half as hard received as much as they did.

The United Order caused many people to leave Bloomington. Then, to add to their troubles, floods along the Virgin River cut its channel so deep that it became almost impossible to get water to the fields. One farmer wrote to his brother, saying, "Farming is very hard here, for we have to run water uphill to grow anything at all!"

Finally conditions became so difficult that many began looking for an easier place to live and left their homes and farms as monuments to wasted effort. Today Bloomington is gone, but near its site a modern retirement community has been built. It's named Bloomington also, but they don't have to run water uphill any more!

ATKINVILLE

Atkinville's chief claim to fame is that it served as a hideout for high ranking Mormons during the comic-opera polygamy trails of the 1880's. Wilford Woodruff, who succeeded John Taylor as president of the church and who issued the Manifesto of 1890 prohibiting further polygamist marriages, was one of those who hid out at Atkinville. A story is told that hiding polygamists would wade out into the neck deep water of a swamp and hide among the bulrushes whenever federal marshals came near. They would signal their confederates by quacking like ducks.

Atkinville was located 7 miles south of St. George on the Virgin River and was named for William Atkin, who with his sons and their families built what was essentially a one family town. There were only a few buildings other than farmhouses at Atkinville. Its most prosperous commercial enterprise was an ice house. During the cold winter months, ice was cut from ponds along the Virgin and stored in a nearby cave for sale to surrounding communities during the summer time. (Has anyone located that cave and checked it for relics?)

Other than its brief notoriety as a polygamist hideout, Atkinville was little more than a sleepy farm settlement. It finally faded and died, its citizens attracted to the brighter lights of nearby St. George.

TONAQUINT

One thing is for sure, the people of Tonaquint had a good sense of humor! They had to, to live where they did, and to call their town the names they did. In 1854 Jacob Hamblin, Thales Haskill and A.P. Hardy built cabins for their families near the mouth of Tonaquint Creek, where it empties into the Santa Clara River southwest of St. George. Although the new settlement was known officially as Lower Clara, its residents called it by such unflattering names as Seldom Stop, Neversweat and Lick Skillet! One man who moved to the little town wrote to a friend, "Our city is really growing, it's got everything now except houses!"

But their perseverance equalled their sense of humor, for by 1861 another dozen families had moved to Tonaquint. At that time it was the southernmost settlement in Utah. Brigham Young was always concerned about his people's welfare. When he wrote to the Bishop at Tonaquint inquiring how the new town was managing, he was answered with a poem written by a local wit who described the hard times settlers were having there.

> The sun it is scorching hot,
> It makes the water siz, Sir,
> And the reason that it is so hot,
> Is just because it is, Sir!
>
> The wind like fury here does blow,
> So when we plant or sow, Sir,
> We place one foot upon the seed,
> And hold it till it grows, Sir!

Tonaquint might have survived the heat and the wind, but the great floods along the Santa Clara during the 1860's washed out its irrigation dams and flooded its fields with red mud and rocks. Its well kept farms, orchards and flower gardens were all destroyed in the twinkling of an eye. They finally lost their sense of humor and left their ruined homes. Most of them moved to new towns being started in the Washington Field. They left little more than memories behind, but by careful searching you might find a reminder of Tonaquint.

HEBRON

Named for an ancient city in Palestine, Hebron was located 5 miles west of Enterprise, near the West and South forks of Shoal Creek. It was settled in 1862 by the four Pulsipher brothers, John, Zera, William and Charles. Although they were Mormons, Hebron became a gentile town. Brigham Young had repeatedly forbidden Mormons to engage in mining and from helping those who did. But Hebron's existence soon depended upon being a supply town for the Nevada silver camps. A small fort was built there during the Blackhawk War, but as soon as the hostilities were over, Hebron moved outside its walls and rapidly grew into a bustling city. It soon sported a fine brick hotel, several stores, freight offices, a church, a schoolhouse and several saloons. An office of the Deseret Telegraph Company began business in 1872.

Church leaders warned the Saints to leave Hebron and its wicked ways. Not all heeded the word, because the booming Nevada camps were good for Hebron's businesses. Hebron grew by leaps and bounds until 1902 when a severe earthquake rattled southern Utah, and the hardest place hit was Hebron! Most Mormons interpreted the ruinous quake as a sign and quickly left the stricken town. Many moved to nearby Enterprise, so named because it was such an enterprising place.

Then in 1906, when the great earthquake leveled San Francisco, Hebron's few remaining buildings were

Sagebrush slowly reclaims the cemetery at Hebron, the Sodom of the southwest.

destroyed. Gentiles said it was coincidence, but Mormons remembered Brigham Young's prophecy that Hebron would be wasted for its wickedness, with "drought replacing abundance and discouragement replacing ambition." Not long after the second quake, severe floods washed a deep gully where the town's main street had been.

Today piles of stone and brick where fine buildings once stood, an orchard of half dead fruit trees, a long row of ancient cottonwoods whose bone-like limbs stand out against the blue desert sky like giant skeletons and a forgotten cemetery lost in the cedars are all that remain of Dixie's Sodom. A Mormon legend claims that Hebron was built where Nephites and Jarradites fought to the death. Early settlers often told of strange things that happened there, and said that there were more ghosts haunting Hebron than there were cedars on its hills. That's an awful lot of ghosts!

NORTHOP
&
THE HURRICANE CLIFFS GOLD

Northop was a hard luck place if there ever was one, located at the divide of Parunuweep Creek, one mile from the Kane County line. It was settled in 1862 by a group of people seeking farm land, led by James Lemon. Lemon's choice for a townsite wasn't the best, for there was little farm land there to begin with, and what there was could be irrigated only by means of the hardest labor. It was said that the people of Northop were so poor that one year they survived on milk weeds and sego lily bulbs.

One way people there made a living was by burning cottonwood trees to obtain ashes, which they sold at more prosperous settlements as a water softener and for making soap. Northop was abandoned during the Indian troubles of the late 1860's, and few cared to return when the troubles were over. By 1890 only 20 people remained. By 1900 the figure had fallen to zero. During its last days, the people still there might have observed the old prospector named Black passing through on his way to becoming a legend.

In 1896 Charles Black rode into Flagstaff, Arizona with $15,000 in raw gold he dug from an old mine he discovered at the base of the Hurricane Cliffs, somewhere south of Northop. Unlike most prospectors, Black didn't spend his hard earned money on some honky-tonk. Instead he purchased a building in Flagstaff and started a general store. Within a few years he had become a wealthy merchant.

Black told several of his prospector friends that he had found his gold in an ancient Spanish mine, in a brown colored quartz ledge, at the base of a towering sandstone cliff. He said that it wouldn't be hard to find, for there was a cross cut into the cliff above the old workings. Strangely, none of those he gave directions to could find the ledge where raw gold glistened in the desert sun.

In 1904 Black agreed to lead several prospectors to the ledge. With a well-equipped outfit, they left Kanab and rode toward the Hurricane Cliffs. Black had boasted that he could go straight to the golden ledge, but eight years had passed and all of the cliffs looked the same to him. They searched from the Vermillion Cliffs and the Little Creek Mountains north to Black Ridge, but didn't see anything that looked familiar to Black. When their supplies ran out they left the desert. Black firmly believed that someone, perhaps Indians, had removed the ancient Catholic cross from the cliff where the ledge was located.

Again, in 1907, Black returned, convinced that if he could trace his trail of 1896 he could find the ledge. Starting at Northop, he located several places where he had camped a dozen years before, at the foot of Gooseberry Mesa and in Gould Wash. From there nothing looked familiar. He couldn't find where the cross had been cut or scratched from the cliffs, probably because the sand had drifted so deeply that it had been covered. Black was already wealthy which probably explains why he gave up. For years he told the tale to everyone who would listen, but there is no record of anyone finding his lost ledge.

Maybe you'll have better luck. It's really not that hard, for the waybill is quite clear. Just go southwest from Northop and search south of Sand Mountain, north of Mt. Trumball, and along the Hurricane Cliffs!

SHUNESBURG

Shunesburg, sometimes spelled Shonesburg, was a sister city to Northop. It was located where Shunes Creek joins Parunuweap Creek, 2½ miles above its confluence with the Virgin River. The first settlers moved there from Rockville in 1862 under the guidance of Oliver DeMill. The site was purchased from Chief Shunes of the Paiutes, hence its name. By 1865 good harvests of cotton and corn were being made and fruit trees were beginning to bear, but the town's location, deep in a dark, narrow canyon, was an ominous warning of hard times to come.

The way out of town up canyon was over "Wiggle Trail", a narrow, dangerous path scratched on the precipitous cliffs leading to the canyon rim thousands of feet above. To avoid its tortuous climb, mail carriers lowered sacks of mail on a long wire cable. Major John Wesley Powell, the famed explorer of the Colorado River, made Shunesburg his headquarters in 1872 while exploring the wonders of Parunuweap Canyon, now better known as Zion National Park.

Like many other settlements along the Virgin River and its tributaries, Shunesburg suffered from floods, and its narrow, canyon bottom site was especially vulnerable. But it was grasshoppers, Mormon crickets, that drove the settlers away. During the 1870's a plague of them destroyed crops and fruit trees. An entry in the *Millennial Star* modestly described Shunesburg's trials and tribulations when correspondent J. J.

Allred wrote, "During the last days of July our farms were severely afflicted by millions of grasshoppers."

When their farms had been destroyed most people moved away, but a few remained to raise livestock. The Harris ranch became quite prosperous. Shunesburg's population dropped to 82 by 1880, and by the turn of the century only Oliver DeMill and his family remained. Since then, most of its buildings have fallen victim to time and the seasons, but not the 20' by 56' cut stone house built by DeMill in the 1880's. Today it stands solid and square, not far from a modern ranch house which probably won't last half as long.

PINE VALLEY
&
PEG LEG SMITH'S LOST LEDGE

Pine Valley is a part time ghost town. During the summer its population numbers in the hundreds, but in the winter, when the snow stands 10' deep, the 100 year old town is nearly deserted. Pine Valley got started in 1852, in its picture post card setting atop the Pine Valley Mountains when Issac Riddle, Robert Rickey and Jeru Blackburn built a sawmill there. That mill was a muley, an early type which used a heavy straight blade that cut with an up and down action. The muley was replaced in 1862 with a more modern circular saw. In the ensuing years several more mills were built.

Much of the lumber cut by Pine Valley's mills was used at the booming mining camps in Nevada's White Pine District.

Pine Valley grew with the mining camps it served, and soon sported a post office, dance hall, cheese making plant, Hancock's General Store and several saloons. But when those camps failed Pine Valley's economy failed too. With its sawmills closed, only a few Mormon stockmen remained, and even they left the little mountain village in the winter. By 1930 its population had dropped to thirty people.

Today Pine Valley is the beautiful little village it was a century ago, with a few new homes having been added recently. During the summer its fourth class post office is open for business and its summer residents attend church in the chapel built by Ebenezer Bryce. It is said to be the oldest church still in use in Utah.

One of Pine Valley's early settlers, Robert Lloyd, figured prominently in one of the most believable of all lost mine stories. It happened this way. In 1828 old Peg-Leg Smith and his band of fur trappers made camp on the Rio Santa Clara where Spanish explorers had camped before them, at the foot of the Pine Valley Mountains. They were out of food so Dutch George hiked down the canyon to hunt. He didn't find any game, but he did return to camp with a pocket full of gold nuggets which he said came from a place on the

A church was always the first building Mormon settlers erected. When they abandoned their towns, it was often the last building left.

river where hand-fulls of them could be scooped up. Peg-Leg examined them, said they were only copper, and threw them away. The starving trappers then broke camp and followed the river south.

In 1852, during settlement of Santa Clara and Pine Valley, Jim Houdon, a gold seeker bound for California, found the same nuggets in a gravel placer along the river. Since it was late in the season, he scooped up as many as he could and hurried on to California before snow caught him in the mountains. Before he left he told Robert Lloyd, a Pine Valley settler, about his find. Lloyd had little interest in Houdon's story, but several years later while digging an irrigation ditch on the river, he too found the nuggets. To insure he'd find the spot again, Lloyd pulled two willow saplings together and tied them in a knot. He then forgot all about his find, so hard pressed was he to make a living in Pine Valley.

Many years later he was visiting St. George when he met W.B. Pace, an old friend who owned the Black Warrior Mine. During their conversation, Lloyd noticed that Pace was using a willow cane that appeared made from a tree that had been tied in a knot. Lloyd mentioned the peculiar cane to Pace, who stated that he had found the knotted willow years before as he hiked along the Santa Clara.

Only then did Lloyd remember the strange nuggets he had found where he knotted two willow saplings together. He and Pace made plans to return to the river, but both were old and time slipped away. It's safe to assume then, that somewhere along the Rio Santa Clara, not far from Pine Valley, Peg-Leg Smith's "copper" nuggets are yet waiting to be found.

DUNCAN'S RETREAT

The little town with the strange name of Duncan's Retreat was settled in 1861 between the communities of Rockville and Virgin City, on Mukuntuweep Creek by Chapman Duncan and others "called" by Mormon leaders to settle in Dixie.

The name wasn't meant to sound romantic or quaint. In fact, it was descriptive; it was where Duncan retreated! Duncan had been engaged to survey a canal to bring water from the Virgin River. The canal was dug according to his survey, but when water was turned into it, it wouldn't run. Duncan had surveyed the canal uphill! To escape the ridicule of the settlers, Duncan retreated! To show their disgust, those who remained called their settlement Duncan's Retreat.

Only a year later the new town was described as a beautiful place, so a new canal must have been dug at water grade. Orchards were planted and soon bounteous crops were being harvested. Although the Saints were frequently admonished not to use tobacco, an 1864 crop census shows that a bumper crop of the vile weed was grown! A post office was established in 1863 and a schoolhouse erected the following year.

Duncan's Retreat was abandoned during the Blackhawk Indian War of the late 1860's. After the war they were hardly resettled before the flooding Virgin River covered their fields with red mud and rocks. A constant battle against the river began, but the river won, and by 1890 Duncan's Retreat was deserted. Today a few half dead fruit trees alongside a long unused irrigation ditch marks its spot. It is said that the present highway passes over the spot where the church once stood. The retreat from Duncan's Retreat is now complete.

DALTON

The village of Dalton was located at the mouth of Dalton Wash, 3 miles west of Duncan's Retreat. It was established in 1864 by a group of Mormon settlers led by John Dalton. Dalton might have become a prosperous farming area if its citizens hadn't been forced to abandon it during the Blackhawk War.

Of those who left during the war, many never returned. Of those who did, most stayed only briefly. Thirty people remained in 1870. By 1880 the little settlement was completely deserted. It is now only one of many similar villages whose pioneers have been forgotten and whose ruins are visited by coyotes and other wanderers of the wasteland. Because settlements like Dalton are now completely forgotten, they are most productive places for relic hunters to seek the treasures of yesteryear.

MOUNTAIN DELL

Mountain Dell was settled on North Creek, 4½ miles upstream form its confluence with the Virgin River, by the Joel Johnson family, and others, in 1861. Good farmground was scarce along the narrow canyon bottom of North Creek, which restricted the growth of the new town. But other settlers did move there, and before long a thriving hamlet grew up. A church was built in 1863. Like many isolated settlements, Mountain Dell was abandoned during the Blackhawk War, but the Indians never burned the little town, so its homes and shops were in good repair when their owners returned. Later more people arrived and more farms were claimed from the wilderness.

1½ miles upstream from Mountain Dell a sawmill was built, and people who worked there established a satellite village shown on early maps as Johnson's Mill. It furnished lumber for many other early towns, including Virgin City and Duncan's Retreat.

Unlike many towns in that country, Mountain Dell's problem wasn't flooding, it was drought. North Creek often dried up. During the 1890's a series of dry years caused many to leave for greener pastures. The census of 1900 counted no noses in Mountain Dell. Since people lived there for quite a few years, and because it is off the beaten path, it's a good bet for today's relic hunter. Good luck!

CHAPTER FOUR

FORTS, CAMPS AND POSTS

When forts of the old west are brought up, one usually pictures the elaborate, polished log garrison of today's TV western, but few early day forts conformed to that image. Most pioneer forts were crudely built of materials readily available, often adobe mud, and were intended only as temporary trading posts or shelter. Forts built by the mountain men and fur traders during the early 1800's were of this type. When Mormon settlers came into Utah, they built forts and walled stockades to protect themselves and their livestock, particularly during the Walker and Blackhawk Indian wars. Some of them, such as Fort Harmony and Fort Santa Clara, were beautifully built of hand cut stone and matched logs, and had well stocked commissaries and comfortable rooms inside. But most Mormon forts were homely places, built of adobe mud mixed with straw. Most were small; Fort Pearce was only 30' square. Fort Deseret, in contrast, was 550' square, with corrals for livestock behind its walls. Some like Fort Kit Carson, are almost unknown today, while others, like Camp Floyd, are known to nearly everyone.

Those old forts were often lonely places, built in remote deserts or canyons to guard now forgotten trails or river crossings. During the Indian wars of the 1850's and 60's almost every settlement had a fort or stockade

for the settlers' protection. Most were torn down when they were no longer needed, providing building stones and logs which in many places are still in use. Many of Utah's old forts can hardly be located today while others, such as Cove Fort, are almost perfectly preserved. Nearly all are ghostly places now, seldom visited or remembered. Most of those described in the following pages can be visited in the family car, but some are beyond road's end, and a few can be reached only by "shank's mare."

Many of Utah's best known lost mine stories are associated with its old forts. Those that have no such tale usually should be remembered for other reasons. With a little imagination a visitor can hear the war-whoop of attacking Indians, and smell the acrid odor of burning gun powder as he stands in the footprints of the mountain men, fur traders, and pioneers who were there before him.

FORT ROBIDOUX
&
THE LOST RHOADES MINE

Other than the nebulous and legendary camps of the Spanish miners, Fort Robidoux was the first white settlement in Utah. It was located where the old Span-

Roosevelt, Utah, 1907.

The trail to the Lost Rhoades Mine passed through Roosevelt on the Ute Indian reservation. -Utah Historical Society-

ish trail from Taos, New Mexico to the Pacific northwest crossed the fur trade trail from the Platte River to the Timpanogos Valley. It stood alongside the Uintah River ¾ of a mile east and 1½ miles south of the present Ute Indian village of Whiterocks in Uintah County. Fort Robidoux was built in 1831 by Antoine Robidoux on the site of an even earlier fort which mountain men knew as Reed's Fort, named for its builder, fur trapper Jim Reed.

Antoine Robidoux was born September 24th, 1794 at the French settlement of St. Louis, and while a young man gained a reputation as a fur trapper, trail blazer and adventurer. During the early 1820's he built Fort Uncompaghre on the Gunnison River in Colorado. Near the mouth of Westwater Canyon, 15 miles northwest of Westwater Station on the D&RGW Railroad in Grand County, there is an inscription written in French, scratched on the soft sandstone walls above the Colorado River. It states: "Antoine Robidoux passed here November 13th, 1837 to establish a trading post on the river Green or White." That inscription was made six years after Fort Robidoux was established, and indicates that Robidoux planned to build another fort. It also supports the belief that it was he who built the old fort on the Green River now known as Fort Kit Carson.

Fort Robidoux was also known as Fort Uintah or Fort Wintey to mountain men, and was an important trading post at the crossing of the trails most used by fur traders. Many famous explorers and trail blazers visited there, including Miles Goodyear, Rufus Sage, Marcus Whitman and John C. Fremont. Ute Indians can still point out a dugout where Kit Carson spent a winter. It was the most important fort in the area until it was burned during the great Indian uprising of 1844.

In 1842 "Old Joe" Williams, a Methodist preacher turned fur trapper, wrote that he was "appalled by the wickedness of the trappers at Fort Robidoux, with their swearing, drinking and debauchery of the Indians," and added, "They are fat, dirty and idle!" The Ute Indians had been enslaved by Spanish miners for centuries, and fared little better when British and American fur trappers replaced them. Their conditions were so oppressive that in 1844 they rebelled, as they had in the great rebellion of 1680, when they first drove the Spanish miners from the land. Forts and outposts throughout the country were destroyed, and Fort Robidoux wasn't spared. Antoine Robidoux was fortunate enough to be gone when the fort was attacked. He died in St. Louis on August 29, 1860. Today the ruins of old Fort Robidoux are the place to begin the search for Utah's most famous lost mine.

Some lost mine stories are based on legend, or on the hand-me-down tales of old-timers. But the story of the Rhoades Mine is built on more verifiable facts than most. Artifacts in the Mormon Temple in Salt Lake City were made from its gold, and gold coins minted at the Mormon capital also had their origin there. Dozens, if not hundreds, of people were indirectly associated with it, and it is mentioned in church, state, federal and congressional records. There can be no doubt it exists.

As the result of a treaty between Brigham Young and Ute Chief Wakara, beginning in 1855 Thomas Rhoades began bringing gold from an old mine located high in the Uintah Mountains. After Brigham Young and Thomas Rhoades died, Caleb Rhoades secretly continued to bring out gold until he died in 1905.

In 1897 Caleb Rhoades obtained a lease on the ground where he said the mine was located, granted by the Ute Indians who themselves no longer knew where it was, thus revealing the long kept secret that only he and a select few Mormon leaders had known. Under the agreement, the mine could not be worked until the Ute Reservation was opened to settlement. Unfortunately, Caleb Rhoades died on June 2nd, 1905 and the reservation wasn't opened until September, only three months later.

Many, including Utah's congressional delegation, knew of the famous mine and the lease agreement, but no one except Rhoades knew exactly where it was located. The Rhoades Mine story is far too lengthy to repeat here, but if you want to read the fascinating story, obtain a copy of *Footprints In The Wilderness*, by Gale Rhoades, a grandson of Caleb Rhoades.

FORT DAVY CROCKETT
&
THE LOST CABIN CACHE

Fort Davy Crockett was one of the first forts in Utah, built in the days of mountain men and fur trappers. It was constructed in 1837 by Phillip Thompson, William Craig and another trapper named St. Clair or Sinclair, on the east side of the Skeetskadee (Green) River, just below its junction with Red Creek at Brown's Hole, in Daggett County. It consisted of three rows of log cabins in the shape of the letter "U", and was protected by adobe walls. It was an important trading post for fur trappers and traders who worked the Brown's Hole country.

In 1825 Brown's Hole was the scene of the first rendezvous of General Ashley's American Fur Company. Fort Davy Crockett provided a place for them to sell their catch and buy supplies as well. The 3,000 Ute Indians who lived in the surrounding mountains also came to trade for knives, hatchets, fish hooks, gun powder and whiskey.

The fort, which was not a pleasant place, was known as Fort Misery. One trapper who spent Christ-

mas there later recalled that an Indian dog was purchased for $5 worth of trade goods and made what he thought was a fine Christmas dinner! In 1844 Fort Davy Crockett was burned by Ute Indians during the same revolt that saw Fort Robidoux destroyed.

Fourteen hundred $20 gold double eagles would be worth nearly a million dollars today. That's how many are waiting to be found in a shallow hole in front of a forgotten log cabin, somewhere near Bird Spring atop South Mountain, at the west end of Brown's Hole, not far from old Fort Davy Crockett. Long before Butch Cassidy's Wild Bunch made Brown's Hole famous as a hideout, five Wyoming outlaws robbed a train of $33,000 in gold coins and led a posse south into Brown's Hole. They lost them in a heavy snow storm, and were forced to hide in the mountains until spring. They built a cabin high on South Mountain near Bird Spring from which they could watch the country below.

The outlaws spent a miserable winter crowded together in a small cabin with only wild game to eat, so when spring came they lost no time heading for town. But they were careful, knowing that the train robbery hadn't been forgotten, and took only $1,000 apiece. The remaining $28,000 in shiny gold double eagles was buried under a large pine tree marked with an "X", located straight in line with their cabin door.

Four of the outlaws made a bee-line for the saloons of Rock Springs, while the fifth went to visit his family in Colorado. The outlaws at Rock Springs were recognized, a mob formed outside the saloon where they were drinking, and a gun battle broke out when they refused to surrender. All four were killed. The fifth outlaw was tracked down in Colorado, killed a posseman, and was sentenced to life imprisonment at the Canon City penitentiary

Fifty years later he was paroled, and as a very old man returned to Brown's Hole. He made several feeble attempts to locate the old cabin and the hidden cache that was then all his, but the country was too rough for him. During the time he searched he stayed with an old sheepherder. When he decided to give up, he told the herder about the cache. He had ridden the mountains there for years and had never seen the old cabin, so he spent no time looking for it.

The train robbers' cache, then, must still be there. All you have to do is find the outlaw cabin, or a large pine tree marked with an "X". But there's one thing you should know. There are an awful lot of pine trees on South Mountain!

FORT KIT CARSON

There is some controversy over who built the fort opposite the mouth of the Duschesne River on the east bank of the Green River in Uintah County. In Kit Carson's journals he described spending the winter of 1833 at the fort, but didn't claim ownership of it. It's unlikely that Carson built it, for the fort was quite elaborate, 78' wide and 95' long, with castle-like turrets at it northeast and southwest corners. It could have been a Spanish fort, judging from its architecture, later added onto by Antoine Robidoux, Carson and others.

Kit Carson described it as a small fort when he was there in 1833. But in 1835 another explorer, Warren Ferris, mentioned seeing three or four log cabins at the fort, something Carson didn't report. In 1838 mountain man Joe Meek described it as a large and substantial fort, but said that it was no longer in use.

Old-timers and Indians who lived in that part of the Uintah Basin always referred to the ruins as Old Fort Kit Carson, so until the mystery of its origin is solved, that seems to be as good a name as any. Over the years flooding by the Green River has nearly obliterated its location, leaving only foundations, the outline of its walls, and a deep hole believed to have been a well. It's a ghostly place today.

FORT THORNBURGH
&
THE TREASURE OF DIAMOND MOUNTAIN

A fort which causes some confusion today is Fort Thornburgh because there were actually two Fort Thornburghs, both in Uintah County and both named for Major T.T. Thornburgh, who was killed in the Meeker Massacre in 1879. The original Fort Thornburgh was built near the present-day Ute Indian trading post at Ouray on the Green River, in 1881. Floods on the Green soon proved its location to be a poor one. Only a year later a second fort was built 3 miles northwest of Vernal near the confluence of Ashley Creek and the Green River.

The second Fort Thornburgh sat on higher ground and was well built. There were two traders, J.B. Adams & Company and Seymour & Company, but Sadler's Saloon was more popular with the troops. Pioneer settlers at Ashley Center also built a small fort where present-day Vernal now stands. It was seldom used, though, for after the Meeker Massacre there were seldom hostilities between the settlers and the Utes.

Not far from Fort Thornburgh there is something strange on Diamond Mountain. It really isn't a treasure, and it's not a lost mine either. I don't know exactly what to call it, but it could be worth a lot of money.

In the fall of 1871 two wily old prospectors named Phillip Arnold and John Slack planned a bunco scheme so elaborate it fooled the most knowledgeable mining men and the most hard-hearted bankers of the time. Like most good frauds, it cost a lot of money to set up.

Arnold and Slack had made some money from their prospects, about $50,000, but they were after a lot more, with as little work as possible. They went to Amsterdam, Holland where they purchased a sack of rough, uncut diamonds. Then they went to a desolate corner of Brown's Park north of where Fort Thornburgh would later be built and carefully planted the

diamonds all over the un-named mountain. They placed the rough gems in rock crevices, along ledges and even on ant hills and gopher mounds. The bait set, they were ready to spring the trap.

In February, 1872 Arnold and Slack walked into William Ralston's Bank of California at San Francisco, looking like two prospectors just in from the diggings. Unshaved and dirty, they presented a leather poke of the type used to carry gold dust to the teller, and told him they wanted it locked in the most secure vault. The teller, expecting to see the usual gold nuggets, opened the bag and had to ask what the odd looking glassy crystals were. When told they were diamonds, he called Banker Ralston, for no one there had ever seen a diamond in the rough.

Ralston almost fainted when he saw the gems. No sooner were Arnold and Slack out of sight than he called in an expert who examined the stones and reported they were of the highest quality. Ralston had the two prospectors brought to his office where he tried to learn where the diamonds came from. Arnold and Slack played it cagey, telling Ralston they didn't need him, for they knew where there was a diamond field worth millions. After several more meetings they reluctantly accepted $300,000 for part interest in their diggings. They agreed also to take an expert chosen by Ralston to their diggings.

Henry Janin, an expert gemologist recommended by Tiffany's of New York, accompanied the two old prospectors to their mine. They travelled on the newly completed Central Pacific to a point in the desert of southern Wyoming. After unloading their horses, the three men rode south into the Uintah Mountains. Janin was blindfolded the last few miles of the trip. There, among the sagebrush and cedars, Janin had no trouble finding all the gems he wanted. In addition to diamonds he found rubies and sapphires as well!

Upon their return to San Francisco, Janin told banker Ralston the sky was the limit, and Ralston immediately incorporated the San Francisco & New York Mining Company, and began selling millions of shares across the country and in Europe. He even gave Arnold and Slack another $300,000 to tide them over until the dividends started rolling in!

By sheer coincidence, an expert geologist named Clarence King was working with the Geological Survey in the Uintah Mountains and heard rumors of the great diamond field. What bothered King was his professional knowledge that diamonds, rubies and sapphires never occur in the same formation. Following the prospector's trail, King found the salted diamond field. Using a microscope, he discovered that some of the planted gems had been cut on a lapidary wheel. The scam exposed, he telegraphed banker Ralston to tell him his great diamond mine was a fraud!

When news of the gigantic swindle hit the newspapers there was a run on the Bank of California, with cries for Ralston's scalp from investors across the country. William Ralston, the richest man in California, committed suicide. Arnold and Slack took their $600,000 and disappeared, but not for long. Arnold went to his home town in Kentucky where he was killed in a fight with a neighbor. Slack surfaced in New Mexico where he lived alone and died a pauper. No trace of the $600,000 was ever found.

Almost any road map will show you the way to Arnold and Slack's salted diamond mine north of Fort Thornburgh. It is rough country frequented only by sheepherders and deer hunters, who occasionally still find diamonds where they were planted more than 100 years ago. You could find a diamond or maybe even a ruby or a sapphire, and they're worth a lot more now than they were when Arnold and Slack hid them. Their gem mountain is shown on almost all maps, so it's easy to find. It's called Diamond Mountain!

FORT DESERET

Fort Deseret, located 10 miles southwest of Delta in Millard County, must hold the record as the fastest built fort in the west. Made of adobe mud mixed with straw, it was erected in 18 days by 93 men divided into two competing teams. It was 550′ square with walls 10′ high that tapered from a thickness of 4′ at their black lava rock base to 1½ feet at the top. Fort Deseret was in active use during the Blackhawk War of 1868-69. Once, a party of 45 men traveling south from Tooele raced Chief Blackhawk and a band of howling Indians from Pack's Bottom to the fort. Once safe inside, the battle became a standoff.

A settlement known at different times as Lake Town and Crofton was established 12 miles to the west in 1874. It boasted only nine families, but was a favorite camping place for Indians, and at times 500 may have camped there. Like so many early desert settlements, a lack of water hastened its end. Few people today have heard of it, so it might be a good place to look for relics, especially Indian arrowheads.

On October 26, 1853 Captain J.W. Gunnison and 7 of his 11 men were killed by Indians in a narrow river bottom 6 miles west of where Fort Deseret was later built. Of the four men who escaped the massacre, two led a burial party back to the scene ten days later. Coyotes had eaten the bodies and strewn bones over a wide area. Capt. Gunnison's body could only be recognized from a few pieces of white hair still clinging to the skull. That tragedy had occured during the Walker War. To prevent similar incidents during the Blackhawk War, Fort Deseret was built. Today the walls of Fort Deseret still stand, but each year's rains are slowly melting them away.

FORT SANFORD

Silas Sanford Smith was a Major in the Iron County Militia, and in his honor Fort Sanford was named. It was built by Major Smith's 76 man company in 1866, a half mile east of the Sevier River on the south side of Sanford Creek, 8 miles north of Panguitch. Its purpose was to offer protection from raiding Indians to the settlers of the Sevier River Valley. Unlike most forts whose log walls were laid horizontally, Fort Sanford's

The walls of old Fort Deseret still stand after more than 100 years. -Utah Historical Society-

were built of cedar posts standing stockade style, side by side 8' above the ground. They enclosed five acres of ground where livestock could be protected during attacks. Around the stockade a deep ditch was dug to prevent its walls from being scaled by attackers.

Fort Sanford had been intended as a defensive fortification, but when the Blackhawk War flared up, it proved to be of little value. The nearby towns were abandoned, leaving the fort an isolated outpost far from the nearest help. After a seige in which an Indian was killed and a defender wounded, a decision was made to abandon the fort. They planned to use the fort again when the war ended. Instead, the settlers along the Sevier River gathered together at Panguitch and the other large cities, and left Fort Sanford to the ravishes of time. Its cedar log walls were used to build corrals and cabins. Only through careful searching can its site be found today.

FORT SCIPIO

The original Scipio was established 2½ miles south of present-day Scipio in 1857. Originally it was called Round Valley and later Graball. At the beginning of the Blackhawk War in 1866, a fort with adobe mud walls was built around the little settlement. The story of how Fort Scipio was named is itself interesting. Old-timers say that not long after it was built Brigham Young visited there and asked what name the settlers had given their fort. One of those present was Scipio Kenner, and as a joke someone said that it was Scipio's fort. The prophet agreed that that was a good name for the fort, and it stuck. Others say that Brigham Young named it for Scipio Africanus, a famous Roman general.

A log schoolhouse was built there, followed by a general store, where tea sold for a dollar a pound. It must not have been very tasty, for there was no drinking water at the fort except that obtained from an open irrigation ditch. The poor water was responsible for a great deal of illness. When the Indian troubles ended the move was made to the present site of Scipio. Most of the original log cabins were moved from the fort to the new location, leaving nothing but an adobe wall to mark the fort's site. A century of weather has reduced them to a mere outline.

FORT SODOM & ITS NEIGHBORS
&
THE POTTER GANG CACHE

Fort Sodom was located 2 miles north of Goshen in Utah County. When it was built in 1857 its adobe walls enclosed two acres, with rows of cabins built along the inner walls. During the tense days after the Walker War it served as protection for the settlers of southern Utah County. After Chief Wakara died, it was seldom used. With the Indian problems over temporarily, Fort Sodom was abandoned, and its settlers moved to several nearby communities.

Sandtown was established in 1859 1 mile southeast of the fort, while Mechanicsville was started across the creek in front of the fort. Both settlements lasted only a few years. Poor soil was the reason for their demise. Goshen soon became the principal town of the valley, and attracted people from each of the abandoned villages.

Juan Lopez was a dashing caballero who dressed like a Spanish Don and flew into a rage if anyone called him a Mexican. He rode with the Ike Potter gang, rustling, robbing and killing, from Utah Valley to the Wyoming line. When Potter was killed in Coalville in 1867, Lopez assumed leadership of the gang. He cached much of the gang's loot in Spanish Fork Canyon, just across the valley from Fort Sodom.

Lopez moved the gang's base of operations from the Cache Cave in Echo Canyon to the high mountains between Heber Valley and Spanish Fork Canyon. With his renegade Indians and deserters from Camp Floyd, Lopez would ride down from secret hideouts on Mt. Timpanogos or in Spanish Fork Canyon to raid Mormon villages or army supply trains. Lopez, like Ike Potter before him, kept all the gold and silver the gang stole, and gave his Indian allies only stolen livestock and supplies. Except for a few dollars for whiskey, he offered the deserters nothing but a place to hide.

Finally the army became fed up with the gang's raids and dispatched a troop of soldiers from Fort Douglas to break up the gang and bring Lopez in, dead or alive. The army caught up with the gang in a mountain valley on the west side of Mt. Timpanogos. From there they chased them along the foothills of Utah Valley and into Spanish Fork Canyon, where most of the gang was killed.

The army deserters were questioned at length, but all said that Lopez alone knew where the gang's cache was hidden, and that he was trying to reach it when he was killed. They searched the area where Lopez died, but failed to turn up the cache.

The cache is still hidden somewhere in Spanish Fork Canyon. In 1974 a man from Springville who was loading a pickup truck with black soil dug up some old coins, several of them Spanish, that dated back to 1790. Of course, it's possible they were lost by early Spanish travelers, but the following year a deer hunter found three more coins when he stopped to rest under a ledge of rock. I wonder what could be found with a metal detector?

FORT RAWLINS
&
A SPANISH MINE FOUND

The little remembered army camp of Fort Rawlins was located 2½ miles north of pioneer Provo City, on the north bank of the Timpanogos (Provo) River. It was established on July 30th, 1870 with two companies of the 13th Infantry from Fort Douglas. Funds were never appropriated for barracks or other quarters, so the troops lived in tents with dirt floors. They didn't even have heat stoves until mid-winter.

Fort Rawlins was a thorn in the side of Utah Valley Mormons, most of whom refused to associate with the troops or let them come into town. For that and other reasons, desertion and drunkenness were constant problems for the fort's commanding officer, Capt. Nathan Osborne. During the short life of his command, one-third of his men were court-martialed for being drunk on duty.

Capt. Osborne could not obtain necessary winter supplies for his men from the army, and Provo merchants refused to sell him anything. In frustration, he often took severe disciplinary actions against his rebellious troops. For minor infractions he ordered men enclosed upright in coffins, only 12" deep and 20" wide! Because of low morale, stemming from their primitive living conditions and the severe punishments meted out to them, Capt. Osborne's troops staged a riot on September 22nd, 1870.

Drunken, swearing soldiers armed with loaded rifles and pistols charged into Provo City during the night, man-handled citizens and shot up the town. They were taking out months of pent-up frustration against their Mormon neighbors. Several forced their way into one Bishop Miller's home and threatened to kill him. Thomas Fuller was cut with a bayonet and other soldiers tried to set fire to the church. The following morning they staggered drunkenly back to camp.

Unbelievably, Capt. Osborne failed to report the riot or the damage done by his troops, and his commander, General C.C. Augur first learned of it by reading a newspaper account. Investigation of the riot brought to light Capt. Osborne's severe punishments and he was relieved of command in April, 1871. He and his troops were fined $308 for damages to Provo City. Capt. Osborne was replaced by Capt. Robert Nugent. Two week later he received orders to abandon the fort. Everything that could be moved was hauled to Fort Douglas, but no doubt a lot of coins and other relics were lost in the dirt floors of its tent barracks.

Upon their arrival, Mormon pioneers in Utah Valley were told by the Indians that bearded miners and soldiers wearing iron shirts had worked gold mines in the mountains hundreds of years before. The Indians told how the Spaniards dug for gold in Pick-quanah-we-woods, their name for Spanish Fork Canyon. The Provo River of Utah Valley has two main forks, Spanish Fork and American Fork, the latter named by "American" settlers. The Spanish Fork was not named, as some suppose, by Mormon settlers, but was called that by even the earliest explorers. It is shown as Spanish Fork on Fremont's map of 1845, two years before the Mormons arrived in Utah and five years before Utah Valley was settled.

Even after the Mormons came to Utah Valley, Spanish and Mexican miners visited the area. Pack trains of ore being brought from the mountains were commonly seen until about 1860, and many pioneer diaries mention them. The journal of Mormon V. Selman describes such a sight in 1852. "A Spanish pack train came down the Provo River and camped near our place for a few days to rest their pack animals. Those pack animals were loaded with very heavy packs which were not very large, but it was all those mules could carry. The men kept an armed guard at their camp, and no one was allowed near. They stayed a few days before going south." Other diaries and journals describe similar pack trains carrying cargo so precious that guards kept anyone from getting near them.

A few early settlers looked for the Spanish mines, but none were found until 1957 when deer hunter Clark Rhoades stumbled onto an ancient shaft hidden in heavy oak brush. It was where the Indians had always said it was, on the first side stream (Diamond Fork) that empties into the Pick-quanah-we-wood (Spanish Fork) River.

The old mine was dangerously caved in and wasn't explored until Rhoades's son Gale and his cousin Gary reopened it. A second shaft was found only 20' from the first. One was 90' deep, and the other 120', and both followed the same ore vein. The shafts had been sunk into the mountain at a 45 degree angle. A series of steps had been cut to make climbing out with heavy ore packs easier. In excavating the shafts, several old Spanish shoulder yokes were found. They were made of cedar with a neck notch in the center and hooks on each end to attach leather ore sacks to.

When the shafts were excavated, a chamber was found at the bottom, and the diggers discovered that the floor of the chamber had a hollow sound. Digging carefully, a rotting log floor was removed and a heavy cross log was uncovered, grooved in the center where a rope of some sort had worn into it while lifting buckets of ore from the black vertical shaft below. Pieces of ore rich in gold were recovered, but the lower shaft was too dangerous to reopen with hand tools.

Rhoades learned that the shafts had been purposely filled in, not caved in by natural means. Their waste dumps were so overgrown with scrub oak that they could not be detected from even a few feet away. The two old mines found by Clark Rhoades were the same ones Indians said were worked by the "iron shirts" hundreds of years before.

When Father Escalante travelled down Spanish Fork Canyon in 1776 he was not unaware of minerals there, for he wrote in his journal, "The veins that are seen in the sierra appear to contain minerals." Escalante wasn't the first nor the last to recognize the mineral wealth of Spanish Fork Canyon. No doubt, other ancient mines are still hidden in its rugged depths. All you have to do is find them!

FORT HARMONY

Fort Harmony was built near the junction of Ash Creek and Kanarra Creek in Washington County, southeast of New Harmony. It was founded in 1851 by a band of emigrants led by John D. Lee. Brigham Young said it was the best planned fort he had seen, and by 1854 it was the strongest fortification in Dixie. It was 300′ square. Its east wall was 10′ high and its west wall 16′. Both had a row of cabins built against their inner sides. There was a schoolhouse and a 100′ deep well to insure a water supply during seige. Fort Harmony served as the county seat of Washington County until 1859.

The fort was in constant use until 1862 when a 28 day rain fell in January and undermined its walls. During the worst of the storm an alert was given to abandon the fort, but Lee refused to leave, claiming it would stand, even against a flood. During the night, swift flowing runoff water combined with an overflow from rain swollen Ash Creek undercut the fort's walls until they began collapsing. Still Lee refused to leave. Then, just before the first light of morning, a huge roof beam collapsed, its full weight falling across the bed of Lee's sleeping children, killing his son George and daughter Margaret Ann instantly.

When the great rain ended and the flood waters subsided, a decision was made not to rebuild the fort. Some moved upstream to what would become New Harmony while others founded Kanarraville, 3 miles to the northeast. Today the old fort's four stone corners and the two stone pillars which stood at each side of its

heavy gates remain intact, and near its center a sunken hole that was its well can be seen. The inspiring view of the towering red spires of Kolob Canyon is still there, just as beautiful as it was when Fort Harmony was the best built fort in Utah and the pride of Dixie.

CALL'S FORT
&
TREASURE RODE IN THE BOOT

Built in 1852, although some say it was 1855, Call's Fort was built by the brothers Homer, Omer and Anson Call at the foot of the Wasatch Mountains just west of U-69 between Brigham City and Honeyville. Brigham Young wanted it: "To protect the settlers of Bear River Valley and guard Zion's northern frontier." He was worried about threats from the federal government to send an army into Utah to "resolve the Mormon problem." When the Utah War finally broke out several years later, Call's Fort was too far north of the armies line of march to guard Zion's borders. It was 125′ square with walls 8′ high and 3′ thick.

By 1858, 35 families were living at or near the fort. No battles were ever fought there against the army or the Indians. A schoolhouse was built at the fort in 1862. But Call's Fort's days were numbered. It would be only a few more years until the transcontinental railroad would be built, and Call's Fort would be far off the beaten path. With the arrival of the railroad, the Utah

George Witherell loaded the treasure onto a buckboard and headed east across the floating bridge on the Bear River.

War in the past, and Indian troubles ended settlers left the fort to build farms throughout the Bear River Valley. In time it was torn down, but by the side of the road 7 miles north of Brigham City, a large rock monument, built of stone taken from its walls, stands to mark its site.

In December, 1870 George Witherell buried one of Utah's biggest money caches between Corinne and Call's Fort. He was a stage driver on the Ben Holloday line from Ogden to Corinne. A few days before Christmas, 1870 four men boarded his stage at Ogden. They had a heavy trunk which was placed in the boot at the rear of the stage. Just south of Brigham City they were flagged to a stop by several tough looking riders who claimed to be law officers. They didn't show badges, but they did take the four passengers and their hand luggage from the stage, and waved Witherell on.

Due to the circumstances, Witherell forgot all about the trunk until he got to Corinne. His curiosity aroused, Witherell opened the trunk to look for identification, but was amazed to see that it was packed with bundles of paper money, while a small chest inside was full of gold coins. Not being above a little larceny himself, and knowing that his passengers were probably on their way to jail, Witherell loaded the trunk onto a buckboard wagon and drove off into the night.

Ed Neal, the stableman, later recalled that Witherell went east from town across the old floating log bridge toward Call's Fort. The old fort was no longer in use and Neal thought it unusual for Witherell to go that way. He also said it snowed all the time Witherell was gone. Two hours later he returned without the trunk.

At that point the "lawmen" who took his passengers from the stage arrived and demanded the trunk. Witherell swore he knew nothing about the trunk, and Neal later said that if he hadn't been present, he was sure they would have killed Witherell. They couldn't seem able to decide whether or not to believe him, and warned him not to try to leave town.

Scared of what had happened to his passengers, and certain the "lawmen" weren't real law officers, Witherell slipped out of town and rode across the mountains into Colorado where he met E.E. Wright and began herding sheep with him. He figured a sheep camp was a good place to hide until he could safely return and dig up the outlaw trunk. On September 18th, 1871 Witherell and Wright killed an old sheepherder named S.K. Wall for $70 and a gold watch. A posse chased them to Sidney, Nebraska where they were arrested. Witherell still had Wall's gold watch with him. He arrived at the Colorado State Penitentiary at Canon City on January 3rd, 1872 to begin serving a life sentence.

After several escape attempts, Witherell was pardoned in 1887. He went directly to Canon City where he purchased a used six-shooter, got drunk in a back street saloon and killed a man in a drunken brawl. He was

seized and hung from a telegraph pole before lawmen could arrive. The secret of his buried cache near Call's Fort died with him.

About an hour's drive by buckboard across the Bear River from Corinne, a fortune waits to be found. The paper money may have rotted away, but the gold is as shiny and bright as ever. And it's worth a whole lot more than it was when George Witherell buried it in a shallow hole more than 100 years ago.

HOYT'S FORT

Hoyt's Fort was located 300' southwest of the historical monument in front of the Mormon Church House at Hoytsville in Summit County. It was built during the Blackhawk War years of 1866-68. At first it was known as Fort Union, but when Samuel Hoyt built a home and grist mill nearby it was renamed Hoyt's Fort. During the worst of the Indian troubles, 25 families lived there. Cabins were built both inside and outside its walls.

Hoyt's Fort also served as a stage station for Kimball's Stage Lines and for the Gilmer & Saulsbury line. Only the shell of one of its buildings and the ruins of Hoyt's grist mill remain. They are on private property. The Utah State Historical Society is presently trying to preserve the fort as an historical place of interest.

ROCK FORT

When Rock Fort was first settled as a farming settlement on the Weber River in Summit County in 1854 it was known as Crandall City., In 1860, with more people arriving daily, its name was changed to Enoch City. When the Blackhawk War threatened settlers during the late 1860's a rock wall 8' high was built around the entire town. This gave it still another name, Rock Fort. The fort soon boasted a schoolhouse that was 18' x 24' in size, built of red sandstone. There was also a combination post office and general store and an office used by its two stage companies, Kimball's and Gilmer & Saulsbury.

For many years an old recluse known only as "Dutch John," described as a "Homeopathic Doctor from Germany", lived in a dugout in the cedared hills above town. He had no farmground, livestock or other means of support, yet when someone became ill, he would mysteriously appear, carrying a pack of strange herbs, pills and potions, which he gave freely to the sick. He never asked for payment and would take food only if it was offered. After the community grew in size and had the services of a regular doctor, "Dutch John" disappeared.

When the Blackhawk War ended, the rock walls surrounding Rock Fort were torn down to provide stone for homes and businesses. In time the name Rock Fort became Rockport, a name it bore until Wanship Dam was built and flooded it with Rockport Lake. Before it went to its watery grave, Rockport had a number of vigorous businesses, among them Seamon's General Store, Vickey's Shoe Shop and Casey & Vernon's Sawmill. At low water level old foundations and streets can be seen. Occasionally, century old coins and trade tokens are found along the submerged sidewalks. That's all that's left of Rock Fort.

KINGSTON FORT

There were few places in pioneer Utah stranger than Kingston Fort. The settlement of Kingston was established near the mouth of Weber Canyon in 1853 by Thomas Kingston, the first Mormon Bishop of Weber County. It consisted of a church, a school, a bowery and two rows of log cabins. When Indians threatened, a wall was built around it, after which it was known as Kingston's Fort. The little town was abondoned when Brigham Young ordered the evacuation of all of northern Utah during the advance of Johnston's Army in 1857. It remained deserted until 1859 when the "false prophet" Joseph Morris and his followers resettled it.

Joseph Morris was an eccentric who believed he was chosen by God for exaltation. He joined the Mormon Chruch in 1849 and came to Utah in 1853, but attracted no special attention until 1859 when he claimed he was receiving divine revelations. When he claimed that he was chosen to replace Brigham Young as leader of the Mormon Church, his troubles really began!

When Young failed to surrender the reins of leadership to him, Morris started his own church, and took over Kingston Fort as his headquarters. By 1862 he had 600 fanatic followers who believed he was a modern Moses. They also believed his prophecy that the Second Coming and the end of the world were at hand. But it was when he imprisoned three men who failed to follow his orders that he got into trouble with the civil authorities as well as with Brigham Young. Friends appealed the illegal imprisonment to Judge J.F. Kinney at Salt Lake City, who immediately issued a writ ordering their release. When Morris refused to accept the order, stating he was an Angel of God and the only law on earth, his fate and that of the Morrisites was sealed.

On June 11th, 1862 Judge Kinney ordered Marshal Robert Burton, who was one of Brigham Young's officers in the Nauvoo Legion, and a 250 man militia to arrest Morris. On June 13th Marshall Burton placed two cannons on a bluff south of the fort and another at its west side. He then ordered Morris to surrender within thirty minutes. Morris refused, saying to his followers, "If you are faithful, your foes will be destroyed, and no harm shall come to you!" Marshal Burton ordered the cannon fired. In the first volley one man and two women were killed and several others were wounded.

The Hoyt Mansion at Fort Hoyt, sometimes called Fort Union.

There was no answer from the fort on that day or the next, when heavy rains halted all operations. On the 15th another volley was fired and another Morrisite killed. Again Morris was called upon to surrender. After several minutes a white flag was raised. Morris appeared at the gate of the fort, dressed in flowing white robes, but instead of surrendering called to his followers, "All who are willing to follow me through life and death, come on!"

Men and women ran to his side, and Marshal Burton ordered the cannon fired. Morris and two of his lieutenants, John Banks and Richard Cook, were blasted into eternity. Two women standing nearby were also killed.

Nearly one hundred men were captured and taken to Salt Lake City where seven were found guilty of manslaughter and the remainder fined $100 each for resisting arrest. Governor Frank Fuller immediately pardoned all of them. The disheartened and leaderless Morrisites gathered up their families and meager belongings and left Kingston Fort forever. Most of them moved to Idaho.

Kingston Fort slowly fell into ruin. Today Interstate 80 passes close by its site, just west of US-89 at the mouth of Weber Canyon. An historical marker stands near the site, but people living there don't talk about it much.

FORT CAMERON & JOHN D. LEE'S LOST MINES

When it was established in 1872 Fort Cameron was known as The Post Of Beaver. It was renamed Fort Cameron on July 1st, 1874 when it was designated a regular army garrison as a result of the tragic Mountain Meadows Massacre. Named in honor of Col. James Cameron, a Civil War hero of the battle of Bull Run, it was home to the 8th Infantry under the command of Major John Wilkins, and consisted of an area 2½ miles square. It was located on the north side of the Beaver River, 2 miles east of Beaver City. It was a well built place of hand cut stone and mortar, that included 4 barracks, a commissary, a hospital and a row of officers' quarters.

The trial of the infamous John D. Lee, leader of the massacre at Mountain Meadows, was held at Fort Cameron. A jury found Lee guilty on September 20th, 1876, 19 years after the massacre. He was executed by a firing squad on March 23rd, 1877 at the place where he and other white men, dressed as Indians, killed 121 men, women and children in September, 1857. Fort Cameron was disbanded on May 1st, 1883.

When the army left Fort Cameron, all of its buildings were sold to John R. Murdock who reopened them

Fort Cameron, The Post Of Beaver, during the 1870's. This was Officers' Row.

Only John D. Lee knows the secret of his lost gold, and he isn't telling!

as Murdock Academy, a branch of Brigham Young University. Several new and impressive buildings went up at that time. When Murdock Academy was closed in 1922 most of its buildings were dismantled for the stone they contained. Mormon churches at Milford and Minersville were built of that stone. Today several of the fort's buildings are in good repair, and can be seen at the edge of the city's golf course.

When John D. Lee was executed he took the secret of two lost mines and a gold cache with him to the grave. They are strange stories, where truth is stranger than fiction.

After Lee led the fanatics who massacred the desert travelers at the Mountain Meadows in 1857 he was a hunted man. For nearly 20 years he hid in the Grand Canyon where he had a secret silver mine as well as a place where he obtained gold nuggets, enough of both to support 18 wives and their families. There is no doubt of the mines' existence. Several times he was trailed almost to the mines before he spotted his trackers, and many people saw the gold he brought from the canyon, including his wife, Emma, who searched for the mine after Lee was executed.

While in hiding Lee lived with Emma at Lonely Dell, a God-forsaken refuge at Lee's Crossing on the Colorado. For several years an adopted boy named Robert Hilderbrand lived with them at Lonely Dell. He would go with Lee into the maze of canyons, but was never allowed to see the mine. In later years Hilderbrand would say that he accompanied Lee to Soap Creek, where he would stay with the burros at a grassy glen. In two or three days Lee would return, carrying a heavy pack of gold nuggets. Hilderbrand was certain the gold did not come from a river placer, since it appeared to be broken from lava rock.

John Hance was an old desert prospector who often saw Lee in the canyons. He met him several times while he was carrying a heavy load of silver ore, not gold, coming up canyon from somewhere far below Soap Creek. His statements confirm that Lee's money rock came from at least two sources.

Many tried to follow Lee, but he knew the mysterious canyons better than anyone, and had no trouble losing them. Lee was later arrested while visiting one of his wives at Parowan, and was executed at Fort Cameron. Not long before he was arrested, Lee and Hilderbrand returned to Lonely Dell from one of his mines and cached a sack of ore under Emma's bed. After Lee was executed, Emma married Franklin French, who sold the ore for $7,000!

French and Emma made many trips into the canyon searching for Lee's mine, but finally gave up and left Lonely Dell. Issac C. Haight, a participant in the massacre with Lee and also a hunted man, somehow obtained a small leather map which supposedly showed where Lee buried seven cans of gold, but in a summer of looking never found the cache.

In 1909 a lone prospector came to Rowland Rider's cow camp near the edge of the canyon in House Rock Valley. The prospector was unfamiliar with the country, yet asked questions about trails and landmarks in Soap Creek Canyon that only someone who had been there would know anything about. Rider gave the information asked for, and several days later the prospector returned to his camp. He had seven old rusty cans filled with gold! Rider remembered that the gold was rough, not water worn. When he asked the old prospector where he got it, the old-timer said, "Down there, where Soap Creek goes into the Colorado!"

Could the prospector of 1909 be the boy Robert Hilderbrand who followed Lee into the canyons long before? In 1909 he would have been in his fifties. There isn't any question that Lee had a mine, or possibly two, one silver and one gold.

If you want to look for Lee's mine, locate Soap Creek 12 miles downstream from Marble Canyon bridge. The canyon is a national monument now, so taking gold from it would be illegal. I'm not suggesting that anyone break the law, but if you happen to be hiking somewhere in Soap Creek Canyon and by accident come across a ledge of rotten lava rock where gold nuggets glisten in the sun, I don't think anyone would blame you for taking a few pockets-full!

Rowland Rider at Lee's Ferry in 1909. He saw Lee's gold! -Rowland Rider-

FORT PEARCE
&
THE LOST PARTNERS' PLACERS

Fort Pierce Wash, southeast of St. George in Washington County, was the site of Fort Pearce, built to protect the trail from Dixie to the Arizona settlements. Today its name and that of the dry wash where it was located are shown on nearly all maps as Fort Pierce. This is an error, for both the fort and the wash were named for John D.L. Pearce, an early-day settler and trail blazer. Originally, the trail south went from St. George to the Washington Field then through Warner Valley along Pearce Creek to the fort. Then it continued east up a dugway over Hurricane Fault and on to Short Creek and Pipe Springs. The fort itself was small, only 30' square, but it was sturdily built of stone and had a high tower equipped with portholes for riflemen.

Fort Pearce was intended to be only a way station where travelers could defend themselves from Indians. Workmen hauling timber and stone used in construction of the Mormon Temple at St. George often sought refuge there. A stone corral with walls 5' high protected their livestock from raiding Indians. It was located atop a bare ridge near a small pool of water at the base of a cliff. It had a roof of cottonwood poles, but they have

been burned by campers over the years. Today the ruins of Fort Pearce keep silent guard over the old Mormon Trail.

Legally the Arizona Strip, that narrow slice of land south of Fort Pearce and the Utah State line, but north of the Grand Canyon, belongs to Arizona. By any other standard it is part of Utah, commercially, geographically and historically. It was settled by Mormon pioneers and almost all of its small population is still Mormon. Utah has made several attempts to annex the strip, but those efforts have always failed. Thus, while the lost partners' gold placer may technically be in Arizona, its story is really a Utah treasure tale.

Three casual prospectors from St. George, who herded cattle near Fort Pearce and Windsor Castle, now known as Pipe Springs, found a rich gold placer on Kanab Creek, not far from the Colorado River. Working part-time while herding cattle, they recovered three fruit jars of nuggets, using sluice boxes built from driftwood found along the river. When they returned to St. George they were severely rebuked by their Bishop for engaging in mining, which Brigham Young specifically forbade Mormons to do. The Bishop reminded them of Brigham Young's warning, that "Some men have a golden God in their hearts, but every dollar earned by mining has cost one hundred dollars. It is gold that causes murders, anarchy, vigilance committees and idleness!" The three partners lost their jobs

Fort Pearce, intended to be a temporary outpost, has survived more transient neighbors. -Utah Historical Society-

with the Mormon owned Windsor Cattle Company and were so shamed in the community that they never returned to the placers, nor would they discuss them with anyone.

Finally, the partners died and their transgressions were forgotten. Times changed as well. Eventually it was no longer a sin for a Mormon to engage in mining. Old-timers remembered the bottles of gold nuggets brought back from the partners' placers, and thus their story was kept alive. In 1941, Louis Arnold, who gave his address only as St. George, was herding sheep along Kanab Creek where the three partners had herded cattle long before. One day he discovered some old log sluice boxes half buried in the sand. Dry panning along the wash he found many small gold nuggets, so he wrote to the Kingman County recorder's office for proper procedures for filing a claim. In his letter Arnold stated the placers were 3 to 5 feet deep and more than 500' long, and were located about 74 miles from the Mt. Trumball Community, a ghost town 65 miles south of St. George.

Kingman County replied to Arnold's letter, mailing location forms to P.O. Box 353, St. George, Utah, but the letter was never claimed. No one in St. George had ever heard of Louis Arnold, nor was he ever heard from again, although his letter to Kingman County is still on file.

There's not much doubt that Arnold discovered the same gold placers on Kanab Creek that the three partners had found 70 years earlier. Since then no trace of the placers has been found. Remember, Kanab Creek and its countless side canyons cover a big piece of country. Arnold said the placers were 74 miles from the Mt. Trumball Community, but he didn't say if that was by trail or as the crow flies. It could be the long way if the crow had to walk and lead a pack burro.

HAMILTON FORT

In 1852 Peter Shirts, second only to Jacob Hamblin as a colonizer of southern Utah, built a log cabin for his family on Sidon Creek, 5 miles southwest of Cedar City in Iron County. Shirts grubbed the head high sage from the sandy soil and turned irrigation water from the creek onto it. His crops grew rapidly under the hot Dixie sun, but Shirts knew there was a constant threat to his security from the wandering Indians whose lands he was claiming. To increase his chances by increasing his numbers, he offered part of his water rights to John Hamilton, Peter Fife and others if they would join him.

The little settlement was just beginning to look like a town when the Walker War began. At Brigham Young's directions, it was abandoned until the Indian threat was over. When the settlers returned to Sidon Creek they were joined by others. They all helped build a fort. When completed its 3' thick walls enclosed all the settlers' cabins.

For awhile the walled town was known as Fort Sidon and later as Fort Walker. Gradually it became known as Hamilton Fort, in honor of John Hamilton, Mormon Bishop there nearly all his life. He was affectionately known to everyone as "Grandfather Hamilton." Hamilton Fort grew into an orderly little community of two story stone houses, but was located too far from the regular trail from Cedar City to the Washington County settlements. When Brigham Young visited there in 1869 he advised the residents to move. Reluctantly, they followed the prophet's advice, leaving their hard won homes to the few determined to stay behind. Before long nearly every home was deserted.

A half century later modern farming methods consolidated many of its small farms. With the advent of the auto, some people returned. In recent years several modern homes have been built giving the old settlement a new lease on life, even though modern road maps list its population as only 26. In sight of Interstate 15, Hamilton Fort dozes under the Dixie sun, a reminder of the Utah of 100 years ago.

COVE FORT

Historic Cove Fort was built in 1867 by Ira Hinckley and others under orders from Brigham Young, for the protection of travelers in central Utah. It was located at the junction of several heavily used pioneer trails and was on the Salt Lake City to Dixie route. Today it is just off U-4 in Millard County, 2 miles east of its junction with Interstate 15. It was built of black volcanic rock, 100′ square with walls 18′ high and cost $25,000. It had a high arched gate on its east side and contained 12 rooms built along its north and south inside walls. A deep well was dug in its center to insure ample water when under attack. About 500′ to the east and 300′ north a lone cottonwood and some cedar corral posts mark the site of Fort Wilden, built by Charles Wilden and his family in 1865.

Cove Fort has always been under someone's care, and today is the most perfectly preserved pioneer fort in the west. Its rooms contain many priceless treasures from pioneer days, while the open area within its walls contains old wagons, buckboards and other relics of the days when it served as a refuge for travelers on trails now forgotten. It's worth going a long way to see; don't miss it.

CAMP FLOYD & DOBIETOWN

Camp Floyd was located in Utah County's Cedar Valley, almost midway between Tooele and Lehi. It was Utah's best known fort, as well as its largest. When first established in 1858 during the Utah War by army troops under the command of General Albert S. Johnston, it had more than 7,000 soldiers and camp followers, and was the largest army post in the country. The well known firm of Russell, Majors & Waddell hauled 16 million pounds of freight to the camp, which soon boasted 300 buildings of adobe, wood, brick and stone. Named in honor of John B. Floyd, President Bucha-

Cove Fort, probably the most perfectly preserved fort in the west.

The older of two cemeteries at Camp Floyd.

nan's Secretary of War, it was designated an Overland Stage station in 1859 and a Pony Express stop in 1860. Dobietown, also know as Frogtown, was located just beyond the camp, and was one of the roughest towns in the state, sporting every kind of saloon, bordello and gambling hall known.

But with the Utah War over, the "Mormon Problem" resolved, and the Civil War threatening in the east, Camp Floyd was abandoned. By then its name had been changed to Camp Crittenden, since Secretary Floyd had become an embarrassment to the administration because of his pro-confederate views. The camp's $4,000,000 inventory of goods was sold for only $100,000, with Brigham Young purchasing half the total. Flour, which cost the government $570 a ton to get to Utah, was sold for $11 a ton. By 1862 the gay times at Dobietown were gone and only 18 families remained.

Today the Stagecoach Inn at nearby Fairfield, built of stone from the camp's buildings, and a little cemetery located a half mile to the southwest, with many tombstones bearing only the words "Killed By Indians" are all that remain of Camp Floyd's past glory. There is a tradition around Utah Valley that when the army left Camp Floyd, they were unable to take all the munitions stored there. Not wanting firearms to fall into Mormon hands, thousands of rifles were secretly buried in a deep pit somewhere near the fort. That would be a cache worth finding!

FORT MONTEZUMA
&
LEGEND OF THE LOST PISH-LA-KI MINE

In 1879 Peter Shirts built a cabin at the mouth of Montezuma Creek on the San Juan River. By the following year six more families had joined him. The settlement was named after the creek, which was called Montezuma Creek because it was believed the Aztec Emperor Montezuma was killed there. That year their first child was born there. One pioneer wrote, "Times are very hard, but we have plenty of white salmon to eat." Those "white salmon" were probably carp or catfish. The settlers were often attacked by Indians, and finally had to build a rock fort, which they called Fort Montezuma. In one week long battle they were unable to leave the fort, and a relief party was sent to their rescue, "To comfort them if they are still alive, if not, to bury them!" But the Saints persevered, and soon their growing settlement boasted a store operated by James Davis, a schoolhouse and a post office.

Living conditions at Fort Montezuma were harsh at best. There was little farmable ground along the river, and the high water often flooded what there was. In 1883, in an unusual policy change, Mormon authorities granted the settlers permission to leave their "mission." A few left, but most remained. Then, in August,

1884, two popular young men from Fort Montezuma were ambushed by Indians on a rocky ridge in view of the fort. Their attackers only wounded the men, and then allowed wild dogs to tear them apart as their horrified families looked helplessly on. Their tragic death was the final straw for the weary settlers, and soon afterwards they moved to Bluff, 19 miles downstream, "Poorer in worldly goods, but richer in wisdom."

The walls of Fort Montezuma are gone now, but by the side of Montezuma Wash, on the San Juan, a trading post by that name remains. On a quiet night, if you listen closely, you might hear the howling of a pack of Indian dogs running along a rocky ridge in the shadow of the old fort.

One of the most intriguing lost mine mysteries is that of the Lost Pish-La-Ki Mine, better known as the Merrick & Mitchell Mine. In 1863 US Army troops with Kit Carson as their scout drove the Navajo Indians from southeastern Utah onto a prison-like reservation at Bosque-Redondo, New Mexico. A few Indians escaped capture, among them Chief Hoskininni's band, who took refuge for six years on Navajo Mountain, south of the San Juan River and north of the Arizona border.

That the Navajos had a secret silver mine on sacred Navajo Mountain is beyond doubt. Many references can be cited, but the most revealing is a personal interview in 1939 between 82 year old Hoskininni Begay, son of Chief Hoskininni, and Utah historian Charles Kelly. In brief, Hoskininni Begay said, "One day father brought some silver rocks into camp, and found they were so soft he could shape them without melting. He and six others took much silver, which was made into ornaments. In those days all silver was made smooth without design."

"When we came from the mountain we had much silver, and were the richest of all Navajos. When the white man saw all our silver ornaments, they wanted to hunt for our mine, but father would not allow it, and none of the old men who knew where it was told any white man, or even another Navajo. I myself do not even know where it is."

But prospectors did sneak onto the reservation, and some of them found the Navajos' sacred Pish-La-Ki Mine. In 1870 John Merrick copied an old Spanish map at Monterey, which revealed a silver mine worked by conquistadores and their Indian slaves 200 years before. Merrick organized a party of Californians, and by following the Old Spanish Trail eastward across Comb Wash and the San Juan River, they located the old mine. The date 1661 was carved on the sandstone cliff above its entrance.

John Merrick and his partners reopened the old shaft and removed a large quantity of nearly pure horn-silver before the Indian descendants of the slave laborers who overthrew the Spanish in 1680 attacked them along the Virgin River. All were killed except Merrick, who made his way to California. He vowed never to return, and gave his prized map to his son Robert on the condition that he not attempt to go to the mine until the Navajos were under army contol.

In 1879 young Merrick began his search teamed with Hearndon Mitchell, son of the trader at Fort Montezuma. With his father's map and directions they easily located the mine and loaded a burro train with silver. Neither was seen alive again! The March 16th, 1880 issue of the *Rocky Mountain News* reported that their bodies had been found by Cass Hite in Monument Valley, one each at the foot of two towering stone monuments located about three miles apart. Empty cartridge cases along the valley floor outlined the running fight they had with the Indians before being killed. The carcasses of their silver laden burros were found nearby. The two towering buttes where their bodies were found are still known as Merrick and Mitchell Buttes.

Hoskininni Begay told Kelly that Merrick and Mitchell were killed by Utes, not Navajos, and added, "My people have been blamed for their killing, but it is not true. Whenever one of our people die, their silver is buried with them, so now little of the silver of Pish-La-Ki remains. I myself have had eight wives, and all of my silver is buried with them."

Navajo Mountain is still the Navajos' sacred mountain, from which white men are forever restricted. So if you decide to follow Merrick & Mitchell's lost pony tracks to the Pish-La-Ki Mine, stop to look at the great Merrick and Mitchell buttes in Monument Valley. Some say their blood still stains the desert sand bright red on the lost trail to Pish-La-Ki!

OGDEN AREA FORTS
&
THE LOST McDONALD MINE

Many present-day cities in Utah were born as pioneer forts, but Ogden is unique in that it is built upon the ruins of four different ones. When the pioneers arrived in Utah, trapper Miles Goodyear had already built Fort Buenaventura on the Weber River just south of present-day 24th Street. Brigham Young purchased Goodyear's Fort for $1,960 in gold and placed James Brown in charge of the Ogden Stake of the church, after which Goodyear's Fort was known as Brown's Fort.

Farr's Fort was built in 1850 at the mouth of Ogden Canyon, where Lorin Farr had located his grist mill a year earlier. It enclosed only five acres, but provided a place of refuge during Indian scares. Bingham's Fort, which grew into Lynne, was located north of 2nd Street and west of Washington Blvd. on the banks of the Ogden River. Built in 1853, its walls enclosed 40 acres. Because of its name it is sometimes confused with Fort Bingham, a small stockade built in 1864, 10 miles east of Tooele near the head of Bingham's Creek, in Salt Lake County. Mound Fort was located between present-day 9th and 12th Streets and west of Washington Boulevard, on the north side of the Ogden River. In 1854 a 9' wall was built around it. In 1884 it boasted a population of 100.

There is a lost gold mine almost in sight of Ogden's pioneer forts. Around 1900 a man named McDonald worked a gold mine in Taylor Canyon, the mouth of which can be seen in the rugged, rockslide cliffs at the head of 27th Street. McDonald must have been working more than just a mine in prospect, since he drove a tunnel more than 100' into the hard granite cliffs, and built a sturdy little log cabin where he lived for at least five years. A man doesn't do that if he's not making enough money to live on.

About 1911 McDonald was called to California. He asked friends to keep an eye on his property, and said he would be back soon. But he didn't return until 1937! When his two sons brought him back to Ogden, he was old and very sick. He had intended to take them to his mine, but was too feeble to climb the canyon. He camped in a tent near the canyon's mouth while his sons hiked day after day, searching for their father's lost mine. Finally they gave up their search for what has been known ever since as the Lost McDonald Mine and returned to California.

About a mile and a half up Taylor Canyon, past the first side gulch to the left, there is a little yellow mine dump hidden in the oak brush. Some say it is the Lost McDonald Mine. Over the years its entrance has caved in and rockslides from the mountain above have almost covered it. But there's a piece of the puzzle that doesn't seem to fit in. McDonald's cabin is much farther up canyon and on the opposite side of the creek. There's not much left of it, and it's very hard to find. But if the little yellow dump was his mine, why did he build his cabin so far from it?

Thus, it could be that the Lost McDonald Mine isn't lost at all, and then again, maybe the yellow dump mine wasn't the real mine. It seems that his sons would have found it with little trouble. If you hike to the top of Taylor Canyon, an almost impossible climb over nearly vertical cliffs and dangerous rock slides, you will arrive at the head of Cold Water Canyon. An old sheepherder I know has picked up lots of pieces of gold float in Cold Water Canyon. It may be coincidence, but McDonald's cabin is closer to Cold Water Canyon than it is to the little yellow mine dump! Could it have been McDonald who dropped the pieces of gold ore the sheepherder found?

If you're a prospector, and have some time, and like to hunt in rough country, you might examine Cold Water Canyon. Surely McDonald didn't spend six years of his life in the canyon, build a solid cabin, and then come all the way from California as a dying man to show his sons where gold was not hidden. There must be something there. There must be!

SOME SMALL FORTS
&
THE LOST PARIA GOLD

In December, 1854 Jacob Hamblin, Ira Hatch, William Henefer and others called to Dixie by the Mormon Church began building Fort Santa Clara in Washington County. It was located on the Santa Clara River 5 miles north of its junction with the Virgin River. Fort Clara, as it was always known in Dixie, was 100' square and built of "hammered rock," with walls 3' thick and 12' high. A traveler who visited there wrote, "It is built very substantial to thwart any purpose of an attack. The inside is partitioned off into 25 rooms, with rifle portholes in each. The doors all open to the center and there is only one opening where wagons can enter." Fort Santa Clara was the forerunner of today's city of Santa Clara.

Hamblin, who was known as the Buckskin Prophet, probably explored more of southern Utah than any other man and was instrumental in establishing a number of forts to protect the trails he blazed and to encourage settlement. One well known fort built by Hamblin was Fort Meek, established in 1869 northeast of Kanab in Kane County, named for a Mormon Bishop who was traveling with Hamblin.

Some early forts which became today's cities included Fort Utah, which became Provo City, Fort Peeteetneet, now Payson, Fort Louisa which became Parowan and Fort Johnson, now Enoch in Iron County.

On the Colorado River near the extreme northwest tip of San Juan County there was a fort shown on the earliest maps as Old Fort Bottom. The earliest trappers used it, but it was old even then, probably built by Spanish explorers or miners.

Pioneer Fort Wah Weap was built in 1869 to guard the Paria Crossing of the Colorado, a place favored by Navajos to ambush travelers. It witnessed the exploration of the Colorado by Major John Wesley Powell and the gold rush on Paria Creek. Long after Fort Wah Weap was abandoned, it witnessed a lone prospector strike it rich, but not wanting the treasures of the Paria known to all, it guarded the prospector's secret well, so well that his lost placer has never been located since.

After the short gold rush of the 1890's at Pahreah, Dake Train became a familiar sight around the Vermillion Cliffs country. An old-time prospector, he made his camp on Buckskin Mountain, southwest of Adairville, not far from Fort Wah Weap.

It was during the summer of 1896, after one of the violent sand storms which blow in from the pink coral sand dunes, that one of Joel Johnson's boys found Train wandering in the desert near Crescent Butte, badly dehydrated and more dead than alive. He was taken to Kanab where there was a doctor. Train slowly recuperated, and told the doctor how he had found a rich gold placer in a hidden box canyon just off Paria Creek. After the gold rush fiasco at Pahreah no one was anxious to listen to his story, but a search was made for his burro. Train's desert canary was found in Buckskin Gulch southeast of Crescent Butte, its pack saddle still intact. Inside it they found a copper kettle full of coarse gold nuggets!

Train explained that he was returning to Adairville from a narrow, slit-like side canyon in the Paria country when he became disoriented in a sudden sand storm. He fell and hit his head, and when he regained consciousness, his burro had wandered off. Visibility in the swirling dust was only a few feet, but he knew that if he kept walking north he would come to Paria Creek. Somehow he lost track of directions and in a brief break in the storm saw the outline of a lone butte far ahead. He staggered to where he was found by Johnson, near Crescent Butte on the east side of Johnson Creek.

After a week's rest, Train was well enough to leave Kanab, and headed back to his camp on Buckskin Mountain, and his diggings in the Paria country. Train had no trouble returning to the narrow box canyon where a small trickle of water seeped from a towering cliff. The tiny stream ran only a short way before it was lost in a sandy wash, but in its gravel bed there was plenty of coarse gold, and enough water to pan it.

For a month Train camped in his secret gold gulch, until his supplies ran out and feed for his burro was exhausted. For several weeks he had been aware that men were prowling around the Paria, probably trying to locate his camp. The abortive gold rush at Pahreah had brought a number of shady characters to the area. With enough gold to fill two dutch ovens, he had no desire to meet any of them.

After two hard-cases passed within a mile of his camp, Train decided it was time to get out. Instead of returning to Adairville, he went down the Paria past old Fort Wah Weap and crossed the Colorado. He made his way to California where he cashed in his gold for over $100,000 and bought a small farm near San Bernadino. There he married a widow with several children. Although his farm kept them alive, in time he felt the need for ready cash and decided to make a trip back to the Paria to get another stake for his old age.

In 1911 Train followed the trail across the Colorado and up Paria Creek, confident he could go straight to the narrow side canyon where a tiny spring bubbled from under the base of a sandstone cliff. For a month he searched every possible side canyon without finding a familiar landmark. Confused, he went back to his old camp on Buckskin Mountain and retraced his trail from there, but never found the secret canyon or a single grain of gold.

Completely bewildered, Train returned empty-handed to California. In 1916 he tried again. He returned to Kanab but no one there remembered him, and when he tried to tell them about his lost placer gold near the Paria, people would only look at him in pity and shake their heads, thinking he was another crazy prospector looking for gold that didn't exist. Train was an old man then and couldn't hike the desert anymore. He returned to his California farm, where until the day he died he told anyone who would listen about the lost gold of the Paria; gold he knew still waited somewhere south of Buckskin Mountain and east of Crescent Butte.

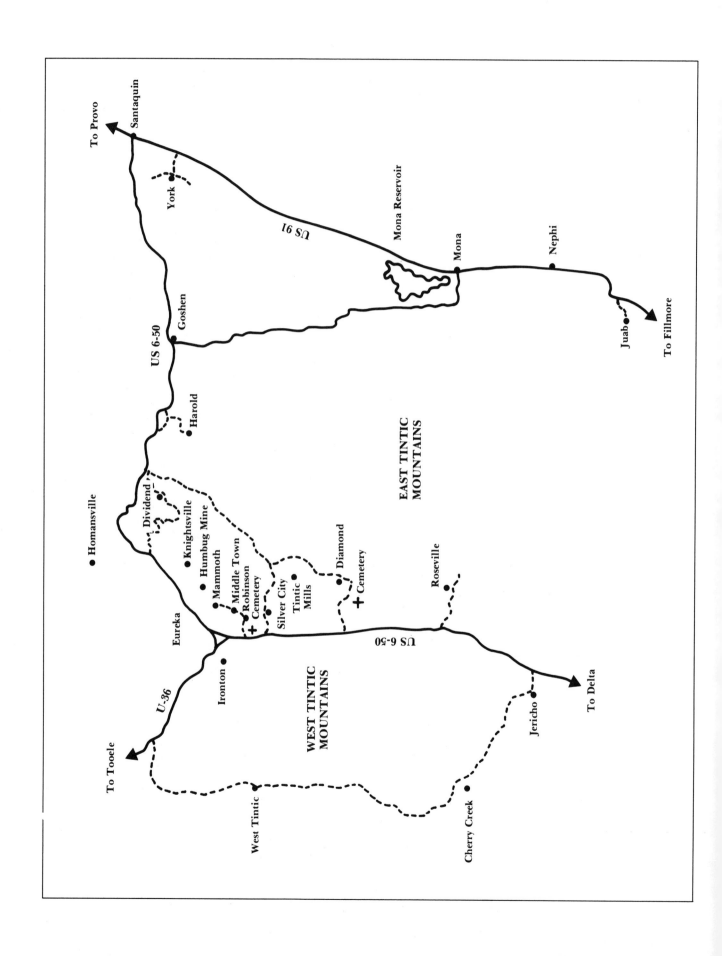

CHAPTER FIVE

TINTIC TOWNS

Mormon settlers of the 1860's undoubtedly were aware of the fabulous wealth of Utah's famed Tintic Mining District, but because they were forbidden to engage in mining silver and gold, the area's wealth remained untouched for awhile. Utah history contains many stories of rich deposits being found by early day Mormons, only to be left unworked or even concealed. Many fascinating treasure tales had their beginnings when rich strikes of precious metals were left untouched by their finders.

In 1865 a young Mormon stock tender accidently discovered silver at what would become Tintic's boom camp of Eureka, but was instructed to keep his find a secret. So it remained until 1869 when a gentile cowboy rediscovered it and started a wild rush to the new Golconda. As if by magic a dozen mining camps exploded along the East Tintic Range, making the newly organized mining district one of the richest in the west. By the end of its first 100 years, Tintic's production of silver, gold and other minerals had exceeded $500,000,000. Although its hills are dotted with ghost towns, it's possible that its second century may equal its first in mineral wealth.

Besides rough-and-ready camps like Diamond and Silver City, Tintic also claimed Knightsville, the only mining camp in the west without a saloon! It could also boast tough end-of-track railroad camps and a little known polygamist colony. Today you can stake your claim on Tintic's ghost towns and their treasures, which range from diamonds in the rough to lost Mormon gold.

RUBY HOLLOW

Ruby Hollow, now known as Eureka, has never achieved the dubious distinction of being a ghost town. Its story in included here because it was the chief camp of the Tintic Mining District, and because the history of nearly all of Tintic's other towns are so closely tied to it. The first discovery of silver in the East Tintic Range was made by Shadrack Lunt, a young Mormon sheepherder who apparently was also a part-time prospector. Lunt took a sample of his find to his Bishop, who in turn reported it to Brigham Young. The Mormon Prophet, who did not encourage prospecting by Mormons, had said, "Whenever I see a prospector going along with an old mule that can hardly stand up, with only a frying pan and a tattered quilt, I say, there goes a millionaire in prospect. These millionaires are all over our country, they are in the mountains, on our roads and in the streets, and they haven't a six-pence between them!''

The ledge of silver found by Lunt was forgotten until 1869 when George Rust, a gentile cowboy who cared nothing about the prophet's ban on mining, camped in Ruby Hollow and rediscovered Lunt's ledge. On December 13th, 1869 Rust and seven other cowboys staked their claims along the silver ledge. The first assays from their claims averaged $1,500 to the ton! Some of the first ore from their mines was hauled by wagon to Lake Point and carried by ships on the Great Salt Lake to the mills at Corinne.

By the spring of 1871 miners' cabins and rough stores and saloons were strung out all along the winding bottom of Ruby Gulch. Already mills and smelters were being built, and more than 500 claims had been recorded. Before those mills were completed, Tintic's best ore was carried by wagon all the way to the Pacific coast and shipped to Wales. Many of those first claims at Ruby Hollow became mines worth millions, among them the Eureka Standard, Chief Consolidated, Eureka Hill and the Bullion-Beck. Several had ore bodies that assayed 15,000 ounces of silver to the ton! And Shadrack Lunt, who discovered it all, never realized a penny.

Early in its boom days the name Ruby Hollow was dropped and the name of Eureka given to the camp. Over the years Eureka has experienced all of the ups and downs that mining camps know, but still keeps going. Today it is one of the liveliest ghost towns in the state!

IRONTON
&
THE OLD SPANISH MINE AT TINTIC

The railroad town of Ironton was located near where US 6-50 and U-36 come together at Tintic Junction 2 miles southwest of Eureka. The rich silver strikes being made at Ruby Hollow gave Ironton its birth. Even before the rails of the San Pedro, Los Angeles & Salt Lake Railroad reached the mouth of the canyon below Ruby Hollow, ore bins had been built, and the ore shipping town of Ironton had been established. One early account describes how 40 wagons were kept busy hauling ore from Ruby Hollow to Ironton.

Because of its location on the railroad, Ironton became a supply town for the mining camps then being built along the mountain front. It soon had a row of stores and shops of all kinds, plus the usual assortment of saloons. But Ironton soon had a rival, for 2 miles south another railroad town named Tintic was surveyed and claimed its own business district. Tintic was the main supply town for the mines at Mammoth, a new camp that rivaled Ruby Hollow as the district's leading silver producer. Businesses at Tintic included Jennings General Store, Freckleton's Store, the Cameron Mining Engineers Building and Mary Madison's Dressmaking Shop.

Both Ironton and Tintic looked forward to promising futures, but their days were numbered. The same railroad which had brought them prosperity would soon take it away. It was inevitable that as richer finds were made at Ruby Hollow and Mammoth, the end of track would be pushed up canyon, and when this happened Ironton and Tintic's day in the sun would be over. As larger mills were built near the mines, the need for the two little railroad towns disappeared, and both soon died. In almost less time than it takes to tell, they were deserted. Tumble-weeds rolled aimlessly down streets where people had walked only days before. Today, a few old houses mark the site of Ironton, while even less remains at Tintic. There is nothing to mark its site except a lonely sign by the track.

The miners in the Tintic District soon found evidence that they were not the first there. The cedar covered hills hid many ancient tunnels and shafts. The Salt Lake *Herald* of May 19th, 1871 reported the discovery of one such find. "Yesterday a miner came to town with some very rich ore taken from an old mine, which when discovered still showed chisel marks and other evidence of having been worked in by-gone days. He stumbled onto the old shaft by accident, within ten miles of Tintic, although he is very reluctant to say just where. The ore he brought in assays at more than $6,000 to the ton.''

Not all of the Spanish mines near Tintic were discovered one hundred years ago, for at least one was found in the late 1920's. I.H. Diehl, a respected mining engineer, reported how it was found. "When boulders were rolled away from its entrance, two ancient skeletons were revealed. The methods used by those primitive miners is a marvel. They had no blasting powder, or even tools, except for what they made by themselves, yet they penetrated the solid rock for hundreds of feet. Some of the old Spanish workings show that fires had been built to heat the rock which was then cracked by throwing water on it.''

Every range of mountains and hills in Utah, from south to north and east to west were explored by Spanish adventurers long before the first Pilgrims and Indians exchanged greetings at Plymouth Rock. The places where they dug for silver and gold are still waiting for you to find them, although they were often cleverly concealed, as was the case in the one Diehl described. The age old hills above Ironton and Tintic might be a good place to start your search.

DIAMOND & ROSEVILLE

In 1869 a cowboy named Steve Moore was hunting stray cattle in an unknown canyon on the north slope of Sunrise Peak when he found some shiny crystals which he picked up and took to his employer. At first the crystals were believed to be diamonds, so the canyon where they were found was named Diamond Canyon. Later it was learned that the crystals were topaz, but by then silver had also been found in Diamond Canyon and the pretty crystals were forgotten in the rush to stake claims. From a rough camp of miners' cabins, Diamond City mushroomed on the mountain side, 6 miles south of Ruby Hollow. Ore from its mines was so rich that it was shipped half way around the world to smelters in Wales. Ore from the Julian Mine was valued at $2,500 to the ton in silver!

Within a year Diamond City boasted 4 stores, 3 hotels, 5 saloons, a post office, a bootmaker's shop and a newspaper curiously named *The Rocky Mountain Husbandman*. The huge Miller Mill, built in 1873, competed with the Tintic Smelter, a 20 ton two furnace plant built in 1871. The Copperopolis-Mammoth Company also built a large mill to process Diamond's ore, but it was located at Roseville, a new town growing up 6 miles to the south, where a more dependable water supply was available. Except for its giant smelter, Roseville didn't amount to much. Today there's nothing left except an old stone wall by the side of a dirt road, a few crumbling foundations of workers' houses and a slag pile from its furnaces. Roseville can be reached by traveling 2 miles along the road to Paul Bunyan's Woodpile, on a dirt road that turns to the east, 13 miles south of Eureka.

Diamond's fortunes paralleled Ruby Hollow's, their mines being discovered at about the same time. In its early days, it was known as a tough camp. In the 1870's Diamond was visited by Capt. John Codman, noted world traveler and author, who wrote, "Diamond is the chief camp of the Tintic District, and is one of the quietest mining camps in Utah. It has been several days now since a murder has been committed!"

Until water began seeping into its shafts, Diamond flourished, but as they sunk below the 300' level the primitive steam pumps then in use were unable to keep them dry. Rich ore strikes were being made all along the East Tintic Range at that time, and Diamond's miners began leaving for easier and richer diggings. Today little is left except caved cellars, broken foundations and a forlorn little cemetery hidden in the cedar trees.

Perhaps some day someone will take another look at Diamond's silver mines. They were never worked out, just abandoned for richer diggings. And somehow in the excitement over silver, everyone forgot all about the topaz crystals they once thought were diamonds. Today they're worth a lot more than silver, and there are plenty of them left at old Diamond, just waiting for you to pick them up.

MAMMOTH & ROBINSON

In February, 1870 a group of prospectors were examining outcrops in Juab County's East Tintic Mountains about 2 miles south of Ruby Hollow when they made the big strike. Their find was a ledge of high grade silver, and one of the prospectors shouted, "Boys,

Robinson at its peak; it's hard to believe hardly a trace remains. -Utah Historical Society-

she's a mammoth strike! We've got ourselves a mammoth mine!" Other miners hurried to the new diggings and before the month was out a rough camp of tents and slab shacks grew up near the mines. By summer the new camp had 4 hotels, a dozen saloons and boasted a population of 2,500. Of course, the new camp was named Mammoth for the prospector's "mammoth mine." Other rich finds included the Golden Chain, Napoleon, and Openhonga mines. A 60 stamp mill was built by owners of the Mammoth Mine and 14 furnaces were kept busy smelting ore from the camp's mines. The Hotel Mammoth, operated by Mrs. Dix, was described as being "The cleanest and coziest of the state," but rates were $2.50 a day, an unheard of price at that time.

Although Mammoth was booming, not everyone was happy there. A mining engineer named G.H. Robinson moved down canyon and started his own town, naturally naming it for himself. Soon Robinson was thriving also, having businesses the equal of those in Mammoth, as well as being the terminus for the newly completed Utah Western Railroad. To help keep his town ahead of its rival, Mr. Robinson hired a large crew of miners and began driving a 4,000' tunnel through the mountains to connect with the Sioux and Utah mines on the opposite side. His plan was to bring ore to his new Sioux Mill, then under construction.

Mammoth and Robinson expanded until they grew into each other, and residents couldn't tell where one ended and the other began. To make it all the more confusing, each had its own post office, and mail intended for one town often ended up in the other. Postal authorities finally ended the confusion by discontinuing both offices and establishing a new one where the two towns met. To keep the peace between the two rivals, it was named Middletown! But the new name wasn't popular with the people, and gradually the newly connected town was called Mammoth. For years afterwards however, local residents referred to Mammoth as Upper Town and to Robinson as Lower Town.

Ore production from Mammoth's mines totaled in the tens of millions of dollars, but as with all mining camps, in time its treasure laden shafts were worked out and hard times came. Its residents kept moving until by 1930 there were only 750 people left, and the town was disincorporated to avoid paying taxes. Mammoth became a ghost town of the first order, and soon even its name was forgotten. Over the years most of its fine buildings have burned or fallen into ruin, but in recent years the rising price of silver has brought a few miners back to explore its abandoned mines once more. Today Mammoth is staging a comeback. Times are getting so lively that even the ghosts are leaving!

Waiting for the mail stage at Robinson. -Utah Historical Society-

Silver City. Those long deserted streets could be a coin hunter's bonanza now. -Utah Historical Society-

SILVER CITY

At the end of a dirt road that leaves U-36 2½ miles south of Eureka stand the ruins of old Silver City, once a bustling mining camp. The Sunbeam Claim was located in December, 1869 and a small but lively camp soon grew up around its workings. The Sunbeam Mine, operated by a British owned syndicate, proved to be a veritable treasure house, and produced more than $50,000,000 during 70 years of operation. Silver City had many more rich mines, among them the Treasure Box, Four Aces, Yankee Girl, Silver Moon, Pocahontas and Cleopatra.

Before the camp's fabulous future was known at least one visitor wasn't too impressed, for he wrote, "Silver City has a billiard hall saloon, a blacksmith shop, one glory hole, numerous tents, several drunks, a free fight, a 90' dry well and any number of imaginary rich mines in the hills!" But his description would have been laughed at less than a year later when Silver City rivaled even Diamond City, then the district's leading camp.

In no time Silver City left Diamond far behind, but her day of reckoning was coming, and sooner than anyone thought. The Sunbeam shaft was the first to encounter water, and by 1890 most of the town's mines were flooded or being pumped dry at great expense. As its marginal mines closed, the town faded. Riter's General Store closed first and then John Legshon's high-class Silver Hotel was boarded up. Its population almost reached zero when it was given a new but temporary lease on life.

Jesse Knight, the "Mormon Wizard" of Knightsville, decided to build his huge new Utah Ore Sampling Mill at Silver City. Overnight the old camp blossomed with new paint on its buildings and new

people on its streets. Knight built the East Tintic Railroad into Silver City and put up new homes for his many employees. Silver City's new prosperity continued until 1915 when Knight's mill could no longer operate profitably, and was closed down. With its great mill boarded up and its mine shafts long since flooded, Silver City's good times were gone. Its long neglected cemetery with its old-fashioned ornamental fence is Silver City's liveliest place today.

TINTIC MILLS

William McIntosh located the Shoebridge Mine in 1870, high in a canyon east of Diamond. By the next year a mill had been built, 25 miner's shacks dotted the mountain side and a general store and saloon were doing a "land office" business. As the rough camp grew into a town, miners living there decided to name it Tintic Mills, but it was just as often called Shoebridge for McIntosh's mine, and many old maps show it that way. Its mines produced so much ore so fast that Shoebridge's mill couldn't handle it all, and until the great new Crimson Mill was built in 1877 much of the ore mined at Shoebridge was hauled to the Ely Mill at Roseville.

Tintic Mills soon sported many substantial businesses and well built homes. Samuel McIntosh, a brother of the town's founder, built a plush palatial mansion there, the equal of any at Salt Lake City. Although other mines shipped ore from Tintic Mills, the Shoebridge was always the camp's bread and butter. As long as the Shoebridge Mine was productive everything went along fine, but when that great mine began to fail, its rich ore veins pinched out, the town began failing with it. By 1890 Tintic Mills was on its last legs. A long, dusty road which winds through the lonely hills from Dividend to Silver City passes by the old townsite, but you'll have to look close to see it, for there's not much left of the town and not a trace of McIntosh's million dollar mansion. For years that fine old mansion was the scene of nearly every party thrown by the "four hundred" of the Tintic District. Its spacious lawns witnessed many gala affairs where coins, watches and who knows what were lost and left for today's treasure hunter. Even after it was abandoned it housed hundreds of cowboys and prospectors who made camp there before it was torn down in 1933. If you're a metal detector fan, it's too good a bet to pass up.

YORK

In the 1870's York was the southern terminus of the Utah Southern Railroad in Juab County. When rails were laid into it on February 25th, 1875 it was a busy place, advertised as "Another Raiload triumph for Utah! Trains will leave this city daily for Salt Lake City, 75 miles to the north." York was located near the north end of York Valley, between present-day Mona and Santaquin, at the base of what is known locally as "Santaquin Hill." Its site was almost due west of the old R. Steele home, known to many as the Starr Ranch, along abandoned US-91. The Starr Ranch, named for Albert W. Starr, was originally known as the Cheney Ranch, and even before that the area was used to pasture livestock. As early as 1858 soldiers from Johnston's Army ranched there, building an adobe and rock wall fort for protection. That old wall still surrounds the present ranch house.

York was a pretty impressive place for awhile, the nearest thing to a city that desolate York Valley ever had. While it was an end-of-track town, York was a main supply point for mining camps in the west desert country and as far away as Nevada, as well as for the farm settlements of Dixie. Many businesses were located there, most in large frame buildings, but a few conducted business out of tents, reminiscent of the Union Pacific tent towns of a decade earlier.

Merchants at York probably stocked more liquid supplies for the mining camps than they did heavy equipment. Miners at isolated camps often ordered whole cases of "tonic" or "elixer", heavily spiced with alcohol and opium. One of the most popular elixers was made by Dr. Higgins, who advertised, "Young men, you can get relief from pimples, bashfulness, aversion to society, stupidness, despondency and the loss of energy and ambition which deprives you of your manhood and makes you absolutely unfit for study, business or marriage. See me before it is too late!" The good doctor also promised "To cure all kinds of fits and to remove tapeworms, including their heads, or no payment will be required!"

York was an end-of-track town for nearly five years, probably a record, but eventually money was obtained to drive the rails farther south and its days

When the rails of the Utah Southern reached York, a new end-of-track town was born.

became numbered. After the line was completed to the next end-of-track at Juab, York became only a whistle stop, and in a few years not even that. A few families remained, many because of the fine brick schoolhouse there, but when an even better school was opened at Mona, nearly everyone moved to that more promising place. Most of York's buildings were torn down for their lumber, or were dragged to nearby ranches where some of them are still in use. They're all that's left of York.

JUAB

During the early 1860's a small band of Mormon farmers settled on Chicken Creek in Juab County. The combination of Indian troubles and swampy ground eventually forced them to move to Levan, 6 miles to the northeast. It wasn't until 1876 that John Widbeck established a stage station on Chicken Creek at the old Mormon settlement. Widbeck's Station was just another isolated stage stop until 1879 when rails of the Utah Southern reached it. The railroad was building south toward the booming silver mines in Beaver County, but its builders often lacked capital to continue construction. It had taken all of their reserves to build from York to Juab, the name they gave the new end-of-track town at Widbeck's Station.

The unplanned end-of-track town quickly became a regular city, where great piles of freight were piled high, waiting for wagons to haul it to places beyond the railhead. The Utah Southern built a first class depot, a large warehouse and shops where many men were employed. Widbeck built a large frame hotel, soon rivaled by another built by Elmer Taylor. A branch of the Levan Co-Op was started, a Mormon ward with James Wilson as Bishop was established and a schoolhouse, post office, dancehall and several saloons were built. Jackman's Saloon was the most popular.

For the next several years, owners of the Utah Southern were unable to obtain financing, and as a result Juab continued to prosper. But in time the necessary funds were obtained and the railroad's grade was slowly pushed toward its meeting with the rails of the San Pedro, Los Angeles & Salt Lake line at Lynndyl. Every day the rails pushed southward, the less important Juab became, and when the junction was finally reached, the once important town had no reason for being. Almost as fast as it had grown along the banks of Chicken Creek, it faded. Like a delicate mountain flower, Juab had blossomed only to die. Today a lone ranch house and a livestock corral by the side of the tracks marks its site. It should be a choice place to look for railroad relics, or for coins where Jackman's Saloon once stood.

DIVIDEND

Dividend was a "company town," built by the Tintic Standard Mining Company, 5 miles east of Eureka, in Utah County. From a camp of rough cabins in 1916, it grew into a regular town by 1918, with stores, shops, a pool hall, schoolhouse and even a brass band. Oddly enough, for a town of its size, it had no church. Before it was granted a post office it was called Standard, but postal authorities thought that name was too similar to Standardville in Carbon County, so they asked the citizens to choose another name. A contest was held to decide the new name, and Dividend was the miners' choice. It is said that the name was inspired by the large dividends the Tintic Standard Company was then paying.

Just a few minutes before twelve on a dark night in March, 1921 four masked men entered the Dividend Store and ordered customers to "Get your hands up, fast!" Apparently the bandits believed the mining company's payroll was in the store safe, and became angry when store manager John Monson told them he couldn't open it. The bandits were excitedly ordering Monson to open the safe or be killed when John Westerdahl, Mine Superintendent for the Tintic Standard Company entered the store to purchase a cigar. One of the masked men whirled around and fired at Westerdahl, the bullet striking him in the head and killing him instantly. The other men then began firing wildly and wounded both store manager Monson and a miner named John Hernandez. Another customer named Peterson was shot in the stomach but managed to crawl outside onto the sidewalk before he died. The four bandits escaped into the darkness, and although a posse was quickly organized, no trace of them was ever found. It was later thought that the bandits were actually miners who lived at Dividend, who had only to run to their homes to avoid capture. They could even have been among the posse members.

For five more years Dividend remained a busy camp. Its mines kept working and the company even built a fine new mill at Harold a few miles to the east. Decreasing metal prices and ore values finally caused mine owners to throw in the towel. Until it was torn down a few years ago the huge mill at the North Lily Mine high on the mountainside above town was a landmark. Like the other homes and buildings at Dividend, it was removed to avoid paying taxes. There really hasn't been any excitement in Dividend since the bandits killed John Westerdahl.

Dividend and the Tintic Standard Mine, where bandits killed John Westerdahl. -Utah Historical Society-

WEST TINTIC & ITS SUBURBS
&
THE LOST LEDGE OF THE LITTLE SAHARA

The strange farm settlement of West Tintic was located at the south end of the West Tintic Mountains near the edge of the white sand dunes. The townsite was established in 1920 by Moses and Octavius Gudmunson and their followers as a "cooperative farm settlement," which was really just a euphemism for the polygamist settlements which spring up throughout Utah's west desert country every few years. A town government similar to the old United Order which was introduced in Utah 50 years earlier was started. All necessary supplies were purchased through wholesale houses and distributed to each according to his needs. All crops were stored in a central place for the use of all. Ten families moved to West Tintic the first year, and their industry was soon responsible for a small village of log cabins, frame houses, barns and corrals and a cooperative store. A large barracks building purchased at Fort Douglas was moved to the new town and used as a storehouse. A garage, blacksmith shop and power plant soon followed.

West Tintic had two neighbors, neither of which was very neighborly. On nearby Cherry Creek a small hamlet of the same name had flourished briefly for a few years after 1883. Starting that year, work on a pipeline began from a dam on Cherry Creek across the desert floor to Eureka. It supplied drinking water for that thirsty town 20 miles to the east. After the dam and pipeline were completed, the tent town of Cherry Creek soon disappeared, leaving who knows what for any relic hunter who can locate exactly where its tent stores and saloons once stood.

Jericho, located 1 mile west of U-36, is a one month a year town. For a few weeks each year Jericho hums with activity, for it is one of the largest sheep shearing centers in the west. As many as 100,000 sheep are sheared of their wool during a three week period, about one wooly every minute. Sheepmen, shearers and camp followers make it a rousing camp for a few weeks, but when the sheep are trailed back to the mountains, Jericho reverts to nothing for another year.

West of Jericho are the great white sand dunes, now a popular recreational area for motorcycles and dune buggies. But back at the turn of the century it was a good place to stay away from, a little sahara where a prospector could lose his way and never be seen again. More than one old desert rat has disappeared out there.

A miner from Tintic was prospecting the sand dune country southwest of Jericho in 1900 when he came upon a ledge exposed by the drifting sand, where diamond-like silver-lead galena ore glistened in the desert sun. He gathered up as much of the heavy black ore as he could carry, and after taking his bearings from far away Tintic Mountain and Buckhorn Peak, he

The old McIntyre Ranch at Cherry Creek. A stage robber's loot is buried near there.

struggled across the drifting dunes to Jericho. As he expected, when the ore was assayed it proved to be nearly pure lead with a rich showing of silver.

The miner, whose name no one around Eureka seems to remember, returned to the dunes less than a week later, but by then the same winds that had exposed his ledge to view had covered it again. He searched on and off for several years. His story became well known to nearly everyone around Eureka, but not many remember it now. But some of the old-timers still remember and will point the way to the Little Sahara Dunes, somewhere west of Jericho.

Not long after West Tintic was settled, a ward of the Mormon Church was set up, but when the polygamist activities there were found out, those practicing polygamy were excommmunicated from the church and federal authorities began prosecution. Two members of the town were sentenced to three years in prison, but Moses Gudmunson, the colony's spiritual leader escaped. In addition to their troubles with church and government, the cooperative farmers learned that the barren wastes of West Tintic had never been intended by nature to be farm lands, and even those not involved with polygamy left for greener pastures. Today West Tintic is a forlorn looking row of weathered houses and barns, strung out along a lonely desert road, burned black by the desert sun. Not even a ghost could call it home.

HAROLD
&
THE STOLEN ORE CAR

Harold was a small town, built at the Tintic Standard Company's reduction mill, located on a steep hillside above the warm springs east of Goshen in Utah

County. The mill at Harold was a modern 200 ton per day plant built at what was then the very high price of $580,000. It was designed specifically to mill ore from the Tintic Standard Mine at Dividend. The problem with the Standard Mill was that it was designed to run steadily 24 hours per day, but the Tintic Standard Mine never produced enough ore to keep it running that way. Nevertheless, from 1921 when it was built, until 1925 when it closed, it supported a little town named Harold, named for Harold Raddatz, a son of E.J. Raddatz, a leading stockholder in the mine.

Harold was a company town like Dividend, and had a company store, a row of look-alike company houses, a company boardinghouse and a post office. Today its crumbling mill foundations still stand on the mountain side above the warm springs, a favorite place for kids to swim or fish for bluegills and small trout. Since Harold isn't as well known as Dividend, it could be a good place to hunt for lost coins and other valuables. One thing you won't find at Harold, which was stolen from the Tintic mines at the same time it was a thriving place, is a stolen railroad car.

The mines at Tintic have been famous for the rich pockets of nearly pure silver and gold they contained. Often miners would find pockets of ore, some as large as a house, worth hundreds of thousands of dollars. One wagon load of ore brought $50,000 while a single railroad car of ore from another mine brought its owner $200,000! High-grading was common at Tintic, with miners stealing rich specimens any way they could, in their pockets, lunch pails or what have you. But one theft took the prize. Somebody stole a fifty ton railroad car of high grade valued at a quarter of a million dollars!

Everyone knew that a very special ore pocket had been struck, for miners coming off duty were asked to change their clothes before leaving the mine and their lunch pails were closely checked. But what really attracted attention was the posting of armed guards on several railroad cars of ore. The whole story isn't known, some say that the guards were slipped a couple of bottles of whiskey, but the next morning a 50 ton railroad car of ore was missing! Someone had loosened its brakes and let it coast down canyon and out onto the main line, but from there its trail was lost forever. Tracers were telegraphed to all railroad stations, but to no avail. Six months later the car was found, empty, in Mexico!

HOMANSVILLE

Mormon stockmen were the first settlers in Utah County's Homans Canyon, named for Sheppard Homans, an early day explorer with Capt. J.W. Gunnison's survey party. The first claims were located there in 1870, and among some of the best known mines were the Calliope, Iowa and Annie Consolidated. The camp that became Homansville soon had a population numbering in the hundreds. Two early smelters were those owned by the Eureka Mining Company and the Utah Smelting & Milling Company, followed in 1873 by the Wyoming Smelter, an up to date 40 ton plant equipped with the first Stedtefeldt Furnace in Utah. It was built by eastern financiers at high cost, but soon made them rich, because they paid mine owners only for the silver content of their ore, and the new plant also recovered large amounts of gold.

It's a long, lonely road to West Tintic, polygamist camp of the west desert.

Homansville grew like Topsy. Each day the Gilmer & Saulsbury stagecoaches brought more people to the booming camp. Owners of the North Spy Mine installed a first class steam powered stamp mill in 1875, and only a year later the railroad reached the busy town. It had stores, shops and hotels the equal of any town in the district, as well as the inevitable row of saloons. In one of those saloons Wall Wilkinson killed Bill Baxter.

Wilkinson and Baxter had been drinking and playing cards when an argument between them erupted. In front of dozens of witnesses, Wilkinson shot and killed Baxter, and then ran from the saloon and up the mountain front above town where he hid in a grove of maple trees. Angry miners tried to reach Wilkinson, but were driven back when he began shooting at them. When Wilkinson ran out of cartridges the miners charged up the mountain and captured him. Angry shouts were heard to get a rope, but cooler heads prevailed, which was kind of unusual around Tintic, and he was taken to the county jail at Provo. Two months later he was legally hanged for Baxter's murder.

Too much water sounded the death knell for many mining camps, but at Homansville water proved to be more valuable than silver. The town's mines encountered water at shallow depths but at nearby Eureka water was at a premium, being sold door to door by the bucket. Springs were scarce at Eureka, and mine shafts there were often sunk a thousand feet or more without striking water. A pipeline was laid from Homansville to Eureka, through which precious water was pumped to the thirsty miners of the larger town.

The coming of the railroad marked Homansville's end, for the railroad could haul ore to the more efficient mills at Eureka, while at many of the mines water had

become more valuable than silver. It was a fast slide once it started; its empty buildings becoming another monument to the miners' never ending search for treasure. But today many people hunt for its little treasures, while larger and better known camps are thoroughly picked over. It might just pay to visit the little camp in Homans Canyon.

KNIGHTSVILLE

The only mining camp in the west without a saloon! That's what they said about Knightsville, named for Jesse Knight, the "Mormon Wizard" who found silver ore where the best trained geologists said it couldn't be found. From a small camp in 1896, Knightsville grew into one of the state's best known, most controversial and strangest mining towns. It all started one day when Knight was resting high on the barren slopes of Mt. Godiva, after a long, hard, fruitless day of prospecting. He wasn't a prospector, only a young man who was the sole support of his mother and a house full of brothers and sisters. All he had ever done was farm work from daylight to dark. But he had seen others grow rich from prospecting, so in desperation he decided to try it himself.

Later Knight said as he stopped to rest, a heavenly voice came to him, saying, "Jesse, this country is here for the Mormons!" Knight interpreted the mysterious voice to mean that he should dig right there to find his fortune. He was so overcome by the heavenly message he had received that he started digging a tunnel into the mountain, even though there was no sign of ore there. Friends laughed at him, and called his claim a humbug, so that's what he named it, the Humbug Claim.

Knightsville, the only mining camp in the west without a saloon! - Utah Historical Society-

He drove his tunnel for 150' through barren rock when suddenly he broke into a tremendous body of silver. Jesse Knight was on his way to becoming a millionaire and a legend. It was the same story wherever he started a new mine. His miners made rich strikes of the Godiva, Colorado, Iron Blossom and Mayday claims even though they showed no evidence of ore. At his Uncle Sam claim a shaft was sunk through barren rock for 350', when for no apparent reason Knight directed that its course be changed, and after only ten more feet of digging a gigantic body of high grade silver was found!

Knight detested the way that miners would work all week and then spend their wages in one night of drunken revelry in the saloons of Eureka, so he started his own town 2 miles to the east, on a wind swept ridge close to his mines. He built 65 homes at Knightsville to provide decent housing for his miners, and they were soon followed by stores, churches, hotels and a post office. But there were no saloons!

Knight paid his miners more than other owners, so he wasn't always popular with them. He also wouldn't allow his miners to work on Sunday, and paid them more on week days to make up for wages lost. As a result Knight's mines attracted the best miners. Others called his properties "The Sunday School Mines," but they made Knight a millionaire many times over, and he put much of his money back into helping his miners.

To stop Knight's liberal policies, the other owners banded together and refused to mill ore from his mines. Knight built his own mill. They coerced the railroad not to haul Knight's ore, so he built his own railroad, the East Tintic. No one got the best of "Uncle Jesse," as his miners affectionately called him, but finally his mines were worked out. Until 1915 Knightsville was one of Tintic's leading mining camps, as well as one of its richest. It's still a good place to look for relics from its heyday, but don't expect to find any purple whiskey bottles!

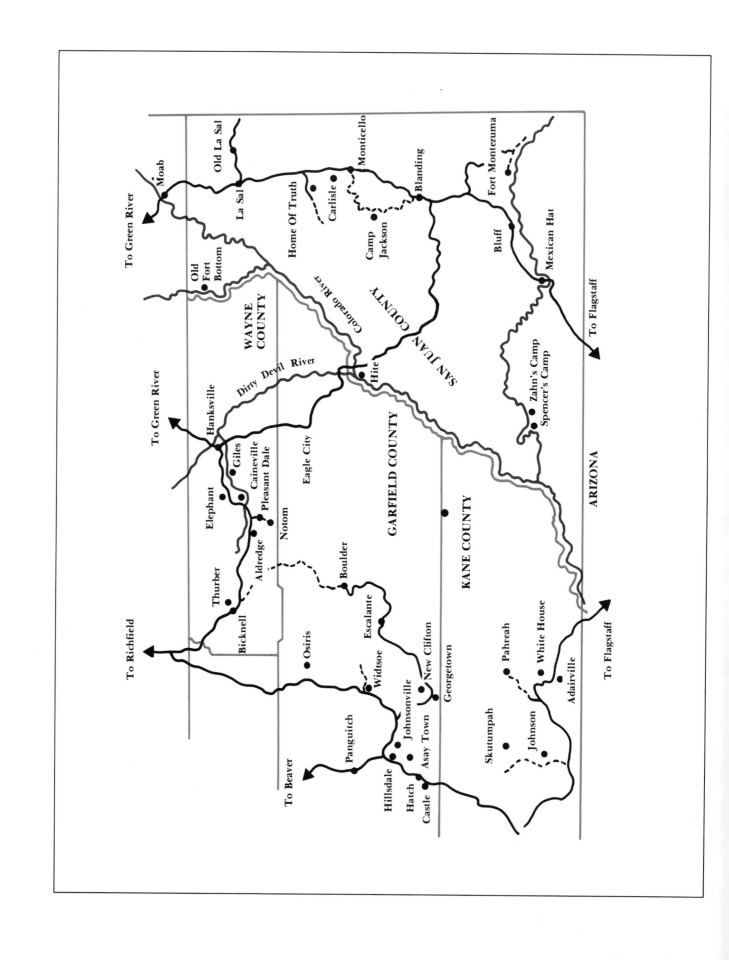

CHAPTER SIX

CANYONLANDS COUNTRY

The deserts and mountains of southeastern Utah's Canyonlands Country harbor some of the Beehive State's most colorful ghost towns. There are pioneer Mormon farming communities like Giles and Georgetown, and ranching towns such as Carlisle and Old La Sal. Several were placer mining camps like Hite and Zahn's camp, and there were even hard rock camps like Camp Jackson and Eagle City.

There were dozens of places in Canyonlands where men toiled and children played, places with strange sounding names like Skutumpah, Elephant and The Home Of Truth Colony, that are now only dots on old, yellowed maps. At most of those old towns, only crumbling stone walls and weathered boards remain, but a few are so well preserved they are used for western movie settings. Some are so seldom visited that rare relics of the past can still be found among their ruins, but at others memories are the only treasures which remain. Those memories are often treasure tales, for there is no part of Utah so rich in lost mine stories as the Canyonlands, probably because it was the first part of the state to be explored by Spanish miners pushing north from Santa Fe. But it is also the least known part of the state, its treasures the most nebulous, its lost mines the most mysterious. That's Canyonlands Country!

PAHREAH

Pahreah often appears on old maps as Paria-no-quint, Piute Indian for Elk River. The Piutes must have had a sense of humor, for it's doubtful there was ever an elk within a hundred miles of Pahreah! The area was first settled in 1865 by Mormon settlers led by Peter Shirts. They built a fort-like stone structure 4 miles down stream from present-day Paria, 40 miles northeast of Kanab, at the junction of Cottonwood Creek and the Paria River. Not long after the original settlement was founded, the settlers were forced by Indians to flee to the newer site of Paria, which could be more easily defended and where there was more level land for farming. They named their new home Pahreah for the Paria River, an Indian word meaning the "dirty water."

It wasn't long before log cabins and buildings of adobe and stone made their appearance. Wm. Meeks was the first Mormon Bishop. T.W. Smith ran the general store. During the polygamy trials of the 1880's, Pahreah was a favorite hiding place for polygamists because of its isolation. Each year saw the growing town prosper from its bounteous crops and increasing herds of livestock, but for some reason it wasn't granted a post office until 1892. But by then almost everyone was leaving. The flooding Paria had washed many of its best farms away. Just when everything looked worst, Pahreah got a new lease on life. Gold was discovered there!

One mining report claimed, "The clay has only to be sprinkled with water to cause it to release the gold within!" Miners' cabins were built next to the homes of Pahreah's farmers, and sluice boxes took the place of plows. But the mining boom was short lived, for the fine flour gold of the Paria couldn't be recovered economically. Once hopeful miners left almost as fast as they had come. Then a series of drought years brought ruin to the farms not washed away by the floods of the 80's. With most of its farmers already gone and the new miners leaving daily, the town on the Paria was soon deserted. Four families remained by 1910 and soon this figure was reduced to one, an old bachelor miner who stayed until 1929.

Pahreah did have a brief respite a few years later when its tired old buildings were given a face-lifting for the filming of a western movie. That day of glory was a short though, for when the movie stars left, the old town was lonelier than ever. The freshly painted signs on its false front buildings soon faded under the desert sun and tumbleweeds rolled under the swinging doors of its honky-tonk saloon. Today, the 5 mile dirt road that leaves US-89 30 miles east of Kanab is seldom traveled, and is dusty in summer and slick with mud during the winter. The road to Pahreah is only 5 miles long, but it spans more than a century in time.

ADAIRVILLE & WHITE HOUSE
&
THE BAKING POWDER CAN CACHE

Adairville, located on the Paria River 8 miles downstream from Pahreah, was located at almost exactly the place that Father Escalante crossed the stream while following the Old Spanish Trail in 1776, at a spot where the narrow river bottom widens between two narrow canyons. The town was named for Thomas Adair, one of the first settlers of the little desert hamlet. Adairville was one of the most isolated settlements in southern Utah. Pahreah had been considered as far from civilization as anyone could get, but Adairville was even farther into the wilderness. It never had much of a chance because the same floods which washed Pahreah away in the 1880's also flooded Adairville.

White House was 3 miles downstream from Adairville. Because it was smaller, White House survived the floods of the 80's, but with the droughts of the 90's, its last die-hards gave up and moved to Pahreah. Today several sagging log cabins remain, built against a yellow sandstone cliff. There is also an old corral and a feed shed, that contained four Model T Ford tires and wheels the last time I was there. They're still there; they wouldn't fit my truck.

A grove of nearly dead cottonwood trees just north of Johnson's Butte marks the site of Adairville, once a promising place, and a supply point for prospectors heading into the Vermillion Cliffs country. Although neither Adairville nor White House could claim much fame as farming settlements, they left a legacy of mystery for today's treasure hunter to solve. In the sand dune country to the southwest, a murdered man's cache of gold coins still waits to be found.

$500 in gold coins is buried in a baking powder can southwest of Adairville, not far from the Arizona border. That may not sound like much, but remember, that was $500 at $16 an ounce, not today's $400 an ounce, without considering the far greater value the coins would have to collectors.

In March, 1886 Sam Clevenger, his wife Mollie and 15 year old adopted daughter Jessie sold their farm and with two hired hands, John Johnson and Frank Wilson, began driving 50 horses to Washington state where they intended to start a stock ranch.

Because the country was full of roving bandits, each night while the men made camp, Mrs. Clevenger would take their $500 fortune, concealed in a large old-fashioned baking powder can, and bury it near camp. Only she knew its location. They crossed the Colorado at Lee's Ferry and on May 19th, 1886 made camp at the base of the Shinarump Cliffs, southwest of Adairville. For several days Johnson and Wilson had been planning to steal Clevenger's gold, and both had more than a passing interest in 15 year old Jessie.

Early the next morning, as Sam Clevenger climbed down from his wagon, Johnson slipped up behind him and killed him with an axe. He and Wilson then tried to force Mrs. Clevenger to tell them where she had buried the gold. Although old and sick, Mollie Clevenger fought her attackers, and during the struggle she too was killed with the blood-stained axe.

Johnson and Wilson searched the red sand dunes along the base of the cliffs for the hidden cache. It turned out to be an impossible job, so with Jessie and Clevenger's horse herd they continued north, turning west to pass through Kanab where they drew only passing interest.

Cowboys from Kanab found Clevenger's camp the following January, and discovered where coyotes had partially uncovered Sam and Mollie's bodies. Folks at Kanab recalled seeing Johnson, Wilson and Jessie pass through town with the horse herd. They also remembered that Jessie had seemed real friendly with Wilson, and soon a marshal was on their trail. Johnson was found at Duckwater, Nevada while Wilson and Jessie were located living as man and wife at Oakley, Idaho.

All three were returned to Prescott, Arizona, the nearest prison to the murder scene, where Wilson was hung for the Clevenger murders on September 23rd, 1887. Both Johnson and Jessie identified Wilson as the murderer, but Johnson was sentenced to life imprisonment anyway at the territorial prison at Yuma. It was thought that Jessie had helped plan the murders, but by then she had had a baby and married a local cowboy, so no charges were filed against her.

With her new husband, Jessie returned to the Shinarump Cliffs to search for the buried baking powder can, but nearly two years had passed and the shifting sands had hidden it well. If Clevenger's camp could be located today, his gold would be an easy target for a metal detector. It's still there, only a day's ride from Adairville, just waiting for you!

JOHNSON & SKUTUMPAH
&
MONTEZUMA'S TREASURE CAVE

Johnson in Kane County was named for the four Johnson brothers, Joel, Joseph, Benjamin and William who with their families settled the community in Johnson Canyon, 12 miles east of Kanab. In 1871 it was known as Spring Canyon Ranch, but as more families moved there its name was changed to Johnson. It soon had a fine brick schoolhouse, a post office, blacksmith shop and two stores, Johnson's and Glazier's.

There are no dancing girls at the old saloon at Johnson anymore!

Orchards, vineyards and green fields proved the town's industry and prosperity until several years of drought caused people there to switch from farming to ranching.

It was during the 1870's that John D. Lee established a ranch 15 miles upstream from Johnson and 14 miles southeast of Upper Kanab, now called Alton. Lee named his ranch Skutumpah, Indian for the "clay colored water." The location seemed to be a good one, and soon other families followed Lee to the site. By 1878 the town had grown until a school was founded, with Willard Lee as the first teacher. By then Skutumpah looked like a regular town, so its name was

changed to Clarkston, for a prominent local family. But the same drought that dried up farms at Johnson also affected Clarkston, and a few people left. It was during the same period that Lee was executed for his part in the Mountain Meadows Massacre, leaving the little town without leadership. It was only a short time until Clarkston was abandoned.

The United Order of Enoch, the socialistic scheme devised by the Mormon Church, was established at Johnson in 1874. Its plan required that everyone contribute to its stores and receive dividends as needed, but as usual, it failed dismally. People put in their five years of labor, but their dividends were never realized. When the order failed, people began leaving, tired of trying to wrest a living from the harsh land. Shortly after 1900 it was completely deserted. Yet, it may be familiar to more people than almost any other ghost town, because it has appeared in many western movies. Though its streets may look busy on the silver screen, the only pedestrians are ghosts. Some say the spirits of Spanish conquistadores and the Emperor Montezuma are among them.

In 1920 a strange treasure hunter named Freddie Crystal began poking around the rugged slopes of White Mountain in Johnson Canyon. He had an old map from Mexico which showed the hiding-place of an Aztec treasure, which he said was Montezuma's Treasure. The map described a place where ancient petroglyphs would point the way to a canyon with four branches surrounded by four mountains, one each on the east, west, north and south. In the center there was another mountain where the treasure was hidden. Everything on the map was found in Johnson Canyon, and White Mountain fit the description of the treasure mountain perfectly!

With the help of almost every man from the surrounding towns, Freddie Crystal started his search. A regular tent town of treasure hunters was established, and even Kanab was nearly deserted as everyone hurried to Johnson Canyon. Just as the map revealed, ancient hand cut steps were found leading up the mountain face. A man made shaft was found, its opening cleverly concealed with closely fit granite blocks cemented into place. To add to the mystery, the perfectly cut blocks were of a stone unknown in that red sandstone country, while close examination revealed the cement was made of a fine sand found only many miles away in New Mexico!

When the granite wall was dug away, a tunnel 14' square was discovered, but 60' from the surface another granite wall was found. It was removed and a maze of tunnels and shafts were found, completely honeycombing the mountain. 160' into the mountain several large rooms were found, and in them deadly concealed booby traps. Huge, delicately balanced boulders would fall without warning. Man-made cement floors and side tunnels blocked by hard granite walls slowed the search to a snail's pace.

Then, hard as it may be to believe, the search was abandoned. It had taken two years, and when no treasure vault was discovered, disappointment set in. With their funds gone, ranchers were forced to return to their farms, women to their homes and children to school. But while it lasted the search for Montezuma's Treasure was as strange as the mysterious money pit at Oak Island. Freddie Crystal disappeared and Johnson Canyon lapsed back into a ghostly silence. No one has probed its ancient Aztec Treasure chamber since.

GEORGETOWN & NEW CLIFTON
&
THE WHITE CLIFFS GOLD CAVE

Just east of Bryce Canyon National Park, in the southernmost part of Garfield County, there are two little towns named for George Q. Cannon, an Apostle of the Mormon Church during the 1870's. One of the towns, Cannonville, still exists, but the other, Georgetown, is a ghost town. Georgetown was built at the junction of Yellow Creek, now Henrieville Creek and the Paria River on the east side of Tropic Valley in 1877, by the Littlefield and Bliss families. The Saints who named the new settlement for their church leader had high hopes of establishing an oasis in the desert, but oases are pretty rare in Garfield County.

Another settlement was made on Yellow Creek 4 miles north of Cannonville. At first it was called Cliff town, but as more families arrived, its name was abbreviated to Clifton. Ebenezer Bryce lived in Clifton, and later Bryce Canyon National Park was named for him. In describing the rugged area, Bryce said, "Sure it's pretty, but it's a hell of a place to lose a cow!" Before long Bryce and several others moved two miles up a tributary of Yellow Creek where they established New Clifton. It thrived and soon outgrew "old " Clifton. A post office was granted to New Clifton in 1886.

With four little towns along its course, Yellow Creek soon began to dry up. New Clifton was the first to go, followed by "old" Clifton. The settlers retreated to Georgetown, and finally to Cannonville, leaving the shells of their towns behind. By 1900 Georgetown was totally abandoned, leaving only Cannonville to honor the Mormon Apostle. Today Cannonville is just a sleepy little village, but Georgetown is even sleepier, as a matter of fact, it's dead!

Old Warren Peters couldn't believe his eyes. He was an experienced prospector, over 60 years old, and had spent 40 on the desert where he had seen lots of gold, but nothing like this. These were golden icicles hanging from the roof of a cavern!

It was May, 1891 when Peters made his way along the White Cliffs southwest of Georgetown. He had passed a hundred crack-like canyons in the broken sandstone face of the cliffs, but there was something different about this one. Perhaps it was only his prospector's intuition, but he climbed over the huge fallen slabs of rock and crawled through a slit-like crack so narrow sunlight had never touched its bottom. The walls were so close together he could see stars overhead at mid-day.

It soon opened out into a canyon 50' wide, with a tiny trickle of water dripping from pool to pool. It wasn't long and ended in a great cave-like overhanging cliff, across the top of which was a heavy streak of red granite which contrasted sharply with the white sandstone. Water dripped from icicle-like stalactites, red in color and streaked with gold!

Peters knew enough geology to know that what he was seeing couldn't be. Years before he had been at the Lincoln mining camp north of Minersville when John Bradshaw discovered the Cave Mine. Bradshaw's cave was jeweled with gold crystals and had gold encrusted stalactites just like the ones he found in the narrow canyon at the White Cliffs. Geologists couldn't explain the formation at Bradshaw's Cave Mine either.

Although his supplies were low, Peters worked hard and soon broke loose enough of the golden icicles to make a heavy load for his burro. They were easily loaded, for when they fell to the cavern floor they shattered like glass. Leaving the canyon, Peters made his way north to Georgetown and on to Marysvale where he boarded the train for Salt Lake City. Peters had intended to return to the White Cliffs quickly, but it took some time to sell his gold. It was late summer when he passed through Georgetown and continued south past Rainbow Point to the west end of the White Cliffs.

Peters traveled eastward along the cliffs, not paying much attention to where he was until he came to Deer Springs, which he knew was east of the gold cave canyon. Upset that he had passed the narrow slit-like gorge without seeing it, he returned westward along the cliffs, checking every opening closely, but never found any that resembled the one he was looking for. He followed the cliffs back to his starting point, but never saw the gold cave canyon again.

Until snow fell, Peters searched the White Cliffs, back and forth, with no luck. When winter came he headed south into Arizona, but the following spring he returned and set up camp at Deer Springs. All summer he searched the face of the cliffs, foot by foot, confused and bewildered. Finally when winter came again he left it for good. He figured that an earthquake or landslide had closed the cave canyon forever. Besides, he was getting old and still had plenty of cash from the gold he had sold at Salt Lake City.

Peters returned to his family home in Kansas knowing that somewhere along the White Cliffs his gold cave still waited. Maybe it's waiting for you.

EAGLE CITY
&
THE LOST JOSEPHINE MINE OF THE
HENRY MOUNTAINS

It is safe to say that Eagle City is one of the least known of all Utah mining camps. Few people living in Garfield County have been to its site, perched like an eagle's nest high in Bromide Basin near the head of Cresent Creek in the remote Henry Mountains. A local legend claims that John Angrove made the first discoveries of gold in the Henrys and was murdered for the wealth he found there. Some say his ghost still haunts the mountains, but if it does it never bothered Jack Sumner and Jack Butler when they located the gold ledge in 1889 that became the Bromide Mine. The following year Kimball and Turner located the Oro Mine. Soon other rich lodes were found, the Ida and Ada claims among them. Owners of both the Bromide and Oro mines built mills on Cresent Creek where gold with values as high as $300 to the ton was milled. High grade silver and copper contained in the ore could not be recovered by those crude mills however, and was lost in the tailings which washed down Cresent Creek.

Eagle City grew up at a fork of the canyon 2 miles below Bromide Basin, and soon claimed a store, a hotel, a doctor's office and a saloon. Long riders from the Wild Bunch often stopped at Eagle City, adding their shoot-em-up antics to the already wild camp. Jack Moore, one of the riders of the owlhoot trail, was a part time faro dealer at Eagle City. Charley Hanks was a young man at Eagle City and he recalled for me how he delivered the mail, carried it by pack horse all the way from Green River, 100 miles to the north across the San Rafael Desert, and then carried gold bricks from the mills back to Green River. Although he remembered several close calls, he never lost a letter or a gold shipment to the outlaws who holed up there.

Water began to seep into Eagle City's mines as they were sunk deeper in search of golden treasure, and flooded the shafts as they neared 300′ in depth. A 3,000′ drain tunnel was planned to drain the shafts, but a lack of financing stopped it after it had been driven half way. To make matters worse, the Bromide Mill burned to the ground in 1911. With its shafts flooded, its leading mill burned and the World War taking most of its young men, the miners left Eagle City. Everyone except Frank Lawler, who stayed, alone, at the forgotten camp for the next 60 years! Except for infrequent visitors, his only company was the deer and wild buffalo that roam the Henrys, the rusted remains of the Bromide Mill and his memories of Eagle City's past.

In that time Frank Lawler had plenty of time to think about the Lost Josephine Mine, richest and most famous of all lost Spanish mines. He never doubted it was hidden somewhere in the Henrys, for both he and Ed Wolverton, another hermit of the Henrys, found plenty of evidence of Spanish miners. Lawler uncovered an ancient Spanish tunnel buried under 35′ of gravel on Cresent Creek, while Wolverton discovered many old Spanish markings, the ruins of a mill, slag piles, primitive arrastras and waste dumps so old they had giant pines growing on them on which Wolverton

counted 175 annual rings. But they never found the Lost Josephine. It's still hidden somewhere in the Henrys.

Without doubt, the Lost Josephine is Utah's most famous and best authenticated lost mine. Numerous references to it can be found in Catholic Church records, Spanish land grants, royal records of gold shipped to Spain on the "plate fleets" as well as in other centuries old journals. It was known by several names over its long history, but most official records at Madrid, detailing shipments from it and the "royal fifth" of its gold claimed by the King of Spain, refer to it simply as the Josephine Mine. In the quantity of gold added to the royal coffers of Spain, it equals such famous Spanish mines as the Tayopa, Planchas del Plata and the El Naranjal.

Records don't reveal exactly when the Josephine was located and first worked, but on the old pack trail leading from the Henry Mountains to the Colorado River, one faded inscription can still be read. Scratched on a sandstone wall is "1642 Ano Dom," and between the Colorado and the Bear's Ears Pass on the Old Spanish Trail is the name and date, "De Julio 1661." Near the north end of the Henrys there is an old burial place where Spaniards and Indians fought and were buried by Jesuit Priests, and the date 1777, a Catholic cross and an illegible name still remains. There are few dates to be found between 1680, when most of the Spanish mines of the northern frontier were lost because of the great Indian slave revolt, and 1765 when Father Rivera's expedition reopened the area.

During his expedition of 1853, John C. Fremont followed ancient steps cut into the stone cliffs at the Spanish Bottoms on the Colorado and noted in his

Frank Lawler, lone resident of Eagle City for more than a half century. He found the gold!

journals that near the Henry Mountains he found, "The very old bones of a pack mule, and on either side of them a pile of gold ore, from pack sacks long since rotted away." Later explorers also found places where Spanish miners had been killed by Indians, and their pack animals left along the desert floor, leaving only scattered bones, rusted buckles from ancient pack sacks and little piles of gold ore by their sides.

The Henry Mountains were the last major mountain range discovered in the United States, and they haven't been fully explored today. John C. Fremont called them the Unknown Mountains. That's still a good name. Who knows what secrets its 12,000' peaks still conceal? The Navajos have a legend that when their ancestors drove the Spanish miners from the mountains, their medicine man placed a curse on the Josephine Mine, "That to him who reopens the mine will come great calamity. His blood will turn to water, and even in his youth he will be as an old man. His squaws and papooses will die, and the earth will bring forth only poison weeds instead of corn." You may not believe in curses, but if you decide to seek the Lost Josephine, it's something to think about!

Few travel the forgotten road to Eagle City nowadays.
-Utah Historical Society-

ASAY TOWN
&
THE JARADITE COIN CAVE

For awhile no one really knew what old Asay Town's name was. It was first settled in 1872 by Mormon farmers at the mouth of Proctor Creek on the Sevier River in Garfield County. The new town was named Aaron in honor of Aaron Asay. Most of its residents were members of the Asay family, but with a new influx of settlers, they were outnumbered by the Hatch family, so the town's name was changed to

Hatchtown! The question of what the town's name would be was settled when a reservoir built upstream from the town on Proctor Creek was named the Hatchtown Dam and the settlement in the canyon below it, Asay Town. While Asay Town was growing into a solid community, several satellite settlements were growing up on the forks of the Sevier River nearby. They included Johnsonville, Castle and Proctor.

A post office was established at Asay Town in 1887 with Joseph Asay as Postmaster. There was also a church, a schoolhouse, a store operated by Abraham Workman and a sawmill run by Tom Jessop and Dan Leroy. The sawmill employed quite a few men, so when it burned in the early 1890's, it was a severe blow to the town's economy.

After 1900 it didn't make any difference what they called Asay Town, for that year the Hatchtown Dam broke and washed it down the river. Instead of rebuilding, most of Asay Town's citizens, joined by people from the outlying settlements, moved to the present site of Hatch. It was a wise move, for in the spring of 1914, the Hatchtown Dam broke again! Only one little tumble-down cabin and a cemetery remain at Asay Town.

Long before Asay Town was settled, its site was a camping ground for Ute Indians. Chief Wakara often led his braves past the very place where houses would later be built. On one such trip Chief Wakara discovered a treasure that remains a mystery to this day.

Many Mormons believe that about 2,000 years ago the Nephite and Jaradite nations fought a battle in which all of the Jaradites were killed, but not before they cached their national treasure somewhere north of a great canyon, believed by some to be the Grand Canyon. There may be some truth to the story.

In 1852 Ute Chief Wakara and a band of his braves were camped near the pioneer settlement of Parowan. The wily old horse thief was just returning from a horse stealing expedition in California. Wakara was always a close friend of the Mormons, having revealed the Lost Rhoades Mine to them. While at Parowan he asked one of the settlers, James H. Martineau, to identify a curious object for him.

Martineau observed that the object was a large but strange looking coin. When he rubbed its surface he discovered it was gold, but unlike any gold coin he had ever seen. Its surface was covered with strange hieroglyphics, similar, Martineau thought, to the kind Joseph Smith had translated the Book Of Mormon from. Immediately Martineau recalled the legend of the Nephites and the Jaradites, and decided the coin was of Jaradite origin. When he asked Chief Wakara where he got the coin, a strange tale unfolded.

Chief Wakara stated that he had followed the Colorado River Canyon to the gorge of the Escalante River, where he and his band turned northward. It becan to rain very heavily. They noticed a cave high in the ledges big enough to hold all his warriors, and took

An 1831 Hindu coin commonly mistaken for the controversial Jaradite coins found by Chief Wakara.

refuge in it. In the cave were countless thousands of the strange coins, piled all over its sandy floor. Wakara said the cave contained many other strange objects made of the same heavy metal, but he could not identify or describe them to Martineau. Martineau noticed that a dozen or more of the Indians had coins with them.

Martineau was allowed to keep one of the coins, and sent it to Brigham Young. After months passed and he had heard nothing from the Mormon leader, he made an inquiry through his Bishop and was told to forget he had ever seen the coins, and to mention them to no one. He was told that the time would come when they would be made known, but that time was not yet here.

Were the old coins and other unknown treasures found in the cave along the canyon of the Escalante of Jaradite origin? Or were they Spanish? There are several legends of Catholic Mission gold hidden in the Escalante country. About all we know for sure is that they were ancient, that they were made of gold, and that today they would be worth a fortune!

HILLSDALE

Hillsdale was first settled in 1871 when Hills Johnson, Deliverance Wilson and their families built a sawmill on the Sevier River 4 miles downstream from Asay Town. During the next year twenty more families moved there, since there was plenty of work at the sawmill. Among the businesses they established was the Hillsdale Mercantile Company, a store which provided a wide variety of goods. In 1874 Nephi Johnson was made Mormon Bishop at Hillsdale, but the town might better have been named Wilsondale, for nearly half of its citizens were relatives of Deliverance Wilson. Homes built at Hillsdale reflected the town's prosperity, many being two stories and built of hand cut stone, with attractive shade trees and orchards surrounding them.

The town prospered until the late 80's when the Sevier River went dry, Asay Town farther up stream having first claim against its small flow. The shortage of irrigation water combined with repeated crop failures at the town's 6,700' elevation started an exodus. A few people moved there after the Hatchtown Dam collapsed in 1900, but by then the town was going downhill fast. After the death of Deliverance Wilson, the town's patriarch, the remaining Wilsons left, leaving Hillsdale deserted. Today, several of the town's sturdy old homes still stand and are occasionally used during the summer season, but the town's only permanent residents are in the little cemetery at the top of a rocky hill just east of the townsite. Most of them are Wilsons also.

THURBER
&
THE LOST FISH LAKE MINE

The now forgotten town of Thurber was built near the mouth of Pine Creek, 8 miles southeast of Loa and 2 miles north of the Fremont River in Wayne County. It was on the southwest slope of the Thousand Lake Mountain, south of present-day Bicknell. Bicknell is a later settlement, an outgrowth of Thurber, and has grown until it covers part of the older town. In 1875 A.K. Thurber drove a herd of 600 cattle onto lower Pine Creek, and other settlers soon followed. Jeremiah Stringham built the first house and before long businesses made their appearance, including Cave's General Store & Saloon.

In 1881 a 20' x 20' log schoolhouse with a dirt floor and roof was built and served the community until 1890, when a fine new frame building was erected. The new school was fancy for a pioneer village. It boasted two cut-glass chandeliers, used when the building doubled as the town's dance hall. It is said that Samuel Chidester, one of the old-timers at Thurber, played the fiddle at more than one thousand dances held there. In 1909 a new stone schoolhouse replaced the older frame building.

Thurber had two problems, and they both involved water. Flash floods on Pine Creek often flooded farms and sometimes washed houses away. But a worse problem was that the town's drinking water came from open ditches which froze in winter and filled with sand during the summer. Several cases of typhoid fever were blamed on the poor water supply. Finally, Mormon Church authorities instructed the settlers to move to higher ground, but few left. When sickness struck again, authorities issued an order, stating, "It is a requirement and a commandment, for your temporal and spiritual salvation!" The settlers left their hard won homes and made the move to Bicknell. Today one building and a grove of trees that once shaded others remain to mark its site.

Thurber was in the shadow of Fish Lake Mountain, astraddle the Old Spanish Trail followed by soldiers of fortune centuries before. There are many references to an old mine somewhere near Fish Lake, in explorers' journals, pioneer diaries, and in oral Indian traditions. Unfortunately for today's treasure hunter, most of those old records refer to trails that no longer

The blacksmith shop was a busy place at Thurber. -Utah Historical Society-

exist, or to landmarks that are unknown. Many refer to the Old Spanish Trail, but over several hundred years the trail from New Mexico to California meandered from the Grand Canyon to the Salt Lake Valley.

In 1540 Captain Lopez de Cardenas traveled north and reached an impassable canyon, believed to be the Grand Canyon of the San Jaun River. Both the expeditions of Antonio de Espejo in 1582 and Juan de Onate in 1598 followed the same trail northward, but left little written record of their journey. As early as 1565 Francisco de Ibarra led an expedition "To the north in search of Indian silver mines," and in 1622 Governor Penalosa personally led a party "In search of Sierra Azul, a blue mountain of silver, somewhere west of Zuni."

In addition, there were hundreds of unauthorized slaving, mining and fur trapping expeditions into what is now Utah. Even Escalante in 1776 wrote of earlier explorations: "That there had been other expeditions to the far north is plain. We are told that Spaniards from New Mexico frequently traded with those distant tribes and remained with them for long periods of time, to gather peltries and to see what they could see." So it is certain that the old Spanish trails were in use for hundreds of years, and that they had many variations.

The old Spanish trails bypass Fish Lake on three sides, so there is no doubt it was known to those early adventurers. Both the famed explorer John C. Fremont and prospector-explorer E.T. Wolverton found pieces of gold ore lost from pack trains along those trails. Mormon explorer Joseph Fish investigated the Fish Lake area in 1857 and wrote, "I have been told there is an Indian tradition of an old gold mine near this place, which was worked by Spaniards at an early time." After leaving Fish Lake and traveling down into the foot-

hills, the Fish party crossed an old trail. "Where we found lead ore that had been dropped along the trail." Later those pieces of lead were found to contain silver!

Many references could be cited at length, but one is particularly interesting. In 1850 Parley P. Pratt, an early Mormon leader, helped settle Parowan, along the Old Spanish Trail, and one of the first things his followers did was to raise a flag pole, "In the protecting arms of the hills at Heap's Spring." Believe it or not, there in the wilderness where it was thought white men had never been before, while clearing ground for their flag pole, the pioneers found two old Spanish doubloons!

Where did those old Spanish coins come from, and who lost the chunks of ore found along the trail if not miners going to and from the legendary Fish Lake Mine? Certainly not Indians. Any guess can be made, but the fact remains that Indians told even the earliest explorers that Spanish miners had been there long before, and that they worked a gold mine near Fish Lake. We can also be sure that the ancient trails into the mountains from near old Thurber to the Fish Lake country were built for a purpose, and that the pieces of gold ore found along them were lost there while being carried away from the mountains, not to them! Some call the case for the Fish Lake Mine circumstantial, but I call it convincing. What do you call it?

ZAHN'S CAMP
&
THE NUGGET GOLD AT LOST OASIS

The "gold excitement of 1892" built Zahn's Camp, one of Utah's most isolated. A placer camp located in the twisting depths of the San Juan River, Zahn's Camp was 60 miles due west of Bluff, but more than twice that far by way of the river. In 1892 the five Zahn brothers discovered fine grain gold in a sand bar 5 miles below the mouth of Copper Creek. The thousand foot rock walls that tower above the river widen out there to form a small basin only two miles square.

When news of the strike leaked out, a wild rush of 1,200 miners made Zahn's Camp boom overnight. Many rich strikes were made; $3,000 in raw gold was dug from the Nephi Claim in only a few days. There were no stores or saloons at the camp, for its isolated location checked any hope of a boom town occuring. The first arrivals had to dare the awful rapids of the San Juan, and many rafts piled high with supplies were lost to the river. Several prospectors were drowned when their frail rafts overturned in the boiling rapids.

Henry Honaker operated a stage line from Cortez, Colorado to Bluff, Utah. To escape the dangers of the river and to get supplies to Zahn's Camp, he had the Honaker Trail built. It started 7½ miles west of Mexican Hat. From the rim of the canyon it zig-zagged 2½ miles down the 1,200′ vertical cliffs. It was intended for pack mules, but the only pack animals to attempt it plummeted from the narrow ledges to the canyon floor below. After that only miners roped together dared its fearsome path. Later a narrow trail was cut in the cliffs along the river's edge from the Piute Farms upstream to the mouth of Copper Creek and then along the foot of towering vertical cliffs to the mines. It required sure feet and steady nerves to pass over it.

Because of its location, Zahn's Camp was a crude place, with only tents, dugouts and slab-rock cabins offering protection from the 125 degree summer heat and severe winters. To add to their misery, most knew nothing about such mining and found it impossible to recover the fine flour gold from the river. Even fewer were fortunate enough to find nugget gold. Zahn's Camp only lasted a few years, but while it did, it was a real rip-snorter.

The general store at Bluff provided most of the supplies for Zahn's Camp, and miners who stopped there often heard a strange tale of a green oasis in a hidden canyon somewhere along the San Juan, a place where only two or three years before a prospector named Brooks had found a fantastically rich placer with nuggets as big as robins' eggs! But who could believe such a story, especially since it claimed there was an oasis in the San Juan country?

In September, 1889 a desert wanderer named Sam Brooks walked into Bluff leading two burros during a blinding sandstorm. He went straight to the general store where he loaded up with the usual supplies: flour, bacon, coffee and tobacco. But he didn't pay for the merchandise in the usual way. Instead, he produced a leather poke of gold nuggets and invited the store keeper to take as many as were needed to pay his bill.

Hard money of any kind was unusual in the little Mormon towns of southern Utah in 1889, and gold nuggets were rarer yet. Several old men who had gathered at the store to tell lies and get out of the wind assured the merchant that the nuggets were real, and while they were jawing over this strange break in their monotonous routine, Brooks packed his burros and strode off into the sand filled air. No one noticed which direction he had come from, and no one saw which way he went. But his gold was the talk of the town for weeks afterwards.

It was six months before Brooks appeared in Bluff again, in the winter during a snow storm. No one saw him until he hitched his burros at the pine rail in front of the general store. Brooks announced that he was leaving the San Juan for good, and was jovial and friendly to all the people at the store, not quiet and secretive as he had been before. Six months earlier he had ignored the store owner's questions about where he got his gold. This time he volunteered to tell where it came from.

Otto Zahn revisits the site of Zahn's Camp on the San Juan River.

Sam Brooks told the hangers-on at the Bluff store that he had enough gold to buy the best farm in Indiana. When they scoffed he showed them a large double-sewn canvas bag too heavy for one man to lift. It was full of water polished, sand worn nuggets, some as large as chestnuts! Brooks said he had all he wanted, and besides, wouldn't spend another season in that hellish San Juan Canyon for any amount of gold. They were welcome to his diggings, he said, all they had to do was to go south past Church Rock, cross Chinle Creek and follow Comb Ridge to the Sawtooths where they would come to a cold water spring and a small green oasis in a narrow box canyon in the cliffs above the river.

It sounded easy and many searched for Brooks hidden oasis, but it wasn't until after he left that they realized that none of them knew where to cross Chinle Creek, and none of them had heard of the "Sawtooths."

Many had lived there for years, but no one knew of the cold water spring, and they certainly didn't know of any green oasis anywhere along the San Juan. To this day no one has ever found Sam Brooks' nugget gold or the lost oasis, at least not yet!

SPENCER'S CAMP
&
THE LOST JIM DOUGLAS PLACER
&
ABEL HERRINGER'S LOST CACHE

Spencer's Camp was a short lived placer gold camp on the San Juan River 3½ miles downstream from Zahn's Camp. During the 1890's when Zahn's Camp was failing, new strikes were made at Spencer's. A trail was built to it, and ladders were used to scale the worst cliffs. At first hopes were high, for several rich finds were made, but Spencer's Camp wasn't destined to be a boomer. Like Zahn's Camp, much of its gold was too fine to be recovered by panning or by using sluice boxes. Stores were unknown. Supplies were brought in from the Bluff general store and whiskey bottles were passed across a rough plank bar, where there were neither crystal chandeliers nor polished pianos. Salt Lake City's *Deseret News* reported, "30 to 50 people a day pass through Bluff, all bound for the gold fields. Those who are equipped to stay and who can take care of themselves may be able to get along quite well, but the poor man who plans on getting work there had better stay away!"

When Spencer's Camp folded up like Zahn's Camp before it, the same hard trails miners used to get there were used to leave. Today, Spencer's Camp is a silent reminder of one of Utah's least known gold rushes. A poor dirt road from Aljato, an Indian trading post south of the San Juan, leads northwest to Copper Creek, then follows it to the river, passing high above the site of Zahn's Camp before it ends at an abandoned uranium mine. The San Juan still isn't a place for the faint hearted or the ill equipped, and it deals harshly with those who disturb its ghosts.

But the San Juan hasn't surrendered all of its gold, for Jim Douglas, an old one blanket, burro-prospector made a bonanza strike on a gravel bar during the low water year of 1909. For years Douglas had been a hard luck prospector. Where others struck it rich, he panned hardly enough to buy beans. Year after year he faced the searing summer heat and icy winter blasts, always just missing the big strikes, but still believing that somewhere along the river there was a mother-lode, rich in gold, just waiting for him.

Douglas watched a miner named Chaffin pan $5,000 in nuggets at Moqui Bar, and witnessed similar finds at Klondyke, Olympia and Rothchild bars, and he was just a little too late when $30,000 was taken from California Bar. But then his luck changed, and the days of being late were over. He found his long dreamed of bonanza at last. In 1909, Douglas was prospecting not far from Mexican Hat when he struck a bar as rich as the mother-lode itself. Working alone, with the river at its lowest level in years, he recovered a small fortune in gleaming nuggets before the spring runoff covered his El Dorado bar.

Douglas marked his secret bar well so that he could find it again, but didn't live long enough to see another low water year on the San Juan. He never strayed far from Mexican Hat, living off his gold and waiting for another low-water year. For 20 years he haunted the San Juan, waiting to return to his bonanza bar. Maybe the wait was too long, or perhaps the thought of his gold just out of reach was too much, but one day in 1929 he walked out on the narrow cable bridge across the river and jumped to his death. He left a pathetic suicide note which read, "When this you see, My old body in the river will be, There is no one in the world to blame for this, Only me!"

Five years after his death, snowfall was light in the mountains, and there was another low-water year on the San Juan. Miners all along the river searched for the lost bonanza bar, but Jim Douglas had not shared his secret with anyone, so today his lost bonanza is still there, somewhere on the San Juan, not far from Mexican Hat. It still waits for another low-water year and some lucky prospector.

Many are the tales of treasure along the San Juan or caches hidden in the shadow of Mexican Hat rock. Old-timers at Bluff still remember Abel Herringer and the stories told about his lost placer mine and the caches he hid. They can tell you those stories are true, for they saw his gold with their own eyes!

Not long after the settlement of Bluff, Abel Herringer began farming along Comb Wash near the San Juan, between Bluff and Mexican Hat. One day, while trailing a lost cow up a side canyon off Comb Wash, he found an ancient river channel, and saw raw gold nuggets gleaming in the morning sun. Being a quiet and secretive man, he told no one, but secretly worked the dry placer when he wasn't at his farm.

No one around Bluff or Mexican Hat suspected that Herringer was becoming wealthy, for he cached his gold in post-hole banks and in old Indian pots which he buried in the garden near his cabin. One day Herringer became critically ill, and was taken by a neighbor to the nearest doctor, at Cortez, Colorado. Herringer was told he had only a few days to live, and since he had no family or close friends, he told the neighbor that after the doctor was paid and he was buried, all of the remaining gold was his, which Herringer estimated to be worth more than $100,000!

After Herringer's death an extensive search was made for his diggings, but every dry gulch along Comb Ridge looked alike to his farmer neighbors, nor were his mining tools found. Several weeks later someone noticed where Herringer had been digging in his garden, and uncovered a small clay pot full of nugget gold, but no more was found although half the garden was dug up. After that Herringer's little farm slowly reverted to nature.

They found gold at Klondyke Bar on the San Juan. Maybe you can too! -Utah Historical Society-

Years passed before a new owner took over Herringer's old farm. One day, while plowing up a long dormant field, his plow cut into a leather bag of gold nuggets. Again only part of the cache was found, and that by accident. Abel Herringer's lost placer and the gold caches he hid are still there, waiting for someone with enough patience to hunt for them. Just stop at Bluff, and have someone point out the way to Comb Ridge and the old Herringer farm. The rest is up to you.

CARLISLE
&
THE GOLD BARS AT RECAPTURE CREEK

During the early 1880's George Washington Johnson built a cabin and started a trap line 5 miles north of present-day Monticello. In 1885 a wagon train of immigrants camped near Johnson's old cabin. After looking the area over they decided to settle there. In short order they erected a number of log cabins and corrals, fenced their fields and started an irrigation system. Their little town was known as Indian Creek until 1898 when it was granted a post office under the name of Carlisle, the name of a local rancher whose place was reputed to be a hideout for outlaws and rustlers. It was a good place for riders of the owlhoot trail to hole up, for it was so difficult to get to that wagons had to be taken apart and lowered down vertical cliffs by ropes before being reassembled to complete their trip to the tough town!

Shoot-outs and killings were common at Carlisle. Tom Mathews, a Texas gunslinger, killed Bill McCord and Moss Walton, both on the same day! The Blue Goose Saloon at Monticello was a favorite hangout for Carlisle's toughs. Henry Honaker, who later built the Honaker Trail to Zahn's Camp, was a young cowboy at

Carlisle, and he recalled that not long after going to work there he was shown a deep ravine filled with the bones of several hundred cattle. He was told, "That's what happens to Mormon cattle that get on our range!"

Farmers who settled near Carlisle discovered that frosts killed their crops nearly every month of the year, while the ranchers stole them blind. And to add to their troubles, Indians were bothersome until after the turn of the century. By 1900 most of Carlisle's citizens were fed up and began moving to Monticello and Blanding. The homesteads they left behind were absorbed by the large ranches. It wasn't long until the process was complete. In 1914 the town's post office was discontinued. Today, most of the area where Carlisle once stood is on land owned by the Scorup Cattle Company, one of Utah's largest ranches. Here and there the dilapidated shells of cabins can be seen next to modern ranch houses.

The list of lost treasures in the Canyonlands is endless. Almost every town has its tale to tell. Some are based only on legends but Carlisle's is based on a fact that anyone can see, on bars of gold that have been found from its first days right down to the present; bars of gold that even you can find!

The mystery of the gold bars on Recapture Creek is an intriguing one, as is the name of the cache itself. Located south of Monticello, Recapture Creek, which flows into the San Juan River was named before the earliest trappers and settlers arrived. When the Hole-In-The-Wall pioneers reached the site of Bluff they found an old hermit living in a brush shack on Recapture Creek. The hermit had followed an old Spanish map into the San Juan country years before, in search of a mine he claimed Spanish miners had worked. He never found the mine, but he did find gold bars, lots of them!

Whenever the hermit wanted to buy goods at the store built by the settlers, he paid in chunks of gold chopped from bars he had found, about an inch square and eight inches long. He told the settlers that when the Aztec Emperor Montezuma fled north with the royal treasury, he was captured by the pursuing Spanish, and escaped only to be recaptured again, along the creek shown on his ancient map as Recapture Creek. The settlers probably didn't believe the old hermit's story, but they had to believe in the bars of gold he had.

For years, people at Bluff and Carlisle speculated about where the hermit actually got his gold bars, but in 1905 the answer became clear. Andy Laney, a young cowboy working for Al Scorup's ranch, stopped along Recapture Creek to water his horse when he noticed something shining in the water. He brushed the sand away and uncovered a crudely cast gold bar, 8″ long and oval in shape, bearing worn markings that looked like a Catholic cross and some Roman numerals he couldn't read. Laney showed the bar to his friends without realizing its worth, but when he was offered $1,800 for it, he quickly sold and quit herding cattle.

Laney took his friend, Elmer Blaine, into his confidence, and the two ex-cowboys became prospectors along Recapture Creek. For a month they searched every inch of the creek where Laney had found the gold bar, and were just about to give up when entirely by accident Blaine stepped on another bar, covered with sand near their camp under an overhanging cliff and 100′ from the creek. Digging in the sand they quickly found four more, all larger than the first, as well as a chunk of melted gold as large as a clenched fist.

With the new found wealth Laney and Blaine were rich, and lost no time going to Durango to celebrate, where Blaine was killed by accident in a saloon gunfight between two men he had never seen before. Laney returned to Recapture Creek and spent a year digging along its banks, but never found another bar. He prospected his way across the San Juan onto the Navajos' Sacred Navajo Mountain, where he was killed by Indians, probably some of Chief Posey's outlaw Pi-Utes.

In time the gold bars of Recapture Creek were nearly forgotten except to local residents. Then in 1964 two relic hunters using metal detectors found another bar and the excitement started all over again. Since then there have been rumors of other bars being found, but everyone is pretty close mouthed now. In 1979 a man and wife camped for the night reportedly found two more bars with the aid of metal detectors.

No one knows where the gold bars at Recapture Creek came from, but the stories told by the old hermit are as logical as any. Perhaps there was a battle between Indians and Spanish miners centuries ago. Who knows? But one thing is certain. Since gold bars have been found there in the past, chances are good that more will be found in the future. Perhaps even by you!

THE HOME OF TRUTH

The Home of Truth colony, or Ogden Center as it was sometimes known, was one of the strangest places you could ever find. It began in 1933 as a religious colony founded by Mrs. Marie Ogden, in the sandy wastes of Dry Valley, 15 miles north of Monticello and 3 miles west of U-160. It was composed of 100 members of a strange socialistic order similar to the Mormon Church's United Order of a half century before. Members surrendered their every possession in exchange for food, clothing and shelter, and were not allowed to use alcohol, tobacco or to eat meat.

The curious colony consisted of three parts. The first, known as The Outer Portal, was located a half mile down a dusty road west of U-160, and consisted of a group of well-kept buildings, including a communal house and a dormitory, none of which had electric lights or running water. The Middle Portal was 1½ miles farther along the road and contained more plain but solid buildings and a chapel built of cobblestones. At the end of the road was The Inner Portal, made up of several barracks and six well-built homes, all high on a windswept ridge overlooking the desert below.

Members of the Home Of Truth colony believed that the Inner Portal was located on the exact center of the earth's axis, and that when the last days came, only those living there would be spared. The rest of the world would be shaken down! On sacred occasions, Mrs. Ogden would climb 9,987′ Shay Mountain, a "holy peak" 15 miles southwest of the colony where, like the prophet Moses, she would receive divine revelations.

If the dreary communal living hadn't been enough to break up the odd colony, its leaders' weird behavior would have been. Stories were heard of efforts to resurrect the dead, so when authorities learned that a body was being kept at the Inner Portal while mysterious ceremonies were conducted, an investigation was started. A badly decomposed body was found before the alter, but before the sheriff could obtain legal papers to seize it, members secretly burned and buried it. A search was made and a dog was seen running with a large bone later identified as a human leg bone. Mrs. Ogden was arrested. After that even the most faithful members of the strange sect began leaving, and the Home Of Truth colony was soon deserted.

Today the road to Indian Creek State Park passes by the strange settlement at Dry Valley. At both the Outer and Middle Portals locked buildings remain. Curtains still cover their windows and inside cobweb covered furniture and shelves of dusty books can be seen. The Inner Portal looks almost as if its occupants were only away for the day, except for the rusty locks on the doors and the cobwebs on the windows. All of the buildings are kept in repair by a caretaker, who keeps barrels under the eaves to catch rain water and piles of chopped wood by each door. Besides the caretaker, who won't speak to strangers, there is no sign of life except the no trepassing signs which warn visitors to stay away.

Mrs. Ogden continued to live alone until she was nearly 100 years old, at the Inner Portal, right on the exact center of the earth's axis, waiting for the world to be shaken down! The last time I passed by the Home Of Truth, the world still looked pretty solid to me.

HITE
&
MORMON JIM'S GOLD

In 1883 Cass Hite and his brothers made camp near the mouth of Trachyte Creek on the Colorado River, 52 miles southeast of Hanksville. They discovered fine flour gold in the sand of Dorothy Bar and organized the White Canyon Mining District. Their find brought a rush of prospectors to the river and in only a few months nearly 200 claims had been located at Dorothy Bar, Olympic Bar, Klondyke Bar and California Bar. A rough camp of rock cabins was built at the ford of the river Hite called a "dandy crossing," but which the miners called Hite's Crossing. When a post office was established to serve the growing camp, it too was named Hite.

For awhile Hite was the scene of a gold rush. A general store opened for business and several saloons parted the miner from his hard earned dust. There was no law at Hite, so plenty of wild ones gravitated there. For awhile it was a ring-tailed-roarer, with Cass Hite one of the toughest of them all. It was common knowledge that he had killed several men in Colorado. Before long the miners learned that the flour gold along the river couldn't be easily recovered by panning, and except for a few rich finds of nugget gold, the rush fizzled out.

Old Cass Hite was tough when being tough meant more than it does now. In September, 1891 he got into an argument in a Green River saloon with a miner named A.F. Kohler over prospects they both claimed. The men went for their guns, but Hite drew and shot so fast that Kohler was killed instantly and Frank Drake, an innocent bystander, was severely wounded. In 1893 several prospectors stopped at Hite's Crossing and asked Hite where they could find gold along the river. Probably to get rid of them, maybe for good, he told them to go to Navajo Mountain and pan the river there. Maybe Hite knew what he was talking about, for that's pretty close to where coarse gold was discovered at Zahn's Camp, but it was also on sacred Navajo land where many prospectors had been killed by Indians. The miners quickly found that it was almost impossible to get down to the river where Hite had told them, and that they had to fight off Navajos every step of the way. It was an angry mob of miners who started back to Hite's Crossing, threatening to kill Cass Hite on sight. But the wily old man heard they were coming and went

into hiding in Green River until things cooled down.

After Hite's first gold rush ended, a stock promotion scheme blew a breath of life into the old camp. The Hoskininni Gold Dredging Company organized the most extravagant of all placer mining projects. A huge floating dredge 150' long and 50' wide was dragged in sections across the desert from the railroad at Green River, more than 100 miles through desolate desert country to the Colorado, where it was assembled. It was powered by three gasoline engines in a land and time where gasoline was unknown. In less than three months the great dredge was declared a failure and left at the river's edge where for fifty years it slowly rotted away.

For years after Hite's gold rush days were over, a ferry operated at the river crossing, but except for a few desert rats the camp was deserted. Its post office was closed in 1915, and after a bridge was built across the Colorado, ferry service was discontinued and Hite joined the ranks of Utah ghost towns. Today most of the site is under Lake Powell. But Cass Hite's ghost still haunts the river, and to those who'll listen it tells a tale of a rich placer known only to the Indians, where nuggets are as big as robins' eggs!

Mormon Jim Black was a prospector at heart. He earned money by cowboying for outfits like the Scorup Cattle Company or Preston Nutter's ranch, but whenever he saved a little he'd return to the wastelands in search of gold. Raised in the San Juan country, Black had often heard of the Lost Merrick & Mitchell Mine and the Indian mines on Navajo Mountain, so he spent a lot of time prospecting along the San Juan.

When winter came in 1897 Mormon Jim was one of the cowboys "let go" until spring, so he headed for a hidden box canyon he had heard old-time cattlemen talk about. Located on the south side of the San Juan, in a deep canyon with 800' sandstone cliffs on all sides, it could only be entered by swimming across the river from another canyon itself almost as hard to get into. Black found the hidden canyon in December, 1897 and built a small cabin of slab-rock and driftwood. There was plenty of grass for his horse and a seep of warm fresh water that never froze.

It didn't take long to explore the canyon. If it hadn't been for an Indian, Mormon Jim might have moved on. He was watching chunks of ice float down the San Juan when he saw an Indian clinging to a log. Black had only a moment to act. He quickly waded chest deep into the icy water and pulled the Indian to shore. The Indian, a Piute, was nearly dead, but Black took him to his crude cabin and cared for him. The Indian had a cough Black recognized as tuberculosis. By then it had become too dangerous to cross the river, so both men were forced to spend the winter in the box canyon.

Mormon Jim prospected every inch of the canyon and found several flakes of gold, which seemed to amuse his Indian friend. One day in late February, when the canyon rim was heavy with snow drifts, the Indian told Black he would be gone all day, and warned him not to follow. After dark the Indian returned, dragging a heavy sack which he threw on the floor at Black's feet. He was coughing terribly and choking up blood, but he managed to open the sack and spill more gold on the ground than Mormon Jim believed existed. None of the nuggets were smaller than a pine nut and many were as large as robins' eggs!

Each day the Indian grew weaker, but would not tell Black where the gold came from. One day, while he lay near death, Mormon Jim hiked up the canyon and learned by accident where the Indian had gone on the day he brought back the gold. At the top of a narrow chimney-like crack in the cliff, hundreds of feet above the valley floor, he could see tracks in the deep snow that had drifted over the canyon rim and down into the chimney. But only an eagle could get out of the canyon that way now, for the melting snow had receded, leaving 50' of sheer, ice covered cliff between the rim and the chimney below.

When Mormon Jim returned to the cabin, the Indian knew where he had been and made him promise never to try to find the gold in the canyon beyond the rim, for it was sacred to the spirit of Navajo Mountain, and if he trespassed he would be killed. When spring finally came, Mormon Jim helped his Indian friend across the river and took him to a government hospital at Phoenix, where he died soon afterwards.

Mormon Jim sold the gold the Indian had given him for just over $56,000 and bought a small ranch. He still made prospecting trips into the desert country, but he kept his promise and never looked for the sacred Indian placers on Navajo Mountain. Navajo Mountain is still off-limits for white men today, but somewhere

Cass Hite, the old outlaw. He started a gold rush and then killed men who tried to find his gold!

south of the San Juan there is a box canyon with an old prospector's cabin in it, and just beyond, up over the rim rock. . .

WIDTSOE
&
THE CAVE OF THE GOLDEN JESUS

The town which became Widtsoe was 25 miles south of Antimony, on the east fork of the Sevier River, near the mouth of Sweetwater Creek. Settlers began moving into the area at the turn of the century, and by 1910 a townsite had been surveyed, building lots sold and the town named Houston for Bishop James Houston of nearby Panguitch. The town was divided into blocks 26 rods square with 4 lots to each block and streets 5 rods wide. When a post office was granted in 1912, the town's name was changed to Winder. That name didn't last long either. Three years later it was changed again to Widtsoe, to honor Apostle John Widtsoe. The town grew rapidly and soon claimed the usual school and church, as well as 2 hotels, 4 stores, a confectionary and offices of the Forest Service. In 1920 its population was 1,100.

Thousands of acres of sage covered desert were cleared for dry farming, but the region was drier than had been bargained for. A long drought starting in 1920 dried its farms until many were forced to leave. When the Forest Service moved its offices in 1925 the end began, with many moving to a new town named Osiris, where irrigation promised an easier life. By 1930 Widtsoe's population had fallen to 200, and a few years later it was zero. For forty years Widtsoe remained deserted while its empty building slumbered in the desert sun. During the 1960's the Forest Service reclaimed several buildings and several families moved back. A few summer homes are there now, but in the winter few choose to stay.

From Widtsoe it is not far to the Escalante Rim and the Kaiparowits Plateau, known locally as Fifty Mile Mountain. A curious tale is told of Spanish gold buried there. The story of the Golden Jesus is a strange one, and goes back to 1810 when Mexican soldiers joined with Apache Indians to drive the Spanish from the land. One small band of soldiers and Catholic priests fled north, to save their lives and their mission treasure. They drove 40 burros loaded with gold and silver ahead of them, but the heavily laden burros moved slowly. Every day more of the Spaniards were killed by their pursuers. Much of their treasure was lost or abandoned by the time they reached the edge of the dread Escalante Desert. With death threatening and their burros exhausted, they decided to cache the remainder of their treasure and flee on foot.

In a cave near the north end of Fifty Mile Mountain, not far from the Escalante Rim, they cached their gold and most treasured church objects, including the Golden Jesus, a 3' high cross of solid gold bearing a figure of the crucified Christ on it. It was so heavy that

The teacher left first, next the students and now even the school bell is gone at old Widtsoe. -Utah Historical Society-

it took four men to lift it. They expected to return one day to recover their treasure, but unknown to them, the land was never to be under Spanish control again.

Fifty years passed before Mormon settlers began exploring the Kaiparowits country. They found evidence of the Spanish soldiers and heard legends from friendly Indians, but they were too busy wresting a living from the harsh land to search for legendary treasures.

In 1875 Bishop Llewellen Harris persuaded some Indians to make him a map of the treasure cave's location. When he tried to find it he found he was unable to understand their signs. But from their descriptions of the objects inside the cave he was sure thay had been there.

Today, Fifty Mile Mountain is still largely unexplored except by cattlemen and hunters who occasionally report finding Spanish spurs and uniform buttons. But so far none of them have found the cave of the Golden Jesus. Maybe you can do better!

OSIRIS

Just off U-22 ten miles south of Antimony are the ghostly remains of Osiris, first known as Henderson, for W.J. Henderson, donor of its 80 acre townsite. It was given the strange name of Osiris when it was granted a post office. It had its birth in 1910, but never amounted to much until Widtsoe, located 14 miles farther south, began to fail. When drought spelled disaster for Widtsoe, many of its people moved to Osiris, the first arriving in 1920.

For several years it looked as though Osiris might be all that Widtsoe had hoped to be. Farmland was cleared, crops were planted and businesses made their appearance. W.E. Halt was the town's chief promoter, building a flour mill, a creamery, a reservoir, many homes and even a telephone exchange, at a cost of more than $300,000.

Large earthen dams were built and an elaborate system of canals dug to bring water to the thirsty land. But the amount of water which could be claimed was gossly over-estimated, and expected summer storms aften failed to come. To make matters worse, frosts at its 8,000' elevation often killed the crops that did grow. After 10 years of fighting droughts and frosts, the once hopeful project was given up and Osiris was abandoned.

Today, few people remember Osiris, but whoever named it was something of a prophet, for Osiris is the Egyptian God of the dead.

CAMP JACKSON
&
THE LOST RIFLE SIGHT LODE

At the south end of the Abajo Mountains in San Juan County a rough mining camp known as Camp Jackson had its brief fling back in the 1880's. Two prospectors named Ducket and Dixon discovered a rich ledge of ore at the top of a steep gulch which showed 150 ounces of gold to the ton. They located the Gold Queen Mine, and not long afterward Hansen and Cooley located the Dream Mine across the ridge near the head of Johnson Creek. Before the first year ended more than 300 claims had been staked in the new district.

Captain Calvin Jackson was the town's namesake. He obtained an interest in the Dream Mine, where he installed a 10 stamp mill and other equipment at a cost of $80,000. Two tunnels were driven into the mountain and three shafts sunk at the Gold Queen Mine at high cost. A second stamp mill was put into service at the Dream Mine in 1901, and a newly built tramway carried ore to it from the mine. Camp Jackson was a camp of rough miners. It couldn't boast fine stores or fancy saloons, but its miners never lacked either supplies or whiskey.

The heavy investment made by the mine owners wasn't justified, because high expenses combined with the isolated location claimed all profits. When its mines closed in 1903, Camp Jackson was abandoned overnight. With its pounding stamp mills idle and its steam engines silent, peace and quiet returned to the Abajos.

Today, the ruins of Camp Jackson can be reached by a rough mountain road 11 miles east of Monticello. A stream of icy water coming from the Gold Queen tunnel tumbles down a rocky gulch past the caved ruins of a wrecked mill and a row of half-fallen cabins. Red Bluff Campground, 4 miles down canyon from the Gold Queen Mine, is a pleasant place to stop while exploring old Camp Jackson.

Long before Camp Jackson reached any degree of fame, there were tales of a lost silver ledge nearby. In 1864 two prospectors camped in the Abajo Mountains. While hunting deer for camp meat, one knocked the front sight from his rifle. At the base of a ledge of shiny rock he picked up a sliver of metal-like rock and pressed it into the dovetail slot where the front sight had been. He was anxious to get the deer so he paid little attention to where he picked up the soft stone, except to remember that the ground at the base of the ledge was covered with similar pieces of shiny rock that had weathered and fallen.

After returning to camp the temporary front sight was examined more closely. Because of the softness of the metal, the two prospectors decided it was lead. There was no market for lead in the wilds of southern Utah so it was forgotten until a year later when they were in Salt Lake City. They took the rifle to a gunsmith to have a new sight mounted and learned that the sliver of metal was silver. Later an assayer verified that it was pure hornsilver.

Every time the prospectors passed through the Abajo Mountains, now the Blue Mountains north of Monticello, they tried to locate the lost ledge, but never found the same place they had trailed a deer several years before, so their hornsilver gulch is still lost today. There are not many clues to go on, but then, if it was easy, I'd have found it myself!

NOTOM & PLEASANT DALE
&
THE MYSTERY MESA TREASURE

Notom was located on Pleasant Creek 5 miles upstream from its junction with the Dirty Devil River, in Wayne County. It was settled in 1885 by a wagon train of Saints led by Jurgen Smith. Smith had been a druggist and for years maintained a regular apothecary at his home. When a post office was established it was named Notom, why, no one knows.

Notom was expected to be a farm settlement, and with great effort some crops were grown, but it was right at the edge of a drifting sand desert and no matter how hard the settlers worked, drifting dunes covered their fields. Finally, except for a few who had built along Pleasant Creek, the town was abandoned in favor of a new settlement on the river called Aldredge. Those remaining on Pleasant Creek sent their children to school at Aldredge, 4 miles away.

It must have taken someone with a good sense of humor to name Pleasant Creek, for there's nothing pleasant about it. But a few settlers chose to tarry there awhile, and named their little hamlet Pleasant Dale, and today atop a dry, windswept bench about midway between Notom and Aldredge the ruins of several rock houses stand stark and bare against the desert sky. They are all that remain of Pleasant Dale, the dreary place with the pleasant name. For awhile it was also called Floral, an even harder name to understand. A dusty road leaves U-24 just east of Capitol Reef and passes by Pleasant Dale, on its way to Notom, now only an oasis of green in a barren desert.

There may be buried treasure not far from old Notom, but to find it you'll have to be able to read a combination of secret signs and pictographs. East of Notom and 25 miles south of Hanksville, on the old road to Hite's Crossing, there is a flat top mesa, about a mile east of the road. On top of it there are five stones with mysterious signs cut into them. They are old, the first explorers found them, and took too much labor to cut to be a hoax, especially since they are in a place where they could never be found except by accident. That is, unless someone had a map leading to them, or knew exactly where to look.

The stones lay roughly in the shape of a three toed animal foot, 26' from the heel to the end of the toes. One stone is where the instep would be, and has the date or numeral 1154 cut into it. The heel stone has the figure of a man, a snake and a three legged animal on it, plus the letters FHP. The first toe stone from the left has a skull and crossbones and an X on it, the center toe stone has a five pointed star with a dot in its center, and the right toe stone is shaped like a human foot with an X on it.

In 1931 a prospector named Alexander was camped at the foot of the Henry Mountains. One day two very old Mexican prospectors came to his camp and asked if he had found any old signs or markings. Alexander told them he had not, and asked for information about them. The Mexicans were very reluctant to talk about the signs, but did give Alexander the impression they had been in that area long before or else had a map that made them familiar with some landmarks. The Mexicans searched for several weeks, climbing ridges and mesas, but finally gave up and left the desert. The following year Alexander found the strange signs.

For fifteen years Alexander prospected the Henrys and the desert between them and the Colorado River. Often he returned to the mesa with the mysterious markings, but he couldn't decipher their ancient message. In time Alexander learned that there were old-timers around Hanksville who knew of the markings. They were very evasive when he questioned them, as if afraid to talk about them.

It's been 50 years since Alexander discovered the mysterious markings the old Mexicans were searching for, but no more is known about their strange message now than was known then. If you want to try to decipher their mysterious message, they are still there, atop the mystery mesa. Alexander spent 15 years trying to unravel their secret. I hope it won't take you as long.

ALDREDGE
&
THE SPANISH CACHE ON
FISH LAKE MOUNTAIN

Aldredge was located just off U-24 east of Capitol Reef Monument in Wayne County. It was built along both sides of the Dirty Devil River, now called the Fremont River. In 1890 after continual drought and drifting sands claimed the farms at Notom, many of its residents moved to Aldredge, hoping to fulfill their prophet's promise that the desert would bloom like a rose. A church, school and blacksmith shop were built. But roses were never intended for the desert and the little community slowly withered and died. At the turn of the century Aldredge was only a memory.

By the side of U-24, 29 miles west of Hanksville, piles of stone that stand no higher than the sage are the ruins of what were once homes at Aldredge. Across the river several long fallen sandstone cabins can be seen at the mouth of a dry wash. A long stone wall built of sun varnished black volcanic rock snakes its way along a bare hillside. Once it protected settler's fields from wild animals and roving livestock. Today their fields are only shifting sand, and there are no wandering animals, except for an occasional coyote!

But somewhere in the mountains north of old Aldredge, not far from Fish Lake, there is a cave, one of many in the area, but a special one. It's a treasure cave!

At the turn of the century Carl Blomquist's father ran a saloon at Richfield. But young Carl wasn't allowed to be seen there, especially with his Indian friends, for Indians weren't allowed to buy whiskey.

One day several of his young Indian friends persuaded Carl to get them some whiskey in exchange for some small gold ingots of curious design. The ingots were crudely made, as though cast in a sand mold, and appeared to be very old. Apparently they were made of a bullion metal containing copper, for they were stained with green oxidation.

In time, after Carl exchanged several more bottles of whiskey with them, the Indian boys revealed where the gold came from. One evening just before dark, while they were returning to their deer camp high in the Fish Lake Mountains north of Aldredge, they took young Blomquist into a concealed cave. Inside Blomquist saw several pieces of Spanish armor, and a pile of rotted animal skins bags. Crudely cast bars and ingots of gold had spilled from them. Blomquist was allowed to look but not to touch anything. He had paid no attention to the surroundings before being taken into the cave, and it was completely dark when he left it.

In later years one of his Indian friends told him that the gold came from mines worked centuries before, high in the Uintah Mountains of northern Utah, and that the cave on Fish Lake Mountain was only a storage place on the long Spanish trail to New Mexico. The Indian said that no one was allowed to go to the cave, and after his elders had learned he had been there warned him against ever returning, for the spirits of murdered Indians who had been forced to work in the Spanish mines guarded the cave. Since the warning he had never returned.

Every time Blomquist was in the mountains he searched for the cave, but he never found it. Fish Lake Mountain is a high weather worn plateau of limestone rock, with countless small caves and springs and seeps indicating many more unseen. There are sinkholes and hollow cavities everywhere. Any of them could be the Spanish cache cave. But if you're deer hunting on Fish Lake Mountain, keep your eyes open, and be sure to take a quick look inside every cave you see. Maybe the next one you see will be it. As the Spanish say, Quien Sabe, who knows?

CAINEVILLE AND ELEPHANT

During the 1880's Mormon Church leaders issued a call for Saints to settle the blue clay desert country of Wayne County. Those who answered the call, led by A.K. Thurber and Elija Behunin, founded a town on the Dirty Devil River 65 miles southeast of Loa. The new community was name for John T. Caine, then a Congressional Delegate from the Utah Territory. By 1892 city blocks had been surveyed and many buildings put up, including a large store called the Fremont Mercantile. For several years Caineville's farms produced good crops of grains, melons and fruits and the settlers prospered. Then, on orders from their leaders, they embarked on what was called the "silk mission."

Mulberry trees and silkworms were imported from the Orient and were taken to Caineville for the town's

The church at Caineville, probably the only Mormon Church with a Star Of David atop it.

new industry, raising silkworms and manufacturing silk. The venture proved to be impractical, to say the least. Caineville's prosperity was rapidly fading when the Dirty Devil River began flooding farm land with blue clay mud and washing homes away. Each succeeding year there were floods and more of the people left. Finally in 1910, church leaders advised people to move to higher ground. Few questioned their advice. Caineville was never destined to become the garden of eden its planners had envisioned.

For a short time Caineville had a suburb which few people today have heard of. For some reason the little hamlet was called Elephant, possibly by someone who had lived at Elephant City, an earlier settlement in Beaver County. Elephant was settled in 1887 when Orson Dalton led a wagon train to where the high bluffs along the Dirty Devil widen out to form a small valley. There they staked out a townsite. More settlers arrived the following year and added their homes to those already built, but hard times plagued Elephant right from the start. Floods washed out dams and irrigation ditches until only three years after its hopeful start Elephant was abandoned. Today, only the gaunt skeletons of three weathered cabins remain at the little town with the strange name.

During recent years, with modern machinery, Caineville's farms are being cultivated again on a large scale, and people have moved back into houses empty for so long. Its fine old church, displaying a six-pointed Star of David atop its steeple, a symbol pretty unusual in Utah, is again used on Sunday mornings. Be sure to stop at that picturesque old chapel where weary settlers prayed for strength so long ago.

GILES
&
THE CLIFF DWELLERS' CACHE

Giles was one of the Wayne County settlements which Mormon farmers under the leadership of Hyrum Burgess started during the early 1880's. By 1883 it had grown into a little hamlet called Blue Valley, named for its blue clay soil. Blue Valley was built along both sides of the Fremont River, then called the Dirty Devil, and had a footbridge connecting its two parts. Irrigation dams were built and canals carried water to its thirsty land. By 1895, with business thriving and more people arriving every day, its future looked quite rosy. At that time its name was changed to Giles, in honor of Bishop Henry Giles.

Solomon Parker owned the general store, Joseph Elliot operated a grocery, Bill Shirts was the town blacksmith, Henry Lords had a sawmill and Mrs. Abbott owned a boarding house. Just as the town was becoming stable, the Dirty Devil began overflowing its banks. Each year saw the river wash more farms and homes away. There were disastrous floods in 1909 and 1910, and by 1919 Giles was deserted.

Today, an empty rock shell that was once a prosperous business stands alone by the side of U-24, 11 miles east of Caineville and 8 miles west of Hanksville. South of the highway an old farmhouse can be seen in a grove of dead trees. Few travelers stop to rest at Giles anymore, and that's just the way the ghosts like it!

There were Indian ghosts in Blue Valley long before there were Mormon ghosts at Giles. Ghosts of the Anasazi, the ancient cliff dwellers of southern Utah, guarded the silent dwellings the earliest settlers discovered high in the rimrock cliffs nearby. One of those cliff dwellings was part of a treasure tale old-timers at Giles often told.

Tine Gray was over 70 years old when he followed his burros through Giles southwest past Escalante in August, 1892. He had prospected all over the Blue Desert country and was now on the trail of a story he had heard of pea sized nuggets Ute Indians once brought from a remote canyon. It took him two months before he found the first gold nugget in a vertical cliff gorge he named Davis Canyon, and another month to trace them to their source. Gray discovered a rich placer where he worked all winter, recovering more gold than he could carry. The placer gravel was in a brown colored quartz vein that had weathered away at the foot of a towering sandstone cliff.

In the spring, Gray went to round up his burros, but found both of them dead where they had eaten poisonous larkspur. He was old and weak from a winter of hard work with little food, and knew that he could never walk and carry all his gold to either Escalante or Giles. While working in the canyon Gray had explored an Anasazi cliff dwelling high on the cliffs above the canyon, and recalled seeing several ancient clay pots in the ruins. He recovered the pots and filled them with gold, burying them deep in a hole at the foot of a high cliff. Then he cached his tools and pack saddles under an over-hanging ledge across the canyon from his clay pot cache.

Gray decided to head for the Mormon settlements at Giles and Caineville, but in the maze of canyons often lost his way or was forced to go in the wrong direction. Summer heat dehydrated his frail body and his meager supply of venison jerky soon gave out. For days he wandered half conscious, until he heard dogs barking and staggered into Joel Johnson's settlement in Johnson Canyon, far to the southwest of where he thought he was.

Johnson knew that Gray couldn't live long without medical help. He sent him by wagon with his son Jesse and John Findley, owner of the Elephant Store, to Kanab where Oscar Lee took the old man in. Gray still clung to an eight pound buckskin bag of gold nuggets he had carried all the way from Davis Canyon. When Gray realized he was going to die, he gave the gold to Lee and told him where the rest of his gold was cached in Davis Canyon. Lee listened carefully to the old man's description of the hidden tools and the buried cache under the cliff dweller's ruins, and never doubted for a minute that once he got to Davis Canyon he could easily locate it. But when he started asking questions about the canyon at Escalante and Giles he was shocked to learn that no one there had ever heard of Davis Canyon. It was a name the old man had made up!

Nevertheless, Lee searched for the mystery canyon, but after a year of hiking he found a thousand canyons just like the one Gray had described. In time Lee married and moved to Kanab, where he raised a family and had no time for treasure hunting. But one day two prospectors passed through Kanab and told a strange story of how they had found the skeletons of two burros and a cache of pack saddles and tools in a remote desert canyon far to the northeast. Lee listened and longed to make one more search, but never did.

Today, modern maps show a Davis Canyon just south of Canyonlands National Park, but it wasn't named until just a few years ago. Is it the same canyon, or is Tine Gray's Canyon and his cliff dweller's clay pot cache still hidden in one of the countless unnamed canyons southwest of old Giles? Only the ghosts of the Anasazi know for sure, and they're not telling!

OLD LA SAL
&
JACK WRIGHT'S LOST GOLD LEDGE

From La Sal Junction on U-160, turn east for 9 miles to "new" La Sal, and then continue over the low pass to Old La Sal. The town itself is pretty well gone now, but for several miles empty cabins and old houses can be seen along the foothills. Several modern ranch houses have been built and a sawmill is kept busy

The Abbott Hotel at Giles. Unfortunately it's temporarily closed for remodeling! -Utah Historical Society-

cutting timber from the La Sal Mountains. Five miles farther east the abandoned buildings and houses of a more modern uranium mining camp dot the mountainside. Old La Sal was first settled along Deer Creek in 1873, and among its first citizens were the Roys, Maxwells and McCartys.

The townsite was located at an elevation of 7,500'. As a result farm crops seldom matured and gradually it became a ranching center. A post office was established in 1878 with William Hamilton as postmaster. Old La Sal was on the pack mule mail route between Salina, Utah and Ouray, Colorado. Winters were harsh at the town's high elevation. During the great blizzard of '85 snow fell 5' deep on the flat and drifted 12' deep in the canyons. Its cold climate, combined with increasing Indian troubles, caused its settlers to seek more sheltered and fruitful homes at "new" La Sal.

Present-day or "new" La Sal was originally known as Coyote, for the large number of coyotes found there. When the post office was moved from Old La Sal in August, 1901, it became La Sal. As the new town grew, the old one died, leaving Old La Sal the forgotten and lonely place it is today. Not far from Old La Sal there is a fabulously rich lost gold ledge! Along the old Indian trail that rises out of the southwest, a cowboy named Jack Wright found an unusual outcrop of red colored rock that assayed at $70,000 to the ton! Although countless prospectors have searched for it since, the ledge has never been found.

Jack Wright was a cowboy always looking over his shoulder to see if a posse was on his trail. With Jack Moore and Bob Ricker for partners, he would rustle cattle and horses from settlements all across southern Utah and then trail them along the Horsethief Trail into Colorado, where they were sold at the mining camps with no questions asked.

Horsethief Trail crossed the Dirty Devil River and went over Sunset Pass to Waterhole Flat, crossing the Colorado at Spanish Bottoms. It then wound up Hart's Draw, passed by Peter's Point to Sagebrush Ridge and continued through Indian Canyon to Old La Sal and the Colorado border.

While trailing a stolen herd somewhere between Peter's Point and Old La Sal, Jack Wright stopped for a few minutes by an outcropping of "pretty red rock," and before he rode on took a few pieces of it. Wright wasn't a prospector, but he knew that gold had been found in the Abajo and La Sal Mountains, and he had heard many stories about lost mines all along the Old Spanish Trail. Neither Moore nor Ricker knew what the heavy red rocks were, so when they got to Durango they had them assayed. Tests revealed $70,000 to the ton!

Wright and his partners were in no hurry to return to Utah right away, for their faces decorated wanted posters all across the canyonlands. Besides, they had plenty of money to spend in Colorado. Months later Jack Wright passed through Old La Sal again, sure that he could go straight to the gold ledge between there and Peter's Point. But from a different direction, nothing looked the same. Sand storms had covered some ledges and exposed others. He spent weeks riding the Horsethief Trail, but when summer passed and snow was dusting the Abajos he gave up and moved on. Wright was never seen around Old La Sal again, and some say he lies in an unmarked grave where cowboys from Carlisle caught him burning the wrong brand on a Scorup Company cow.

There's no doubt that Jack Wright found an outcropping of red colored gold somewhere along the Horsethief Trail, between Peter's Point and Old La Sal. Both Moore and Ricker saw the samples he took to Colorado, but neither of them knew where Wright found them. And it's known that Wright spent a lot of time looking for the gold, something a wanted man wouldn't risk if he wasn't sure of what he was doing. Every passing wind changes the face of the desert. New ledges are uncovered while others are buried. Who knows what the next wind might reveal?

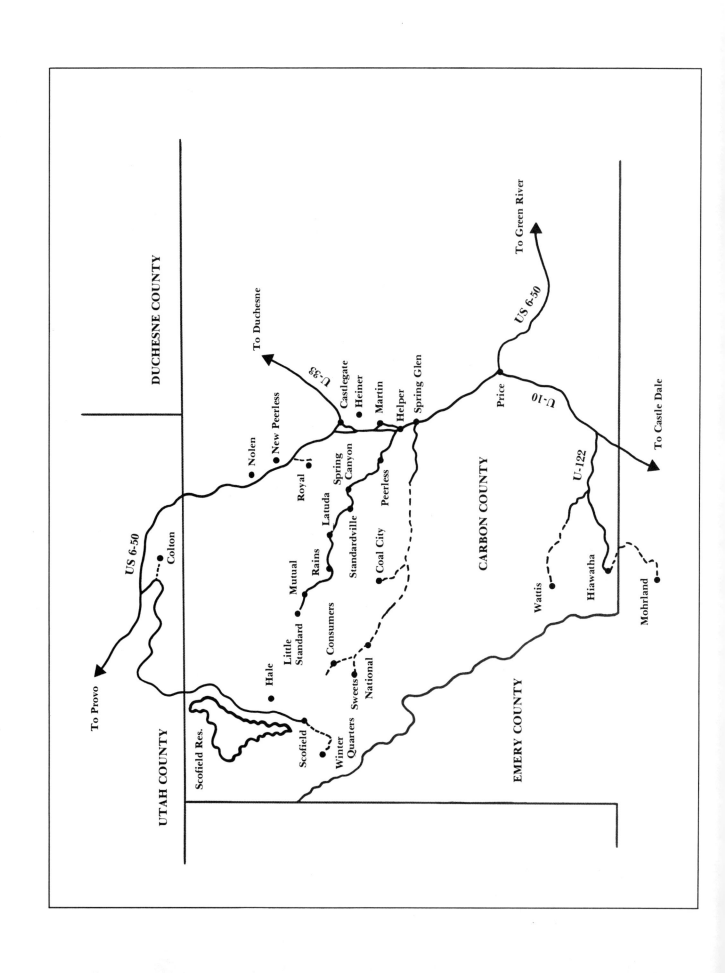

The Wasatch Store at Winter Quarters, no longer the center of town.

CHAPTER SEVEN

COAL COUNTRY

The valley of the Great Salt Lake was a harsh place when the Mormon pioneers arrived there in 1847. Many of the things thought of as necessary for starting a new life in the wilderness were lacking. There was little timber for lumber or fuel, and it soon became apparent that coal would be needed. There was none near the valley so the pioneers directed their search to the vermillion cliffs and purple mesas of what would become Carbon County.

By 1849 extensive coal deposits had been found in the area's colorful canyons, but they were too far from the Salt Lake Valley to be mined economically. In 1854 Brigham Young offered a reward of $1,000 for the discovery of a coal vein at least 18″ thick within 40 miles of Salt Lake City. Soon coal mines were developed near Wales in Sanpete County and at Coalville in Summit County, but they didn't qualify under the terms of Young's offer, and the reward was not paid. After the railroad was completed in 1869, the discovery of coal almost anywhere was reward unto itself, since the steam engines relied on it.

Caleb Rhoades of Lost Rhoades Mine fame is credited with making the first discovery of coal near Price City, and in 1877 Peter Morgan located the famous Winter Quarters Mine near Scofield. Overnight coal camps such as Nolen, New Peerless and Coal City became booming mining camps. Almost all of the coal mines were within the borders of Carbon County, and over the years it has accounted for 75% of the state's production

Nearly all of the coal camps are ghost towns today. Brush-choked canyons and mile high plateaus hide those long deserted and forgotten places, sometimes only a few moss covered cabins, but often an entire town of solid rock buildings. Each has fascinating treasure tales to tell those who who will search them out and take time to listen. There are not as many lost mine stories in coal country as in other places, because coal hasn't the glitter gold has. Who could get excited over a lost coal mine? Perhaps the stories of those old coal towns and the miners who built them are the real treasure.

WINTER QUARTERS
COLTON & HALE

To visit the site of Winter Quarters, turn west off US 6-50 onto U-96 in Utah County, 6 miles southeast of Soldier Summit. It is 17 miles to Scofield. From there continue west a half mile on a poor dirt road to a barbed wire fence. A half mile walk beyond the fence, either along the rocky road or on the abandoned railroad grade that parallels it, will bring you to the old townsite. When coal was discovered in the dark canyon beyond during the early winter of 1877, the discoverers, led by Peter Morgan, were caught in a savage blizzard and held snow-bound until the following February. They named their forced camp site Winter Quarters.

The camp that grew up where the snowbound prospectors wintered was first named Pleasant Valley, but was later renamed Winter Quarters. It became one of the most impressive cities in the state. It is hard to reconcile the ruins of today with the shining city of yesteryear. Its business district was more than a mile long and boasted dozens of substantial stone buildings, many of them as fine as any in Salt Lake City.

The Pleasant Valley Railroad was built into Winter Quarters in 1879, and connected with the Rio Grande line at Colton, 20 miles north. For awhile Colton was called Pleasant Valley Junction, but its name was changed to honor William F. Colton, a Rio Grande official. Its businesses included Covington's Hotel, Higney's Store and five saloons. It burned to the ground three times! But Colton's future was tied to that of Winter Quarters, and unknown to either, that future wasn't very bright.

On May 1st, 1900 the Winter Quarters #4 mine exploded, killing 199 men in one blinding second that left 105 widows and 270 fatherless children, and a town that never recovered from the shock. Every available coffin in the state was sent to the stricken town, and still more had to be brought in from Denver. 150 miners were buried at Scofield while two special funeral trains took the remaining caskets to other places. The terrible tragedy cast a pall of gloom over the entire town, and the deaths of its miners seemed to signal the death of Winter Quarters also. From that day on the town slowly died. Caved cellars and broken foundations are all that remain.

Coffins stacked up at the Wasatch Store after the mine explosion at Winter Quarters, May, 1900.

Scofield, where most of the dead from Winter Quarters were buried, is only a shadow of the boomtown it was a century ago when immigrant miners rubbed elbows along its crowded streets. Scofield isn't a ghost town, but it's not far from being one. Hale, another has-been coal camp, was located just off U-96 north of Scofield. Its site is now marked by a couple of tumble down shacks at the edge of the hillside. Some of the mines at Hale were located downstream from Scofield Reservoir, while the lake covers the upper part of it. If you're going to camp overnight, the lakeshore near Hale is a more pleasant place than the dark canyon at Winter Quarters. The ghosts of 199 dead miners don't make very good company!

Of interest to treasure hunters is the fact that many of those killed at Winter Quarters were bachelor miners. No doubt many of them had secret post-hole banks near their cabins. Over the years others were killed or died there, and many of them hid money they never recovered. When the town was abandoned, who knows how many other caches were left behind, unknown, forgotten, lost or buried by someone no longer able to recover them? They are the lost treasures of Winter Quarters today.

COAL CITY

To find Coal City drive south from Helper 2½ miles to the junction of U-139, and take its gravel route northwest for 9 miles to where a narrow dirt road turns to the right. Watch closely and you can see a line of weathered old buildings perched atop a windswept 8,000′ high ridge about a mile ahead. Those tired old relics are all that remain of Coal City.

First settled in 1885, Coal City was known as Oak Springs Bench, and later as Cedar Mesa Ranch. In those days its settlers were more interested in farming than they were in mining coal. But the 8,000′ elevation and the dry desert foothills soon proved unsuitable for farming. Then ranching was tried, but too little feed and too many coyotes quickly put an end to that scheme.

But when coal was discovered and the town became Coal City, everything looked rosy. New people moved in, business boomed and for a few years prosperity reigned. But Coal City had a problem. It was just too far away, over primitive roads, to compete with coal camps along the railroad. Its mining days came to an end, at least temporarily, and its homes were abandoned.

Year after lonesome year the little ghost town waited until its rebirth as Great Western. During the 1920's mining promoters tried to reopen its mines, and during its second life things looked so good that a new schoolhouse was built. Andienini's Store catered to housewives, and a railroad, known locally as the National Coal Railroad, was built into town. The timing couldn't have been worse, for the great depression

Grass grows on the streets at Coal City, and its railroad cars are rusted to the rails.

struck and the price of coal fell until it couldn't be given away. Except when heavyweight champion Jack Dempsey called Coal City home and trained for several of his fights there, the tired old town fared no better as Great Western than it did as Coal City. It wasn't long before tumbleweeds were rolling down its empty streets again.

Today, the skeleton of Andieini's Store, several other businesses and a few miners' homes are all that remain. An occasional visitor walks those silent streets to take photos and peek into empty doorways, or search along the sage covered foothills for relics of yesterday. Items that were tossed into cellars or thrown into cloudburst gullies as junk are antiques now. A visit to Coal City could be a relic hunter's dream come true!

NATIONAL

The town of National was located 12 miles from the highway and 3 miles up canyon from Coal City. Some coal had been mined there as early as 1908, but the real boom came in 1926. Miners rushed there to get in on the high wages being paid by the National Coal Company. Naturally, the town they helped build was named National. It soon boasted all the usual businesses and saloons, but there was never any doubt that it was a company town. Almost all of its buildings were constructed of the same red colored block stone, and its houses were all look-alikes.

During the late 1920's National grew by leaps and bounds, but by the 30's, like other coal towns, National felt the sting of the depression. By the time the great depression ended, National was through. Today a long row of empty red rock houses stand one above the other along the canyon bottom, looking down on a sagging red rock mine building by the side of Gordon Creek. Caving shafts and leaning gallow frames dot the canyon sides above the town. For some reason many modern road maps still show National and give its population as being 300. Funny, the last time I was there, no one was home!

CONSUMERS

To visit Consumers, follow Gordon Creek upstream from National 1 mile to where the road forks, and take the right hand fork to an unlocked gate in a barbed wire fence. Leave the gate closed if that's how you find it. You'll come onto main street about a half mile up canyon. Consumers was one of the most prosperous coal towns in Carbon County, as evidenced by the large, impressive buildings there. Yet, it retains the unmistakable stamp of a company town.

Coal had been found there right after the turn of the century, but it wasn't until 1920 that A.E. Gibson discovered a high quality vein large enough to be mined profitably. The tent town that grew up was named Gibson, but when the National Coal Railroad laid track into town, it was renamed Consumers for Consumers' Coal Company. It soon had some of the finest business buildings in coal country. Its huge four story hotel still stands, dwarfing the smaller buildings around it.

Many comfortable company houses were built
along both sides of Gordon Creek, but many independent miners built their own houses or shacks farther up
canyon, where evidence of them can still be found
hidden in the heavy brush. They are the places for relic
hunters today. Old bottles and other junk, now valued
as relics, were thrown down the hillside or onto trash
piles. The post office was located in the mine office
building where several wooden mailboxes still remain,
one marked, "For the townsite." Old record books and
ledgers strewn at random on the floor provide reading
material for ghosts who wait in vain for the postmaster's return.

SWEETS

Sweets was located 2 miles up canyon from
National on the main fork of Gordon Creek, 14 miles
from US 6-50. From National follow Gordon Creek up
the main canyon instead of turning right to Consumers. The town there was named Sweets for the Sweets
Mine, which with the Gordon Creek Mine accounted
for most of the camp's coal production. During the
1920's Sweets was an impressive place, its buildings
extending almost to the edge of National. Old-timers
still remember the wild times to be had there.

For several years after the Sweets Mine began operations, miners and their families lived in a tent town.
(Just think how many coins could be lost in a tent
town!) The National Coal Railroad built its line into
town and set up its shops there. A high trestle was built
across the narrow canyon above the town to bring coal
from the Sweets Mine, located high in the cliffs above,
to the railroad. Both the Sweets and Gordon Creek

The snow piled up at Consumers. - Utah Historical Society-

Note the young boys who worked in the mines at Sweets.

mines shipped 2,000 tons of coal a day, seven days per
week.

Sweets went sour when the great depression struck,
and today its name is hardly remembered. Its site is on a
dead end road, so few people visit there now. A long
unused coal tipple at the Gordon Creek Mine still
towers above the canyon, while on the opposite side of
the canyon the caved in tunnel of the Sweets Mine can
be seen. Although no buildings remain at Sweets, places where they stood or where miners cabins were built
can still be seen. All could be good places for coin-
shooters to detect coins lost 60 years ago. Some of them
could be gold! Today its grassy creekside location, sheltered by towering cottonwood trees, makes Sweets a
pleasant place to camp while exploring nearby
National and Consumers.

MARTIN

Until 1918, when angry citizens started a petition
to make it a separate community, Martin was part of
Helper. A long narrow line of houses joined it to the
larger town down canyon, but it was always treated like
a poor step-child. It was winter when a fight broke out
over something, now long forgotten, and quickly
spread into the streets and involved a whole neighborhood. Helper police couldn't get through the deep
snow and mud to the upper canyon. The battle finally
ended, but angry citizens who were tired of depending
upon Helper's poor police service voted to break away
and start their own town. They named it Martin for a
popular railroad engineer who lived there.

Martin was a pleasant place at the mouth of Price
Canyon. "Welcome to Martin" was posted by the side
of the highway and names of businesses were changed,

but no one seemed to take the new town seriously. Martin never fared well as a separate community. Its police and other services were worse than ever, because there were no funds to pay for them. Many citizens left in disgust when water and power services failed. When the highway was rerouted around it, Martin's time had run out.

Although it has never been completely deserted, Martin is only a shell of what it once was. Don't miss its old stone hotel and tavern, built of hand quarried rock by one-armed Ross Gigliotti, who for many years operated the town's small store and gas station. It's been empty for years, but remains Martin's most impressive building. It's all that's left from when Martin parted company with Helper.

WATTIS

To find Wattis go south from Price on U-10 to its junction with U-122, then west 3 miles to U-50. Follow it 8 miles up very steep grades to the townsite. First settled in 1912, the town was named for William Wattis, a major stockholder in the Lion Coal Company, which owned the mines there. Wattis grew into one of the more promising coal camps and had one of the largest business districts. From its lofty location, perched 7,500' high on Castle Valley Mountain at the foot of a towering cliff, Wattis looked down on a sweep of colorful desert country larger than many eastern states.

Like many coal camps, Wattis was a company town, with rows of houses as much alike as modern sub-divisions. There were neat frame houses for family

men and boarding houses for bachelor miners, and even a separate section for the large number of Japanese miners employed there. The town went out of business long ago, but its mines are still worked. During the 1930's the mines closed and everyone left, but in recent years coal has come into demand again and the mines have been reopened. Except for a few custodial people, no one lives there now with miners preferring to live in Price and commute to work.

The present owners have posted "No Trespassing" signs everywhere, although it is hard to see what a ghost-towner or shutter-bug could damage. Row after row of empty company houses still stand, as well as many of its old business buildings. Old fashioned mine cars and unused equipment stand rusting among the ruins, replaced by high speed modern machinery.

HEINER

Two miles north of Helper, where Panther Creek empties into the Price River, a coal camp named Heiner once stood. To find it today, start at the store at Martin and follow the dirt road north along the Price River for a half mile. Cross the river at the mouth of a rocky canyon where old foundations and half dead shade trees can be seen. The site can only be reached by crossing the river on a railroad trestle, so watch out for trains!

When it was first settled in 1911, Heiner was known as Panther, for the Panther Coal Mine, but for a short time later it was called Carbon. In 1914 a single room schoolhouse was built, at which time its name was changed to Heiner, for Moroni Heiner, vice presi-

Water was free, but gas cost 15¢ a gallon at the Martin general store! - Utah Historical Society-

dent of the US Fuel Company, which owned several of the camp's leading mines. The following year a social center was built for the miners and their families. By 1917 a post office had been built and a Co-Op Store was doing a thriving business. The little one room schoolhouse was replaced with a new eight room brick building in 1923.

For awhile it was expected that Heiner would be listed among Carbon County's biggest towns, but the coal veins at its mines began to pinch out and it couldn't continue to operate profitably. Slowly but surely the town began to fade. Today everything is gone including the buildings. Only the shade trees they planted remain, and like the town, most of them are dead.

Heiner is so close to the highway that treasure hunters pass it by, believing they will do better at another camp far from the highway, at the end of some rocky road. It ain't necessarily so! Coins, rings and relics were lost wherever people lived, and people lived at Heiner. Give it a try. You might be surprised!

ROYAL

Royal was located 2 miles north of Castle Gate, just off present-day US 6-50. It was one of Carbon County's first coal camps and was originally known as Bear Canyon. Later it became Cameron, when Frank Cameron purchased the mines there, and after that, Rolapp, when the mines were sold to Henry Rolapp. All that happened in the 1880's, and it wasn't until 1940 that the town became Royal when the Royal Coal Company purchased it, lock, stock and barrel. Coal was first discovered when road builders in Price Canyon blasted off a cliff side and uncovered a thick vein of coal, at the junction of Bear Creek and the Price River.

The pink colored cliffs of Castle Gate dwarfed the little town, but at the same time gave it a setting of unequalled beauty.

Royal, or whatever it was called at the time, was a hell-for-leather camp, with a reputation of being a wild place. In addition to its saloons, it had the usual general store, post office, school and church. Most of the structures at Royal were look-alikes, for it was a company town no matter who owned it or gave it their name. While it lived, it lived fast, and when it died, it died fast.

Today Royal consists of rows of empty houses and mine buildings, side by side along the narrow canyon bottom. Discarded time books and safety inspection ledgers left at the time keepers office have slowly yellowed with age, while boots, gloves and rusting pieces of machinery seem to be strewn everywhere. Dusty diggers still hang from the ceiling in a silent change room at one of the mines. Some old tunnels are still open, while others are badly caved. If you listen closely you can hear traffic speeding by a half mile down the canyon, but a world away in time. The noise doesn't seem to bother the ghosts.

NEW PEERLESS

For there to have been a New Peerless, there must have been an "old" Peerless. There was, in Spring Canyon. For now it will suffice to say that when "old" Peerless failed, the mine owners there opened a new mine 3 miles north of Castle Gate, about a mile up canyon from Royal, and they called it New Peerless. Coal had been discovered there as early as 1900, but it wasn't economically feasible to mine until 30 years later. New Peerless was born right at the start of the great depression, and in part because it was born dur-

Homes at Royal were built to last. They outlasted the town!

ing hard times, its life was hard. Its population never exceeded 300 even though its mines worked off and on all through the 1930's.

There isn't much left of New Peerless because a salvage firm removed many of its buildings. Along the present canyon highway an old stone wall remains while in the canyon below there is an old rock building as solid and square as it was 50 years ago. Caved in cellars pockmark the canyon sides, while in a side gulch the mine's old powder magazine can still be seen. Today, while autos speed by unaware, New Peerless continues to disintegrate, hidden in a forgotten side canyon.of yesterday.

There are a lot of places like New Peerless. Almost every canyon hides a ghost of some kind. Seek them out, look them over, decide where the picnic grounds were, or the bowery, or the park or school yard. People there lost coins, rings and other valuables just as they do today, except the coins they lost weren't our modern coins that turn black or rust away. Their coins were silver, and some were gold, and whatever they lost is still there. Just waiting. All you have to do is find it. What are you waiting for?

NOLEN

The long forgotten town of Nolen was located 6 miles up canyon from Castle Gate, by the side of the Price River. It was one of the earliest coal camps in the state, settled in 1883 by miners sent to develop the coal fields of central Utah. The origin of its name is now unknown. Most of its mines were dug into the canyon walls right at river level and the waste from them dumped into the river. It solved a problem for its mine owners, but it caused a worse one for people living down stream!

The miners and their families who settled there hoped to build a town and stay, but their hope was a frustrated one, for Nolen wasn't destined for lasting inhabitation. Its mines were located much farther up canyon than were those of its rival camps, and its coal had to be hauled down over the worst kinds of roads. Mine owners found they couldn't compete with coal mined closer to the railroad, and one by one Nolen's mines began to close. And when its mines closed, its people left.

Today a newly completed freeway winds through the canyon bottom while the Price River claims most of the rest. Nolen is little more than a memory now, and there're not many left old enough to remember it. Even its foundations are gone, and it is only with a careful search that its caved mine tunnels can be found. Scarcely a token of Nolen remains.

MOHRLAND
&
THE EMERY PAYROLL CACHE

Emery County's ghost town of Mohrland can be reached by going south from Price to U-122 and following it to Hiawatha. Before the comeback of coal, Price was almost a ghost town itself. From Hiawatha a dirt road leads west for 5 miles to a fork. The right fork leads up canyon 1 mile to the old townsite. When coal was discovered in 1906, miners began a rush for the new strike. Many sent for their families and by 1909 a townsite had been surveyed. The new town was named for the first letter in the names of its four leading promoters: Mays, Orem, Heiner and Rice, to form M-O-H-R-land.

Mohrland soon sported a fine business district, including a new hospital, doctor's office, company boarding house and many new homes. Errol Charlestrom ran the Wasatch Store, a post office was built and several saloons made their appearance. By 1922 Mohrland's population exceeded 1,000, and to serve the growing town, a hotel, theatre, an amusement hall and more than 200 new houses were built. Like many mining camps, Mohrland was divided into several sections where the different nationalities lived. At Mohrland they were called Knob Hill, Centerville and Tippletown. Although it was located at the edge of the desert, Mohrland was not an unpleasant place, for trees shaded its streets and lined the canyon bottom where a small snow-fed stream splashed its way to the dry sandy washes below.

The early 1920's were Mohrland's most prosperous years. Profits began eluding mine owners after that. On March 1st, 1925 Mohrland's mines were closed without notice, leaving a town full of miners without jobs and the wives with no credit at the company store. By summer the town was deserted. After it was abandoned, many of Mohrland's frame buildings were moved to other locations, but its solid rock business houses were left to time and the elements. Today little is left but broken stone walls and foundations half hidden in the head high sage. You may not see any ghosts, but watch out for rattlesnakes!

Some of the first settlers at Mohrland came from Emery, a few miles to the south. Mohrland and Emery were on the old Owlhoot Trail used by long riders like the Wild Bunch, and one day three toughs who had been hanging around Mohrland rode into Emery and started a local legend of buried outlaw gold that is still told today. As the old-timer who told me the tale said, "I can not say how true it may be, I only can tell the tale as it was told to me!"

The old-timer said that back when Mohrland and Emery were busy places a mine payroll was placed in a store safe at Emery, since the town had no bank. But the payroll wasn't there long, for it had hardly been locked up when three toughs rode into town, forced the store keeper to surrender the gold, and raced out of town without a.shot being fired. A quickly organized posse followed the outlaws south across the San Rafael Desert and into the canyon of the Dirty Devil River.

After several days of hard riding the posse and the

outlaws came face to face in a narrow canyon. In the confusion dozens of shots were fired, and when the smoke cleared, two of the outlaws were dead. The third was badly wounded, and was later sent to prison where he died, but not before writing a letter to his sister. He told her that after the robbery, while the posse was still hot on their trail, they came upon an old cabin hidden in a side canyon joining the Dirty Devil River. Knowing they might be caught any minute, they pulled up a cedar post from a corral by the cabin and dropped the gold into the hole, replacing the post as it had been.

For several years the outlaw's sister came from California and searched the desert country south of Mohrland and Emery, trying to find the old cabin, but she finally had to admit that the country was too big and the cabin too small. Before returning to California she told several people who had helped her about the cache, but none of them had any better luck than she. If you plan to look for the Emery payroll cache, you'll have to find an old cabin in a side canyon not far from the Dirty Devil River. And in the San Rafael country, that's a mighty big order!

PEERLESS &
THE NEW FOUND ROBBER'S
ROOST TREASURES

Peerless was without peer as a coal camp in Carbon County, located 3 miles northwest of Helper along the Spring Canyon Road, which turns west near the north end of town. Peerless was settled in 1912, and was named for the Peerless Coal Company. A booming city grew up around the Peerless Mine, and by the First World War years its production reached 2,000 tons of black gold per day. While coal was in strong demand during the war years the town's economy hummed right along. Then the war ended and demand for coal lessened. Every year saw increased use of fuel oil and

The Emery payroll loot is cached near an old cabin built into the cliffs, not far from the Dirty Devil River.

natural gas, causing the town's marginal mines to close. By the 1930's Peerless was a shadow of the camp it had been.

Mine owners at Peerless opened a new mine in Bear Canyon near Royal and built a new town there they called New Peerless, which has already been decribed. Many miners left "old" Peerless for New Peerless. The war years of the 1940's gave Peerless a brief respite, but with the war's end it renewed its downhill slide. Windows were boarded up and doors were locked for the last time. Only a few die-hards remained and in time even they left.

Today many well preserved old buildings remain, many more than 70 years old. One large stone structure still has the famous "Scowcroft's Never Rip" clothing advertisement painted on its west wall. Many other empty buildings and abandoned houses still stand, all very photogenic, making Peerless an adventure for the photographer as well as the ghost-towner. Peerless could also be the start of an adventure in treasure hunting, for back when the Wild Bunch made Price and the Carbon County coal camps their headquarters, Peerless was right on their outlaw trail. Many a long rider stopped to have one for the road at Price after riding down Spring Canyon on their way to hideouts in the San Rafael country. A recently found hideout not far south of old Peerless could be a gold mine for some modern day metal detector equipped treasure hunter.

Nearly every story told about the Wild Bunch tells of their well planned robberies and daring riding escapes to Robbers' Roost. But something that was always puzzling to posses was why they needed a hideout as remote as Robbers' Roost, when there were countless places closer to Price that would have been equally safe from pursuit. Not even the Wild Bunch could have enjoyed that hot, dusty ride 150 miles across the San Rafael Desert from Price to Robbers' Roost! It had long been suspected that they had another hideout much closer to Price, and now it has been found! It's probably the hottest treasure hunting news in years!

After such daring holdups as the payroll robbery at Castle Gate, newspapers often described the gang's flight to Robbers' Roost as a long, hard three day ride. It would take a good rider and a better horse at least a week to cross the San Rafael Desert, cache his loot at Robber's Roost and return to Price, yet on many occasions they would be seen around Price only a day or two later, rested up and riding fresh horses! Lawmen looked for another hideout, but it was never found.

The San Rafael country around Castle Valley, Secret Mesa and the Head of Sinbad is such a wild, broken wasteland of towering vertical sided mesas, bottomless box canyons, jagged cliffs and trackless desert that it was thought that the Wild Bunch's secret hideout would never be found, except by accident. As it turned out, it took luck and an airplane to find it! A secret, known to only a few insiders around Price, can now be told.

A few months ago a local pilot flying north from the canyonlands country spotted an old log cabin atop a nameless mesa, and while making a turn around its vertical cliffs to take a closer look spotted two more. There were no signs of a trail leading to them, and all were built close in among the broken cliffs and twisted cedars. Had the light been at even a slightly different angle he would have never seen them.

The pilot could see not way up the mesa's sheer, vertical cliffs, but he marked it on his topographic map and several weeks later drove a jeep into the area. It took several days of driving sandy washes and exploring dead-end canyons to locate the mesa on the ground. There appeared to be no way up its sides, although he walked 10 miles or more around its base. It took three more trips and several months to figure out how the long riders got to the top.

With binoculars a faint trail can be seen zig-zagging down a steep chimney and onto a narrow ledge, where it appeared to end. It took a hard day of climbing to find where horses' hooves had worn steps into the sandstone as they were led through a narrow crack up onto a shelf-like ledge that led to the mesa top. A vertical cliff rose on one side where a mis-step could send either man or horse hundreds of feet to the rocks below.

The mesa top covered only a few square miles and was yellow with bunch grass and covered with acres of twisted cedar trees and broken crags of sandstone. Several pot holes collected snow and runoff water in deep green pools, enough for a half dozen horses. Although the cedar log cabins had turned silver-gray with age, they were just as they had been left when the Wild Bunch broke up. Except for a cover of gray dust and cobwebs across the windows there was little to indicate that the owners would never return.

Treasure hunters around Price are close-mouthed and aren't saying what has been found, but a lot of turn of the century relics have suddenly turned up in antique shops, including several old pistols reportedly found buried in a dutch oven. And it may only be coincidence, but an unusual number of old silver and gold coins are being sold to dealers from Price to Salt Lake City, Strangely, all of the coins are dated before 1897, the year of the Castle Gate payroll robbery!

The new found Robbers' Roost isn't easy to get to, and a four-wheel-drive vehicle is almost a necessity. Go 26 miles west of Green River on Interstate 70 to where a dirt road turns to the north, and leads up Cottonwood Draw to Buckhorn Wash and on to the dry bed of the San Rafael River. Follow the riverbed northwest as it circles the base of the mesa until you see the old trail under the rimrock. Or you can turn west at Cliff Siding on the D&RGW on US 6-50, 22 miles north of Green River or 45 miles south of Price, and go through Joe's

Hole Wash to the San Rafael. But by either route it's dangerous country, where a lost person or a stranded vehicle might not be found for a long, long time. Take plenty of water and gas, and I'd suggest that you carry a Price Geological Survey Map and a Stinking Springs Quadrangle Map. Even then it wouldn't hurt to pray a little!

A lot of long riders who rode with the Wild Bunch hid out at the outlaw hideout atop the mesa at the edge of Castle Valley, and no doubt many hid caches there. Few if any had the chance to return, so most of the loot they hid is still there. Fred and Bill McCarty were killed during the Delta bank robbery in September, 1893, Joe Walker and "Blue John" Herron were killed near Thompson in 1898 and Jack Moore died in a gunfight that same year at Green River. "Flat Nose" George was shot near Thompson in 1900 while Bill Carver died in a shootout at Sonora, Texas in 1901. Camella Hanks and "Gunplay" Maxwell were both killed in 1902, Hanks in Texas and Maxwell at Price. Harvey Logan, the worst of the lot, committed suicide in 1903, while Ben Kilpatrick was shot to death during an attempted train holdup in 1911. Only Butch Cassidy and the "Sundance Kid" died natural deaths, and there is no reason to believe they ever had a chance to return to the outlaw mesa. If they did, they only recovered their own caches.

There hasn't been time since the hideout's discovery for anyone to search it thoroughly. It would take a treasure hunter months just to check all the possibilities around the old cabins, and there are dozens of other likely spots for a cache; under giant cedars, in wind worn caves, at the foot of rock monuments or a hundred other places that might have caught the eye of an outlaw. If you make your way to the top of the new found Robbers' Roost mesa, look around and try to think like an outlaw. Where would you hide a cache? That's the place to look! Maybe I'll see you there!

SPRING CANYON

Spring Canyon was located 1 mile up canyon from Peerless. When first settled in 1912 it was known as Storrs, for the mine manager, but when a post office was granted several years later it was renamed Spring Canyon for the coal rich canyon it was located in. Jesse Knight, the Mormon Wizard of Knightsville, built Spring Canyon, and even ran his own railroad to it, just as he had at Knightsville. He built 60 modern homes for his miners before the mine began operation. Knight also built the first Mormon Church in the district as well as a modern school, business buildings and water and sewerage systems, something few mining camps had. Many of its beautifully built stone buildings still stand, although they haven't been used in years.

The population of Spring Canyon exceeded 1,000 for many years. After Knight built his railroad into town, the Utah Railroad also laid tracks up the canyon to his mines. For years the railroads shipped as much as a million tons during the town's life. But during the 1940's demand for coal slacked off, and by the mid-50's most of the town's miners had been laid off.

Today, Spring Canyon is one of the most impressive ghost towns the state has to offer, with entire blocks of well built stone buildings still standing. Scores of businesses and rows of abandoned homes line the canyon bottom for a mile or more. Spring Canyon is a photographer's delight, where many hours can be spent taking pcitures or just prowling around its ruins. Don't miss it!

STANDARDVILLE

Standardville, often simply called Standard, was located 5 miles northwest of Helper and 1 mile from Spring Canyon. It was settled in 1911 and was named for the Standard Coal Company. Standardville soon became one of the major coal producing camps of Carbon County and had a business district and homes that were the envy of all its neighbors. The mine owners spared no expense making Standardville a show place, building the most elaborate stores and modern steam heated homes, all surrounded by well kept lawns and shrubbery. It became a standard that other towns tried to match, but which few could better.

From its extensive coal beds miners often dug huge pieces of petrified wood, many of which can still be found where they were thrown over the waste dumps, to the delight of today's rockhounds. But not everything was rosy, for on February 6th, 1930 twenty miners were killed in an explosion at Standardville. Before that, in 1922 a young coal miner named John Tenas was killed

in a gunfight with a Deputy Sheriff over an unpopular Ku Klux Klan meeting. In the riot which followed the killing, a Deputy named Art Webb was also killed. Standardville became an armed camp. In order to stop the riots, Governor Mabey sent a company of state police. Before the fighting finally ended, one of the radical Ku Klux Klan leaders was captured and later sentenced to life imprisonment.

When Standardville's bubble burst during the depression years, the once attractive town quickly faded. By the 1940's all of its easily mined coal was gone. Today, extensive ruins, mostly of great rock buildings, still stand. An empty saloon with a broken bar mirror and a floor strewn with playing cards leans wearily against a large commercial building whose roof has long since caved in. Standardville is every bit as interesting to visit as nearby Spring Canyon, and is a bonanza for shutter-bugs and coin hunters.

LATUDA

The town of Latuda was located 6 miles up Spring Canyon and 1 mile from Standardville. When it was first settled in 1917 it was named for the Liberty Coal Company, but since Utah already had a town named Liberty, postal authorities insisted that another name be chosen. The town's citizens decided to rename their town Latuda, to honor an immigrant coal miner who had become a wealthy mine owner. In 1923, when Latuda was a booming place, a new schoolhouse was built and prosperous looking shops lined its main street. A fine, two story mine office building was built. Its top floor was a hotel for visiting stockholders.

A glorious 4th of July in Standardville, also called Standard. -Utah Historical Society-

They don't give credit at the general store in Mutual anymore.

Today's visitor to Latuda might have good reason to wonder what happened to it all. The Liberty Mine office building is in nearly perfect condition, with carpets on the floor, by all appearances awaiting the next pay day. The polished counter of the payroll office, though a little dusty now, still shines beneath the fancy grillwork of the teller's cage, and in a corner a huge locked safe still hides its unknown treasures. On the mountain front above town the ruins of the old Maple Creek Mine stand guard over the sleeping town below.

In 1927, an avalanche roared down from the mountain, killing two people and wiping out an entire row of company houses. That marked the beginning of the end, for after that the coal veins at Latuda began to pinch out. The 1930's saw Latuda deteriorate, and the 1940's saw it die.

RAINS

The little ghost town that miners once called Rains is located 7 miles from Helper and 1 mile up Spring Canyon from Latuda. It was named for L.F. Rains, a prominent mining engineer of the early 1900's. He had been a grand opera singer before making his fortune in mining. From the years just before the first World War until the late 1940's, Rains was a thriving town. A seemingly unending stream of coal poured from its mines and the mark of prosperity could be seen everywhere. It was a typical company town with all the usual businesses and a double row of 60 company houses lining each side of its main street. Most of the coal mined at Rains came from mines owned by the High Heat Coal Company.

Rains blossomed when the other coal camps in Spring Canyon bloomed, and it faded and died when they did. Most of its mining came to an end by the late 1930's, although one tunnel produced coal for another ten years. The ruins of several large business buildings and many homes remain today, but they are not as extensive as those at Spring Canyon or Standardville.

There are some old wooden coal cars slowly rotting away in the canyon bottom where they were left long ago, while just up canyon there is a strange looking building of uncertain architectural ancestry. Today Rains is a lonely place, maybe even too lonesome for ghosts!

MUTUAL AND LITTLE STANDARD

Empty buildings are all that is left of Mutual, a deserted coal mining camp 8 miles northwest of Helper in Spring Canyon. It was named in 1912 for the Mutual Coal Company. Other mines there included the Day, Vulcan and Western. During its heyday they produced more than 2,000 tons of black gold every day. Its business district was equal in every way to Spring Canyon's or Standardville's, with many buildings three and four stories high.

Spring Canyon forks at Mutual, right where the old Mutual Store still stands, and up the right hand or north fork many fine homes were built, boasting well kept lawns and shade trees. For 30 years Mutual kept its place as the prettiest town in Spring Canyon, but it fared no better than the ugliest, for time and economics claimed them all.

Mutual had a suburb called Little Standard, across the canyon and about 1 mile up the left hand or south fork of Spring Canyon. But unlike the fine stone buildings at Mutual, Little Standard was a poor country cousin town of tents and shacks. One of its tents was so large that it housed a 14 bed bunkhouse, and miners lived there for more than twelve years! When the company mine at Mutual closed in 1938, its residents quickly left their fine homes, but they weren't vacant long, for the families from Little Standard lost no time moving in! But even the mines at Little Standard were worked out by the 1950's, and Mutual was abandoned for good.

Mutual is a favorite place for ghost town photographers, for its impressive buildings make excellent photos, especially the Mutual Store. Most are as solid as the day they were built, although a few are starting to sag. Some road maps still show Mutual's population as 200, but that must include a lot of walking dead. Even with coal making a come-back, only one or two families have returned. You might be pleasantly surprised at what you can find with a metal detector among its old buildings, and don't overlook the old tent town at Little Standard. There are local tales of post-hole banks and miser's caches there. One of them could make your day!

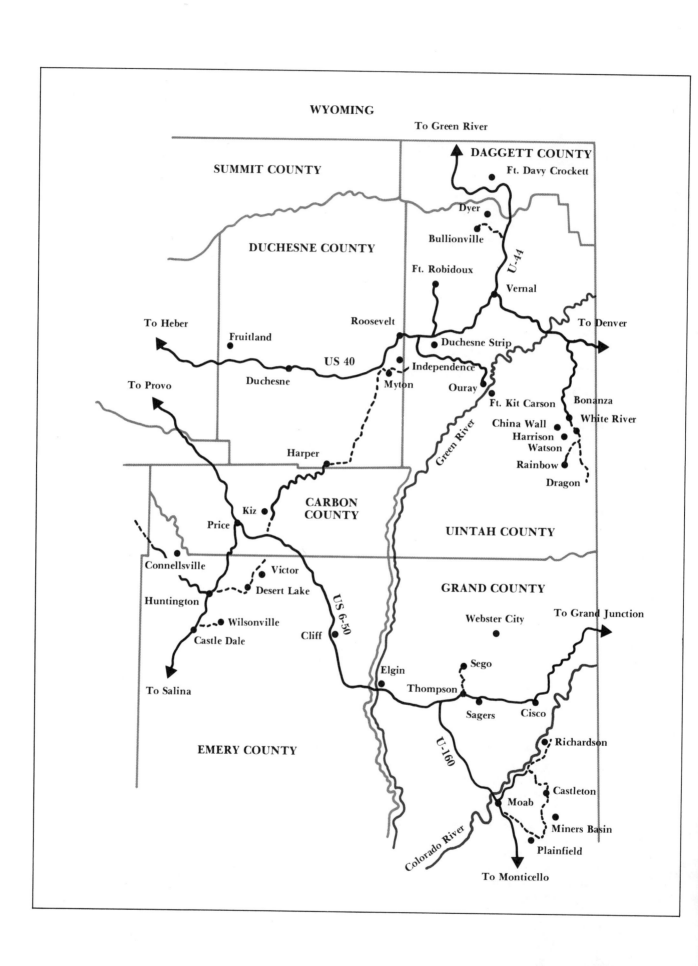

CHAPTER EIGHT

INDIAN COUNTRY

El Dorado! It's somewhere out there in Indian Country. It might be a long lost Spanish mine, or an outlaw cache. Be it a post-hole bank or a much sought ofter relic, it can become your personal El Dorado. The directions are clear, Edgar Allen Poe described them: "Shadow," said he, "Where can it be, this land of El Dorado?" "Over the mountains of the moon, and down into the valley of the shadow, ride, boldly ride," the shade replied, "If you seek for El Dorado!"

Eastern Utah was Indian Country centuries before the first white man explored its high deserts and canyon cut plateaus. Emery and Grand counties make up the southern half while Duchesne and Uintah counties form its northern section. Its first settlers were fur trappers at Fort Robidoux in the north. Mormons at the Elk Mountain Mission initially colonized the southern part. The fur trade died and the Mormons were driven out by Indians, thus it remained Indian Country until prospectors came in search of the Leprechaun's treasure.

The argonauts found gold in the Sierra La Sals and uranium in the desert places of Spanish Valley. They founded placer camps and rough and ready hard rock towns, and even a coal camp or two. Mormon settlers returned and established several farm commun-

ities, but they were exercises in futility, for none survived.

The northern half of Indian Country remained a stronghold of the red man much longer than the southern half, although several "boomer" camps were located within its borders before the reservation was officially opened for settlement. It even boasted a railroad, a fact many present-day residents of the Uinta Basin are unaware of. But the towns the railroad built are gone now, as are the mining camps and farm settlements. Many are hard to find, for Indian Country is a big land of snowcapped peaks, the highest in the state, scorched desert wastes, bottomless canyons and purple mesas, where a day's hike may take you only a mile or two. Don't wait, there's something lost beyond the mountains and deserts. Go and find it. It may be your El Dorado!

DRAGON

The oddly named town of Dragon was located 1 mile from the Colorado state line on Evacuation Creek, a tiny trickle of alkali water in eastern Uintah County. Sam Gilson discovered the strange looking black solidified oil which scientists name Uintaite, but which nearly everyone else called gilsonite in honor of him.

Although Gilson located the black, oily stuff in 1885, the Black Dragon gilsonite mine wasn't in production until 1888. The Dragon Mine camp didn't flourish until 1904 when rails of the narrow gauge Uintah Railway connected it with Mack, Colorado. Gilsonite was used extensively in the manufacture of many things at that time, including phonograph records, stove polish and high grade lacquer paint.

When the Ute Indian Reservation was opened to settlement in 1905, the newly completed railroad was kept busy bringing in homesteaders and land speculators. Dragon became the most important town along its route. Stagecoaches left Dragon daily for the Uinta Basin. With every incoming train bringing more people and every outgoing train heavily loaded with gilsonite. Dragon was a busy place, soon boasting a fine hotel, stores, saloons and well built homes.

The Uintah Railway was the steepest in the world! It crossed 8,500′ Baxter Pass on a 7½ grade with 66 degree curves, crossing 75 bridges in 53 miles! Standard locomotives couldn't climb its extreme grades. Shay-type engines, where every wheel was a driving wheel, had to be specially built. The line wound so sharply that the corners of regular cars hit each other going around curves. In response, cars with round corners were built. On the zig-zag switchbacks the engine would often be going one direction while the caboose passed it going in the opposite direction on the switchback below! The best railroad engineers of the day said

the line could never be built, but old Sam Gilson and his friends didn't know that, so they just went ahead and built it anyway!

For a half dozen years Dragon boomed as the end-of-line town, but in 1911 the rails were pushed 10 miles farther to a new camp named Watson. Dragon continued to be a stable place because the railroad's roundhouse and shops were located there. But its days were numbered. The day was coming when gilsonite would no longer be needed. Although still several years away, the end began when Watson became the end-of-track town.

By 1920 the Black Dragon Mine was pretty well worked out, while better producers were opened at Watson and beyond. Their payrolls gone, Dragon began fading. The saloons were first to go, followed by the general store and the school. Its fine hotel was torn down, leaving only a pile of rubble to mark the site. Today only broken foundations, caved cellars and shells of homes remain. A sidewalk still winds its way to where the schoolhouse had been. The iron rails of the Uintah Railway turned red with rust before they were salvaged for scrap, but by then the last resident had pulled stakes and left. A forlorn little cemetery stands on a barren, windswept ridge above the ruins, but is seldom visited now. You can still climb the hill to the old Black Dragon Mine and peer into its dark caverns, but don't be afraid. Utah's Dragon is dead!

WATSON
HARRISON & CHINA WALL

Watson owed its existence to the Uintah Railway. Settled in 1905, about a year after Dargon hit its peak, Watson was an end-of-track railroad town. It was named for Wallace Watson, the engineer in charge of surveying the railroad's route. As well as being the jumping off place for homesteaders rushing to the Uinta Basin, Watson was an important ore shipping point, where gilsonite from its mines and those at nearby Harrison and China Wall was shipped to the main line Rio Grande at Mack, Colorado.

Harrison was a small mining camp located 9 miles up canyon from Watson. China Wall was a one-mine camp between the two. There were several fine homes at China Wall, including one owned by Mr. Zane, superintendent of the Harrison Mine. Miners' children living at Harrison and China Wall attended school at Watson. A favorite sport of school age children was catching and riding the wild burros that ranged in the rocky canyons above the towns.

Watson claimed many of Dragon's citizens who followed the railroad's terminus. Joseph Gurr owned the hotel at Watson which he later sold to Jack Winkler, while C.E. Eaton ran a general store that had originally been built by Henry Lee, a long-rider with Butch Cassidy, who had a saloon in the same building. Although Watson's life blood was gilsonite, it was

Utah's Dragon is dead!

The narrow gauge Uintah Railway crossing Vat Creek heading for Watson.

common bricks that made it famous.

In 1914 the US Postal Department dropped the cost of parcel post to 1¢ a pound. It didn't take merchants in the Uinta Basin long to realize they could ship goods cheaper by mail than they could by freight. One merchant at Duchesne ordered 50 tons of cement, all boxed in 50 pound packages, the heaviest size mailable by parcel post, but was a piker compared to the Vernal banker, Colthorpe. He had his entire two story brick bank building shipped by mail!

Countless 50 pound packages of brick were mailed from Salt Lake City to Vernal by parcel post. Soon 35 tons of bricks were piled up at the station at Watson, while freight wagons broke down under the heavy loads or sunk into sand until teams couldn't pull them. Thousands of bricks were strung out and piled high all the way from Watson to Vernal. Everyone from mail clerks with aching backs to freight haulers complained to Washington, until mail regulations were changed to prohibit large or unusual packages. But by then Vernal had its new bank building, the only one in the world shipped by mail, and Watson had enjoyed its brief moment of fame.

Three years later the Uintah Railway pushed its rails on to Rainbow, and Watson, like Dragon before it, lost its end-of-track status. Synthetic products began replacing gilsonite, and the end was in sight. In only a few years Watson's name was added to the roll of Utah ghost towns, but while it lasted it was a fun place considering bricks, burros and all. Many old half caved mine buildings and miners' cabins, rock front business buildings and collapsed cellars still remain, but none of them would provide decent shelter today, not even for a ghost!

RAINBOW

The origin of Rainbow's name is as obscure as its beginnings. Located in eastern Uintah County, Rain-

bow was a companion town to Dragon and Watson. Although never much of a town until 1920, gilsonite miners and oil promoters were there long before that. Gilsonite mines were developed by 1900, but Rainbow's star didn't reach its zenith until oil was struck in 1920. That same discovery well is still flowing, one of the longest pumping wells in the state.

The narrow gauge Uintah Railway was built from Watson into Rainbow, winding and twisting its way 4 miles up the mountain side. The old gilsonite mines at Rainbow are still impressive today, and pretty dangerous as well. Many of the gilsonite veins were only two or three feet wide, but they ran vertically and often 2,000' deep. Those narrow, deep and dangerous mined out veins snake their way across the mountains, and woe to anyone who should fall in, for there would be no chance of getting out.

One result of the technology represented by the oil exploration was that by the time Rainbow boomed, motor trucks began replacing the narrow gauge railroad, just as autos had replaced horses. Railroad owners had hoped to push their line into Vernal, but the mountainous terrain gave trucks much greater versatility. Hence, it became a railroad no one needed, 100 miles from nowhere.

The oil and gilsonite easily outlasted the town, for almost nothing remains of Rainbow today. Rubble foundations and forgotten cabins half hidden among the cedars hide artifacts from Rainbow's past, where a metal detector has probably never been seen. A weathered sign by the side of the abandoned railroad grade can hardly be read. But there is one word on it. Rainbow!

Gilsonite miners stacking sacks of black gold at Rainbow.

WHITE RIVER

The old log cabins at White River, silver-gray with age, stand alone along a high ridge above the crossing of the White River in Uintah County. But just before the turn of the century, they weren't weathered or old, and they weren't alone either. In those days White River was a busy town, a stage station and planned end-of-track town between Watson and Vernal. The Uintah Railway's official name for it was Ignacio, but few people ever called it that. From White River the stage road climbed through a deep, narrow canyon and wound across desert and mesa country to the Bonanza Mine and Kennedy Station; then on to the ferry across the Green River, at what was known as Alhandra, and on to Vernal.

Gilsonite mining at nearby Harrison and China Wall helped White River keep going when the railroad changed its plans to build its line there. But when the Uinta Basin had been subdivided, and land hungry homesteaders no longer rode the Uintah Railway and the stage line beyond, White River ceased to be. Today there is a group of deserted houses, built more recently than those of White River's heyday, strung out along the north side of the river. But it is the weathered row of tired looking log cabins which stands at the edge of the high bluff above the south side of the river that marks the site of White River, one of the Uinta Basin's last frontier towns.

20 miles east of Vernal on US-40, state road U-45 turns south to the Bonanza Mine. From there it is only 3½ miles to White River, down a steep, narrow canyon which shouldn't be entered if cloudbursts threaten. If you can decide which of its old cabins was the stage station, or perhaps a saloon, you could have good luck with a detector. The dirt road beyond leads to Watson and Dragon. But be sure to leave before sundown, for that's when the gilsonite ghosts come out!

SEGO & WEBSTER CITY
& ITS OUTLAW CACHES

The Grand County coal camp of Sego was located 5 miles north of Thompson at the end of a narrow dirt road, which twists and winds its way up canyon, following the grade of an abandoned railroad. In its climb up the canyon the road crosses nine wooden bridges, most of which are pretty shaky, and should be carefully checked before crossing. Sego once produced a good grade of anthracite coal, not unlike that found in Pennsylvania. The first discoveries were made by Harry Ballard, and the original camp was named for him. When Ballard sold out to the American Fuel Company, the growing town was renamed Neslin, for the mine's general manager.

The new owners built a fine rock store building, company houses and a bachelor boarding house. An impressive two story hotel was next, and was followed by other new businesses. But Neslin's management led

There are a lot of unfound treasures around the old outlaw town of Webster City.

the company into financial troubles and he was fired. To get the town off to a fresh start it was renamed Sego, for the Utah state flower. Prosperous times returned temporarily when the Utah Grand Coal Company took over and added more homes and hired more miners. But it was poor timing, for they didn't foresee the coming of diesel engines, which sounded the death knell for coal.

The old two story hotel still stands, and even retains a touch of its former glory. But time has not been so kind to the general store across the street. Only its rock walls remain, and they are frail and cracked. Just below the townsite, on a bare and windy ridge, there is an old cemetery. A bouquet of faded plastic flowers by a weathered wooden cross seems strangely out of place. Still farther down canyon, ancient Indian petroglyphs are carved on the sandstone walls of the canyon, left there centuries before white men searched the canyon for mineral wealth.

Although it has been many years since Sego was abandoned, smoke still issues from its deserted mine shafts, the product of underground fires which have burned for decades. In places they have burned close to the surface, creating a deadly trap for the unwary.

The strangest thing about Sego's mines were the dinosaur tracks found at many places in the coal beds. One set measured 53″ in length and were 32″ wide! Examples are now preserved at Pennsylvania State College and at the American Museum Of Natural History. There are no dinosaurs in Sego today!

Something relic hunters shouldn't overlook is the policy mine owners had of letting Sego's miners build cabins wherever they wanted instead of requiring them to live in company houses. All along the canyon and its side gulches you can find places where cabins or shacks were built. Under high ledges, dugouts where less fortunate miners and their families lived can be spotted. All sorts of things were lost or discarded wherever people lived. But watch where you step, for if you see a wisp of smoke seeping from the ground, back up quickly. It could be one short step to hell!

High in the Book Cliffs north of Sego, in a canyon accessible only by foot or horseback, stand the crumbling remains of Webster City, the outlaw town of the Book Cliffs. During the 1880's many British syndicates purchased western ranch lands, one of which was the Webster City Cattle Company. Far back in the Book Cliffs they built a log-cabin ranch-town for their cowboys. It boasted a combination commissary and saloon, so large that dances were held there almost every weekend. They also built a school for employees' children and a large first class boarding house with a dining room, known as the Webster City Hotel.

Webster City might not have been as large or important as some towns, but it was as wild as any, with long riders from a dozen outlaw bands making it a stop along the Owlhoot Trail. Fights and even a few shoot-outs kept things lively, for there was no law closer than Vernal, two days hard ride away. No doubt more than a few post-hole banks and shallow caches were left behind by men who cashed in their chips before the game was finished. It should be a great place to hunt for coins and caches hidden in the 1880's. Your best bet is to inquire about the roads at Vernal, for the old town can't be reached from Sego. It's near the head of Willow Creek on the Hill Creek Indian Reservation, but flash floods change trails every time it rains, so ask for last minute directions and be prepared to hike, for it's beyond the end of the trail. Good luck!

CONNELSVILLE

Connelsville was located 15 miles east of Fairview, in Coal Canyon, near the head of Huntington Canyon in Emery County. Back in the 1870's and 80's it was a busy place. One of the characters who lived there when things were booming was Sam Hill, Manager of the Bear Creek Mine, and a deputy sheriff. One summer several sheepherders used the creek up canyon from the town to water their flock, in spite of continued pleas from the townspeople who drank the creek water. Finally a complaint was made to the sheriff, and a warrant of arrest was sent for Hill to serve.

Now, Sam Hill was a hard working and conscientious deputy, but he couldn't read! Still, it had been explained to him what the warrant said, so he went to the sheep camp, took the warrant from his pocket and appeared to study it closely for several minutes, then informed the herders that they were under arrest. "Good hell man!" one of them said, "You can't arrest us with that piece of paper, why you can't even read it! You're reading it upside down!" Before the herders knew what was happening, Hill drew his six-shooter, aimed it dead center, and answered, "I don't give a damn if its upside down, sideways or backwards! No matter how I hold it, it says you're under arrest!" And by heck, they were!

Besides Sam Hill's Bear Creek Mine, there were the New York, Deer Creek and Deseret coal mines at Connellsville. It was named for another coal mining town in Pennsylvania, and was essentially a company town, built by the Fairview Coal & Coke Company. Several of the old log buildings built 100 years ago still stand, even if they sag a little now. In the canyon just below them are the ruins of three beehive shaped coke ovens. The half-mile long trail to old Connellsville starts at a still used log cabin at the mouth of Coal Canyon, at the head of Huntington Canyon, right on the Emery/Sanpete County line.

DESERT LAKE
&
THE LOST LOOT OF THE WILD BUNCH

The farm town of Desert Lake was settled near Cedar Mountain 6 miles east of Cleveland in Emery County, in 1885 when John Thayne, W.J. Powell, and Thomas and Samuel Wells built a dam to store irrigation water. There were only a dozen or so houses throughout the 80's, then it picked up and soon there was a new school and church and Silas Winder was operating a general store. At that time the Desert Lake townsite was described as beautiful, surrounded by shade trees and produced an abundance of crops.

Then in 1896 the dam broke and many of the settlers lost their homes and farms in the raging flood waters. But the dam was rebuilt, and the settlement continued growing. By 1898 the school housed 45 students and additional lots were being surveyed. A post office was granted, but its days were destined to be short. The lake behind the settlers' dam was the cause of its namesake's unplanned end.

The lake raised the water level of the surrounding countryside, bringing concentrations of underground minerals to the surface. By 1910 the land had soured and glaring patches of white alkali began spreading over the land. It didn't take the alkali long to ruin the land and soon left Desert Lake a deserted village. A large two story house still stands, surrounded by corrals and out-buildings which will never be used again. The farm houses that dot the alkali marshland around the lake are the ghosts of Desert Lake today.

If Butch Cassidy had cached all the loot old-timers say he did, he would have been kept busy just digging holes! Most of the stories told about his buried caches are simply that, stories, but a few are true. One that is concerns the unsigned money from the Wilcox, Wyoming train robbery.

At 2:18 AM, June 2nd, 1899 the Wild Bunch robbed the Union Pacific's Overland Flyer near Wilcox, taking $30,000 in gold and $60,000 in paper money. The gang escaped across the line into Utah, a few stopping at Brown's Hole and the rest riding hell-for-leather to Robber's Roost in Wayne County. The paper money taken at Wilcox proved to be nearly worthless. The bills were unsigned, and required the signature of the officials at the banks they were destined for.

Banks throughout the west were notified to watch for the unsigned money. Trying to spend it soon got several of the gang arrested. Some of it was spent with forged signatures, but most of it was buried in the hope that it could be more easily spent after excitement over the robbery died down. Elza Lay told Queen Ann Bassett that he buried his share at Brown's Hole, and George Curry reportedly cached his in Desolation Canyon near the Green River. If any of those bills are ever recovered they would no longer be negotiable, but they would still be of great value to collectors, worth many times their face value.

There are also stories that Cassidy hid part of the nearly $9,000 in gold taken during the mine payroll holdup at Castle Gate on April 21st, 1897. Some believe it is hidden at the gang's hideout at Robber's Roost, others say it is hidden on Sid's Mountain 15 miles straight south of Desert Lake. An old outlaw cabin was found there recently, and several small caches recovered.

No doubt there are many caches hidden at Hole In The Wall, Brown's Hole, Robber's Roost and points in between. Many of the Wild Bunch's robberies were spectacular, like the $65,000 robbery of the Great Northern Railroad, $60,000 from the Union Pacific, $30,000 from the Winnemucca bank and $7,000 from both the Castle Gate and Montpelier holdups. The loot was divided up between a half dozen or more men on each "job," and not all of them lived to spend their shares. They all had to cache part of their shares at one time or another, for none was fool enough to open a bank account! They just didn't think their money was safe in banks!

There's no question that there's outlaw loot still buried along the Owlhoot Trail that ran from Brown's Hole past Price, Desert Lake and Hanksville to Robber's Roost. Many caches were never recovered, their owners buried in nameless graves all along it. So if you get a good lead, go for it. Even a few gold coins would be worth a small fortune now, and who knows, maybe you'll hit the big casino!

VICTOR

Victor, located 5 miles southeast of Elmo in Emery County, was born when Desert Lake died. When alkali began ruining farms at Desert Lake, new land was sought. Manassa Blackburn, who had been a school teacher at Desert Lake, was one of the first to move to the new site of Victor in 1896. Victor grew at about the rate Desert Lake died. Blackburn's new town soon claimed a school, church and post office. In 1908 O.B. Cooley opened a general store.

All ghost towns result from an intractable problem or great calamity that its residents cannot overcome. In this arid country the desire to live atop water ruined many settlements because of the resulting erosion. Victor suffered from the more common affliction, lack of water. At Victor sand dunes continually threatened farms, drifting over fences and burying crops. Farmers waged a never ending battle against the dunes, which eventually drove many away. When their Bishop gave up and left, most of the weary settlers soon followed. Many moved to Elmo, a new town started in 1909.

Within only a few years sand dunes reclaimed the farms at Victor. Here and there pointed roofs of long abandoned farm houses, their lower half buried in sand, stick up above the head high sage. Its old school-

Century old cottonwoods stand guard over the ghost town of Desert Lake.

house stands on a parched alkali plain. In the shadow of a low cliff just to the northeast is the loneliest graveyard in Utah, a forlorn reminder of the hope that was once Victor's. Victor, like Desert Lake, was astradddle the old outlaw trail, so in addition to the relics to be found among its forgotten homesteads, there is the same chance of cashing in on an outlaw cache. You'll never know if you don't try.

Who knows what secrets the Icebox Cave hides?

WILSONVILLE
&
THE OUTLAW CACHE AT SWAZEY'S CABIN

Nestled in a deep, narrow canyon 5 miles east of Castle Dale, the county seat of Emery County, stand the lonely, sun-burned ruins of Wilsonville. The now forgotten little town was settled in 1878 on the Gunnison Trail, a 250 mile mail line from Salina, Utah to Ouray, Colorado. It was named for Sylvester Wilson, one of the first settlers and town postmaster. A large log schoolhouse served as a dance hall on Saturday nights.

Wilsonville was located on Cottonwood Creek near its confluence with the San Rafael River. Although small, it was the most important town in Emery County; the officials at the county seat had to send a rider to Wilsonville to get their mail. When the Rio Grande Railroad was built into Castle Valley, it

signalled the end of Wilsonville, for locomotives could carry the mail faster than pony riders.

Wilsonville was a pretty little oasis in the desert, and as long as the Gunnison Trail was used by mail carriers and other travelers it was an important place, but when the trail fell out of use, it began to die. Its school closed and the post office and churchhouse were moved to Castle Dale. Only a few seldom used buildings owned by a local ranch remain to mark its site. On a hillside there is a little cemetery with five neglected graves, while farther down canyon there are two more, without head stones to mark them. A local legend claims those are outlaw graves, and that the long riders buried their cached gold close by, not far from Wilsonville.

The San Rafael Reef is outlaw country. It was tough country a hundred years ago, and it's tough country now; not a place to run out of gas, or water. Tom McCarty and his band of bank robbers holed up there, as did Indian Ed, Silvertip, Blue John, Jack Wright and Jack Moore. Butch Cassidy's Wild Bunch crisscrossed its lonely miles many times. Probably all of them cached loot there at one time or another. But none stayed long enough to call its desert wastes home, except a few who are buried there. None, that is, until the Swazey brothers arrived, and they came to stay.

Joe Swazey carved his initials in Coal Wash in 1874, and it wasn't long before brothers Sid, Charlie and Jack joined him. Joe and Sid were big men, over 200 pounds of solid muscle each, while Charlie was tall and thin. Jack was an adopted brother, and full blooded Indian. Sid had the reputation of being a bad one to tangle with, and at times rode with the Wild Bunch. But all of the brothers were hard cases.

The Swazeys discovered a seep spring in a narrow slit in the sandstone cliffs, where the ice cold dripping water kept the cave cool even during the hottest summer day. They called it the ice cave and hung a meat pole inside where fresh beef was kept hanging for cowboys and long riders alike. Next to the cave they built a hidden corral and sturdy log cabin. There were towering cliffs on two sides of the cabin while behind it was a bottomless canyon. Miles of unbroken desert to the north made it a perfect hideout for men on the dodge.

Every outlaw crossing the San Rafael country stopped at Swazey's cabin. What stories those old log walls could tell of long riders, posses, hidden loot and treasure chests! Many a long rider cached his gold in a shallow hole before riding up to Swazey's cabin, and more than a few of them never rode away again. Their nameless graves are hidden in unknown canyons, their caches hidden in forgotten places in sight of Swazey's cabin.

The recently completed interstate highway from Green River to Fremont Junction has opened the San Rafael and Sinbad Desert country to treasure hunters for the first time. 34 miles west of Green River a faint trail leads south. It forks many times, most branches leading to petrified wood diggings, but a fork to the west that crosses a deep sand wash leads to Swazey's cabin. Its hard to find, hidden as it is in a heavy stand of cedar trees. The ice cave, now sometimes called the refrigerator cave, is just a short hike beyond. The old meat pole put there by the Swazeys remains.

With places with strange names like Secret Mesa, Devil's Canyon, Cliff Dweller's Flat and The Head Of Sinbad surrounding it, Swazey's cabin is a scary place to camp overnight. Ghosts of men who died along the trail keep a lonely vigil, and they're not friendly to those who seek their treasures!

FRUITLAND &
THE LOST JOSEPHINE MINE ON
CURRANT CREEK

Fruitland, in Duchesne County, was settled in 1907 by a group of more than one hundred well-educated and prominent people from Nebraska, most of them professionals in search of a place to start a perfect community. They located their town 3 miles west of the present Fruitland post office, 25 miles west of Duchesne City. Many of their log houses can be seen from the highway where they stand not far from a more modern ranchhouse and several house trailers. When the first group of settlers arrived from Nebraska, they named their new home on Dead Ox Flat, Rabbit Gulch, but when a post office was granted to the growing community two years later it was renamed Fruitland, because the area was expected to be a fruitful place.

Fruitland's 7,000' elevation proved to be anything but fruitful, and the settlers despaired of ever growing crops where frosts were common every month of the year. Most were unfamiliar with farming and the hard life they had committed themselves to. It was only a few years before they began leaving, many moving to Canada where they started a new settlement not dependant upon farming. The cedar covered, red clay hills they left behind were better suited to stock raising than to farming, thus Fruitland is now a ranch area, where cattle graze peacefully among sagging cabins built three fourths of a century ago.

Fruitland was built on the Old Spanish Trail followed by Father Escalante in 1776 and by Spanish miners and explorers before him. Early explorers and settlers discovered many old prospect holes and mines left by the Spaniards. One of the most fascinating is only a few miles from Fruitland on Currant Creek.

"An old mine found near Currant Creek is thought to be the long lost Josephine Mine!" So proclaimed headlines in Heber City's *Wasatch Wave* in 1908, "Ancient picks and other tools have been uncovered, and ore values are sensational!," it continued.

Local residents were undoubtedly excited, especially if they'd forgotten the earlier reports by the *Wave* in 1897 of the discovery of the same Lost Josephine

"near the shores of a mountain lake, where the ruins of an ancient arrastra have been found." At that time, ore values were sensational as well.

No researcher questions that the Lost Josephine Mine existed in early day Utah, and most believe it was somewhere in the Henry Mountains, but periodic reports have placed its re-discovery everywhere from the Escalante Desert to the Uintah Mountains. And no wonder, it had been the most sought after lost mine of all time. But the reported finding on Currant Creek was special, because there was no doubt a Spanish mine of considerable importance had been discovered. I have listened to lost mine stories at old mining camps, along desert trails and around camp fires, but the story of the Currant Creek Josephine came to me first hand from an old man in a rest home, and he ought to know, for he was there!

George Olson of Heber City was one of the men who reopened the mine on Currant Creek, and he recalled it for me many years ago. It is a strange story. Olson stated that after its discovery, some Provo City businessmen provided the funds to hire a small crew of miners, and they opened the badly caved tunnel for 125' into the mountain. Many ancient, strange looking tools and relics were found, but from the size of the waste dump it looked like a long and dangerous dig to reach the tunnel's end. When Olson and his crew ran out of supplies the investors were reluctant to spend any more until the mine produced some ore, so one of the businessmen devised a scheme to satisfy them.

A quantity of gold nuggets was obtained and used to salt the mine. The investors were taken to Currant Creek so they could see for themselves the wonderful ore that had been found. The businessmen were convinced to put up the money required. But several of them were Olson's friends. He refused to let them be taken in, and exposed the swindle. With the fraud public, work stopped and the tunnel was never reopened to its original depth. It has caved in again since 1908 and today large aspen trees grow in its portal.

12 miles up Currant Creek Canyon from US-40 a steep, rocky road climbs 3½ miles to the east to where some towering red ledges can be seen. A half mile hike through an aspen grove reveals the old mines, that appear as almost invisible scars on the mountainside. Mounds of dirt and rotted logs show where cabins once stood, and mine dumps overgrown with brush and trees testify to the great labor expended by those unknown miners of long ago. Remember, the tunnels and dumps were old at the turn of the century.

George Olson and his miners never learned what was at the tunnel's end, and they only tried to open one tunnel. There are two tunnels close together. The Spanish miners of long ago know what is there but their ghosts aren't telling!

BULLIONVILLE
&
THE MINE OF LOST SOULS

In June, 1880 the Carbonate Mining District was organized by a group of miners who had gathered at the Vortex Cafe at Ashley Center, now Vernal in Uintah County. Only a month later, on July 3rd, the town of Bullionville was surveyed near the head of Brush Creek, 27 miles north of Vernal. In early issues of the *Vernal Papoose* the new town was sometimes referred to as the Bullion Townsite. Although a mining camp, there often were more outlaws than miners there, for it was only a few miles from Brown's Hole, a hideout often used by men on the dodge.

Bullionville's mines weren't all that rich, but when the famous Dyer Mine was discovered only 4 miles to the north in 1887, business picked up, and when gold strikes were made near Gilbert's Peak in 1894 and at Marsh Peak in 1897 it got still another boost. Outlaws from Brown's Hole rubbed elbows at the bar with miners, and more than once gunshots echoed from behind its swinging doors. Some of Bullionville's ore was hauled all the way to Park City, but most of it was taken by teams over Carter Road, a corduroy road built over the 13,000' Uinta Mountains to Carter, Wyoming. Ore would be stockpiled during the summer and hauled in the winter, because sleds could be pulled much easier than ore wagons.

Although several of Bullionville's mines contained high grade copper ore, most of its diggings were shallow, so when the gold strikes in the Uintas fizzled and the nearby Dyer Mine closed, Bullionville folded up like a house of cards. It never was more than a camp of log cabins and frame buildings. Over the years the high mountain winters have wreaked their vengeance on it, almost as if nature wanted to erase its scar from her face. Only a few caved and rotted cabin walls hidden by the encroaching pines and a board sidewalk that leads to nowhere prove that men once lived and worked at Bullionville. A half century and more before Bullionville, Spanish pack trains carried heavy loads of silver bullion from the Uintas. Miners at Bullionville found evidence of their passing, rusted tools, lost spurs and an ornate sword, but they never found their mines, for they didn't have enough information.

If you haven't all the pieces to a jug-saw puzzle, the picture isn't complete. Long ago, before the Indian uprising that drove the Spaniards from the mountains and burned the old forts of the Uinta Basin, a rich silver mine was worked in a canyon whose landmarks were peculiar to that canyon only. Most of the miners were killed and their bodies thrown into mine shafts. Only a few managed to escape, one of them a small girl who, with a few others, made her way to the Spanish settlements in New Mexico.

Years later, as a very old woman, she recalled the terrible battle, and the dead miners whose souls would never be saved. She called the old mine in the Uintas where the miners' bodies were hidden, the Mine Of Lost Souls. She still remembered the mine and the landmarks near it. There is only one place that matches her description, and that is on the Dry Fork of Ashley Creek, northwest of Vernal.

The old woman recalled that the mine was located on one side of a high point of land where two streams came together. One of the streams sunk into a swirling sink hole, leaving its bed dry until it resurfaced several miles downstream. There was a natural stone bridge that spanned a side canyon, and not far from the bridge, a cave where some of the miners lived. The mine was not very far from the cave. As a young girl she and her mother had been picking berries near the stone bridge when the Indians attacked and killed the miners and covered their shafts and tunnels.

From Maeser, 3 miles west of Vernal, follow Dry Fork upstream. Pass the Red Cloud Loop Road and continue past an old ranch. About 17 miles from Maeser the road forks to each side of a high point of land where two streams come together. The rocky road to the left goes only a short way. After a half mile a stone bridge spanning a side canyon to the right can be seen. Another half mile or so farther on there is a thick stand of brush. Hidden in it is the mouth of a cave, exactly like the old woman described it.

Be careful if you crawl into the cave, for it narrows to no bigger than a man's body, and then drops into a bottomless abyss. At the end of a mile hike upstream there is a swirling sink-hole, where Dry Fork disappears. Below the sink-hole the stream bed is dry, but if you put your ear to its bed you can hear water flowing beneath it.

The clues are complete, the old woman's waybill was correct, the point of land, the two creeks, the stone bridge, the cave and the sink-hole. And the mine is not far from the cave. It should be pretty easy to find... but it isn't!

DYER
&
THE LOST EWING MINE

Dyer was a copper mining camp built around the workings of the Dyer Mine, 4 miles north of Bullionville. At its peak Dyer claimed more than 100 miners and their families, and an additonal 30 families living at the camp's smelter site 2 miles to the northwest, on Anderson Creek. The Dyer Mine operated from 1887 through 1900, producing more than $3,000,000 worth of high grade copper. Its ore was shipped to the railroad at Carter, Wyoming and to the huge Marsac Mill at Park City, 150 miles by rough wagon road across the Ute Indian Reservation.

Pick Murdock, a full-blooded Indian, discovered

Forgotten cabins in the pines are all that remain of Dyer on the trail to the Lost Ewing Mine.

the Dyer Mine, but sold it to Lewis Dyer. Dyer had no money left to develop the mine so he sold an interest to a Salt Lake City banker named Gates, for $30,000. After receiving the money, Dyer apparently had second thoughts about the hardships of mining and left for parts unknown, leaving Gates to run the mine. Although its location was terribly isolated, the camp which grew up near the mine thrived for several years. Since it was close to Bullionville, the same toughs who hung out there frequented Dyer also.

Dyer was basically a one-mine camp, and when the mine closed, the little town it supported failed also. Today, only a few sagging log cabins remain, their vacant windows staring like empty eye sockets in some giant skull. When the Carbonate Mining District was organized in 1880, one of its by-laws stated, "No Chinaman shall be tolerated in the district." There are no Chinamen at Dyer today, nor anyone else for that matter!

Almost anyone can tell you where to look for the Lost Ewing Mine, but no one knows where it is! All you have to do is go to Jesse Ewing Canyon on the Green River in Brown's Hole and locate Ewing's old cabin. Actually there are three cabins, and his grave is near one of them. There's also a 1,500' tunnel he dug, but that's not his lost mine, only a low grade copper working. Jesse Ewing's lost mine is somewhere close by, but it's still lost.

In the spring of 1868 Ewing rode a raft down the Green River into Brown's Hole, long before it became an outlaw hideout. He stopped to prospect and discovered an outcrop of copper ore in a steep canyon that later became Jesse Ewing Canyon. He was a powerful man, kin to the old-time mountain men. One who knew him well said that he never saw him wear a coat in a country where temperatures were often 40° below

zero! Ewing thrived on hard work and lost no time driving a long tunnel into the solid rock canyon side.

But Ewing was not a friendly man, and avoided company. A grizzly bear had clawed his face, leaving him "the ugliest man in the mountains!" A miner, who knew him for years, called Ewing "an odd freak of humanity who cared little for his own life and even less for others!" Ewing had one habit that bothered other miners and prospectors. He liked to take in new mining partners, work them till they fell, and then kill them!

Ewing would talk someone into becoming his partner, always someone with money to invest in his mine, and preferably one who was a hard worker. But when his new partner's money was gone, Ewing would pick an argument and drive him off, and if they wouldn't leave he'd kill them. He shot several partners, knifed another and even poisoned one.

But one who Ewing never got the best of was Pick Murdock, the full-blooded Indian, who discovered the Dyer Mine and was sometimes a partner of Caleb Rhoades of Lost Rhoades Mine fame. He was also, incidentally, the author's great-uncle. Ewing gave Murdock some pieces of nearly pure copper ore heavily laced with gold to entice him, but Murdock knew what had happened to Ewing's other partners and declined the honor. Instead, he sent a young outlaw named Duncan to help him. Duncan was different than Ewing was used to, and when he tried to run him off, Duncan grabbed Ewing's rifle and blew his head off with it. Duncan was already wanted by the law so he fled the country, taking Ewing's common-law wife with him. Other miners buried Ewing on a little hill near his cabin.

After Ewing's death, Pick Murdock showed mining men around Vernal the chunk of gold ore Ewing had given him, where it caused great excitement. No.

one had ever seen anything quite like it, almost pure copper shot through and edged with lacy gold. Some claimed later that the ore actually came from the Dyer Mine which Murdock had discovered, but the ores were entirely different. To settle the argument, Murdock let an assayer test both ores. While ore from the Dyer Mine was rich, assaying several hundred dollars in copper, Ewing's chunk of ore went $5,000 to the ton, mostly in gold!

Pick Murdock was a knowledgeable mining man, having made discoveries at Park City, on the Ute Reservation and with Caleb Rhoades. He certainly didn't believe Ewing's ore came from the same formation as that at the Dyer Mine, for he spent much of the rest of his life looking for Ewing's Mine. But still people will tell you it shouldn't be hard to find, just go up Jesse Ewing Canyon and . . .

DUCHESNE STRIP
&
THE BURIED GOLD OF THE RED SASH GANG

The string-town known as the Duchesne Strip, located 3 miles east of Fort Duchesne in Uintah County was a no man's land. When the Ute Indian Reservation was created in 1861, a narrow strip of land was left unattached to either the reservation or the county, and as a result there were no provisions for either government or law enforcement in the strip. When Fort Duchesne was built, it didn't take long for outlaws of every kind to take advantage of its refuge. Saloons and gambling halls ran 24 hours a day, liquor was sold to all, including Indians, and every kind of vice flourished.

Elza Lay, one of Butch Cassidy's lieutenants in the Wild Bunch, was in partnership with Henry Lee, another tough nut, in one of the strips worst gambling-hell saloons. County records contain the names of at least 16 men who were killed in gunfights in the strip, but several times that number were actually killed in shoot-outs there in Lay's saloon. An Indian gunfighter named Tabby Weep once faced three desperados in a gun fight and killed them all!

Besides saloons there was a large dance hall, a hotel, blacksmith shop, stage-line and telegraph office as well as several mining company offices. Between the strip and Fort Duchesne there was a trail that passed through Bottle Hollow, a place where soldiers from the fort cached bottles of whiskey and went on drunks, liquor not being allowed at the fort. For many years relic hunters collected those old bottles where they had been thrown away 100 years before, but now a man-made lake, appropriately named Bottle Hollow, covers its site.

In 1887 Adolphus Busch, of Budweiser Beer fame, purchased the St. Louis gilsonite mine which was located within the strip's boundaries, and his miners added even more wild life to the outlaw town. Several violent explosions occurred at Busch's mine, each one claiming many lives. It was finally closed in 1904 after a particularly tragic explosion. It all came to an end in 1905 when the Ute Reservation was opened to homesteading and the strip was included, bringing law at last to no man's land. Gambling halls and saloons were closed, the outlaws left for safer havens and the strip became only a bad memory. About 3 miles east of Fort Duchesne, close by present Gusher, a pile of stones that was once a general store still stands in the sage, all that's left of Duchesne Strip.

Among the outlaws and hard cases who holed up on the strip were Matt Warner, Cleophas Dowd, Isom Dart and Harry Tracy, all killers of the worst kind. Another, not so well known but just as bad, was "Red Bob," leader of the notorious Red Sash Gang, long riders who were the predecessors of the Hole In The Wall Gang and the Wild Bunch. Red Bob buried a gold cache in the Uinta Mountains, not far from Duchesne Strip, in Sheep Creek Canyon. There may be more, but there's $85,000 for sure.

The Red Sash Gang robbed the Union Pacific mail car of $85,000 in gold near Bryan Station, Sweetwater County, Wyoming in 1898 and rode across the state line into Utah. Few people know much about the Red Sash Gang, but it was a loose knit band of rustlers and train robbers started by outlaw Nate Champion about 1890. After Champion was killed at the Hole In The Wall the gang saw a series of leaders, all worse than the one before, ending up with a roughneck known only as Red Bob. The gang members all wore red sashes around their waists, hence their name.

Three jumps ahead of the posse, the five man gang bypassed Manila and entered the mountains at Long Park, heading for the safety of the strip. Several cowboys later recalled that when the outlaws passed Long Park they were still leading the pack horse which carried the robbery loot. They dropped into Sheep Creek

This posse wiped out the Red Sash gang, and with them, the clues to their buried treasure.

Canyon where Cleophas Dowd, an outlaw turned rancher, traded fresh horses to them. But they didn't trade or unload the pack horse. It was later found where the outlaws turned it loose, between Dowd's ranch and the head of Sheep Creek, where a second posse from Burnt Fork, Wyoming met them. That wasn't quite fair from the outlaw's point of view, for posses were supposed to stop at the state line. But one thing everyone agreed on afterwards was that the pack horse had been relieved of its heavy load and turned loose before then.

The outlaws were trapped between two posses at Dowd's Hole. Caught in a deadly cross fire, three outlaws were killed and one badly wounded. He later died in jail. Red Bob was sent to prison for life, which in his case wasn't very long. He died soon after of tuberculosis. Since he knew he was going to die in prison, Red Bob drew a map showing where the gold was buried, and gave it to another inmate named Turner. After he was released, Turner followed Red Bob's map to Long Park, Dowd's ranch and Sheep Creek Canyon, but he couldn't match reference points on the map with the cache.

Several of the posse members as well as Pinkerton detectives working for the Union Pacific searched for the outlaw loot, knowing it had to be somewhere between Dowd's ranch and Long Park, where the gang was caught. Dowd might have had some idea where the loot was hidden, but had no reason to look for it. It was common knowledge that he had several substantial caches of his own hidden somewhere near his ranch. Dowd was a character, an occasional outlaw and confidant of Butch Cassidy and Tom Horn. But even if Dowd had had an interest in the outlaw gold, he wouldn't have had much chance to look for it, since he was killed only two months later by Charlie Reaser, an outlaw neighbor he had had trouble with for years.

There's at least $85,000 in gold buried in a shallow hole somewhere near Dowd's Park in Sheep Creek Canyon. There may be a lot more than that, for no one knows how much Dowd himself buried, and it's all worth many times its face value now. If you want it, it's yours, all you have to do is go get it. It won't do Cleophas Dowd or Red Bob any good now!

INDEPENDENCE

In 1905 a brand new town was born on Dry Creek near its junction with the Duchesne River, 4 miles southeast of Myton and almost on the Duchesne-Uintah county line. It was named for the Independence Townsite & Development Company. The Ute Indian Reservation had just been opened to homesteading, and Independence was one of the new towns started by the modern pioneers. A number of substantial homes were built and a trading company store was established by the development company, But Independence had two strikes against it right from the start.

Most of the farmland near the site proved to be highly alkaline, while that nearer the river included many acres of swamps and sloughs, thick with red willows and cat-tails. Although the settlers tried to make Independence a model farming community, nature had stacked the cards against them. At that time there was plenty of good land left to homestead, thus the farmers began leaving for other places before the best land was taken. Only a few years after its hopeful birth, Independence was becoming a ghost town.

At that time Myton was the Uinta Basin's leading town. Many moved there, while others moved to a new townsite named Roosevelt. By 1912 Independence was deserted, except for a few ranchers. Today it is still listed as an election district, but except for a few scattered ranches, there is nothing left, only caved cellars and dugouts and a few abandoned log cabins.

PLAINFIELD
&
THE GOAT MAN'S MONEY

Plainfield, one of Utah's first uranium mining camps, was located southwest of Moab in Grand County, near what was then called Blue Hill, but what is now known as Cane Springs Park. Several early day uranium mines were located at Plainfield and along Mill Creek, a few miles farther north. When Plainfield was first settled during the 1870's it was as a farm and ranch settlement, known at that time as Bueno, and later as Poverty Flat. When a post office was established on November 26th, 1879, it was named Plainfield. In 1885 a churchhouse was built, followed by a school the following year.

At that time experiments with radioactive ores were being conducted in Europe, so when rich deposits of uranium were discovered near Plainfield, the fledgling community became a center of the infant uranium mining industry. The McArthur Chemical Company mined most of Plainfield's ore and shipped it to New York and Scotland for refining. One shipment of 400 pounds was the richest uranium ore mined up to that time anywhere in the world.

But though its ores were rich, there was demand for only limited quantities. Then, uranium ore much cheaper to mine was discovered in Africa, and Plainfield's role as a mining center came to an end. The area had never been suited to farming, and Indian troubles hastened the exodus already begun by its miners. By the turn of the century Plainfield was deserted. Today, few people who pass its site as they travel the Warner Creek Scenic Drive have even heard of it. Because of that it may be a real sleeper for treasure hunters, a place where relic and bottle hunters and detector users have never stopped. Why not give it a try? You may even want to look for the Goat Man's money.

The Goat Man hid his money near Plainfield. That's about the only part of the story everyone agrees on. His name is unknown. He was always called the Goat Man because he kept a herd of goats near his little cabin by the side of the river south of Moab. When he first appeared is unknown, but most people say he was living there by 1945. His cabin burned to the ground in 1965, and the Goat Man burned to death in it.

That the Goat Man had plenty of money and that he never put it in banks is certain. He was well educated, gentlemanly and always had plenty of money to buy whatever he needed. He had few acquaintances, but one woman who knew him better than most, said that he told her he had plenty of money, and that he had it cached near his cabin. He never volunteered how much "plenty" was, nor did he tell where his money came from.

So when you're through visiting old Plainfield, stop at Moab and talk to some of the old-timers there. They'll tell you that no trace of the Goat Man's cache has been found, and they can show you where his cabin was. After that, it's up to you.

RICHARDSON

It is 30 miles along a rough, dirt road that follows the winding Colorado River upstream from Moab to the deserted camp of Richardson, on Onion Creek just above its confluence with the Colorado. The town was born when high grade vanadium and uranium ores were discovered in 1898. The Welsh and Lofftis Rare Metals Company was organized that year, with the Jessie D #1 and #2 claims being among the company's best properties. Ore from Richardson's mines was shipped to New York City for processing, and in 1903 one shipment was made to France where it was used in experiments conducted by Madame Curie.

The price of radium soared to $210,000 per gram by 1911, and Richardson's ore production soared with it. But the cost of refining the ore into radium was high as well. The Standard Chemical Company once spent $480,000 to produce radium valued at only $220,000! Nevertheless, Richardson's future looked bright, for there were few places anywhere in the world where uranium could be mined at any price. But during the 1920's rich deposits of the radioactive mineral were found in the Belgian Congo, where mining and labor costs were far less than they were at the little mining camp on the Colorado. The price of refined radium skidded from $200,000 per gram to only $70,000. Since there was no way for the mines at Richardson to compete with those in far away Africa, before another season came, it was only another has-been mining camp.

The boom at Richardson did lead the way for the great uranium rush that came to the Colorado Plateau a half century later. Modern jeep-prospectors restaked its old diggings, but none of them even heard of Richardson. The Charlie Steens and Vernon Picks who became millionaire uranium kings made their fortunes where one-blanket burro prospectors dug with picks and shovels 50 years earlier. Today, by the side of the Colorado, there is a dirt roofed dugout, and close by a solitary grave enclosed by a rough pole fence. To the east, right in Richardson's back yard, are the beautiful red spires of the Fisher Towers, great minarets of blood-red sandstone that will stand guard over the camp for eternity.

Dream mines, valuable ore deposits located through dreams are phenomenon not yet understood, but they do exist. For proof of that, witness John Bradshaw's Cave Mine at Bradshaw City, Bishop Koyle's Dream Mine near Salem, Sam Hair's John The Revelator Mine at Park City or Jesse Knight's Humbug Mine at Knightsville, all examples of mines whose locations were revealed to their finders in dreams. One such mine was the Yellow Circle Dream Mine near Richardson.

In 1915 Charlie Snell, a Moab cowboy who knew nothing about mining, had a dream in which he saw a place where there was a yellow circle on a red sandstone boulder, and behind the boulder a fortune in rich uranium ore. Snell's dream was so graphic that he remembered every landmark, even though he had never seen any of them before. Snell convinced a Moab businessman to grubstake him and began the search for his dream mine.

In a wild desert place where he had never been before, Snell came upon landmarks he recognized from his dream. He followed them to a place where great blocks of red sandstone had fallen from the cliffs high above. On one of them there was a yellow circle, just as in his dream! Snell staked his claim at the base of the cliff and gathered ore samples which he had tested at Moab. They were high grade carnotite ore.

Snell and his partner dug more than a million dollars worth of ore from the Yellow Circle Dream Mine. You still don't believe in them? Well, if you're interested in seeing the red block of rock with the yellow circle Snell saw in his dream, just stop at Moab, it's on display there. Perhaps some day you'll have such a dream!

HARPER
&
THE TREASURE AT CLIFF STATION

The town of Harper was located on Argyle Creek, 2 miles from where it empties into Minnie Maude Creek in Nine Mile Canyon at the south end of Duchesne County. During the early 1880's a man remembered only as "Brock" built a saloon on the stage road between Price and Fort Duchesne. Later, Frank Alger opened a store alongside the saloon, a hotel was built across the road, settlers began moving in and before long a little town with a post office appeared. A telegraph line connected the new town with Fort Duchesne, its single wire strung on iron posts to keep Indians from burning them. The townsite had been used as a camping place by Indians for centuries, and many ancient artifacts were found. On the canyon walls above town there are many caves where ancient pictographs were found, and ledges where early day explorers, Spanish miners and mountain men carved their names or strange signs and dates.

In 1902, Preston Nutter, Utah's most prominent rancher, purchased the Brock saloon and made it his headquarters for his far-flung ranching operations. Pete Francis had been operating the saloon, but a gun fight with a wild one abruptly ended his career. His widow sold out to Nutter. Nutter's ranch holdings consisted of hundreds of thousands of acres and uncounted cattle. Today Harper can be reached by following U-53 from either Wellington in Carbon County or from Myton in Duchesne County, but because it follows the deep, sandy washes of Nine Mile Canyon where flash floods are frequent, take care during stormy weather.

The stagecoach road from Brock's saloon, now the site of Harper, to Myton, passes by the ruins of Cliff Station, 18 miles south of Myton. Many are the tales of outlaws and Indians those crumbling old walls could tell, but their strangest story would be of a huge gold cache and a mysterious stone map that showed where it is hidden.

Back in those days, five desperados stole a large shipment of gold being brought from a mine somewhere in the Uintas. One outlaw took his share and traveled along, leaving the other four. Soon one was killed and another wounded by a purusing posse of Mexican miners. The outlaws took refuge in the rough broken country where in later years Cliff Station would be built. They had eluded their pursuers and built a crude sandstone slab shelter, where the wounded man died, leaving only two to share the miners' gold. Although they had lost the miners, Indians found their horses and stole them during a short fight in which one of the remaining outlaws was killed.

The last outlaw remaining was an old man, a trapper who had been in the mountains for years. He didn't dare stay where he was and he couldn't carry the heavy gold without pack horses, so he buried it and scratched a cryptic message on a sandstone slab which he placed, carved side down, over the grave of his dead partner. The old man eventually made his way out of the Ute Country and in time back to St. Louis where he told a nephew how to find the stone slab map that was the waybill to a fortune in gold.

The nephew owned a prosperous freight outfit and couldn't take time for the long trip west, but he did tell several trapper friends about it, and they told others, and so the tale of the lost cache had its start. A few old-timers in the Uinta Basin knew of it, but it would have been dismissed as just another story, if not for what happened a few years ago.

A group of rockhounds from nearby Roosevelt uncovered the sandstone slab mine, and thinking it only a curious relic, took it home. A well known treasure hunter familiar with the lost cache story heard about their find and obtained permission to examine the map, but found that its meaning had been lost when it was moved, for it was oriented to landmarks surrounding the outlaws grave. One rockhound agreed

to return to the canyon near Cliff Station where it had been found, but was unable to find the outlaw's grave again or even the place where the rough slab cabin had been. Since then several hikers have mentioned coming across an old slab cabin, but none have been able to return to it. Perhaps you'll be luckier and find the old ruin not far from Cliff Station, and the dead outlaw's grave where an old Mountain Man buried a hoard of stolen gold back when the country still belonged to the fur trappers, Spanish miners and Ute Indians.

But even if you don't find the treasure near Cliff Station, you can visit the treasure that is old Harper, and see its old cabins and climb up to the cliffs where names a century and more old remain. Some of the old cabins are still in use by the Nutter Ranch which is doing business as usual in Nine Mile Canyon. The iron poles of the original telegraph line still follow the canyon bottom, and a few still have the original rubber insulators prized by collectors today. When Preston Nutter purchased the old Brock saloon a beautiful peacock was included in the sale. A mate was obtained and over the years they have multiplied, until today peacocks have become a colorful and curious part of old Harper.

KIZ
&
THE OUTLAW LOOT OF THE SINBAD DESERT

Only 5 miles north of US 6-50 on State Road 53, the road to Harper, a faint dirt trail turns east into Clark Valley, named for an old-timer who was ranching there when the first settlers arrived. Clark had established a large bachelor ranch with solid log cabins, stables, a grainery and even a blacksmith shop. He abandoned his hard-won foothold in the desert during a long and severe drought, and it wasn't until 1906 that his pioneer ranch was homesteaded by Ephraim and Kiziah Dimick, and some two dozen other families.

The newly arrived settlers developed the land for farming instead of ranching. A large reservoir was built by 1916 and in 1924 a school made its appearance in one of Clark's old buildings, with Mary Tidwell as its first teacher. She was paid the splendid salary of $40 a month plus board and room! So many children attended that a new schoolhouse was built the following year. A post office was established in 1926 and George Mead opened a general store.

A name was needed for the new post-office. The name Kiz was proposed and accepted to honor Clark Valley's first woman settler, Kiziah Dimick, affectionately known to about everyone as "Aunt Kiz." But it didn't turn out to be much of an honor, for by the time postal authorities accepted the name, most of Kiz was drying up and blowing away, just as it had when Clark ranched there. A series of dry years combined with the depression of the 1930's brought the end. The ruin and desolation around its sad little cemetery gives no hint today of the dreams its settlers had when they staked their hopes on Clark Valley.

Kiz and the desert around it abound with abandoned farms and ranches, many dating back a century and more. All hide little treasure for today's coin hunter, relic seeker or bottle digger. Nine Mile Canyon was the outlaw trail from the Uinta Basin to Price and the Robber's Roost country farther south, so Clark Valley saw many a wanted man ride by.

When one thinks of outlaws on the Sinbad Desert, the Wild Bunch comes to mind but there were other bands in the Sinbad country before and after Butch Cassidy's long riders. Tom McCarty taught Cassidy a lot of tricks, and after the McCarty gang was wiped out at the Delta bank robbery, the Sinbad Desert saw the coming of the Red Sash gang, the Tip Gault gang and the Blue Mountain gang as well as a whole bunch of loners. There's a lot of loot hidden on the Sinbad, and not all of it was cached by the Wild Bunch.

In 1910 George McCarty, one of the last living Utah outlaws, gave a man who had befriended him a dying description of how to find a cache worth $100,000. It's worth a million dollars today if you can find it! Before he died McCarty admitted that he was the last of a band of eight who for 15 years hid their profits from bank robberies and train holdups along the old outlaw trail between Nine Mile Canyon and Robber's Roost.

High atop a vertical sided mesa half way between Green River and Hanksville they cached all of their hard money, gold coins, bullion, gold and silver, keeping only paper money to spend. The mesa top covered about a square mile and was pock-marked with shallow depressions which became small ponds when winter snow melted or thunderstorms struck the desert. A hole was dug and the hard money was cached in the bottom of one of those seasonal ponds. It was a perfect hiding place, for every passing storm and season erased all evidence of new deposits made to their growing cache.

Each outlaw band intended to recover his share, but four were hung or shot by posses in Utah, two died in a shootout in Colorado, and McCarty admitted that he killed another in an argument. McCarty was the last of the gang, and he knew he would never see the Sinbad country again.

The first World War took McCarty's friend to Europe. After that earning a living for his family kept him from looking for the outlaw mesa. Time passed until the outlaw's story became a family legend, just another tall tale from long ago. But those who research such legends believe McCarty's story is gospel. The holdups he described happened and the payrolls taken were never recovered. Both Bill and Fred McCarty were killed during the Delta bank robbery while other gang members filled lonely graves in forgotten desert places.

The outlaw cache mesa remains there in a desert world that looks the same as it did when the long riders cached their loot. Flat topped mesas can be seen shimmering in the desert heat all along the old outlaw trail from Green River to Hanksville. Most of them have vertical sides 500 to 1,000 feet high, and there is no way

A prospector grinds his ore samples at the diggings at Castleton.

M.I Fowler (at spring), George Hepburn (sitting) and McKee (standing) found the gold that started the camp of Miner's Basin. -Utah Historical Society-

to get to the top of most of them. You can be sure the outlaw mesa has no easy trail up its sides. McCarty said the hard money cache mesa was about half way from Green River to Hanksville, but there are still a lot of mesas out there. It won't be easy, but for a million dollars in hard money, it might be worth it!

CASTLETON

Castleton was located on Castle Creek, 3 miles above its junction with the Colorado River and 18 miles northeast of Moab in Grand County. Settled during the 1860's, Castleton was originally a placer gold camp, but it failed after the placers were worked out. The old camp was frequented by occasional wandering cowboys or sheepherders until 1888 when gold in quartz was discovered at Miner's Basin in the La Sal Mountains. When Miner's Basin roared to life, Castleton was reborn as a supply town for its mines. Freight companies were kept busy, a large general store supplied the miners' needs, Miller's Hotel catered to miners hurrying to the new diggings and "Plug Hat" Kelly's saloon provided liquid refreshment for the inner man. The revived camp also had a restaurant, livery stable, blacksmith shop and a deputy sheriff.

As long as the mines at Miner's Basin kept working, Castleton kept going as a supply town, but when the great financial panic of 1907 closed the hardrock

mines, Castleton suffered also. Closed mines and out of work miners need few supplies and for the second time Castleton found itself facing extinction. Before long its only residents were stockmen whose herds grazed on the mountain front above town. But the old town may yet stage another comeback. Recently tourists have discovered the beauty of its blood red hills and the giant Castle Rock in the center of its valley floor. A dude ranch has been started and several new homes have been built. It has taken 60 years, but once more people are coming back to Castleton, a two time loser at the edge of the La Sal Mountains.

MINER'S BASIN

The first gold discoveries in the Sierra La Sal Mountains of Grand County were made in the early 1860's, but the first lode claims weren't staked until 1888. Among the first claims were the Clear Crystal, which according to owners Miles, McGraw & Howell had gold values of $200 to the ton, and the High Ore and Tornado claims owned by Fowler, Hepburn & Wolf, as well as the promising Green Mountain and Jennings Bryan claims. On May 27th, 1898 a group of miners met at George Hepburn's cabin and organized the Miner's Basin Mining District.

Before that summer was over a regular mining camp with a general store, livery stable, shoemaker, two restaurants, two saloons (one operated by blind Sam McGraw), a sheriff's office and even a Sunday school was flourishing in the little mountain basin below the mines. The following year the new town was granted a post office with the name Basin, however to miners then and visitors today it was always known as Miner's Basin.

During the next few years Miner's Basin produced a wealth of gold for its mine owners. G.R. Propper, a stockbroker and land agent, advertised the district as a "bonanza field," and in reference to the Alaska gold rush then taking place, asked in his advertisements, "Why go chasing rainbows in the frozen north when Miner's Basin is a bonanza field?"

In 1905 the Interstate Mining Company installed a huge new 125 ton cyanide mill in a canyon east of the camp where there was plenty of water. Its construction was poorly timed, for the great financial panic of 1907 was just around the corner. When it struck, the price of gold dropped so fast the mines were forced to close. Everyone but Gordon Fowler left. He stayed for the next 50 years, all alone, always promoting Miner's Basin and the gold he knew was still hidden there.

Until Fowler died in 1966 he kept Miner's Basin one of the most beautiful areas in the state, a delight to visit. He kept all of the old cabins in repair, freshly chopped wood by each old iron range, beds made for unexpected visitors, curtains on the windows and a welcome for everyone. There were few visitors, and deer walked among century old cabins while black bear kept watch from the edge of the forest. Its little alpine basin of towering pines and clear snow water streams was the best preserved mine area in the state. Gordon Fowler was one of my treasured friends.

After Fowler's death, Bill and Edith Connors moved into his old cabin, the same one that had been the camp's post office when Miner's Basin was booming. Recently Connors has engaged the Cyprus Mining Company to core-drill for the gold ore that Fowler always insisted would be found. Maybe Miner's Basin will become a "bonanza field" after all, but even if it doesn't it will always be a treasured place. The road past Castleton from Moab is paved now, but the 4 mile rocky trail up to Miner's Basin certainly isn't. If you do visit Miner's Basin, watch out for bears. The last time I visited there one ate a pan of beans that Connors put outside the cabin door to cool, beans, pan and all!

SOME FORGOTTEN
D&RG RAILROAD STATIONS &
THE TRAIN ROBBER'S CACHE &
THE JAPANESE COOK'S CACHE

As the Denver & Rio Grande Railroad built across the Colorado state line into Utah, it left a long line of lonely end-of-track camps. A few remained as isolated desert settlements, some became only water stops or sidings and others disappeared completely. Those old stations from east to west were Utaline, West Water, Cottonwood, Agate, Cisco, White House, Pinto, Sagers, Thompson's, Crescent, Little Grand, Elgin, Solitude, Sphinx, Desert, Cliff, Grassy and Cedar before the rails reached the coal camps of Carbon County.

Many strange tales are told of those old camps, and many are tales of lost treasures and secret caches yet unfound. With time and a good 4x4 you can explore them all, and find countless little treasures, but there are a few "biggies" you might want to spend more time on. One is an outlaw cache just inside the Utah state line.

In 1906 a D&RG train was held up and robbed near Grand Valley, Colorado. A payroll consisting of gold coin was taken by two robbers who fled westward with their loot, racing a hastily formed posse for the safety of the Utah line. They crossed into Utah and the Colorado posse, whose jurisdiction had ended, fell behind, but they lost no time notifying Utah authorities who stopped the pair near Moab. The outlaws didn't have a dollar of the stolen loot with them.

The two were kept in custody and taken to Price where it was learned they were wanted for other crimes for which they were soon jailed. Their names have been lost somewhere along the way, but twice told tales claim that the payroll they took in Colorado was buried as soon as the outlaws crossed into Utah, under three large cottonwood trees near the railroad tracks at Utaline. It might pay for some four-wheeler to follow the old D&RG line along that desolate desert route. Who knows? Those old cottonwoods may still be standing!

Farther west at the camp called Sagers, in the heart of the desert half way between Utaline and the Green River local legend tells of a Japanese cook who hid a cache that has yet to be found. It was common knowledge that the cook had a great deal of money all of it in hard coin that wouldn't rot or tarnish in a post-hole bank. Apparently he didn't trust paper money. Whenever railroad workers approached him for a loan, always given at high interest, the cook would disappear down one of several draws or washes behind his restaurant, and after a short time would return with the desired amount.

One day two Mexican gandy-dancers broke into his rickety cabin and tried to force the cook to tell them where his cache was hidden, but they overestimated the old man's strength, and when he refused to tell its secret hiding place their beatings killed him. The Mexicans tore his tiny cabin apart in a frantic search for his wealth, before being discovered and fleeing ahead of a gang of irate track layers. Later, others dug and prodded into every wash and gulch, but not a dime was ever found.

Perhaps some modern day metal detector equipped treasure hunter will find the Japanese cook's cache, but first you'll have to find where his cabin was located. And that might be a little hard to do, for no one has lived at old Sagers for a long, long time now.

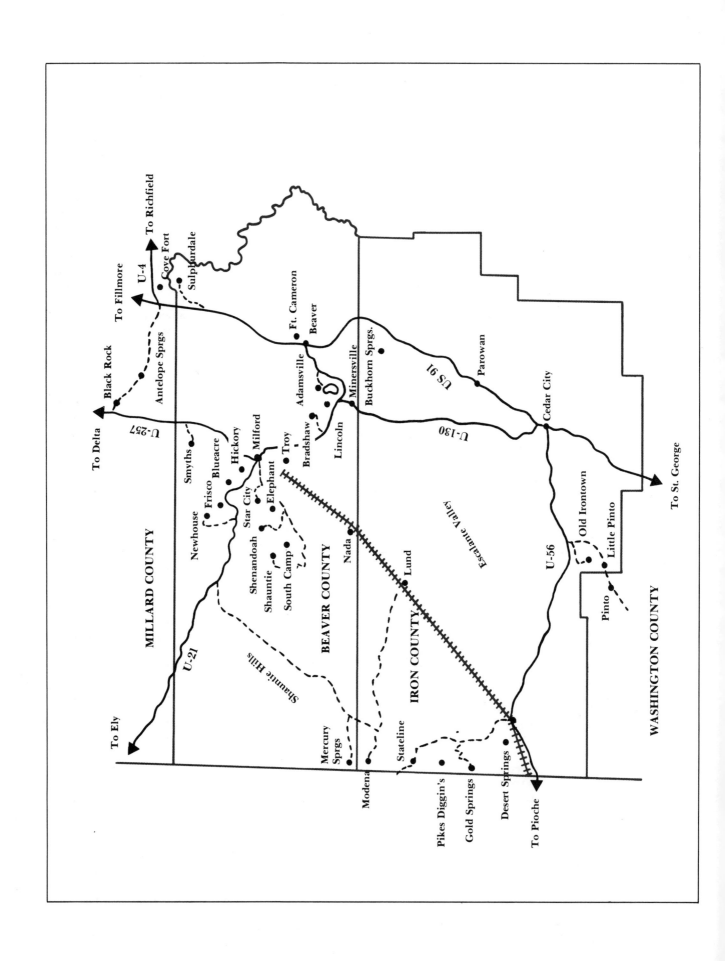

CHAPTER NINE

IN THE SOUTHWEST

Beaver County, butted up against the Nevada border, and Iron County adjoining it on the south make up Utah's southwest, a color country of deserts, mesas and mountains that is a ghost towner's paradise and a treasure hunter's dream come true. There are dozens of has-been towns in Beaver County alone, many dating back from its silver mining days. Older camps like Lincoln were built on the ruins of earlier Spanish camps, while late bloomers like Stateline were outlaw hideouts before they became mining towns. There were towns like Frisco where the cemetery grew almost as fast as the town did, and places as quiet as old Adamsville, where the chirping of crickets kept people awake at night.

The Star Mining District spawned a whole cluster of towns that hardly a man alive has heard of, such as Shenandoah and Elephant, places that have never heard the buzz of a metal detector. And along the Nevada border there were others equally unknown and forgotten, isolated places like Mercury Springs and Pike's Diggings. Today they are only sleepy little ghost towns at the ends of long dusty roads.

Several of these southwest towns were built by sturdy pioneers, while others were built on silver and gold dust. Each is a monument to fickle nature, which topples one dream and nurtures another. A treasure hunter could have a field day at any one of them. But don't expect any company, for all of the ghost towns of Utah's Southwest couldn't muster enough live ones for a game of cribbage! What are we waiting for? Let's get going!

LINCOLN
& BISHOP ROLLINS' SPANISH MINE

There is no mining camp in Utah more historically significant than Lincoln, a long forgotten camp that grew up around the workings of the Lincoln Mine, 5 miles north of Minersville on the west slope of the Mineral Range. No one really knows how old the diggings there are. When Mormon Bishop James Rollins and his party discovered the ancient workings in 1858 they described them as "an old Spanish mine." Even though it was obviously very old, dug long before the earliest explorers crossed the Rocky Mountains, it was not badly caved in, since it had been dug into solid rock. Bishop Rollins and his men explored the old workings, finding rusted remnants of tools left behind perhaps a hundred years before. They also found a vein of what they thought was pure lead, which the Mormons badly needed at the time, because the arrival of Johnston's Army into the Salt Lake Valley was threatening their very existence. The Rollins Party wondered why the bullets they cast from the old mine's lead were so hard, but when the ore was assayed they soon learned the answer. It wasn't lead at all, but nearly pure silver!

In short order a bustling mining camp named in honor of Bishop Rollins grew up near the mine. It didn't take long for gentiles to outnumber the Mormon miners, though, and when they did the town's name was changed to Lincoln by pro-northern Lincoln supporters. In 1862 a Salt Lake reporter wrote, "Lincoln is a goodly town, with over 100 houses and fully 500 people. Business is lively and all signs point to permanent prosperity." Other mines at the new camp included the Pioneer, Rattler, Golden Gate, Dunnenburg, Yip-Yap, Home Ticket, Richmond and Coral Reef. Owners of the December Mine claimed it had ore values as high as 3,000 ounces of silver to the ton.

The first Mormon miners built several smelters near the Lincoln Mine, but since they were unfamiliar with mining they never operated them efficiently or profitably. They were able to recover lead, but most of the silver ended up in the slag pile, and in recent years much of that slag has been shipped to modern smelters at high profit. More experienced Gentile miners built an efficient smelting works at nearby Minersville, recovered both lead and silver. The Lincoln Mine operated until 1900 when a British syndicate purchased the property. As was so often the case, the new owners had little knowledge of mining and the company went bankrupt, which closed the mine and put its miners out of work.

Underground water had already closed most of Lincoln's smaller mines, and in time, depressed silver prices or lost veins closed the rest. Lincoln became a forgotten place, and for years sat idle, but recently rising silver prices have caused prospectors to take a second (or is it a third?) look at old Lincoln, and today miners are probing its ancient shafts and tunnels again. A modern air compressor now powers jackhammers where Spanish miners once chipped the hard quartz rock with crude chisels in what could be one of America's oldest mines. There is still silver in the Mineral Mountains. To find it, just follow the centuries-old trail Spanish miners followed while Coronado was still seeking El Dorado and the Seven Cities Of Cibola.

BRADSHAW CITY

The story of the Cave Mine and the little mining camp which grew up around it, 7 miles north of Minersville, is the story of John Bradshaw and his dream. Bradshaw wasn't a miner or even a very good prospector. Instead, he owned a small store. He watched with envy as mine owners at nearby Lincoln became rich, and wished that one day he would be wealthy also.

One night Bradshaw had a dream in which he saw a cave high on a mountain, and in the cave he saw a pack rat's nest filled with gold nuggets! His dream was so real he told friends about it, but they only laughed at him. Bradshaw was not s strong man, and he had no horse to ride, so he set out on foot to find his dream mine. As he hiked north from Minersville he tied pieces of string on cedar tree branches so he wouldn't become lost. He had never been in the mountains before, but was able to follow landmarks he recognized from his dream. Finally, when he could go no farther, he found his cave, high on the side of the mountain, just as it had been in his dream. Bradshaw climbed up to the cave, and inside its dark opening was a pack rat's nest, and in the nest were handfuls of glistening yellow gold nuggets! The interior of Bradshaw's dream cavern proved to be a great limestone cave, with stalactites and ceiling heavily encrusted with sparkling crystals of silver and gold.

A line of cabins was soon built in the canyon below the cave, while a boarding house and saloon made their appearance on a level spot across the canyon. W.S. Godbe started a general store soon afterwards. The little camp was reputed to be a wild one while it lasted, which wasn't very long. It took only a few years to strip Bradshaw's cave of its wealth. Ore from his Cave Mine was hauled to Minersville and to the Old Hickory Mill at Hickory.

Around Minersville and Lincoln the little town was usually just called the Cave Mine Camp, but many old maps show it as Bradshaw City. The honor of having a town named after him was about all John Bradshaw realized from his dream. It would be nice to say he made a fortune from his Cave Mine, but he didn't, for other more knowledgeable men beat him out of it. Yet, it is another example of the many "dream mines" that are mysteries the best minds still can't explain.

Today, just inside the Cave Mine, where sunlight filters down through the natural opening found by John Bradshaw, there is an old forge and the fire blackened walls of an underground blacksmith shop. With careful search broken pieces of ancient stalactites can be found on the waste dump outside the cave. At the edge of the cedars on a hillside across the canyon there is a single tombstone. It bears a simple inscription, "John Hayes, 1886." It could very well be the epitaph for John Bradshaw, the Cave Mine and Bradshaw City also.

SOME SP, LA & SL RAILROAD CAMPS

After the trans-continental railroad was joined at Promontory in 1869 other railroads soon came to Utah. Most were narrow gauge short lines, but a few became the railroads of today. The Utah Southern built south from Salt Lake City, and underwent many name changes before it became the Union Pacific route of today. Its original purpose was to reach the silver mines of Beaver County, but in time it joined the San Pedro, Los Angeles & Salt Lake to become the line we now know as the UP. There were many old end-of-line camps along its route, any of which could be of interest to today's treasure hunter. Among them were Neels, Cruz, Zenda, Opal, Laho, Latimer, Sahara, Beryl, Tomas and Uvada. Some of them have tales to tell.

The old railroad camp of Smyths, 12 miles north of Milford, looks just like an artist might paint a picture of a deserted desert ghost town, slowly being buried by drifting dunes. The restless sands are so deep that at some cabins they drift through broken windows and out open doors. A long neglected windmill creaks for want of a few drops of oil, but it still pumps a tiny trickle of water which sinks into the thirsty sands only a few feet from the outlet pipe. Scraggly trees lift their dead limbs against the desert sky like giant skeletons from another age.

When the dunes shift before the never-ending wind, relics of the past are exposed to view. But there's no one to see them, for Smyths has been deserted for more years than anyone can remember. Only a few hundred yards away in distance but a world away in time, motorists in shiny autos speed by, unaware of the lonely little ghost by the side of the road. It's maybe best that they don't know or stop, for when the wind whistles through the empty cabins and the sands shift like a homeless spirit, Smyths is a dismal and ghostly place.

While exploring the route of the old SP, LA & SL be sure to stop at the depot at Black Rock, 12 miles north of Smyths. When the railroad was hauling silver ore from the mines of the Star District, Black Rock was an important place, with many fine homes and well built buildings. Today only a few shacks and the old depot, which shouldn't be missed, remain. Unfortunately, the Union Pacific may tear it down to avoid paying taxes on it. Its red tiled roof and yellow adobe walls look like something right out of old Mexico.

A good bet for coin and relic hunters is the virtually unknown resort built at Antelope Springs during the 1860's, 7 miles southeast of Black Rock and 7 miles straight south of the old Cudahy Mine. It is on the old Devil's Gate & Meadow Valley Stage Road between Black Rock and Cove Fort. Long ago, it featured a hotel and saloon where settlers and outlaws alike came from miles around to dance and party. Any coin or relic found there would be very old, and very valuable!

Clear Lake was 19 miles south of Delta just west of a natural body of water by the same name. As hard as it may be to believe, settlers dug a 7 mile canal from Clear Lake to their little town on the railroad, to get water for farms and to drink. It was an exercise in futility, because the lake rose and fell with every storm and season, and drifting sand filled the canal almost as fast as it was dug out. By 1900 the town was a thing of the past, and today, foundations half buried in sand show where homes and businesses once stood. About the only person who could have any interest in it would be a treasure hunter!

If you're interested in ancient Indian artifacts, visit the ghost of Nada. Nada was built just south of the Iron County line between Thermo and Latimer, atop an ancient Indian ruin. When the winds blow, and that's all the time, arrowheads, grinding stones and pottery are exposed. For twenty years settlers tried to farm that desert, but it was impossible. When crops didn't burn up in the desert sun, they were blown away. The settlement is gone, but artifacts remain. "Nada" in Spanish means "nothing," an appropriate name if I've ever heard one.

There are dozens of old camps along the San Pedro, Los Angeles & Salt Lake Railroad, and there are little treasures at all of them. But it's a big country where gas stations and stores are few so be careful; take lots of water, and don't get lost. If there are ghosts in any of Utah's towns they're there, so watch out!

WHITE MOUNTAIN STATION
&
THE LOST WHITE MOUNTAIN SILVER

Not far south of Fillmore are the ruins of the old White Mountain Stage Station, a stop of the Devil's Gate & Meadow Valley route during the 1860's. It was on the route from Fillmore, then the territorial capitol, to the mines of the Escalante Desert country. White Mountain Station is shown on Froiseth's 1878 map of Utah as being about 11 miles southwest of Fillmore, near what is shown as the White Crystal Mountain. There is hardly a trace of the old stage road today, no sign of the station and no White Crystal Mountain, only dozens of black volcanic cones at the edge of the Black Rock Desert.

Nevertheless, you might want to visit the station site, for in 1859 an emigrant party bound for California made a fantastic silver strike on the White Crystal Mountain, but when they returned the following season they couldn't find it, or even the mountain it was on! Somehow Orrin Porter Rockwell, Brigham Young's bodyguard, obtained several peices of the silver, and he also claimed it came from the White Crystal Mountain. And no less a person than the famed Sir Richard Burton mentioned the silver strike and the mountain it was made on. In his book, *The City Of The Saints,* Burton said, "At the western extremity of the White Mountain there is a mammoth cave, of which only 1 mile has been explored, by the enterprising Major Howard Egan."

Still other accounts of the silver strike can be found in rare books and pioneer journals, written by different people at different times and places, each unaware of the other, giving an unquestioned degree of authenticity to what otherwise would be only local legend. Find the old station and you might find more than just great relics, you might find a lost ledge of silver. It's been lost a long time now, somewhere out there on the White Crystal Mountain!

A scene at Frisco. Note the street paved with boulders!

FRISCO

In September, 1875 Jim Ryan and Sam Hawkes set up a prospecting camp at Squaw Springs at the foot of the San Francisco Mountains. Each day, as the prospectors left their camp, they passed an unusual looking boulder. One day, as they stopped to rest, Ryan broke a piece from it. Almost without interest he picked the broken piece up to look at it. He then took a quick second look, for it was nearly pure silver! They staked a claim they named the Bonanza, and then hurried off to town to sell it. They got $25,000 cash, not bad for two old desert rats, but not too good either, for the Bonanza Lode produced $50,000,000 in silver!

The claim's new owners discovered that the boulder of silver was only the apex of a giant outcrop of nearly pure silver. It was so soft it could be cut with a knife, and then it curled like an animal horn. Thus they called the mine the Horn Silver. Only a few weeks after they bought it for $25,000 they sold it to Jay Cooke, owner of the Great Northern Railroad. But they did a little better than Ryan and Hawkes had, for Cooke paid them $5,000,000!

At the foot of the San Francisco Mountains the west's toughest mining camp exploded into being. In only weeks it had 21 saloons where whiskey sold for two shots for a quarter. Water sold for 5¢ a bucket, but it was too thick to drink. So many men were murdered and killed in gun fights that city fathers hired a "meat wagon" to pick up the corpses and bury them. Frisco soon had not only the biggest but the fanciest cemetery in the state. The Utah Southern Railroad built into

town, bringing every kind of gambler, shady lady and gunman known. Frisco was a ring-tailed roarer, a wild son of a gun, and the devil's delight.

From an open pit 900' long, 400' wide and 900' deep Jay Cooke's miners dug out $50,000,000 in silver, without doubt the richest single body of silver ever found, anywhere. And there were other mines, the Carbonate, Comet, Jay Hawker, Hoodoo, Dolly Mack and Grand Republic among them, and they produced another $10,000,000. You couldn't count all the businesses at Frisco. In addition to the 21 saloons there were fine hotels, Sackett's the favorite, a whole row of stores and shops, B.F. Grant's the largest, freight and stage companies and the new railroad, not to mention houses of ill fame, gambling halls and opium dens along the back streets. It was Dodge City, Tombstone, Sodom and Gomorrah all rolled into one. There was nothing else like it, anywhere.

Murders were daily fare at Frisco. Two men killed each other over a 50¢ bet! As many as a dozen men were killed each night. If you doubt it, count the crosses on boothill! Finally, it got so out of hand that city fathers hired Marshal Pearson from Pioche, Nevada and gave him a free hand in cleaning out the outlaws and murderers. Pearson made his policy clear the first day. He would have no jail, make no arrests and there would be no bail or appeals. Outlaws were give two choices, get out or get shot! Some didn't think he meant business, but they changed their minds when he killed six men his first night on the job! He still had to convince a few, but most got the idea and left for easier pickings. Frisco and the San Francisco Mountains were named for St.

Francis, the Patron Saint of Wildlife. It was a good name, for Frisco certainly had plenty of wild life!

Then in one day it came to an end. On February 13th, 1885 the Horn Silver Mine caved in. It hadn't been a conventional mine, but just a great open pit 900' deep braced by a jungle of cross timbers. It's hard to see why it didn't cave in sooner. Luckily the cave-in occurred during shift change when no men were in the mine. The disaster shook the earth so violently that thousands of tons of rock crashed off the mountain front and rolled into town, and store windows broke in Milford 15 miles away. In one day Frisco was deserted, but while it lasted is was really the toughest of the tough.

Although it has been picked over countless times, Frisco is still a favorite place for treasure hunters. It seems that every rain storm and summer cloudburst washes more old coins from under its wooden sidewalks, or uncovers another bottle cache. Metal detector users have a field day there. Only last year a man and wife uncovered a solid gold Buddha in the old Chinatown, using a beat up $25 detector they purchased at a pawn shop. I know, for I was there! One of the best places to find relics seems to be across the highway and down a deep wash below town. Nearly a hundred years of storms have washed hundreds of relics there. Be sure to visit Frisco. Don't miss it. I'll see you there!

Boot Hill at Frisco, the toughest of the tough.

NEWHOUSE
&
THE POT HOLE PLACERS

The site of Newhouse is located 30 miles northwest of Milford at the end of a dirt road that leaves U-21 6 miles west of Frisco. A few prospectors lived there in crude cabins and dugouts as early as 1870, but the camp never amounted to much until 1900 when Samuel Newhouse purchased the Cactus Mine. It had been located early, along with the Belmont, New Years, Purity and Cupric claims, but its record of production was something less than spectacular until Newhouse obtained it.

Newhouse established a model city 2½ miles southwest of his newly acquired mine, building comfortable stucco homes for his miners, which he rented to them for $10 a month, including all utilities. His ideas were much like Jesse Knight's had been at Knightsville thirty years earlier. Newhouse apparently liked the name of his Cactus Mine, for he also built the Cactus Trading Company, the Cactus Club, the Cactus Dancehall and a restaurant called the Cactus Cafe. He allowed only one saloon, and that was built a mile from town! There was a clubhouse at the center of his model city, containing a well stocked library, pool tables and a small bar. But it was a very proper place, for no drunks were allowed! When the Utah Southern laid track into town, Newhouse had them stop at the saloon, wanting its influence and the people it brought no closer than that.

Mr. Newhouse offered a $50 prize to the parents of the first child born at Newhouse, and at Christmas time he provided free gifts for all the children in the town. Samuel Newhouse died before his model town was completed, but his brother, Matt Newhouse, completed it and kept it up until 1910, when the ore in its mines ran out. By then more than $3,500,000 in silver, gold and copper had been produced. Two of the finest buildings of Salt Lake City's skyline are monuments to Samuel Newhouse today, the Newhouse Building and the Newhouse Hotel.

In 1914 the Cactus Mill was torn down, and in 1921 several of the town's buildings burned. Still others were moved away. The Utah Southern depot was hauled 5 miles across the valley to a ranch where it is still in use. In 1922 one of the most famous of all silent movies, "The Covered Wagon," was filmed at the old town. That was the last time there was any excitement at Newhouse!

Somewhere out there, not far from Newhouse, in the bleak sun-burned wastes of the Sevier Desert, where it butts up against the mysterious Confusion Range, there are some wind-worn potholes eroded into the desert floor, and in those potholes there are gold nuggets, lots of them!

In 1870, Frank Lane, a trained geologist, was one of the first to prospect the hills where Newhouse was later built. While out in the Confusion Range Lane became lost. He would have died of thirst if he hadn't discovered some wind-worn pot holes where a few inches of green stagnant water still remained from the last desert rain. Even through the slime he could see the sun reflecting from the shiny flakes and nuggets of yellow gold that lined the bottom of each hole.

The water saved his life and let him stay a few more days in the unknown, mind-boggling Confusion Range before the summer sun burned even the pot holes dry. Working only during the early morning or late afternoon, when the sun was at its lowest angle,

The blacksmith shop at the Cactus Mill, Newhouse. -Utah Historical Society-

Lane was able to dig nearly 30 pounds of sand size gold dust and grain size nuggets from the pot holes. Traveling only by night he managed to hike eastward between the San Francisco and Crickett mountains and across the Sevier Desert to Cove Fort.

Six months later Lane returned outfitted with pack burros to the Confusions. For two months, before the summer heat drove him away, he searched for the pot holes. Confusion reigned in the Confusions, and Lane couldn't tell if he was in the wrong place or if drifting sand had covered the pot holes. For three more years Lane returned and searched the desert country from Fort Deseret to Cove Fort, and from the San Francisco Mountains through the Confusion Range into Snake Valley, but he never found the pot hole placers again.

It's a tough country, below zero in the winter and hotter than Hades in the summer time. And the Confusions are no place for a greenhorn. They are located in probably the most inhospitable part of the western desert country. Every mountain looks like every other, and every gulch looks like its neighbor. There are plenty of rattlesnakes, but no water. But I can see that you've decided to look for Lane's lost pot hole placers anyway, so all I can do is warn you, don't get lost in the Confusions!

ADAMSVILLE

Adamsville was located on the north side of the Beaver River, 9 miles west of Beaver City. It was named for David Adams, a settler who came into the area about 1862. It was surveyed as a townsite in 1867. A stone church was built the following year. It was soon joined by a schoolhouse with a row of benches around its walls and the teacher's desk in the center of the room, instead of the rows of desks usually found in country schools. One of the first stores in Adamsville was operated by John F. Jones, but he soon had competition from J.H. Joseph. J.T. Evans was the town blacksmith.

In 1914, when the little town's population had reached 121, a land development company purchased most of the area to build Minersville Reservoir. The impounded water soon backed up and flooded Adamsville, forcing people to leave their homes and farms. The churchhouse was taken apart in sections and moved to Beaver, while other buildings were moved to nearby ranches and farms.

When Minersville Reservoir filled to capacity, Adamsville ceased to exist. Though it is still shown on some maps, the present Adamsville is not the old town, but a shadow of it. The election district is made up of a handful of ranchers and farmers who live by the man-made lake. A few small businesses have made their appearance in recent years. Most cater to tourists who stop to fish in the lake. When it is at low water level, places where people once lived can be seen. Ghosts must have muddy feet at old Adamsville!

BUCKHORN SPRINGS
&
THE FUR TRAPPER'S GOLD

In the northeast end of Iron County, near the north end of desolate Little Salt Lake Valley, stands an old cabin, the lone survivor of what was once the promising community of Buckhorn Springs. John Eyre, a brick mason from Parowan, organized the settlement in 1879, 10 miles north of Paragonah and 18 miles south of Beaver. Eyre believed the virgin land at the mouth of Cottonwood Creek was an oasis in the desert. When he led the first settlers there, he found a fine set of mule deer antlers near a large cold water spring. Eyre mounted that set of "buck horns" atop a high pole, and for many years they served as a symbol of the town's namesake.

Buckhorn Springs grew slowly, for settlers were few in southern Utah during the 1880's. Since he was a brick mason, it didn't take Eyre long to build a fine brick home for his family, and later a new schoolhouse near the springs. More people arrived to call the new settlement home, and in 1910 a ward of the Mormon Church was organized. The future looked promising until a long drought began, in time drying up the town's fine cold water spring. When the flow in Cottonwood Creek became too little to irrigate farms, the move to other places began.

Every month saw more people leave until by 1920 nearly everyone was gone. Only a few die-hards remained, and even they left after a few more years. A ranchhouse by the side of the highway now marks the old dirt road that winds through the cedars to the last remaining cabin. Buckhorn Springs is a lonely place today.

The Old Spanish Trail passed close by Buckhorn Springs, and not far to the south of its lone cabin a cryptic message carved on a volcanic rock is the waybill to a lost mine. At the mouth of Winn Canyon, 20 miles south of Buckhorn Springs, a group of mountain men made camp alongside the Old Spanish Trail in January, 1831. Their discovery of gold nearby is well documented, but it is their waybill carved on stone but eroded by 150 years of desert storms that baffles treasure hunters today.

William Wolfskill, George Yount, Lewis Burton and several others left the Spanish outpost of Taos, New Mexico on September 30th, 1830 to trap beaver and trade with Indians along the Old Spanish Trail to California. They reached the Little Salt Lake in a blinding winter storm and took refuge in the mouth of Winn Canyon. The storm was one of the worst they had ever seen in the mountains, so cold their horses froze to death. For days they huddled together, thawing frozen horse flesh for food.

It was probably while searching for firewood that they found gold, but it held little interest for them,

stranded as they were in a mountain blizzard a thousand miles by trail from the Spanish frontier in California. Several of the trappers climbed Summit Peak at the head of Winn Canyon, where Wolfskill recorded in his diary, "It is a cheerless prospect, calculated to cause emotions by no means agreeable to even the stoutest heart!" Though their gold find was of no immediate use to them, they probably intended to return to it one day, for they left a cryptic message cut into a black volcanic boulder at the mouth of Winn Canyon.

Carved onto the rock is the word "Gold" and the date "1831." There are several signs or drawings long since worn smooth by the desert winds. They seem to be parts of words. The letters "AW" or "TW" might be part of Wolfskill's initials, while "LB" almost certainly refers to Lewis Burton. There isn't any doubt what the word "Gold" means!

Eventually, the trappers made their way to Monterey where both Wolfskill and Yount became wealthy ranchers, with no need to ever return to their horrible winter camp at Winn Canyon. Burton and the others faded into the obscurity of time. Only the gold remains, waiting for some modern day mountain man to find it.

IRONTOWN

The ruins of Irontown are a monument to perseverance in the face of extreme hardship and continual defeat. In a speech before the territorial legislature on December 2nd, 1850 Brigham Young told his followers: "In the neighborhood of the Little Salt Lake exploring parties have discovered inexhaustible beds of the very best iron ore, and a settlement is being made at that place." It's interesting to note that Young was only opposed to mining precious ores, not iron or lead which the Saints could use. And it's also interesting that the first arrivals found the ruins of an old Spanish arrastra, on the exact place they built their foundry.

The new settlement was called Irontown, and it was located on Little Pinto Creek, 1 mile east of the Washington-Iron county line. The first group of 120 men and 30 women called to settle the Iron Mission soon had a townsite laid out and work started on an iron foundry. A furnace was built of sandstone, 21' square with sides 12' high before tapering another 21' to its peak. Its weight was estimated at 650 tons, all built by hand with the hardest labor. Six beehive shaped charcoal ovens were built and a coal mine was located in the mountains to the west to provide fuel for the furnace.

Irontown was immediately incorporated as a city, with stores, shops and well built rock homes. During one week in March, 1853 a ton of iron was manufactured, but it required 600 bushels of charcoal to produce it. Although some badly needed iron was made, it was at great cost and greater labor. More than $150,000 had been spent on the project by 1855 with very little to show for it, so Brigham Young grudgingly gave the order to abandon the mission. Irontown became Utah's first ghost town, but its demise was only temporary, for during the 1870's another attempt was made to manufacture iron there.

In 1868 a second iron mission was authorized, and a group of new settlers led by Ebenezer Hanks returned to Irontown. Financing was obtained in England, resulting in the organization of the Great Western Iron Works Company. Predictably, the new venture also failed and it was succeeded by a Mormon Church owned cooperative named the Iron Manufacturing Company of Utah. For awhile Irontown buzzed with activity, and the defunct Pioche & Bullionville Railroad was purchased in Nevada and hauled by wagons and by hand all the way across the Escalante Desert to Irontown where it was rebuilt and used to haul coal from the church mines to the iron foundry. The work involved is incomprehensible today.

Production eventually reached 800 pounds of good iron every eight hours, but its costs were very high, and couldn't compete with iron being shipped on the newly completed transcontinental railroad. The foundry was shut down once again and Irontown returned to ghost town status. Today its site has been set aside under state control to stabilize its present condition so that everyone can see it as it was more than 100 years ago. The ruins of its huge furnace, an old stone house, and a silent charcoal kiln remain as lasting monuments to the perseverance and industry of those settlers called to serve in the iron mission.

HICKORY AND BLUEACRE
&
THE MURDERED MINER'S CACHE

Hickory was a mining camp organized in 1882 at the southeast tip of the Rocky Range, 5 miles northwest of Milford in Beaver County. It was named for the Old Hickory Mine, and was shown on some maps as Old Hickory. The Old Hickory was one of the camp's best mines, its ore assaying 40% copper and 8 ounces of silver to the ton. Other mines at Hickory included the O.K., Rob Roy and Montreal. Owners of the Old Hickory Mine installed a stamp mill in 1883 at a cost of $45,000 and almost paid for it in one season. Its noisy stamps pounded out $12,000 in bullion from Old Hickory ore and $19,000 from gold ore hauled from John Bradshaw's Cave Mine at Bradshaw City. The following year the mill was sold at a good profit and moved to Nevada, and from then on ore from the old Hickory was hauled to the Miller Mill, located on the site of the present-day library at Milford.

At the foot of the Beaver Lake Mountains 5 miles northwest of Hickory, a small mining camp named Blueacre was Hickory's neighbor for awhile. It gave promise of becoming a copper mining center and a number of substantial homes and buildings were built, but its ore was too low grade to be recovered by processes then in use, hence, its boom was a short one. Only one old stone building remains at Blueacre, and it

Sage 'n cedars have reclaimed the once busy streets of old Irontown.

is being used as a powder magazine by the American Mining Company, presently working Blueacre's low grade copper ore deposits.

Hickory wasn't a large camp and its daily doings were easily eclipsed by its wild and wooly neighbors of Frisco and the camps of the Star Range a few miles to the south. But Hickory did have one exciting day, long after it was a dead and forgotten place, and that moment of excitement left a mystery cache still unfound.

During the late 1930's, a Finnish prospector named Gus Knuts began reworking one of the old mines at Hickory. He was a quiet old man who kept to himself, living alone in a fifty year old cabin at his mine. It would probably be fair to describe him as a hermit. During the early 40's the war in Europe drove mineral prices up, and Knuts made several ore shipments at a good profit. Whenever he went into Milford for supplies, which he did as seldom as possible, he always paid in cash for whatever he bought. It soon became common knowledge around town that the old miner was well to do, and had a secret cache buried somewhere near his cabin.

On November 18th, 1941 after someone mentioned that he hadn't been in town for months, the sheriff decided to investigate and found that Knut's cabin had been torn to pieces and search holes dug all around it in a haphazard fashion. The old man's body was found where it had been thrown into his mine shaft. His throat had been cut.

No arrests were ever made, nor did anyone around Milford appear to become suddenly wealthy. There was no indication that any cache had been uncovered at his cabin. A few half-hearted searches have been made since his murder, all in a hit or miss way without benefit of a metal detector. It's unlikely that Gus Knut's cache has ever been found, and few today have even heard of it. So if you just happen to be in the neighborhood, stop at old Hickory and take time to look around. It could be the most profitable thing you'll ever do.

STAR CITY
&
THE LOST RATTLESNAKE MINE

Star City was the namesake of the Star Mining District and was located 6 miles southwest of Milford. During the 1870's Star City grew from a tent town into a raw new mining camp on the north end of what was then called the Picacho Range, now the Star Range. More than 1,600 claims were located in the Star District, among them the Little May, Rebel, Copper King and Osceola at Star City. Ore from them was hauled to the railroad at Milford or to the mills and smelters there and at Troy, a mill town located on the Beaver River 5 miles south of Milford.

Star City was a boomer, but remained a bachelor camp because there wasn't any water there. In the winter miners melted snow, but during the summer water was peddled door to door at a cost of 10¢ a bucket. Miners claimed it was cheaper to drink beer! With no water, few women chose to live there, and its businesses were therefore saloons and the like.

For nearly a decade Star City's mines produced large quantities of silver and lead ore, but as the diggings sunk deeper, veins pinched out. Each time one of its mines closed Star City died a little, until there was no one left. Today caving mine shafts pock-mark the mountains where towering gallows lean crazily like skeletons of primeval dinosaurs, and great waste dumps mark the places where Star City's miners searched for sudden wealth.

Old-timers around Milford claim that somewhere in the mountains beyond Star City there is an abandoned shaft full of rich ore, and that it's gold, not silver! They say an old miner had lived alone too long and gone crazy from "cabin fever." He had a cabin at a working he called the Rattlesnake Mine, which was a good name, for the area is full of Great Basin rattlers.

The old hermit worked his mine only when he felt like doing so. The rest of the time he lived alone in his tumble-down shack and took pot shots at anyone who came too close. Once or twice a year he would bring a wagon load of hand sorted ore to the Miller Mill at Milford. It was always high grade gold, unlike any ore found in the Star Range. But he was a real closed mouth loner, and answered no questions. A couple of local toughs tried to jump his claim one day, but after dodging a hail of rifle bullets they left the old man alone.

The recluse lived alone at his mine back in the hills long after Star City became a ghost town. His trips into town became more infrequent and in time everyone forgot about him and his Rattlesnake Mine. Years later two young hikers chanced upon his cabin and found his dried up body where he had fallen who knows how long before. In a shed by his caving shaft were rotting sacks of ore, all heavy with stringers of yellow gold. Although the shaft appeared to be dangerous to enter, the old hand whim above it appeared to be solid, and one volunteered to search for the rich vein in the black depths below. With his foot in a knotted loop at the end of the hoisting rope, his partner lowered him into the foul smelling pit.

Near the end of the rope the man in the shaft suddenly dropped his candle and screamed in terror. His partner worked feverishly to lift his dead weight from the awful pit, but when he reached daylight he hardly recognized him, for his face was white as snow, his eyes were filled with terror and he was babbling incoherently. From his wild ravings his partner learned that from the cold winter air outside the shaft, he had lowered his friend into a hot, stinking den of thousands of twisting, writhing rattlesnakes, all coiled together in a hideous, nauseating mass!

The awful sight and sickening smell of the terrible den had so deranged his friend that be became violently insane and had to be committed to a mental hospital.

His partner, in a state of shock over what happened to his friend, refused to talk about it or even tell where the old miner's cabin and shaft was located. He left the area soon afterwards, but it was later learned that his partner's fate had so unnerved him that he committed suicide.

According to the tales old-timers tell, somewhere in the countless canyons and ridges beyond Star City there is an old cabin with a hermit miner's skeleton still in it, and on the mountain side close by there is a deep shaft where thousands of rattlesnakes have their den. According to the legend, there's still lots of gold in the shaft, but the old hermit's ghost haunts it, so you better tread softly if you plan to look for the Rattlesnake Mine!

ELEPHANT CITY

At the foot of the Star Range about 1 mile southwest of Star City there is a dusty road that turns northward and climbs steeply to an old cabin standing close by the ruins of the Vicksburg Mine. It may not look like much today, but over a hundred years ago it was one of Elephant City's leading mines. It was also a popular place for miners to gather, for the camp's baseball field was at the Vicksburg Mine. On Sundays miners would hike from nearby mines or ride from other camps to meet at Elephant City to play ball. There was a fierce rivalry among the different camps along the Star Range, and many a gold coin changed hands because of bets won and lost. Liquor and beer flowed freely because there was no water at Elephant City. That old ball field and the spot where the camp saloon was located shouldn't be overlooked by coin hunters today.

Elephant City was named for nearby Elephant Canyon, but don't ask me who named the canyon! During the 1870's it was a thriving camp. Rich mines like the Golden and the Era kept miners busy, as did the Estelle and Maude properties. The town's post office was located at the Crown Point Mine. The strangely named camp hit its peak during the 1870's and 80's when other camps along the Star Range did, and it hit the skids when they did. Some of the best mines in the Star District were at Elephant, but today it is probably the least well-known of the five towns the district supported.

There are not many who can recall its name today, although one grizzled miner at Milford told me he'd never forget those wild ball games played there. There's not much left now, just the old ball field and the ancient looking cabin at the Vicksburg Mine. Old-time miners had a saying that when they had seen it all, they had seen the elephant. But they will never see it again, for the Elephant is dead!

SOUTH CAMP

On the south side of the Star Range there is a long black ridge covered with cinders and volcanic ash, where the Earth erupted a million or so years ago. 8 miles southwest of Milford a hardly visible dirt trail turns to the right and climbs steeply for a mile and a half through stunted sage alongside that black ridge to the ruins of South Camp, once one of the leading camps of the Star District. Near the end of the trail a lone cabin, burned black by the desert sun, stands alone, while just beyond are the few sad remnants of the town. Pieces of "desert amethyst," sun purpled bottles, sparkle in the sun, while here and there the broken rubble of old foundations poke up through the yellow straw grass.

South Camp may be dead today, but it wasn't one hundred years and more ago. It was a rough and ready place then. In those days the stagecoach road from Milford, at the end-of-track, led west through South Camp to the Nevada diggings. Many wanted men passed through town. One day Tom McCarty, leader of the McCarty gang of bank robbers, stood watching as passengers boarded the coach. One passenger was a woman with a babe in arms, and when her turn came to climb onto the wagon, she turned and asked a man in line behind her to hold her child while she climbed aboard. The man quickly snapped back that he wasn't "no damn baby tender!", and forced the woman to get aboard unassisted. After the stagecoach left town, McCarty followed it far out into the desert, where he stopped it and ordered the driver to "throw down the box!" He then ordered the man who had refused to hold the woman's child to get off the coach. McCarty took his boots and told him, "Start walking! Maybe a nice long walk back to South Camp might teach you some manners!" McCarty may have been an outlaw, but he was still a gentleman!

Today, sun-baked mine dumps, sprinkled with enough shiny iron pyrites and chunks of blue-green copper to gladden the heart of any rockhound, line the canyon above South Camp, and on one old dump an ancient looking one horsepower "whim" hoist lays rusting in the sun. Stone outlines in rows along the mountainside reveal where buildings once stood, houses, stores and saloons. With lots of free spending miners and outlaws like the McCarty gang frequenting its saloons, many a coin was lost along its busy streets or on sawdust floor saloons where no one took time to look for them. South Camp's miners couldn't be bothered looking for a few lost silver or gold coins. There were plenty more where they came from, and besides, weren't they digging more silver every day? Lately there have been stories of doodle-bug prospectors finding fabulous coins at South Camp, so don't wait too long, you might be too late!

SHAUNTIE

After the Star Mining District was organized in 1870, Shauntie quickly became its chief camp. While mining records are almost silent on the district's other

A sagging gallows frame stands its lonely guard over the old Moscow Mine at Shauntie.

towns, they are full of the daily happenings at Shauntie. Newspapers reported the shoot-outs there and recorded the camp's bullion shipments. From a tent town in 1870, it soon blossomed into the busiest camp in the district. It had all of the usual, and most of the unusual, businesses miners patronized.

The Nellie Mine, located by Jack Forgie, was probably the first claim staked. Other mines at Shauntie included the Moscow, Flora, Hub, Lady Bryan and Savage. For a short time after the Moscow Mine began operations, the camp's post office was located there, so some old maps show Shauntie as Moscow. How a town so large could exist where there was no water is hard to comprehend today. Fires were a constant threat. In 1876 a fire fanned by a desert wind roared through town and, according to newspaper accounts, burned most of the business district and more than 40 houses. Almost before the ashes were cool, Shauntie was rebuilt.

A mine owner named Shumer built a smelter at Shauntie in 1873 to smelt ore from the Savage Mine. It burned down, was rebuilt, and burned again! Ore from other mines was shipped to Troy, a mill town 5 miles south of Milford. One shipment of 12,000 tons of ore reportedly produced 3,000 tons of bullion, valued at $325,000 in silver and $10,000 in gold! No wonder Shauntie was a boomer, with or without water.

But all good things must come to an end, and Shauntie's end came in worked out mine shafts. As mine after mine ran out of ore and closed, Shauntie fell into a decline that ended in closed stores and boarded-up windows. Fire visited the old camp after it was nearly deserted, and today little remains. Leaning frames stand guard over long forgotten shafts while rusting bits and pieces of ancient looking mine machinery lay where they fell a century ago. It may not look like much now, but once Shauntie was the brightest star in the Star District.

SHENANDOAH & TROY

Shenandoah was the southernmost camp in the Star Range, and thus, the most remote from Milford, and is therefore the least remembered today. When first

built, Shenandoah was known as North Camp, but when its mines proved to be bonanzas, it was renamed Shenandoah, some say by confederate war veterans. Mines like the Wild Bill, Mowitza, Red Warrior, Hoosier Boy, Cedar Tailsman and Silver Bug poured out what miners thought would be a never ending stream of silver. Like other camps of the desolate Star Range, Shenandoah didn't have green lawns or flower gardens, Like other camps of the desolate Star Range, Shenandoah didn't have green lawns or flower gardens, because there was no water except for what could be dipped from its mine shafts or recovered from melting snow. There are no springs or flowing streams in the Star Range.

A smelter was needed to reduce the camp's ore into bullion, but the closest place there was water enough to operate a smelter was along the Beaver River, 10 miles away by wagon road. In 1875, owners of the Mammoth Mine at Shenandoah built the Troy Smelter on the river bottom 5 miles south of Milford. Old-timers said it was located "on the flat between Hay Springs and the horseshoe bend" and recalled it was built by E.W. Thompson and James Low. For five years, until it burned in 1880, it produced bullion from Shenandoah's ore. During that time a mill town known as Troy existed along the Beaver River. It folded when the smelter burned and wasn't rebuilt, for by then Shenandoah's ore values were declining and silver prices were dropping.

After the price of silver plummeted, lessees continued to work the mines at Shenandoah for awhile, but in time they all closed for good and the camp was deserted. Today only one house and a shed used to store mine equipment still stand, and they are used by property owners who have claims in the canyons above the townsite. Almost no one has hunted the little treasures at Shenandoah or Troy. The last time I was at Milford I couldn't even find anyone who had heard of either place! Both Shenandoah and its little mill town could be real bonanzas for you, so go ahead, check them out, but walk softly, for you don't want to disturb the ghosts!

SULPHURDALE
&
THE LOST MORMON MINT MONEY

Mormon pioneers first discovered and mined sulphur at the foot of the Tushar Range near the northeast end of Beaver County in 1869. Sulphur, then called brimstone, was in great demand for the manufacture of gunpowder and medicines. Others became interested in the brimstone and by 1883 the Dickett & Myers Mining Company was working an open pit. *The Millenial Star* reported in its November 26th, 1883 issue that, "A sulphur mine is being worked near Cove Creek, turning out 25 tons of ore each day, assaying up to 90% pure."

A settlement that grew up near the sulphur mines soon featured a store, a fine two story hotel and a row of

30 look-alike company houses. It quickly took on the appearance of a permanent camp, and its mine production remained steady year after year. At one time the mines changed ownership and the town was renamed Morrissey for the new owner, but the name never became popular and the town remained Sulphurdale.

For awhile, Sulphurdale's mines produced a steady supply of yellow sulphur, and the old-fashioned town with its wide veranda hotel and tree shaded streets kept on its slow but steady course. Then the mine owners decided to double production and a new 100 ton per day mill was built. For some reason the new mill wasn't as efficient as the Mormon built mill, and that, combined with falling sulphur prices, knocked the supports from under the town. Black gunpowder became a thing of the past and about the only thing sulphur was used for was matches, and how many matches did the settlers use? Sulphurdale disappeared as fast as an April snow in the desert sunshine.

Today the road to Sulphurdale is closed and there is a watchman on duty to prevent trespassing, but if you can talk your way past the guard and his locked gate you will find the old town still there, just waiting for the miners to return and the mill wheels to turn again. You might even get a chance to rest in the shade of a hundred year old tree on the porch of the hotel. Sulphurdale is a good place to start your search for a fortune in gold coins, Mormon coins stolen from the mint at Salt Lake City and lost somewhere on the Sevier Desert to the west.

In 1850 the mint was robbed, but it didn't make national headlines, because it was the Mormon Mint at Salt Lake City. In 1849, Thomas Bullock and John Kay began minting gold coins for Brigham Young, in denominations of $2.50, $5, $10, and $20. All coins minted until 1851 carried an 1849 date, and are the most valuable today. From 1851 to 1862 all coins carried the 1851 date.

Dies used to mint the Mormon gold coins the Baldwin brothers hid somewhere on the Sevier Desert. -Utah Historical Society-

Dave and Reg Baldwin were two California bound prospectors passing through Salt Lake City in 1850. They stopped at Bullock's Money Mill as the mint was then known and couldn't believe their eyes. It was only a small single wall adobe brick building without even bars on the windows. To the Baldwin brothers it looked like a golden goose waiting to be plucked.

During the night they broke into the flimsy, unguarded mint and scooped up 250 freshly minted coins from Bullock's work bench. The little mint didn't even have a safe, for Salt Lake City was only three years old, and there probably wasn't one closer than the Missouri settlements. Before dawn they headed west, avoiding the usual trail south, to throw pursuers off their track. A posse led by Hosea Stout searched the regular emigrant trail, but of course, no sign of the Baldwin brothers was found.

Two years later Mormon scouts crossing the bleak Sevier Desert between the sulphur mines and Sevier Dry Lake came upon the coyote scattered bones of two men, far off any known trail. From scraps of clothing and their rusted pistols the remains were later identified as the Baldwin brothers. Over the next few years the bones of their horses were found, scattered across a mile of desert, half buried by the drifting sands.

Somewhere out on the Sevier Desert a pack horse carrying a prospector's outfit and 250 newly minted gold coins fell and died of thirst. It may have lost its pack before it fell. The coins could all be in one place, or they could be strewn across several miles of desert. It sounds almost hopeless. Maybe it is, but wherever they are, they're worth $10,000 each. Think of it. 250 coins at $10,000 each. The trail starts at Sulphurdale!

DESERT SPRINGS
&
IDAHO BILL'S CACHE

"Something hidden. Go and find it!
Go and look, beyond the mountains.
Something lost beyond the mountains.
Lost and waiting for you. Go!"
                                                        Kipling

It's strange that so few people today know of Desert Springs or the outlaw's cache hidden there. During the 1870's Desert Springs was headline news almost every day, one of the most notorious places in the state. It was an important station of the Devil's Gate & Meadow Valley stage route, at a main junction with Hugh White's Silver Reef to Pioche line and the Old Bailey Road north to the mines at Mercury Springs. It was in Iron County, according to most maps only 2 miles from the Nevada border, but by most written accounts 9 miles, close by present-day Modena. At either location, it was a tough place, an outlaw hideout, and a place of buried treasure.

Nate Hansen had a ranch nearby, where outlaws of every description made their headquarters, chief of whom was the notorious Idaho Bill, murderer and highwayman. Stagecoaches were robbed and lone travelers murdered on both sides of the line, with the outlaws meeting at Desert Springs to celebrate and spend their ill-gotten gains. The *Beaver City Enterprise* reported, "Desert Springs is fast becoming notorious. Yesterday the mail rider reported that Idaho Bill and Al Winn have taken possession of the station and are running things to suit themselves, stopping travelers, turning the liquor loose and making everyone indulge, practicing with six-shooters on the windows and riddling the place generally." Another account several days later added, "Because of Idaho Bill's gang, bullion shipments from Silver Reef and Pioche have stopped, and no passengers are coming by stage. The highwaymen have complete possession of the road, and will no doubt hold it until ousted by force!"

After stage station operator Ben Bowen was run out of town and the outlaws controlled everything, the editor of the *Salt Lake Herald* wrote, "We don't advocate lynchings, but if the towns-people at Desert Springs have to resort to violence for protection, we hope the telegraph poles will prove of sufficient strength to bear their burdens!"

On the night of December 13th, 1875 Idaho Bill single-handedly robbed the stagecoach as it stopped at Desert Springs, and dragged the treasure box off into the dark where it was found empty the next day. It was thought that Idaho Bill buried the large bullion shipment it had contained close by, because it was too heavy to carry far, and he was back at the station soon afterwards, carousing and shooting the place up. He was captured soon afterwards by Wells-Fargo Special Agent Frank Blair. He had none of the loot with him, and refused to tell where it was hidden. The box was found as stated, but no sign of the loot, although the sand and sage was probed and searched, was ever recovered.

For more than two years Idaho Bill was moved from jail to jail, from Beaver to the territorial prison at Salt Lake City, where he made a daring escape on September 5th, 1877. A posse chased him into Wyoming where he was killed, strangely enough, by his father-in-law, leaving no clue to the buried bullion cache at Desert Springs.

For several more years Desert Springs remained an important stage station and desert town, but in time the rails of the San Pedro, Los Angeles & Salt Lake Railroad reached nearby Modena. When rail cars replaced stagecoaches, Desert Springs was left to wither away under the desert sun. There may be a few old-timers at Modena, now almost a ghost town itself, who can point out the spot where Ben Bowen's station stood, but even they can't tell you where Idaho Bill cached his outlaw loot. You'll have to find that yourself. As Kipling wrote so long ago, "Something hidden. Go and find it! Go and look, beyond the mountains. Something lost beyond the mountains. Lost and waiting for you. Go!"

PIKE'S DIGGINGS

During the early 1890's placer gold was discovered on the cedar and pine covered slopes of Buck Mountain, near the western end of Iron County where it meets the Nevada state line. Among the first claims located were those of an old prospector known as "Pike." Others soon ventured into the area and in a short time the raw new camp of rough log cabins and dugouts built near their claims became known as Pike's Diggings, reminiscent of similar names give to placer camps during the days of '49 in California.

The little placer camp became the center of the Stateline Mining District, organized in 1896. Some of the placers at Pike's Diggings proved to be exceptionally rich, and many pockets of nugget gold were found. There was little water for sluice boxes or panning, so the easily worked placers were soon worked out, and a search was begun to find the mother lode where the placer gold originated. It was the discovery of the quartz ledges that were the source of the placer gold that signaled the end of Pike's Diggings and the birth of a new hardrock camp.

The new town of Gold Springs soon stole Pike's Diggings brief hour of glory. But while it lasted it was a typical frontier placer camp of tents, cabins, huts and dugouts, of which little is left. Its draws and gulches where miners once panned for color are still fascinating places to visit, if you love the desert. You can still pan a little color, and sometimes find a relic of long ago. What more could you ask for?

GOLD SPRINGS

Gold Springs was a direct outgrowth of Pike's Diggings, and came to life along the Utah-Nevada border in 1897. Two prospectors, C.A. Short and H.R. Elliott, discovered the rich gold outcroppings that were the source of the placer gold at the earlier camp. Short and Elliott staked several claims which they called the Jennie group. Ore from their mines was so rich that it was shipped to Salt Lake City under armed guard. When news of their find leaked out, a swarm of eager prospectors started a wild rush to the slopes of Buck Mountain.

Surface ore at Gold Springs was fabulously rich. Owners of the Snow Flake ledge claimed that their ore averaged 1,000 ounces to the ton, but that report was eclipsed when owners of the Rafferty and Mountain View properties boasted their ores exceeded 2,000! Other early claims where high values were found included the Wild Irish, Gold Bug and Horseshoe. Short & Elliott's Jennie Mine was the town's leading producer. A two compartment shaft was sunk deep into water and had to be drained by an 800' long drain tunnel lower on the mountain.

A mining camp, modern for its time, mushroomed on the slopes of Buck Mountain, with such conveniences as electric lights, a telephone exchange and a water

Old mines like the Snowflake at Gold Springs are relic hunters bonanzas today.

system. It also had a store, a hotel and daily stage service to Modena on the railroad. The town straddled the state line so closely that a later survey revealed that the compressor plant at the Jennie Mine was half in Utah and half in Nevada.

Several fine mills were built at Gold Springs, including a modern 100 ton per day plant built by the Jennie Mine. In 1907 two new cyanide type mills were ordered for the mines there. That was the town's downfall, for they were hardly completed when the great financial panic of 1907 struck. Bankrupt mining companies were unable to meet their payrolls. Then store owners quit giving credit, and began boarding up their buildings. Short & Elliott used the last of their company's treasury to hire a special train to bring stockholders to Gold Springs to prove the Jennie Mine was still full of gold ore, but the bankers had no money to loan, and left the Jennie Company broke and Gold Springs a vagrant with no means of support. Out of work miners left town and by 1910 Gold Springs was deserted.

Today a dirt road turns north from U-56 2½ miles west of Modena and follows the state line 12 miles to the townsite. The road climbs steeply over a mountain pass where snow often lasts until early summer. Several still solid homes built of logs stand hidden among the pines and cedars. One or two of them are occupied by modern 49'ers. Just over a ridge, the towering gallows frame of the Jennie Mine stands guard over the caving ruins of its old mill on the mountainside below. Higher on the mountain mine buildings remain, visited only by passing deer and mountain lions, their tracks fresh daily by the spring above town. After the sun goes down, a great horned owl hoots from his perch atop the ancient looking building at the Snow Flake Mine. After dark Gold Springs is a lonely place, maybe even too lonely for ghosts.

STATELINE

The Stateline Mining district was organized in 1896 when placer gold was discovered at Pike's Diggings. Miners searched for the mother lode, the place where placer gold originated. One of the places they found gold in hardrock quartz was in Stateline Canyon. The Burro, Ophir and Creede claims were among the first properties located. Ore from Stateline's mines was rich from the start, owners of the Burro Mine claiming values of $800 in gold and $600 in silver at their property. A mining camp named Stateline blazed into quick fame. with a mile long street of impressive stone and false front buildings.

Three large mills were built during Stateline's palmy days: the Ophir, Johnnie and Big 14. Stateline was on the main stage road between the end-of-track at Milford and the Nevada mines, so it was a busy place night and day, the dust from a dozen or more freight outfits never having time to settle.

Stateline was an outlaw hideout as well as being a mining camp, for Stateline Canyon had early proved its value as a quick and easy route to move stolen Mormon cattle into Nevada. In those days it wasn't considered much of a crime to steal from the often mistreated Mormons, and many herds of cattle stolen from them were driven through Stateline Canyon to Nevada buyers who asked no questions about blotched brands or forged bills of sale. Rustling was Stateline's biggest business until the Mormon ranchers finally decided to stop turning the other cheek.

One day an angry posse of Saints gave chase to a rustler named Nate Hansen, the same one who was Idaho Bill's partner at Desert Springs. Hansen was hurriedly driving a herd of stolen cattle through Stateline Canyon, and was only a mile from the Nevada border when the posse ordered him to stop. But Hansen only spurred his horse on, determined to reach the safety of the state line. The long suffering ranchers were just as determined that he be stopped, and only a few yards from the border he was shot from the saddle.

By the time Nate Hansen's gang was broken up, many of Stateline's mines were playing out. Although its ore veins were rich, often they were shallow. It wasn't long until Stateline joined Gold Springs in unwanted ghost town status.

The last time I was there there still stood several homes in good repair, one with an ornate marble fireplace. In the canyon above town the ruins of an old mill slowly disintegrate. To reach Stateline, follow the dirt road leading north out of Modena for 16½ miles to where a fork turns to the left. It is only 2 miles along that dusty trail to Stateline, the mining camp where outlaws outnumbered miners. Because so many outlaws such as Nate Hansen died there, Stateline would be a real good place to search for the places they banked their coin.

MERCURY SPRINGS

Don't start checking your oil company road map for Mercury Springs because you won't find it. But if you look at a century-old map such as Froiseth's New Mineral Map of 1878 you'll see it, right on the Old Bailey Wood Road on Spirit Mountain in the Old Home Range. Unfortunately, none of those places are shown on modern maps, which is fortunate for treasure hunters, for almost no one has been there!

Prospectors ranging north from Silver Reef or west from Minersville probably made the first silver discoveries on the mountain Pah-Utes called Quich-U-Ant-Ta, or Spirit Mountain, in what was then the Old Home Range. Today it is called Indian Peak in the Needles Range. The Washington Mining District was organized in 1879, and years later was renamed the Indian Peak District. Among the earliest locations were the Arrowhead Mine, 2 miles south of the Iron County line, and the Silver King, Cougar Spar and Holt Bluebell mines 6 miles north in Beaver County. Ore values ran 50% lead and 30 ounces of silver.

An organized group of miner's cabins and clapboard shacks grew up in the cedars and pinyons at the foot of the mountain below the Arrowhead Mine, then the district's most promising property. Although it remained a bachelor camp, it was a pleasant place, high above the desert heat and shaded by tall pinyons at the edge of the mountain where all kinds of game abounded. The main camp, where the post office and general store were located, was near the workings of the Cougar Spar Mine, in the next canyon north. There the mining companies built several large boarding houses, barns and blacksmith shop, and offices as well as numerous cabins and smaller structures.

Miners at Mercury Springs were first interested in silver, but gold finds attracted more people and after that, mercury discoveries brought still more miners to the rugged Needles Range. That was probably when the camp was named Mercury Springs. Even later tungsten was mined in great quantities, but over the years fluorspar has probably bought more whiskey and put more bread and beans on the miners' tables than anything else. Mercury Springs was a terribly isolated camp then, and it's still 100 miles from a gas station. It's a long, dusty road to the old camp today, where desert winds play hide 'n seek in lonely canyons and coyotes prowl around empty buildings.

From Cedar City go north 3 miles to where a narrow paved road turns northwest and follow it 31 miles across White Sage Valley to Lund, a railroad siding in the desert. Cross the track. 14 miles beyond on a dirt road a side canyon on the right hides the old Red Bud Mine, an interesting place to stop awhile. 6 miles farther (20 from Lund) a narrow track to the left leads 11 miles to the Arrowhead Mine, now shown on topographic maps as New Arrowhead. There are many old cabins in good repair, complete with furnishings, but they are private property and occasionally used, so please respect owner's rights. High on the pinyon covered ridge to the west stands the gaunt gallows frame of the Arrowhead Mine. Old mine buildings are built into the mountain side, but watch your step, for several shafts are dangerously caved. It's a forgotten place, where there are more cougar tracks than footprints.

To get to the main camp return to the road from Lund and continue north for 6 miles to where a second side road turns to the left. It is a better road that passes by a state Fish & Game camp and goes up a long ridge and into a basin where the Cougar Spar Mine and other properties were located. Here and there old cabins can be seen hidden among the cedars while a large log barn and corral where the blacksmith shop was located stands at the edge of the forest just below an old office building. The boarding houses have been torn down in recent years to avoid taxes for new owners who are taking a close second look at the camp's silver veins.

A rockhound can have a field day at any of the old mines at Mercury Springs or at the New Arrowhead Mine camp across the ridge to the south. Iron pyrites, blue-green copper and violet fluorspar can be found in its old mine dumps, while at the Holt Bluebell property on the 9,500' peak above the Cougar Spar Mine there are numerous beryl crystals free for the taking. From the two mile high pass beyond you can see 100 miles or more into Nevada, and look back across the Escalante Desert into southern Utah. Mercury Springs country is big, where almost every lonely canyon or rocky peak hides some treasure for today's prospector or rockhound.

This was a miner's home at Stateline, Utah's gold camp.

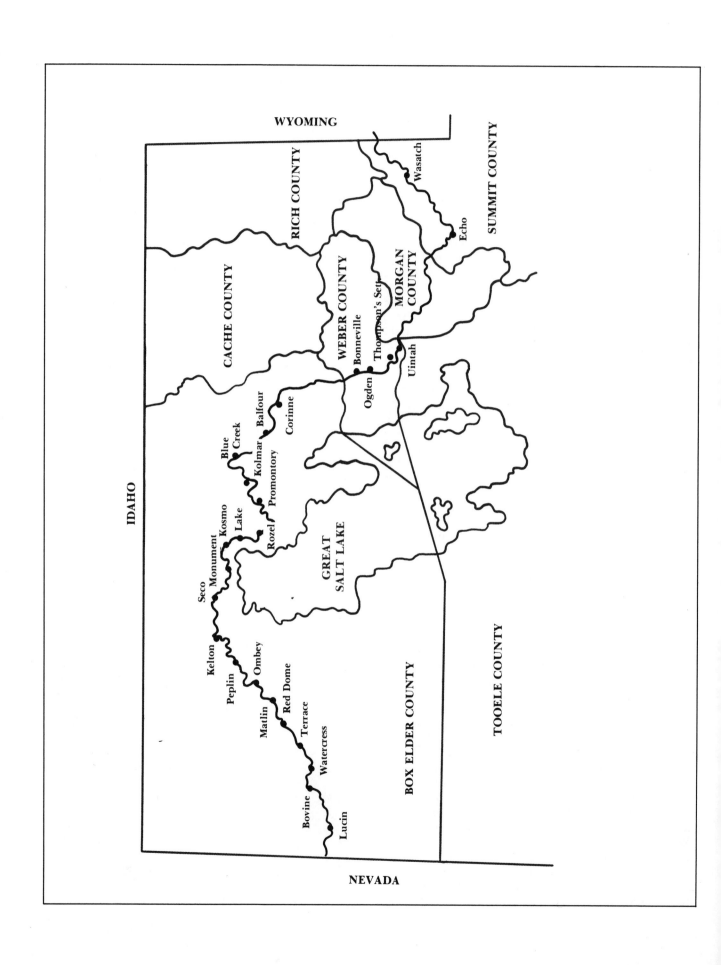

The *What Cheer* dining hall at Wahsatch. now a ghost town near the Wyoming border.

CHAPTER TEN

GOLDEN SPIKE COUNTRY

During the closing months of 1868 track laying crews of the Union Pacific building westward from Wyoming and those of the Central Pacific building eastward from the Nevada desert were rapidly approaching their historic meeting on May 10th, 1869 at Promontory, then only a desolate spot of wasteland in the heart of the Great Salt Lake Desert. As the Union Pacific's Irish "Micks" and the Central Pacific's Chinese "Celestials" came closer together they worked at a furious pace, for each company was paid for the miles of track they put down, often as much as $250,000 a mile! The U.P.'s "Micks" once laid 7 miles of track in one day, but the C.P.'s "Celestials" beat them with 10 miles in only 12 hours, a record still unbroken.

Along each company's right of way construction camps and supply towns were built. Some blossomed only to die while others became cities of today. The "Hell on Wheels" camps of the U.P., with their tent saloons and gambling dives, were wild and wooly places, but were short-lived, moving lock, stock, and barrel as the end-of-track moved west, leaving unmarked graves and piles of empty bottles to mark their passing. While the U.P. was built through a sparsely settled area, the C.P. was built through wild and empty land, and had to depend upon a long thin line of single track across the Nevada desert and over the Sierras to California for every rail, cross-tie and spike. Thus, the towns it built were far different places from those built by its competitor. Many of the C.P.'s railhead camps were built of rock and adobe, often with false front wooden buildings, where opium pipes were smoked in incense filled rooms and rice wine was sipped from thimble-sized silver cups.

Most of the U.P.'s camps soon disappeared while the C.P.'s towns became supply points for desert ranches and the "northern mines," such as Elko, Kelton and Terrace. But in time even they were abandoned when the rails were rerouted, leaving deserted and forgotten places in the silence of the salt desert. Now their only visitors are relic hunters seeking old opium bottles, strange looking brass coins or other little treasures from the days of '69. In the following pages are a few brief glimpses into the colorful and exciting times those towns had. Most are Central Pacific towns, for the Union Pacific built few camps substantial enough to be remembered. But even a caved Chinese dugout or a cemetery whose tombstones are so weathered that the Irish names on them are no longer readable still recalls that historic day when the last rail was laid and the east and west were tied together with twin ribbons of silver steel, joined with a spike of solid gold.

LUCIN
&
THE RANCHER'S LOST GOLD

Lucin was the first Central Pacific camp in Utah, 7½ miles from the Nevada line in Box Elder County. In its heyday when it was a booming construction camp, it was often known as Pilot Peak, but when it became a main supply point for railroad workers and desert dwellers it was named Lucin, for the large numbers of Lucina-Subanta, a type of fresh water fossil found there. When the end-of-track moved farther east, Lucin didn't just dry up and blow away as many camps did. It remained a supply town for ranches and farm towns in the Grouse Creek and Goose Creek mountains to the north.

During the 1870's prospectors discovered gold, silver and copper in the mountain ranges near Lucin and it became the center of the newly organized Lucin Mining District. Rich mines brought a stampede of miners to the mountains, and for several years Lucin enjoyed boom times. The district's chief mining camps were Copperfield in the Desert Range to the south and Dunnstein in the Lakeside Mountains to the southeast. But they were short-lived camps, and when they faded, Lucin died a little also.

Today Lucin is little more than a few dreary looking, dusty houses at the edge of a sun-baked desert, strung out along the rails, just barely clinging to life. But some still call it home, and now and then a stranger stops to ask about the old stage roads north, for Lucin is still the jumping off place for treasure hunters searching for the rancher's lost gold.

On May 10th, 1879, exactly ten years to the day after the wedding of the rails at Promontory, stage driver Harold Roost awaited the arrival of the eastbound train from Sacramento. Only one passenger got off at Lucin, and Roost helped him load a small but heavy locked chest onto the stage before starting the long, dusty trip north past Grouse Creek, Burley and on to Boise Basin.

Roost and his lone passenger followed the stage road north along the east side of the Grouse Creek Mountains, and then turned west to circle the west end of the Sawtooth or Raft River Range. Suddenly, five bandits spurred their mounts from behind some huge rocks alongside the trail, killing the passenger instantly with a shotgun blast of buckshot and wounding Roost badly. He fell from the coach as though dead and laid face down in the sand, covered with blood and too paralyzed with pain to move.

Between periods of unconsciousness, Roost could hear the bandits breaking open his passenger's locked chest and hear their cries of glee when they found it full of gold coins. Luckily for Roost, it wasn't long after the outlaws left when a rancher discovered the holdup scene and bound up his wounds. Taken to the nearest

doctor at Burley, Roost learned that the passenger's locked chest had contained more than $100,000 that he had intended to buy a nearby ranch with.

A posse was soon on the outlaw's trail and followed them into the strange, wild, broken rock covered country along the Utah-Idaho border between Lynn and Almo. They found the outlaws strictly by luck. The posse made camp just before dark in a canyon where the only spring in the area was located. One of the posse members walked down canyon to check on the horses and just by accident saw one of the outlaws slip up to the spring where he filled five canteens with water, unaware that he was being watched. The posse quietly followed him around a point of rocks and into the next canyon.

At first the posse was under fire, ambushed by unseen outlaws hiding in the rocks. Posse members retreated into their own cover and all night shots were exchanged on both sides. When morning came and the smoke cleared, two of the posse had been shot and all of the outlaws except one were dead. The last bandit called for help, claiming he was badly wounded, and two of the posses went to his aid. As they neared the wounded outlaw, he turned and fired point blank with a 12 gauge shotgun, killing one of them instantly and wounding the others. The bandit was also killed in the wild exchange of shots.

A thorough search of the box canyon where the outlaws had camped was made, both then and later, but no trace of the stagecoach holdup loot was ever found. The Independence Pass area of house size rocks and the City of Rocks farther north hides many lost treasures, as it was an outlaw hideout for many years. Two years ago ago a metal detector equipped treasure hunter found some rotting pieces of hardwood with heavy metal hinges still riveted to them. They looked as if they could have been the remains of the treasure chest taken off Harold Roost's stagecoach in 1879. As a relic it was too rotted to have much value. But if you find the gold that was taken from it and buried some place nearby, probably in a shallow hole by hunted men who had no time to make an elaborate cache, well now, that might just be worth looking for!

BOVINE AND WATERCRESS

The second Central Pacific camp in Utah was Bovine, 12 miles east of Lucin and 20 miles from the Nevada line. It was named for the large herds of wild cattle which roamed the area, lost by pioneer stockmen. When the rails reached Bovine, the railroad provided an outlet to market for the cattle, and soon large corrals and shipping pens were built. For a short time a Dodge City like end-of-track cattle town flourished. Marshall Dillon and Kitty Russell weren't around; nevertheless, for awhile, it was a tough town.

The thousands of Chinese laborers, often called "Crocker's Pets" because they had been hired by Charles Crocker, an official of the Central Pacific, built their town there, where they had their opium dens and countless dugouts and rough cabins that they called home. Bovine's life as a construction camp came to an end in due time, but the station itself remained active for several years as a shipping point for cattle and a supply town for ranchers in the area.

Watercress was a water station located 5 miles east of Bovine. It had a high water tower which was kept filled with spring water piped from springs to the north where watercress grew in abundance, hence its name. Watercress was an important stop since it was the only place steam engines could replenish water supplies before continuing into the desert ahead. Track was laid rapidly because of easy going near Watercress, as was reported by the Salt Lake City *Daily Reporter:* "The Central Pacific is now passing the south end of the Grouse Creek Mountains and is coming on at the rate of three or four miles every day."

As a town Watercress didn't last long, but its water tower made it a necessary stop for years after its few shaky buildings were abandoned. Today both Watercress and Bovine are pockmarked with holes dug by relic hunters in search of opium bottles and strange oriental coins lost by "Crocker's Pets" so long ago.

TERRACE

Terrace was the largest of the Central Pacific towns built in Utah. It was located 7 miles east of Watercress and 32 miles from the Nevada border. The company built their huge 16 stall roundhouse and repair shops at Terrace. It also had a large depot and many supply warehouses, as well as schools for employees' children, stores, saloons and other businesses. Some of the firms doing business at Terrace included Cave & Hinley's general store, William Grose's meat market, Smith's fruits and vegetables, Parry's Saloon, King's Hotel and the Pearson & Eager Livestock Company. Railroad employees were taxed $1 per month to maintain the library.

Terrace's population quickly soared to more than two thousand, not counting the six to eight thousand Chinese laborers who called it home for a time. Many of them remained or returned to operate stores and shops, and built a Chinatown second only to San Francisco. The Chinese shops featured items like wild rice, seaweed, duck and dried fish. Opium was sold openly for $7 a bar, enough to last a careful smoker one month. Terrace's population 30 years later was still 900, by that time nearly all Chinese.

Until the famed Lucin Cutoff was built across the Great Salt Lake in 1903, Terrace remained the Central Pacific's largest town and maintenance station in Utah, but after the line was shortened, most of the shops were moved to Elko and Carlin, and the big town slowly faded away. Since it was a busy place for three decades, it is a favorite place to hunt for relics. Except for the 60 people buried at its Lone Hill Cemetery, no one remains at Terrace today.

RED DOME & MATLIN

Red Dome was a station 5 miles east of Terrace, located at the point where the rails turned northward after they had followed a due east course along the edge of a dry, barren hillside. Only a temporary end-of-track camp, Red Dome was too close to Terrace to ever achieve much fame on its own. It had a neighbor named Matlin, a similar camp located 7 miles farther to the east, where the rails left the sun-baked hard clay foothills and entered the soft gray mud flats, heading toward the Hog Mountains which could be seen dancing above the shimmering heat waves on the great salt desert.

Both Red Dome and Matlin were short-lived places, where for a few weeks great piles of rails and cross-ties stood alongside the long rows of little white tents used by the Chinese track layers. The railhead had hardly moved to the next line camp before the tents were taken down and the transient camp left behind, leaving little to mark its site except discarded sake jugs, opium bottles and coins lost where "Crocker's Pets" played high stakes Fan-Tan using the desert sand for a gambling table. It is at such little known places as Red Dome and Matlin that today's treasure seeker has his best chance of finding precious relics of yesteryear.

The Central Pacific route from Terrace to Red Dome and past Matlin was paralleled for many miles by a hastily surveyed grade built by rival crews of the Union Pacific. Both companies were allowed to grade their right of way 300 miles beyond their actual end-of-track, and since they were being paid $32,000 a mile in the desert areas, both built their grades as quickly and as cheaply as possible. Because congress had failed to designate a meeting place, Union Pacific survey crews were working as far west as Elko while Central Pacific engineers were surveying beyond Echo Canyon. Red Dome and Matlin were places where both grades paralleled each other, often only a few hundred feet apart. Both grades can still be seen today.

OMBEY & PEPLIN

Ombey was a fuel station, a place where engines stopped to load up wood to fire their boilers. It was named for the Ombey Mountains, a cheerless, barren, waterless range nearby. Great piles of cordwood cut far to the north in the Raft River, or Sawtooth Mountains were stacked high along the track, waiting for engine tenders to load up before work trains pushed off into the barren mud flats ahead. For a few months Ombey served as home to thousands of Chinese laborers, many of whom lived like desert coyotes, in dens and burrows dug into the hillsides. The caved dugouts where they lived can still be found, and are now favorite places for history buffs to dig for relics of Ombey's brief but sometimes hectic past.

Maps of the old Central Pacific route at the north end of the Great Salt Lake reveal that its rails were laid in nearly a straight line, but just east of Ombey they suddenly veered sharply to the north, and after a mile turned southward, forming a great gooseneck bend. The big bend was in a deep cut driven through the north end of the desolate Hog Mountains. It was a cut where progress was slow, where large crews of laborers inched their way along as they dug the great cut ever deeper.

Four miles beyond Ombey by rail, but only two miles as the crow flies, a camp named Peplin was built. While the slow work on the long horseshoe shaped cut through the mountains was being dug, Peplin bustled with activity. Hastily built joss houses and opium dens served the "heathen chinee" while shacks and cabins replaced the little white tents usually used for shelter. Because they built in rocky cliffs and hillsides, many of the relics they left behind are still being found. Ombey and Peplin are completely forgotten places today.

Kelton is a forlorn ghost in the desert, but you have to start here to find the City of Rocks Treasure.

KELTON
&
THE CITY OF ROCKS TREASURE

Kelton was located at the northwest end of the Great Salt Lake 64 miles from the Nevada border. At first it was called Indian Creek but was later named Kelton for an early stockman. It quickly grew from a rough end-of-track camp into a prosperous city and important stop on the Central Pacific line as well as a supply point for the northern mines and stage station on the road to Boise Basin and the Snake River diggings.

There was nothing shoddy or temporary about Kelton. It boasted several fine two story hotels, well stocked stores, comfortable homes, a whole row of saloons and gambling halls and even a telephone exchange. The stage road from Kelton north went by

way of 10 Mile, Hard Luck and Strevell to the rich gold mines in Idaho and Montana. Nearly all the supplies for the northern mines were shipped from Kelton and stagecoaches heavily laden with gold and silver bullion returned the treasures to the railroad there. Wagon trains headed north daily while stagecoaches brought back lucky miners carrying pokes tightly packed with yellow gold.

Until the Lucin Cutoff was built across the Great Salt Lake, Kelton remained a booming place, but after the rails were rerouted it quickly faded. In 1934, when it still claimed a small population, Kelton was at the epicenter of one of the most severe earthquakes ever recorded in Utah. Deep cracks three feet wide opened in the earth's crust, releasing a flood of muddy water and black, oily slime to cover the desert floor. Houses and other buildings were rocked violently and the schoolhouse was tilted at a crazy angle. Residents tried to prop it up with long poles, but it had to be abandoned.

After the earthquake Kelton became completely abandoned, and today a few broken foundations hidden in the sage, long dead trees and a vandalized cemetery are all that is left of what was once a promising place. Not even a ghost would want to live there, and few visitors pass that way, but to treasure hunters, Kelton is still important, for there were probably more stagecoaches robbed there than anywhere else in the west. There are at least two treasures hidden near Kelton, somewhere near the Idaho line.

The Wells Fargo stageline from Kelton to the northern mines was the most often robbed stageline in the west. Records reveal that stages were held up nearly every week, occasionally daily! As was their policy, Wells Fargo never admitted what their losses were, but on the Kelton line they had to be large.

On July 9th, 1871 the Kelton stage was robbed of nearly $100,000 by three men who were soon caught, minus the loot they took. Another band of long riders robbed the Kelton stage on October 18th, 1879 of $90,000, and a lone bandit on January 3rd, 1881 made off with a bullion shipment worth $144,000. But the company reached the end of its patience in July, 1882 when the same gang robbed them twice in one week!

On July 25th, 1882 Jack King, Francis Hawley, Bill Adams, and Dave Francis held up the Kelton stage near the Idaho border, and made off with what Wells Fargo grudgingly admitted was a large haul. The gang escaped into the safety of the weird City of Rocks country before a posse could be organized. The City of Rocks is a strange moon-like landscape of twisted, towering rocks that looks, from a distance, like a medieval fortress. It was named by very early explorers, and outlaws who took refuge in its 25 square mile area found it to be an almost impenetrable maze of box canyons, tortuous trails and countless wind blown caves.
caves.

Wells Fargo hadn't seen the last of the bandit quartet, for less than a week later they struck again. On

July 30th they robbed the same stage as it was returning to Kelton from the rich mines at Albion Basin. The bandits made off with a gold shipment said to be the largest ever, and it was only a few hours until a posse organized at Park Valley and Strevell was in pursuit. The outlaws were cornered just north of the state line, where a blazing gun fight resulted in the capture of King and Adams. Neither had any of the loot with them. Hawley and Francis escaped on horseback, but they were followed so closely it was obvious that they had none of the heavy gold shipment with them either.

King and Adams were both sentenced to life imprisonment and incarcerated in June, 1883. Over the years both admitted the loot had been cached just before their capture, but neither threats nor promises could make them tell where. Meanwhile Hawley and Francis fled into Nevada. They tried to return to the City of Rocks several times, but were spotted by posses each time.

Only two weeks later, on August 14th, 1882 Hawley and Francis robbed the Wells Fargo stage between Humboldt Wells and Cherry Creek, Nevada. There they didn't have a City of Rocks to hide in, and both were soon caught and jailed. They entered the Nevada penitentiary on March 2nd, 1883 to begin serving 14 year sentences.

More than one outlaw cached his loot in the mysterious City Of Rocks, but it should be easy to find the loot from the Kelton stage holdups. Both Hawley and Francis died in prison, but before they did they confided to fellow inmates that they buried their gold in a rocky gulch in the center of a circle formed by five cedar trees. The only problem you'll have is that there are an awful lot of rocky gulches at the City Of Rocks, and there are just about as many cedar trees are there are rocks!

SECO
&
THE IRON DOOR TREASURE CAVE

After leaving Kelton the iron trail of the Central Pacific headed for Seco, 7 miles to the east. There the roadbed turned southward around the north end of the Great Salt Lake. The thousands of Chinese laborers pushed hard by their American bosses laid track rapidly, for there wasn't even a stand of sage to slow their progress. Square cross ties cut hundreds of miles away in the California Sierras were laid mile after weary mile on a roadbed of soft gray mud, where hardly a stone could be found for ballast.

Although an end-of-track camp was built at Seco, it was little more than a transitory place of tents and shacks, for it was built in the shadow of Kelton. Every passing year helped erase its memory. A reporter for the *Alta California* described its demise in only a few words. "The rows of white tents which dotted every brown hillside and every shady glen have been taken down, and the places where their owners lived are now abandoned." Nothing remains to mark its site, but not far from Seco may be one of the most unusual of all treasure caches, outlaw gold hidden behind the solid iron doors of a stolen bank vault! It's an oft told tale in the desert country, which I repeat as it was told to me.

The story of the iron door treasure cave is something like a jig-saw puzzle with some of the pieces missing; it's awfully hard to put together. Every version of the tale agrees that somewhere in Box Elder County, probably not far from old Seco and the low desert hills of Hansel Valley, there is a door from an old safe, cemented over the entrance to a cave where outlaws cached a fortune in stolen loot.

Some accounts claim the iron door came from a bank vault at Salt Lake City while others say it is part of a large safe stolen at Corinne. But they all agree that over the years a gang of outlaws led by Jim Polk robbed banks, stagecoaches, stores and travelers, caching their loot in a cave whose entrance was covered with the iron door.

The end of Polk's gang apparently came at Malad, Idaho, either when they rode into town to pull a robbery there, or when they came to buy supplies and were recognized by the local sheriff. Accounts differ in specifics but it's certain that a gun fight wiped out the entire gang as well as a lawman and several citizens. Old-timers recall that one of the outlaws, a man remembered only as "Dakota," tried to tell where the iron door cache cave was, but died before anyone could piece his incoherent words together.

The iron door cave is the kind of story most people would pass off as being too fantastic to believe, if there weren't so many local stories about it, or so many reliable people who claim to have seen it. The Polk gang used to trade or buy horses at the Bar-M Ranch in Howell Valley, and on several occasions let slip a clue or two about the cave. At the time no one paid much attention, but over the years several transient cowboys have ridden to the ranch and asked about the strange vault door they saw in a remote canyon while chasing cattle. Howell Valley and adjoining Hansel Valley are big pieces of country, so big that the cowboys couldn't find the vault door again.

And then there are the rockhounds and relic hunters who have never heard of the iron door, but while passing through nearby towns have casually mentioned seeing it. One man, an aged Mormon patriarch who would rather die than lie, personally told the author how he saw the vault door years before when helping to develop a mining claim. And so the stories go, too many and too similar to be made up or mere coincidence.

The low, rocky hills of the Hansel Valley - Howell Valley area north of the old Central Pacific route are made up of volcanic rhyolite rock, as full of holes as a giant piece of swiss cheese. Caves are everywhere, and any one of them could be the cave with the iron door. So stop awhile if you're out that way, it doesn't cost anything to look!

MONUMENT

From Seco it was 7 miles of cross ties, ballast and heavy rails to Monument. Other than its role as an end-of-track camp like so many before it, Monument never amounted to much. Only the crudest kind of shelter, tents, shacks and empty box cars were home to the nearly eight thousand "Celestials" who labored there. The *Alta California* reporter who kept his readers advised of the railroad's progress called it Parker's camp, for a reason now unknown, and described it as three separate camps of Chinese, most living in their little white tents all lined up in neat rows.

The old and the new came face to face at Monument, marking the end of an era. What is believed to have been the last California bound wagon train to cross the country before the railroad was completed met the Central Pacific's first eastbound passenger train at Monument on April 18th, 1869. A photo taken by an unknown photographer (very likely C.R. Savage of Salt Lake City) recorded the meeting for posterity.

Years after the last Chinese laborer was gone and forgotten, a salt works was built at Monument. But its life was almost as short as the railroad camp had been before, because a series of drought years had shrunk the lake, leaving the plant miles from shore. Eventually, Monument made one claim for fame, as the rabbit hunting capitol of the world. The Morgan, Utah based Browning Arms Company held a rabbit hunt there, and in one day more than 8,000 rabbits were killed!

KOSMO

It wasn't all work and no play at the tent towns along the Central Pacific, for many sported the wild attractions of the day. Kosmo was such a place, at least for a few days. Sometimes spelled Cosmo or Kosmos on old

The old meets the new at Monument on April 18, 1869. The last westbound wagon train meets the first eastbound passenger train.

maps, Kosmo's most famous story concerns one of the wildest fights in railroading history. Ironically, when it was over there was still some question of who had won.

The story goes that a boxcar full of Chinese Coolies, who were being taken to the end of the track, was stopped at Kosmo when a small group of drunken Irishmen from the approaching Union Pacific line crept up to a boxcar and placed a fused keg of gunpowder under it. A few moments later an awful blast ripped the boxcar to bits, tossing bleeding and battered Chinese high and wide! A mob of angry "Celestials" rushed to the blast site, carrying picks, axes, shovels and clubs. The Irish "Micks" were spotted and a wild fight of flying fists and swinging clubs began. When the dust cleared the "Micks" had lost the battle, but with blast torn bodies scattered across the right of way, the "Celestials" had lost the war!

A reporter from Salt Lake City's *Deseret News* described the intensity of the explosion: "Mr. T.E. Ticks showed me a boulder of three or four hundred pounds weight which had been thrown over a half mile by the blast, and which had completely buried itself in the ground within twenty feet of his restaurant!" (Businesses like Tick's Restaurant often followed the camps as they moved across the desert, as did stores and other business ventures, all catering to the tracklayers' needs.)

The Chinese were not as knowledgeable as the Irish about handling gunpowder, as was shown in another incident when several Kosmo laborers used an iron bar to tamp gunpowder into a drilled hole. One was blown 300' into the air by the explosion, the fall breaking nearly every bone in his body. The Deseret News reporter wrote, "Fun is fun, but standing astraddle four or five kegs of gunpowder and working it into the rocks with a crow-bar is a particular kind of sport that most men wouldn't relish!"

Many years after its railroading days were over, Kosmo became the site of a large potash plant. At that time the reoccupied townsite boasted more than 40 houses and several stores, but all that came to an end when the venture failed. Today both the railroad camp and the potash plant are gone, and old Kosmo is only a swampy marshland where hunters seek a different kind of wildlife.

LAKE & ROZEL

Lake, located 5 miles southeast of Kosmo, entered the record books on April 28th, 1869. On that day Central Pacific tracklayers established a record which has never been broken. They put down 10 miles of track in only 12 hours!

The record was the result of a wager made by Charles Crocker of the Central Pacific and G.M. Dodge, chief engineer of the Union Pacific. Crocker claimed his Chinese coolies could beat the U.P.'s record of 8 miles of track in one day. The starting point was just south of Lake Station and ended four miles beyond Rozel Station. It was accomplished with great precision as well as speed. 16 railroad cars of iron rail were unloaded in only 8 minutes! The actual placing of the rails on the cross ties was done by "eight strong Irishmen" as fast as the heavy rails could be carried to them by Chinese laborers. Those eight men lifted 3,250 rails that day, or more than 125 tons each!

When the remarkable record was made, Lake Station was a name flashed to every newspaper across the land, but a few months later hardly a soul remembered it. Even that great feat couldn't keep Lake from joining the long line of ghost camps stretched out behind it, as the track laying crews raced eastward toward their rendezvous.

Rozel was not only a railroad camp, but a seaport as well, where great steamships from Corrinne and Lake Point stopped to unload cordwood used as fuel by steam locomotives like the famed Jupiter. When the 10 miles of track in one day crew worked into Rozel, the new camp was called Camp Victory, but later its name was changed to Rozel for the nearby Rozel Hills.

Usually, Charlie Crocker's long suffering and hard working "Pets" caused little trouble for his company, but at Rozel a Tong War suddenly exploded. It was later learned that the See Up and Teng Wo tongs fought each other over a $15 debt! A visiting newspaper reporter wrote, "Spades were used as clubs while crowbars, spikes, picks and infernal machines were hurled. Several shots were fired, resulting in the death of one heathen."

Indians had frequented the site of Rozel for centuries before the coming of the railroad, to obtain the natural asphaltum which seeps to the surface there, which they used as a medicine. Chemically, the asphaltum is very similar to natural rubber, but it has long defied attempts to produce it in quantity. It seeps from the ground at a temperature of 130 degrees, and quickly cools, congealing in pipe lines and storage tanks. A large plant was built there, but it became a white elephant for its owners and was shut down. As a railroad camp, seaport and asphaltum field, Rozel has been a three time loser, and today is known only to the relic hunters who visit its forgotten ruins.

PROMONTORY

This was it! The historic meeting place where Engine #119 of the Union Pacific and the Central Pacific's Jupiter engine touched cowcatchers on May 10th, 1869. The meeting place, 26 miles west of Corinne and 103 miles from the Nevada line, had been designated by Congress, and was named for the high promontory of land rising out of the desert above the lakeshore. The rails of the Central Pacific had been laid into Promontory on April 30th and most of the company's dignitaries were on hand by May 7th, but the Union Pacific's VIPs were delayed until May 10th by floods in the Wasatch Mountains.

Promontory in 1868, a tent and false-front town awaiting the coming of the rails.

Rain had fallen for days, and Promontory's buildings were draped in soaked bunting, but it was welcomed by many, for Promontory had no other water source. There were plenty of saloons however, more than enough to quench the thirst of every track layer. Once account described the hastily built town as being "Dozens of tent saloons and rum holes, located 9 miles from the nearest water!" The editor of the Utah *Reporter* described it pretty well when he wrote, "Promontory is 4,900' above sea level, but it ought to be 49,000' below it, for it is for its size, morally nearer to hell than any town on the road!"

On the great day a golden spike was placed in a hole already drilled into a cross tie of laurel wood, while California's Governor Leland Stanford stood by ready to drive home the gold spike with a silver hammer. Telegraph stations across the land waited breathlessly for the final spike to be driven, while a telegrapher tapped out a message saying, "We have got done praying, the spike is about to be presented." Governor Stanford swung a mighty blow - - -, and missed! At that same instant the telegrapher tapped out, "The last rail is laid, the last spike is driven, the Pacific Railroad is finished!"

The Union Pacific had laid 1,085 miles of track at a cost of $90,000,000 while the Central Pacific put down 690 miles that cost $75,000,000. When the ceremonies were over and the crowds gone, the last cross tie and the golden spike were returned to California. The tie burned during the San Francisco earthquake, but the spike was saved and is now on display at the Stanford Museum at Palo Alto. With the celebration over, Promontory couldn't live up to the great things expected of it, and soon faded into obscurity. When the route was abandoned in favor of the Lucin Cutoff, it lost its only reason for being.

In 1969, at the exact spot where the "Wedding Of The Rails" took place a century earlier, the driving of the golden spike was reenacted and the site designated a National Monument. A fine museum has been built where visitors can view scenes from the building of the railroad in air-conditioned comfort Chinese and Irish laborers couldn't even dream of. Two replicas of the Jupiter and #119 engines are fascinating tourist attractions. But when the darkness falls and the ghosts gather, Promontory is still a lonely place, not much different than it was when Chinese and Irish track layers sipped champagne together.

KOLMAR

From Promontory the rails turned north before reversing and turning east again, forming a great inverted "V," with the Union Pacific's most westerly camp located at its apex. On March 28th, 1869 a *Deseret News* reporter described Kolmar, then called either Lampo or Junction City as, "The largest and most lively of all the new towns. Built in a valley near where the grade commences the ascent of Promontory, it is completely surrounded by grading camps." A California writer included compulsory teasing of the Mormons when he wrote: "Several dancehalls are now going full blast, astonishing the natives by the manner in which they are developing the resources of the territory. I will venture to say there are not less than 300 whiskey shops between here and Brigham City, all developing the territory's resources and showing the Mormons what is needed to build up this country!"

Kolmar was the Union Pacific's last camp before Promontory, but the Central Pacific's Chinese built roadbed to it. Since no meeting place had originally been designated, both companies built grades beyond the other's end of line. On April 14th, 1869 Central Pacific President Stanford ordered all grading work stopped when an agreement was reached for the Central Pacific to purchase the Union Pacific's completed track from Promontory to Ogden for $3,000,000 and pay the U.P.'s debts to the Mormon firm of Benson, Farr & West for road work completed by that company.

Just west of Kolmar and north of the old roadbed, about two thirds of the way up to the Promontory Range, is the Chinese Arch, a natural rock formation named in honor of the 10,000 Chinese laborers. It is the only monument named in honor of the hard working Chinese. When Promontory was chosen as the meeting place, the Chinese withdrew and left the arch along the U.P.'s right of way. Today it still stands in a seldom visited spot in a lonely land as a silent tribute to the often ill-treated and long-suffering men in whose honor it was named.

Today people think of the Union Pacific's camps as being more substantial and long lasting than the Chinese end of track towns, but today Kolmar is just as forgotten as any Central Pacific camp. For a few years it was an important construction camp, and later a water station, but when the long roadbed around the Great

Salt Lake was abandoned in favor of the trestle across the lake, and its rusty rails were salvaged for scrap, Kolmar was finished. Ghost are ghosts, no matter whether they're Chinese or Irish!

BLUE CREEK

It was a wild place. People who lived there called it Deadfall, or Hell's Half Acre! While it lasted it was a ring-tailed son-of-a-gun. One reporter told his readers, "It seems as if all the toughs in the west are gathered here. Every form of vice is in evidence, and drunkenness and gambling are the mildest sports known. It is not uncommon for two or three men to be shot or knifed every night!"

The Union Pacific's camp east of Kolmar was officially called Blue Creek, for a spring of beautifully colored blue water found there, but nearly everyone called it Deadfall. An Alta *California* reporter wrote, "The loose population which has followed the Union Pacific is turbulent and rascally, and several shooting scrapes have occurred between them lately. Last night a whiskey peddler and a gambler had a fracas in which the sport shot the peddler. Friends of the slain man then shot the gambler, falling upon him with rifles and pistols. Thirty or forty shots were fired at the unfortunate wretch as he ran, one hitting him in the face." C.R. Savage, famed photographer of railroad scenes, wrote to his wife, "There have been 24 men killed here in 25 days. Whiskey is sold everywhere at Deadfall. Men earn their money working like horses and spend it like asses!"

Blue Creek, Utah also called Dead Fall and Hell's Half Acre.
-Utah Historical Society-

But Blue Creek's days were numbered, for like all of the Union Pacific's Hell On Wheels camps, it packed up lock, stock and barrel to move to the next end-of-line camp. All that was left behind were dozens of nameless graves whose locations are now unknown, and the great piles of empty whiskey bottles that relic hunters still occasionally stumble upon. The clear blue pool of water that gave the camp its name is still there, but the big black steam engines that stopped to take on water there are gone forever.

First the tents were set up, then the rickety slab saloons were built. When they were gone, a well-filled cemetery remained!

BALFOUR

Balfour was 8 miles west of Corinne and, like most of the Union Pacific's camps, was a fly-by-night kind of place. It consisted of several gambling hall tents 100′ long and 50′ wide, a number of similar size saloon tents as well as dozens of smaller ones where Irish laborers holed up when they weren't working or drunk. Balfour had what was described as a tri-weekly stage, that is, it went to Corinne or Promontory one week and tried to get back the next!

Balfour was one of the places where both companies built parallel grades almost side by side. In one of his letters, Central Pacific President Stanford wrote to a colleague, "From Bear River to Promontory the Union Pacific is very close to us and their grade even crosses ours twice. They have so many lines surveyed, some coming very close or crossing ours that I can't tell you exactly how the final line will be." It was later learned that sections of both roadbeds paralleled each other for over 200 miles, adding millions of dollars to the cost of the final line.

Unlike the Central Pacific's camps which were at least intended to become permanent places, those of the Union Pacific were always transient places at best. When the rails moved west, their tent towns picked up and moved with them, leaving only abandoned shacks or dugouts, perhaps a water tower, and thousands of empty whiskey bottles to mark their passing. Balfour was such a place.

CORINNE

Corinne was the exception to the rule of Union Pacific camps. It was intended to be a permanent place,

with railroad shops and roundhouses. It quickly became Utah's second largest city and had hopes of becoming its capitol. When first surveyed and named Connor City for General Patrick Connor in 1868, it was an unknown spot in the sagebrush, but with the coming of the railroad, previously worthless alkali-covered lots sold for $1,000 each. Only weeks after the rails arrived the new town boasted a population of 1,500, not counting the thousands of railroad employees, and had more than 500 buildings.

Besides 28 saloons and two dozen gambling halls, there was a cigar factory, a flour mill, a brickyard, several fine hotels, one a block long, two theatres, an opera house and even a block set aside for a university! Corinne was also the center of the Liberal Party in Utah, headed by General Connor, who hoped to defeat Brigham Young and the People's Party in the governor's election and move the state capitol from Salt Lake City to Corinne. The general's hopes were in vain however, for after several stinging defeats during the 1870's the Liberal Party broke up, and in time General Connor and Brigham Young became friends.

The booming town's name was changed from Connor City to Corinne, but why is now forgotten. Some say it was named for the first child born there while others claim it was named for an actress, Corinne LaVaunt, who appeared at its grand opera house. It quickly became a main supply point for the northern mines and its freight companies were busy night and day. One company reported it had over 100 wagons and 500 mules on its line, and there were dozens of such companies! The wild, raw town boasted five newspapers, and in one of them a reporter observed, "The city is fast becoming civilized. Several men have

Corinne, the Union Pacific's boomtown. Witherell's treasure cache is buried within sight of the old Wells Fargo office.

been killed already!'' Murders were daily fare and became so commonplace that Brigham Young warned Mormons living there, "To keep a whistle in every home, to be sounded in case robbers or murderers try to break in!"

During its palmy days a large smelter was built to reduce the ores from the mines at Rush Valley. Several large steamships carried the ore from Lake Point across the lake. The primitive milling processes then used weren't very efficient, and much of the gold and silver value of the ore was lost and thrown out with the slag. That slag was used to pave Corinne's streets to help control the dust, but when more modern milling methods were discovered, the city's streets were torn up and put through the mills again, making mine owners a little richer, but Corinne's streets a little poorer.

Corinne suffered through disastrous fires, epidemics and Indian troubles and remained the stronghold of the Liberal Party, but it took another railroad to put it on the skids. Brigham Young saw his chance to cash in on the wealth of the northern mines and deal wicked Corinne a death blow at the same time. He pushed the Utah Northern through Brigham City and Logan north into Idaho, by-passing Corinne and bringing his railroad hundreds of miles closer to the mines, leaving Corinne and its dozens of freight companies high and dry. The final blow came when the Lucin Cutoff was completed, leaving Corinne a railroad town without a railroad. Today Corinne is a sleepy little farm town, not quite a ghost, but it isn't even a shadow of the wild and wooly place it was when people called it "The Burg On The Bear."

BONNEVILLE
&
THE GOLD NUGGETS AT WILLARD CANYON

The Union Pacific's right of way south from Corinne passed the Hot Springs to Bonneville, and then continued to Ogden. Although the Union Pacific built the line from Ogden to Promontory, that section of the road was sold to the Central Pacific, making Ogden the junction city for the two competitors, as well as the junction for the Utah Central south to Salt Lake City and the Utah Northern north to Idaho. Bonneville was the main point between Corinne and Ogden.

The Hot Springs became an important loading station for ore being mined in the El Dorado Mining District high on Mount Ben Lomond. The mines there built long tramways to carry their ore to mills built near the Hot Springs at what became Bonneville. The little mill town never amounted to much since it was so close to Ogden, but it was an important shipping point as long as the rich mines of the El Dorado District were working. Most of the mines there were basic metals, lead, silver and manganese, but one has become a legend, a lost mine, a rich gold placer hidden somewhere close by, most likely in Willard Dry Canyon.

Brigham Young once said he could stand in his doorway and see where veins of gold and silver were hidden in the mountains, but that the time had not yet come to mine them. Perhaps he was looking at Willard Dry Canyon, a deep water worn gash in the Wasatch Front above the sleepy little town of Willard.

There are many early day pioneer reports of nugget gold being found in Willard Dry Canyon. Some tell of a rotten white quartz ledge where nuggets of pure gold could be picked up. Others claim seeing gold being panned from the spring runoff creek in the steep rocky canyon. Both Ivan Peterson of Willard and Ories Jeppesen of nearby Brigham City saw handfuls of nuggets found by a young fellow who worked at a CCC camp at the mouth of the canyon during the early 1930's, and others tell the same story, too many not to be true.

Bill Thorpe had said that when he was a young boy, Indians would bring nuggets from the mountains above Willard to trade for the white man's trinkets. A monument south of Brigham City marks the place where some of Bill's family were killed by Indians. Sometime after that Bill Hunsaker took a short cut over the mountains from Mantua to Willard, and while passing a broken ledge to a dry wash he picked up enough nuggets to fill his pockets. Hunsaker waited too long to return, for several days later one of the violent cloud bursts that regularly strike the Wasatch Front flooded the canyon, covering where he thought the ledge was with tons of silt and boulders.

During the late 1920's several large floods raced out of Willard Dry Canyon, burying houses along the foothills. Scars of those terrible floods still remain. But the gold ledge is still there, and it sends flakes and nuggets downstream with every passing rain. Only last year a boy hiking in the canyon picked up several large nuggets.

The Sierra Madre Mine built the Hot Springs Smelter and started Bonneville, now a forgotten place.

But be warned, all of the canyons along the Wasatch Front are rough, the roughest you'll ever see, and Willard Dry Canyon is the worst of the lot! It's impossibly steep. Its little snow water creek can often be heard bubbling along under tons of loose rocks and boulders, but only rarely can it be seen, usually during spring runoff. There are vertical cliffs hundreds of feet high, and during the heat of summer flash floods race down its steep slopes without warning. There are even rattlesnakes!

JACK THOMPSON'S SETTLEMENT
&
THE UTAH CENTRAL'S LOST LOOT

The Union Pacific went south from Ogden to Jack Thompson's Settlement before turning east toward Weber Canyon. Jack Thompson's Settlement was called Taylor's Mill before the railroad arrived, and after the iron rails were laid quickly became a booming place. From a sleepy village it blossomed into a town that had no less than eight restaurants, where meals cost $2 each, more than most people there had ever seen before the railroad came. It had the usual saloons, but not the usual drinks, for only beer could be served, there being a city ordinance against selling whiskey.

Jack Thompson's Settlement soon became a main junction for travelers, especially those going to Salt Lake City and points south, for they could leave the Union Pacific and board the newly built Utah Central for the Mormon capitol. Today almost all of Jack Thompson's old settlement has been swallowed up by present-day Riverdale.

The greatest excitement the old town ever saw was when the Wells Fargo express car on the Utah Central Railroad was robbed of $35,000 at 8:10 PM, September 14th, 1876, near the Hot Springs a few miles north of Salt Lake City. Every newspaper in the city reported it, and within days four men were arrested for the robbery. But that's all we know. We don't know what happened to the arrested men, and more important to treasure hunters, we don't know what happened to the loot.

When the train stopped at Woods Cross at 8 PM everything was in order, but when it arrived at Salt Lake City at 8:20 Wells Fargo Messenger Billy Williams was tied up with strips of canvas and the safe had been cleaned out of just over $35,000, $15,000 of that in gold. Wells Fargo offered a reward of $500 each for every robber caught, plus one fourth of any money recovered. No one took them up on it.

Messenger Williams claimed he surrendered the safe keys on demand at gunpoint, and that two bandits jumped from the speeding train, carrying the loot, including the heavy gold with them. Investigating Wells Fargo Agent J.E. Dooly decided that William's story sounded just a little too thin, and the next day he was arrested. Dooly traced the canvas strips used to tie Williams to the Walker Brothers Store, and learned that Williams and a man named Frank Treseder had pur-

chased them. Treseder was arrested and jailed with Williams, but searches of their homes and property failed to turn up a dime of the loot.

The following day two more men were arrested. One was Clem Lee, a known hood who had robbed Wells Fargo stagecoaches in the past, and George Rose. To the great embarrassment of Wells Fargo, Rose turned out to be one of their special agents! Now two Wells Fargo employees were in jail, Rose and Williams. Suddenly the investigation ended, and nothing more appeared in the newspapers. Reporters couldn't learn a thing, and when they went to the city jail to interview the prisoners, their cells were empty and all four were missing!

Court records then and now are silent about their fate. There is nothing to show that they were tried, transferred or released. Nothing! Then to add to the mystery, on October 12th, Wells Fargo published another reward notice, offering $500 for information leading to recovery of negotiable bonds of the Wasatch & Jordan Railroad taken during the Utah Central robbery on September 14th. Why Wells Fargo waited a month to report the theft of the bonds wasn't explained, but soon stories began circulating that the amount of money taken was far greater than the $35,000 originally reported.

At this late date the mystery is difficult to unravel. What happened to the four men will probably never be known, they simply disappeared. Perhaps the company's well known motto gives a clue to their fate: "Wells Fargo Never Forgets!" Nor do we know exactly what was taken during the robbery, for Wells Fargo did not detail their losses. There probably was a conspiracy among the four, with Treseder and Lee actually pulling the robbery. But what they did with the loot is unknown. Certainly none of the arrested men had it. There isn't a clue.

Any large amount of gold suddenly appearing in Salt Lake City or other small towns would have been noticed. And what about the railroad bonds? They would be worth a fortune today. Since nothing was ever found it is reasonable to believe the loot was hastily cached in a shallow hole somewhere along the Utah Central tracks where the bandits jumped from the train near Hot Springs. Who knows? That's probably as good a place as any to start looking!

UINTAH &
THE SPANISH TREASURE CAVE
OF PARRISH CANYON

Uintah didn't actually start as a railroad town. Mormon settlers built a 500' by 1,300' walled fort there in 1850 and called it East Weber. But there wasn't enough farm land to support much of a town until the rails of the Union Pacific reached there in 1869. Its location was ideal, because stagecoach connections could be made there to Salt Lake City. Railroad officials renamed the town Easton, but several years later it became Uintah, named for a Ute Indian tribe.

Uintah's tent and board shack business district covered two acres, and was described by one traveler as "The most repulsive place I ever saw! Every building is either a saloon, a gambling hall or what passes for a restaurant." Another said that its hastily built stores and saloons were "huddled closely together as if afraid of their own frailty." Among the firms doing business at Uintah were Bowman Brothers Groceries, De La Baume's General Store and the Corey Brothers Construction Company.

Until the Utah Central connected with the Union Pacific at Jack Thompson's Settlement, Uintah was the main junction for travelers who left the rails for the long, dusty stagecoach ride to Salt Lake City. Travelers could stop at Kay's Creek, Parrish's Settlement or Session's Settlement before reaching the Mormon Zion. At the Parrish Settlement, now Centerville, a Spanish treasure of historical significance was found and then lost again.

Early journals of fur trappers and diaries of explorers mention the ruins of a stone building, usually referred to as a Spanish fort, where Kaysville City now stands. Mormon settlers discovered the ruins in 1847, and later wrote about them. "The Mormons believed the Salt Lake Valley to be uninhabited until their arrival, but white men whose identity will probably always remain a mystery had in the long ago lived here."

Since there was no one but the defenseless Digger Indians in the area it's safe to assume the ruins are not of a fort. Fur trappers would never have built a stone house there, for there were few fur bearing animals in the valley. Besides, early fur trappers and mountain men had said the ruins were old when they first saw them.

In 1848 Samuel Parrish established a settlement between Bountiful and Farmington at the mouth of what became Parrish Canyon. Over the years the little town of Centerville grew, and in 1909 Thomas Christensen moved there. Christensen operated a grist mill on Parrish Creek and grazed a few cows and sheep in the steep rocky canyon above. It was he who solved the mystery of the stone cabin.

One day Christensen took his wife and children high into the mountains, where they had a picnic lunch at a place he later called "a glade-like meadow." There, at the top of a rock slide at the base of a towering crag, Christensen spotted a small cave-like opening, and decided to explore it. He wiggled inside and waited a few minutes until his eyes became accustomed to the dark. There before him, covered with the dust of ages, was an ancient cross-bow and pieces of heavy Spanish armor!

Christensen pulled several pieces of armor out of the hole, including a curious looking breastplate, and carried them down the canyon to his mill. For the next several years many of his neighbors saw the ancient artifacts, and some mentioned them in their diaries and other records. After a few years Christensen moved to the Pacific Northwest, and no one knew what happened to the "old Spanish junk" he found. It was probably thrown into some nameless gulch or wash.

Why was the Spanish armor cached in the cave in Parrish Canyon? Who put it there, and when? Did they intend to return for it? Was it left behind because they had an even heavier load to carry, perhaps a fortune in gold? The answers may never be known, but there's probably a connection between the armor cache and the old stone building at Kaysville.

Many years later gold was found in Farmington Canyon only a few miles south of Kaysville. During the same period several shipments of rich ore were made from the Morning Star claims in Parrish Canyon. Could there be a connection between those finds and the old stone cabin? Could Spanish miners have lived there? In 1891 a minor gold rush began in the small un-named gulch between Farmington and Parrish canyons, but fizzled when the source of the rich float couldn't be found. Maybe other miners a century or more before had mined the source and dropped the pieces of float where they were later found. Perhaps they also left an old stone cabin near Kaysville, and some pieces of armor in a cave high in Parrish Canyon, where who knows what else may be hidden? Perhaps, but we will probably never know.

ECHO CITY

Echo City had its start as Weber Station on the Overland Stage route. When the rails of the Union Pacific reached the mouth of Echo Canyon a city was surveyed, with numbered building lots and named streets where the old stage station had been. Within a month after its birth Echo City had a business district of more than 50 false front business buildings. But behind those wooden false fronts customers found only a huge white tent, the same one as the last end-of-line camp.

Echo City was a tough place. Outlaw bands like the infamous Potter Gang holed up there and killings were everyday stuff. Finally the Union Pacific brought in Jack Slade, a hired gun, to help clean the town out. Mark Twain visited there and was appalled by the daily murders. One visitor described the wild town in the following way: "Echo City is in direct communication with all the gilted enticements which wanton pleasure decks herself with!" After it became a ghost town and its buildings were torn down, the bodies of seven murdered men were found under the floor of one it its saloons!

But while it lasted it was a humdinger. The Asper House Hotel was the leading hostelry while stores, restaurants, saloons and even a dance hall quickly separated the track layers from their pay. When the railhead moved on, Echo City faded, but unlike most camps it didn't completely die, for in time it became a junction for the Utah Eastern Railroad into the silver camp of Park City. But don't confuse present-day Echo with the Echo City of old, for they are not the same. Echo is northwest of the original town which was built on an east to west axis directly in line with the canyon entrance.

A later visitor described Echo City after the thousands of Irish track layers left: "Everything at Echo City is so still and quiet that one wonders what businessmen do to pass the time. Store doors stand open while their owners sleep. Every saloon boasts two or three occupants, but they are all stretched out in the sun along their canvas sides." Of interest to treasure hunters is the fact that Echo City had more than its share of toughs who spent, and no doubt lost, many a gold coin in its sawdust floor saloons. Years after the town was deserted an enterprising farmer tore down its one room rock jail, and in a hollow space behind a loose rock he found a gold watch, a pair of spectacles and a bag of gold coins. Who knows what other little treasures still wait to be found?

WAHSATCH

The first Union Pacific camp in Utah, west of the Wyoming border, was Wahsatch, located near the head of Echo Canyon on a high, windy divide between the Weber and Bear River drainages. Wahsatch lasted longer than most Union Pacific towns because at that point a long tunnel had to be driven through the mountain. While the 772' tunnel was being dug, a rickety temporary track was laid on a makeshift roadbed built on piles of logs and rubblestones piled along the mountainside. A few small work trains could use the temporary track, but until the tunnel was completed Wahsatch remained a shoot-em-up wild and wooly place.

Unlike most Union Pacific camps, Wahsatch had many wooden buildings. This was probably because of its relatively long life and because it was located on a cold, windswept ridge. The What Cheer Dining Hall was a well built wood frame restaurant. Irish laborers spent their money in tent saloons as fast as they were paid and killings were part of the day's activity. The town didn't have a regular cemetery, thus many lonely and now forgotten graves were dug on the sage covered hillside for men whose only mistake was that they were a little too slow on the draw.

A reporter for the *Deseret News* accurately described Wahsatch when he wrote: "A man was shot and then hung at Wahsatch last night. The reason? He was a damn nigger!" Finally the long tunnel was completed and the railhead was pushed farther down Echo Canyon, leaving Wahsatch in the discard pile. Many of its buildings were moved to another newly built camp named Evanston. Because it lasted much longer than most Union Pacific towns and was such a wild place, Wahsatch should be a profitable place for lost coin and cache hunters. Good Luck!

Uintah, also called Easton, once an important place. The treasure of Parrish Canyon is not far from here. -Utah Historical Society-

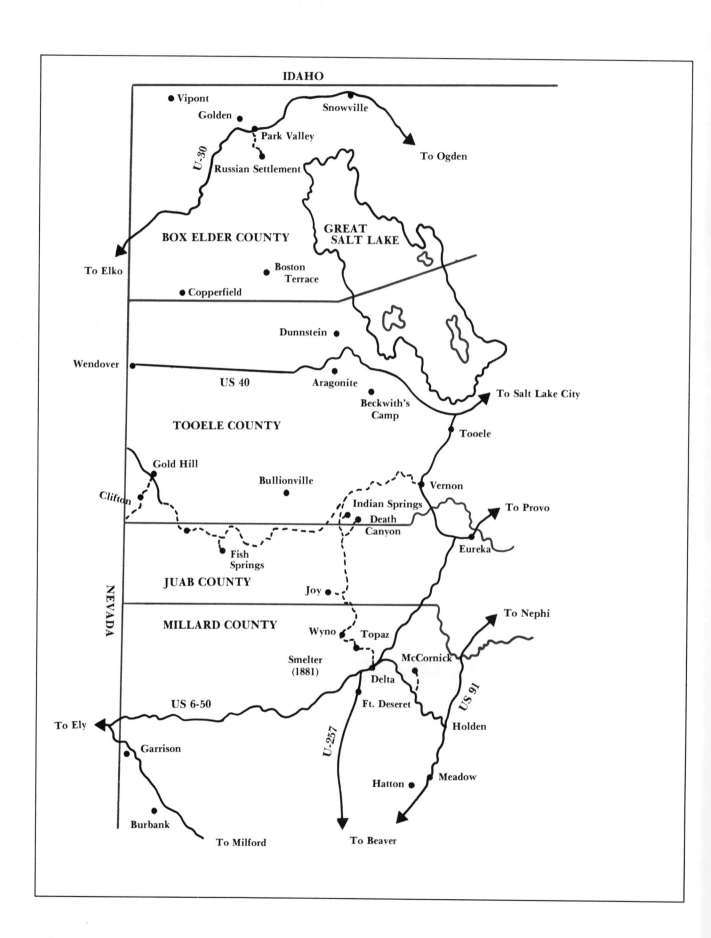

A miner left his buckboard at Boston Terrace and never returned.

CHAPTER ELEVEN

IN THE WEST DESERT

From the Idaho border on the north to the Sevier Desert on the south, the northwestern part of Utah is an arid, sparsely settled land of alkali flats, low sun-baked hills, black volcanic cones and snowcapped peaks. Dirt roads snake across its endless miles, following trails made by homesteaders, prospectors and cowboys 100 years and more ago. Many of the farm settlements, ranch towns and mining camps they built still dot the sage covered flats and barren hills, but no one walks their streets anymore, for now they are the ghost towns of the West Desert.

Most maps don't show those old places. Except for a few old-timers and wanderers of the wasteland they are forgotten. But they are still there, hidden in lonely canyons or standing forlorn beyond road's end. The howling winds from a hundred winters and the burning sun from as many summers have taken their toll. Towns far from the beaten path or located in sheltered places often have a few houses and business buildings standing. Sometimes they are almost as their owners left them so long ago, but more often time and the elements have done their work so well that only crumbling walls and sagging roofs remain.

The West Desert is a big land of quiet solitudes and purple distances, and the towns which blossomed and

died there were as varied as its moods. Many were booming mining camps such as Bullionville and Fish Springs, where glistening streams of silver poured from thundering stamp mills and whiskey flowed even faster across rough plank bars. Some, like McCornick and Hatton, were farming settlements while Burbank and Garrison were ranching towns where horse thieves outnumbered cowboys. And there were strange places like Russian Settlement and Topaz. From the salt desert to the wastelands of Juab and Millard, the West Desert is a ghost-towner's dream come true, where lost mines still wait to be found and buried caches taunt the treasure seeker. Why wait, maybe it's your turn to strike it rich!

BOSTON TERRACE
&
RELIC TREASURES OF THE NEWFOUNDLANDS

Because it is located in one of the most isolated mountain ranges in the west, completely surrounded by the great salt desert, the old mining camp of Boston Terrace is unknown to most ghost towners. Long after most of the Utah Territory had been mapped, Box Elder county's desert ranges were unexplored and unknown. Mormon stockmen called the little known ranges far out in the west desert the new found land, but avoided their barren, waterless slopes.

During the late 1860's silver was discovered in the mountains of the new found land, and a group of Swedish miners started a little mining camp on one of the desert ranges they called the Newfoundlands. There isn't much in the way of written records, but local legend has it that the Swedish miners had an agent at Ogden who sold their ore, sent them supplies when needed, and banked their profits. After a long year of hard work the miners came to town to celebrate and settle accounts, but discovered that their agent had gone south with their money, reportedly about $100,000. With nothing to show for their hard work and no funds to buy supplies with, the miners lost heart and never returned to the Newfoundlands. Today old mine dumps strewn with ancient looking machinery, old cabins hidden in out of the way places and a large fort-like building of closely fitted stones remain to prove they were actually there.

In 1880, the Box Elder Mining District was organized and once more prospectors began searching the Newfoundlands, locating several promising silver outcrops. A mining company was organized at the Central Pacific town of Terrace, its purpose being to reopen the old mines abandoned by the Swedes years before. When their old camp was reoccupied it was named Boston Terrace for the Boston & Terrace Mining Company. Ore shipped from the mines assayed 86 ounces of silver, 27% copper and 15% lead. Other companies were soon started, including the Ogden & Lucin Copper Company, Utah & Nevada Gold Mines and the Shepard Mining Company.

For nearly a decade miners stayed at the isolated camp, until the richest and most easily mined ore was gone. There are almost no records to tell what kind of a camp Boston Terrace was, but from foundations and ruins it appears that most of its buildings were clustered at the northwest tip of the range near the Nephi Mine. Then in 1905 a new camp called Dunnstein sounded its siren call from across the desert in the Lakeside Mountains. Almost overnight Boston Terrace was deserted. Trunks filled with clothing and barrels of dishes were left in empty cabins, while buckboards and ore wagons were left behind by miners who never returned for them. Never well known except to those who lived there, Boston Terrace was easy to forget, and today it is probably the least known of the ghost towns of the West Desert.

But because it is so isolated and forgotten, Boston Terrace can be a relic hunter's dream come true. There are countless reminders of yesteryear strewn all across the range. At one old cabin I picked up a beautiful and most unusual cobalt blue colored eight sided bottle embossed with the name "McAlister's Mocking Bird Food." During the 1950's I spent two years in the Newfoundlands and shipped some 1,300 tons of ore from

them. There is every kind of ore to be found there, from large deposits of tungsten, copper and manganese to veins of silver and pieces of gold float. One geologist called the range a prospector's paradise. I know that it's a treasure hunter's paradise, for every rocky canyon and boulder basin hides secrets from the past. I found still locked cabins from the 1880's and mine buildings no one had entered in a century. Not much has changed since then.

But be warned, the Newfoundlands are for desert rats, not for armchair treasure hunters driving air-conditioned motor homes! The rugged canyons are steep to hike and temperatures are extreme, often over 130 degrees in the summer and far below zero in the winter. The few water seeps hidden back in the deep canyons are full of arsenic, so it is necessary to carry water. And there are no roads to speak of, the only access being along the Southern Pacific tracks from Lakeside on the south or Lucin to the north, and the railroad isn't very happy about people using their road. But if you like to get away from it all and don't mind getting lost or poisoned, then Boston Terrace and the Newfoundland Mountains are for you!

DUNNSTEIN, ARAGONITE
&
BECKWITH'S CAMP

A small mining camp located near the south end of Tooele County's Lakeside Range was named Dunnstein, its origin now unknown. Miners first hurried to the diggings there in 1905 when silver and copper were discovered. Of the mining companies operating there, the chief ore producers were the Lakeside Copper Company, the Lakeside Mining Company and the Monarch Gold Mining Company. Again, few records remain to tell what kind of a camp Dunnstein was. Of the firms doing business there, none remained in 1909, for the camp was described as being deserted at that time. As was the case at many desert mining camps, transportation of ore to distant smelters or mills was a major problem, and many mine owners stockpiled ore waiting for a railroad that never came.

Today a dirt road leaves I-80 just west of the Lakeside turnoff and winds back into the hills to the old Monarch Mine. Other old mine dumps and shafts can be found farther along the range, and just beyond "grassy" on the mountain's east slope, there is an old Indian burial ground. Most of the Lakeside area is on the Air Force's bombing range and permission to enter should be obtained, for unexploded bombs are often encountered.

Eight miles west of the Lakeside turnoff another dirt road turns south towards the Cedar Mountains. It leads the way to Aragonite, a small camp that owed its life to the mineral aragonite, a pure white crystalline calcium carbonate, used as a decorative building stone. Although Aragonite came later than Dunnstein, it is still an interesting place to visit. Several tumble-down houses remain and a number of shafts can be seen along the mountain front. One mine is still being operated on an irregular basis, so watch for heavy ore trucks coming down the canyon.

The road beyond Aragonite climbs to the head of a rocky canyon, where it crosses the crest of the Cedar Mountains, then drops steeply down the eastern slope to the desert floor below. This is Hasting's Pass, followed by the Donner Party in 1846. At the edge of the foothills, where the cedars meet the sage, a small army post once existed, In 1853 Lt. E.G. Beckwith of the Army Topographical Corp led a survey party there and established a camp which was used for the next five years. Lt. Beckwith was searching for a route to be used by a proposed trans-continental railroad, but found no way across the endless miles of salt and sand of the Great Salt Lake Desert. He was replaced by Capt. J.H. Simpson who surveyed the famous trail around the south end of the great salt desert which later became the route of the Overland Stage and the Pony Express.

Early maps show the location of Camp Beckwith, but it is only through careful searching that it can be found today. Because so few have ever been there, and fewer yet have searched for relics or metal-detected, it could be an unexpected bonanza for ghost towners visiting Dunnstein or Aragonite.

COPPERFIELD
&
THE DONNER PARTY GOLD

Copperfield was a small mining camp at the north end of the Desert Range in Box Elder County, 30 miles across the salt flats northeast of Wendover. It was born in 1870 when copper-galena ore was discovered in the newly organized Lucin and Silver Islet Mining Districts. Among the earliest mines were the Tecoma, Empire, Rising Sun, Mary Ann and Bald Eagle claims. Ore from the Goldstone Mine assayed up to 50% lead while at the Black Warrior Mine, hornsilver with values up to $4,000 a ton was found! The Silver Island Coalition Company was one of the district's best producers.

Copperfield mine owners built a smelter near Salt Lake City, but they might just as well have built it on the moon, because heavy ore wagons bogged down in the soft gray mud of the salt flats almost before they were out of sight of the mines. The same mud that stopped the Bidwell-Bartleson Party in 1841 and spelled doom for the Donner Party in 1846 hastened the end for Copperfield 30 years later.

When mining at Copperfield proved unprofitable, its mines closed and miners left for easier diggings. It never did amount to much as a town, and there is no record of its businesses. There must have been some, though, if only a store and a saloon. But they were left behind when the miners left, and in the harsh world of

the salt flats it wasn't long until their empty shells were claimed by time and the seasons. On some old maps Copperfield is shown as Copper Hill, but by whatever name it is one of the state's least known and shortest lived mining camps. And it will probably stay that way, for the Great Salt Lake Desert is just as inhospitable today as it was 100 years ago.

George Donner believed the lies that Lansford Hastings told about a short cut to California across the Great Salt Lake Desert, and it cost him his fortune first and his life later. While at Fort Hall in August, 1846 Donner decided to take his wagon train across Hasting's Cutoff and Utah's salt desert. Hastings had ridden a horse across the desert three years earlier, but no wagon had ever crossed it before, and after the Donner Party tragedy, none ever would again.

It was the first of September when the Donner Party began the desert crossing which Hastings said would take only two days. After a week of pure hell Donner's wagons were abandoned and left scattered across the desert, buried in salt, mud and sand. The emigrants were without feed for their livestock or water for themselves. Everything not necessary for life was thrown away to lighten the loads, from pistols and rifles to dishes and furniture. Near Floating Island George Donner buried a heavy wooden chest containing $15,000 in newly minted gold coins that he had hoped to start a new life with in California.

When the burning sun rose the next morning, Donner's oxen were gone, and he staggered on across the glaring salt to find water for his family. Finally Donner collapsed and fell near Silver Zone Island, where he was found and saved by Jim Reed. With the greatest effort, all of the party made it to Pilot Spring and pushed on across the Humboldt Desert, leaving all of their valuables behind on the great salt desert, including George Donner's cache of gold worth more than a million dollars today.

There's no doubt that Donner cached his gold, for everyone with the wagon train knew it, nor did they question that some day they would return to recover their valuables. But unknown to them, that was never to be. All treasure hunters know the story of the Donner Party, how they were so delayed by their terrible ordeal on the salt desert that they started too late in crossing the Sierras and froze to death in the mountains. George Donner was one of the first to die, and the secret of his cache died with him.

No one tried to follow the Donner trail again until 1927 when historian Charles Kelly traced the route and recovered countless dishes, pieces of clothing from rotted trunks, chests of silverware and pistols and rifles. The tracks of the Donner Party can still be seen today, and the great salt desert is as terrible now as it was 136 years ago when George Donner cached his chest of gold. But the gold is still there, and if you decide to go look for it, don't say I didn't warn you.!

HATTON
&
THE OLD SPANISH MINES COMPANY

The sorry remains of Hatton, a town settled in 1851 by pioneers led by Peter Robinson, are located 1 mile west of US-91 between Kanosh and Mendon in Millard County. For awhile there was a stage stop known as Petersburg, but when a town was surveyed at the spot it was named Hatton. In addition to the Gilmer & Saulsbury Stage Station, an important stop on the route between Salt Lake City and the mines near Milford, Hatton had the usual store, church, school and post office. It also boasted a confectionary and candy shop, a rarity in pioneer settlements.

From the first, Corn Creek flooded farms every season and washed badly needed crops away. In 1867 Brigham Young surveyed the results of a disastrous flood and advised the Saints to move farther upstream. The settlers lost no time following the prophet's directions, and before another season came most had moved upstream and established Kanosh. After their relocation, irrigation dams and canals lessened the threat of flooding and most of Hatton's fields were cultivated again, but the farmers never returned to live. Since then most of the original homes have fallen with the weight of years.

A few of those long empty cabins and log houses, nestled in the shade of giant cottonwoods planted long ago, wait patiently for their owners' return. In one of them a man said to have been a well-known artist lived for awhile, and while there painted the upper part of the living room walls with outdoor scenes whose color and detail are still beautiful today, providing an unexpected bonus for today's ghost towner.

At the head of Corn Creek not far from old Hatton there is living proof of Spanish mines in Utah, which some historians still question. Everyone familiar with Utah's old Spanish mines knows of the Lincoln Mine, a centuries old silver mine discovered by Bishop Rollins, north of Minersville in 1958. Other well documented accounts describe the discovery of the ancient lead mines at Potosi, and the Spanish diggings near Eureka and other places. Stories of the Lost Josephine, the Pish-La-Ki and the Lost Rhoades are legion. But somehow they all seem nebulous and unreal since they depend upon thin accounts by nameless Jesuit Priests hidden in musty church records at Mexico City or Madrid. But old Spanish mines in Utah are real, and ancient histories as well as modern accounts of their rediscovery do exist. I refer skeptics to the Old Spanish Mines Company.

After the settling of Hatton and Fillmore during the 1850's, pioneers frequently saw pack trains of ore being brought down Corn Creek Canyon from the mountains above by Mexican miners. Several miners told the settlers they had worked the mines all their lives, and that their fathers had worked them as well. But the settlers were aware of Brigham Young's admonitions against mining, and were in any case more interested in growing corn than digging gold, and thus paid little attention to the pack trains. During the Walker War of the 1850's and the Blackhawk War of the late 60's many of the ore trains were attacked by Indians, and the miners killed. In time they were seen no more. The locations of their mines were forgotten, if in fact the pioneers ever knew the locations.

In 1893 Robert M. Keen was operating a hotel at the Baldy Mining Camp in New Mexico. There he became acquainted with a Mexican named Joe Guiterez, who told him that when he was eight years old his father and other miners were killed by Indians near a gold mine in Utah. Guiterez was one of seven who escaped. None of them ever returned to the mines. Keen was fascinated with the story and in June, 1900 convinced Guiterez to lead him to the mine. Guiterez remembered that the creek (Corn Creek) that ran from the area of the mines flowed into a valley of black volcanic cones (the cones are 14 miles south of Fillmore) where a large and permanent Indian village (Kanosh) was located.

It took Guiterez and Keen nearly two years to locate the proper landmarks. Finally, near the head of Corn Creek, they discovered several sunken depressions in the ground which proved to be the ancient shafts, cleverly concealed by timbers with grass and sage planted on them. Several tunnels that had been concealed with giant boulders and brush were also found. One of the shafts was uncovered and a windlass hoist built over it. When men were lowered into it they found four different levels in its 140' depth. The landings were made of large flat stones set into the sides of the shafts in fitted grooves. Steps were notched in the shaft walls, worn by Indian slaves who had climbed them with heavy packs of rock and ore. Pieces of ore broken from the shaft bottom assayed $22,100 in gold!

The old shafts were too dangerous to work in, so late in 1901 a tunnel was driven from lower on the mountain to connect with the shaft bottom. In digging the tunnel an ore body was struck, which the Salt Lake *Mining Review* reported as being "A large body of telluride ore, with average values of $263 to the ton, although some of the ore assays more than $1,400. This begins to look encouraging!"

Robert Keen, Guiterez and several prominent mining men organized, with tongues in cheeks, The Old Spanish Mining Company! The Salt Lake *Mining Review* as well as all the leading newspapers of the day and state mining records reported the story. If you remain unconvinced that there are old Spanish mines in Utah, let me know who you think dug that deep shaft.

Century old cabins hidden in forgotten canyons near the ghost town of Golden could be a cache hunter's bonanza.

GOLDEN & VIPONT

6 miles west of Park Valley in Box Elder County, a silver camp ironically named Golden had its beginnings at the turn of the century. John Angove made the first ore strike at the foot of the Raft River Range in 1899, and the following year Dr. J.F. White and a party of prospectors from Salt Lake City staked the claim which became the Planatary, Deer Trail, El Amigo and Sussanah mines, while at the west end of the district a not too promising claim named Vipont was staked.

The first ore taken from the newly located mines was rich in gold, so the camp that grew up around them was named Golden, but as shafts were sunk deeper, the ore changed from gold to silver, often with values of up to 1,000 ounces to the ton! A five stamp mill at the Century Mine produced $500 a day for its owners. Everything looked so promising that the original Century Mill was replaced with a larger 16 stamp plant in 1906, and the next year one of the first Chilian Rod Mills was installed at the Sussanah Mine. The camp's population was estimated at 500 at that time.

Along with the mining industry as a whole, the great panic of 1907 struck Golden a severe blow. Hard money was replaced by nearly worthless script, mines closed daily and unpaid miners left for more hospitable climes. E.H. Jones closed his general store and moved its inventory to nearby Park Valley and Rosette. Golden had a brief rebirth in 1910 when several of its mines were reopened, but it wasn't until 1920 when owners of the Vipont uncovered an ore body with values of 12,000 ounces of silver to the ton that a second boom began.

A long tramway was built from the Vipont Mine down the steep mountain front to a new concentrating mill. 300 men were hired, with none being paid less than $4.50 a day, a large salary for the time. The Vipont proved to be a real treasure house of silver, and it was mined steadily until the depression years of the 1930's. After that lessees shipped ore from it through the 40's. But as a town Golden died in 1907, though silver was shipped from some of her mines for another 30 years.

RUSSIAN SETTLEMENT

There is a forgotten little cemetery in Box Elder County not far south of Park Valley that is a monument to forlorn hope. It marks the site of Russian Settlement, one of Utah's strangest ghost towns. At the little ranching town of Park Valley a narrow dirt road turns southward across a sage covered flat. There, in 1914, a band of Russian peasants came to start a new life in a new land. Where they came from is uncertain, but legend claims they traded valuable business property in San Francisco for the desolate arid acres in Park Valley which, according to the story, was owned by an old Chinaman who had won it in a fan-tan game during the days when the Central Pacific was laying track south of there. No matter how they got there, before long they were putting up houses, churches and schools in the strange architectural style of Czarist Russia.

For six long, lean years the Russian peasants battled the hostile desert. But after repeated crop failures and a death to match every birth they gave up and moved on, no one knows where, leaving their strange looking homes to the desert. Over the years they've been torn down for the lumber, dragged to nearby ranches and used as farm buildings.

In 1937 a cowboy hunting coyotes rode his pony onto the rotting planks covering a forgotten well, and both he and the pony fell 30' to its bottom. With his lariat, a lot of hard work and plenty of luck the cowboy got out of his underground prison, but it took two days and the use of a derrick to get his horse out. Today the little cemetery hidden in the head high sage and the caved in well where the cowboy nearly lost his life are all that remain of the Russian Settlement.

INDIAN SPRINGS AND DEATH CANYON

The little remembered mining camp of Indian Springs was located south of Simpson Springs, on the Overland Stage route, north of Death Canyon almost on the Tooele-Juab county line. The springs there were a camping place for the Indians of Skull Valley long before the coming of pony express riders or miners. Some early day maps show them as Good Indian Springs, a name that leaves little to the imagination!

After silver was discovered in the Simpson Range in the late 1890's, a small but wild mining camp was established at Indian Springs. It had several well built boarding houses, a store and a saloon where 40-rod whiskey was sold. The broken rock walls of one building still stand not far from the mouth of a caved mine tunnel. The ore veins were exposed at Indian Springs. They snaked their way across the mountain fronts for long distances, and were mined from the surface down wherever they turned and twisted, leaving dangerous shafts only a foot or two wide but hundreds of feet deep. Watch carefully where you walk, for they are a death trap for whoever falls in one.

Probably the most exciting day Indian Springs ever had was in 1902 when Barney Dunne shot and killed his partner, Bill Dryburn. The two miners had been drinking at the saloon all day long and continued in their cabin after it closed. They argued over just about everything, including which was the best shot. Finally Dryburn bet that Dunne couldn't shoot the hat off his head with only one shot. The wager was made, but both men lost. Dunne lost his partner and Dryburn lost his head!

To get to Indian Springs follow the Pony Express Trail west from Simpson Springs to a weathered sign-post that points south to Death Canyon, another old mining camp of more recent vintage. Five miles along the Death Canyon road a narrow, almost overgrown trail turns sharply to the left and climbs steeply up the mountain front. If you have a low-slung auto it is safer to walk the half mile to the rock ruins of the old store building. Foundations of old mine buildings can be seen against the mountainside. Here and there relics of yesteryear lie in the desert sun. Apparently, each miner at Indian Springs had his own salt and pepper shakers at the company boarding house, for I found several with names etched into the ornately cut glass, one marked "Ben - 1902."

At the point the trail to Indian Springs leaves the Death Canyon road there are the ruins of an old smelter. In the brush and rocks just below the road one can

find its crumbling rock walls. About 8 miles farther, at the south end of the Simpson Range, the road to Death Canyon doubles back to the left, then goes up canyon to a double row of solid cabins. At the end of the road stands an often used house with a fine spring of cold water. Although no one lives there anymore, the cabins at Death Canyon are still used by prospect owners, so treat them with respect. Neither camp, Indian Springs or Death Canyon, became world famous, for like the good, both died young.

JOY & IBEX
&
PEDRO'S LOST PLACER GOLD
&
THE SPANISH MINE IN THE HOUSE RANGE

There is nothing joyful about Joy! Located in a wild, windswept canyon at the south end of the desolate Thomas Range at the edge of the bleak Sevier Desert, it would have taken someone with a warped sense of humor to name such a woeful and desolate place Joy. The explanation lies in the fact that it was named for Harry Joy, one of her promoters. The god-forsaken desert town was the only place between the Overland Trail and the railroad, far to the south, where travelers could find water. At that there was hardly more than a trickle of mineral laden moisture. Prospectors who camped at the seeps first discovered large outcroppings of manganese which was of little value then, but later uncovered promising ledges of gold and silver ore. Several mines were developed, the Major Drum, Howard, Deseret and Ibex properties among the most promising.

The Drum Mining District was organized in 1872, and reorganized in 1879 as the Detroit District, but most miners knew it as the Joy District, for Harry Joy. Owners of the Howard Mine built a smelter but it proved impractical since there wasn't enough water to operate it. Harry Joy purchased the useless smelter and moved it to Wyno, another small camp to the south. Until it was in operation much of the ore from Joy's mines was shipped to Chicago and some was even sent across the Atlantic to Wales. Incidentally, Mr. Joy became quite rich and helped found the Packard Motor Car Company a few years later.

Many early references to Joy, as well as many maps, refer to it as Detroit, since it was the chief camp of the Detroit Mining District. When a post office was established there, mail addressed to Joy, Detroit, or even to the Drum Post Office, was delivered there, all of which is somewhat baffling for researchers today.

Even more confusing is the camp known as Ibex. Ibex was a small camp built around the Ibex Mine, and for a time it rivaled Joy. It had the reputation of being a wild and wicked place, boasting several saloons which never closed and one hotel. Its population was said to be 200, and apparently for a time there was a post office named Ibex. Oddly, it was located at the Charm Mine, not the Ibex Mine. The little camp was almost exactly on the Juab-Millard county line. To further upset ghost-towners, there was another Ibex Mine located some 40 miles farther south, in the Confusion Range, and it was known at times as Ibex Camp. The townsite of Ibex located near Joy was definitely short-lived, because a government water survey report for the year 1900 describes it as being deserted at that time.

While its mines operated Joy was a lively place though never an attractive place to live. When it became a vagrant, the veins pinched out, only those who had to remained. "Aunt Mary" outlasted them all. She lived alone at the deserted camp for the rest of her life. Prospectors and passing cowboys knew her as "No Nose Maggie," since she had lost her nose years before.

But now even "No Nose Maggie" is gone, and her sun-burned shack by the side of the road has fallen into a pile of twisted boards, stove pipe and broken furniture. Broken foundations of mill buildings, decaying mine structures in surrounding canyons and piles of rusting tin cans are all that remain. I doubt that even a ghost could call it home. No, there is nothing joyful about Joy!

Prospectors from Joy fanned out into the surrounding desert ranges. Some of those who drifted into North Canyon in the desolate House Range southwest of Joy were amazed to find the ruins of ancient sluice boxes made from hollowed out logs. There are no trees larger than scrub brush within a hundred miles of the House Range, so where did the logs come from? And even if there had been timber, there is no water to operate a sluice, not a drop. No one knows who built those ancient sluice boxes, but we do know why, for there is gold in the House Range!

Early desert travelers and pioneer sheepherders discovered ample proof of early Spanish miners in the House Range. Ancient metal picks were found near the sluice boxes, so old they crumbled when touched, and in a centuries old shaft, ladders made of notched logs still remained. Wooden shoulder yokes with pieces of rotting leather ore sacks still clinging to them were found in ancient mine tunnels. Buckles, spurs and remains of unknown metal tools have also been uncovered in old diggings. No one familiar with the House Range doubts that Spanish miners were there in the distant past, but where the ore they washed in the giant log sluices came from remains a mystery.

The House Range is unbelievably rugged. Its west face is a 35 mile long vertical cliff towering 2,700' above the desert floor, while Notch, Sawtooth and Swasey peaks are jagged exclamation points against the desert skyline. Knowledgeable mountain climbers consider the cliffs of the House Range among the most challenging anywhere. Only a few stunted bristlecone pines stand twisted and wind torn atop the high ridges, and there's not enough water in the entire range to make a cup of coffee. Don't venture into its forbidding depths without adequate supplies; it's more than a hundred miles across the desert to the nearest drive-in.

Prospectors have found the House Range to be rich in minerals. A great deal of tungsten has been shipped in recent years, but only a few clues have been found to explain the old Spanish workings. In North Canyon, miners dug into an old tunnel, and inside uncovered ancient hand tools, which are now on display in Delta. Another tunnel, also in North Canyon, led into a series of stopes, or rooms, where log ladders and leather ore buckets were found before the workings caved in.

The best waybill for today's treasure hunter who plans to find the Spanish gold of the House Range came from Pedro, a Mexican sheepherder who walked into the office of Dr. J.E. Stains, a Delta dentist, in 1938 and offered a poke of gold dust and nuggets for sale. Dr. Stains bought the gold and asked Pedro where he got it. Pedro said he panned it from a rich dry placer where he'd been herding sheep. Dr. Stains later learned that was in North Canyon!

A few months later Pedro came into Delta again, but this time he brought a pack sack containing 20 pounds of gold! Dr. Stains had no use for that much gold and declined to buy it. In search of a buyer, Pedro quit his job and left town. He was never seen around Delta again.

There is one other thing. Dr. Stains talked to the rancher whom Pedro had worked for, and he recalled that Pedro spent more time prospecting than he did herding sheep. He also remembered that Pedro had had an old map that was supposed to show where there were old Spanish mines in the House Mountains. But the rancher didn't believe in that kind of thing. All he wanted was somebody who knew how to herd sheep. I wonder what happened to Pedro?

WYNO

Wyno is a strange name for a town, but then Wyno was a strange town, one that moved around a lot! During the 1870's a smelter was needed to make bullion from the silver and gold ore being mined at Joy and Ibex, but there wasn't enough water at either camp to take a bath, let alone run a smelter. 14 miles west of present-day Hinckley in Millard County, where several springs promised an adequate supply, a smelter was built in 1881. Shortly a store, a saloon and a row of cabins turned into a small town which, for some strange reason, was named Wyno. But the enterprise wasn't very well investigated and Wyno's days were numbered; the springs which looked so promising in April dried up when summer's heat scorched the Sevier Desert.

When the springs failed, Wyno's citizens founded Smelter Knolls, 11 miles to the northwest, where there seemed to be plenty of water to operate their smelter. Wyno was rebuilt at the new location. Soon ore shipments began arriving from Joy and Ibex, but then more unexpected troubles developed. The water at Smelter Knolls was heavily laden with salt and other minerals which fouled up the whole process. After repeated unsuccessful smelter runs, the entire plant was sold to the Tintic mine owners who moved it to their properties at Eureka.

Wyno probably would have died then and there if still another move hadn't been made to yet another smelter location. In 1888 a blast furnace smelter was built at Hot Springs, 11 miles north of present-day Abraham. The new plant proved to be an instant success, and during the next two years it produced 130,000 pounds of high grade bullion. Cabins and shacks that could be moved were dragged from the old camp at Smelter Knolls, and others were built. A regular little town grew up by 1890. Then disaster struck; the fine new smelter caught fire and burned to the ground!

By then good wagon roads were being built across the West Desert, so when a modern smelter was built on the railroad at Leamington in 1893, there was no need to rebuild the one at Hot Springs. Wyno's main value for ghost-towners may be that since few people know where it was, it hasn't been thoroughly picked over. While it takes some looking to locate its three sites, when you do you'll be on virgin ground, for I saw no evidence that anyone had ever dug a hole there.

TOPAZ

It was Utah's fourth largest city, yet many have never heard of it. Topaz, located in central Juab County north of Delta and 20 miles south of its namesake Topaz Mountain, is not only Utah's most recently abandoned ghost town, but probably its most completely obliterated one as well. Topaz was a wartime internment camp built to house suspected Japanese-American security risks, who began arriving at the desolate, remote desert site in September, 1942. The well planned town consisted of 42 city blocks with 12 military type barracks buildings on each block. There was also a large 128 bed hospital, a theatre, 5 churches, a recreation hall and even a newspaper named *The Topaz Times*. In all, the Topaz townsite contained 19,800 acres with more than 600 buildings, enclosed behind a four-strand barbed wire fence. The number of Japanese confined there reached a high of 8,778, making it Utah's fourth largest city.

Not long after Topaz was established, authorities realized that there was no need to confine most of the people who had been brought there, because nearly all were loyal American citizens. Most had been brought from the Pacific coast, and in time were allowed to return to their homes. But while living at Topaz, the so-called prisoners were allowed to roam the desert, prospecting or searching for topaz crystals. One group discovered a 1,164 pound meteorite which was later sent to the Smithsonian Institute.

Topaz was closed in 1945. Contracts were given to salvage everything, as if to erase the shameful blot from the desert's face. The job was done so well that practically nothing remains to show that people once lived there. It's not a very good place to go treasure hunting.

BULLIONVILLE

The mining camp of Bullionville in Tooele County's West Desert country can be reached by following the old Pony Express Trail west from Faust and over Lookout Pass to the foot of the desolate Dugway Range. A poor dirt road turns north from the Pony Express Trail and follows the eastern edge of the range almost to its north end, where an almost invisible trail turns up a rocky canyon to Bullionville. It is a track better suited to trail bikes or four-wheel-drive vehicles than it is to passenger cars.

After the first discovery of silver in the Dugways in 1870, a small camp named Bullionville appeared, with a store, saloon and even a butcher shop. One eastern visitor wondered where the fresh meat came from but later observed that the quantity of meat sold stood in direct proportion to the diminishing numbers of wild horses that roamed the desert. Bullionville's leading mines were the Silver King, Black Maria and the Queen Of Sheba while smaller properties included the Yellow Jacket, Harrison, Cannon and Buckhorn.

Distances in the desert country were too great to make hauling ore to the railroad profitable, so a smelter was erected in Smelter Canyon. Mine owners built it at great expense, but after it was completed they learned that smelters require a great deal of water to operate, and water is one thing the Dugway Range had little of. When its smelter proved to be useless, mines closed, and by the late 1880's Bullionville was a deserted camp, with piles of high grade ore stacked up waiting for the day when the proposed railroad would arrive. It never came.

Several years later a reporter for the *Stockton Sentinel* passed by the abandoned camp and wrote for his readers, "Tons of high grade silver ore is sacked up and piled on the Silver King dump, just waiting for the day it can be converted to coin!" Today only a few log cabins still stand. At one long closed mine a locked and still privately owned house awaits its owners return. Dangerously caved shafts are everywhere. Rockhounds often search the foothills of the Dugway Range for geodes which are abundant there. Few know of the old camp in Smelter Canyon, because the north end of the range is off-limits. Signs warning it is part of the Dugway Proving Ground, a test area for explosives and poison gas, keep them away.

If you get up that way, stop and look around, and be sure to visit the old Silver King dump. The last time I was there those tons of silver ore were still waiting to be converted to coin!

The First Issue of the New $5 Gold Piece

Obverse   Reverse

Mormon gold can be found at a hundred places like Burbank and Garrison. -Deseret News-

BURBANK
&
MORMON GOLD CACHES

11 miles from the Nevada border, just west of U-21 in Millard County, a ranch house and some weathered log cabins can be seen, where the colorless desert country of Snake Valley butts up against the Nevada foothills. They are all that is left of Burbank, a Mormon farming community that dates back to the 1870's. Burbank was surveyed as a townsite in 1876 and named for Margie Burbank, the maiden name of the wife of Judge E.W. Clays, a prominent early day settler. The little town grew as more farmers arrived each year. A post office was established and a store was started at Dearden's Ranch, close to present-day Baker.

Farmers at Burbank and at nearby Garrison, now also a ghost town, sold their produce and livestock for gold, often Mormon gold coins, but usually bought what they needed through barter. There were no banks in Snake Valley, or even a store or business building with a safe, so post-hole banks and backyard caches hid many farmers' life savings.

For awhile Burbank prospered, but then years of drought came to Snake Valley and farms began to dry up and blow away. Snake Valley was right on the "Horse Thief Trail," used by rustlers to move livestock stolen from Mormon farmers to the mining camps of Nevada, where no questions were asked or forged bills of sale questioned. With chasing horse thieves and fighting summer droughts and winter blizzards, Burbank's settlers began to find that farming in Snake Valley was an uncertain proposition at best. Gradually they left for greener pastures, leaving the town to disintegrate.

It is at forgotten Mormon settlements like Burbank that treasure hunters hear intriguing tales of money caches, usually only a few coins hidden away as a hedge against hard times. It seems that many of those old-timers hid Mormon gold rather than US currency, perhaps because they had more faith in church minted gold. Some caches were simply forgotten and some

were lost when the only person who knew where they were died. Isolated places like Burbank are probably the best places to look for lost Mormon gold caches.

It's amazing that so few treasure hunters know that the Mormon Church minted gold coins from December, 1848 to March, 1862. Tens of thousands were minted, but only a few can be found in coin shops, museums and private collections today. The rest are lost, hidden or cached, and they are worth no less than $10,000 each today!

When the flood of emigrants hurrying to the California gold rush passed through Utah, only non-Mormon merchants who had plenty of hard money to conduct transactions benefitted from their lucrative trade. Coin poor Mormon merchants who could deal only in barter couldn't compete. Salt Lake City Marshal Hosea Stout commented on the phenomenon when he wrote in his diary: "Men will not buy or sell anything except for gold dust or coined money."

To cash in on the California trade, Brigham Young directed Thomas Bullock and John Kay to establish a mint which was located where the Hotel Utah now stands. The Mormon Mint was known as Bullock's Money Mill and began operating in December, 1848. The coins made there were minted from what one observer described as being, "A considerable quantity of gold dust brought from California by the Mormon Batallion, melted down Spanish doubloons and a large amount of raw gold brought in from the Rhoades Mine."

Coins bearing an 1849 date were minted in values of $2.50, $5, $10, and $20. The $20 coins were the first of that denomination ever minted in the United States. The obverse side had the coin's value, two clasped hands, the words "Pure Gold" and the initials "GSLC," for Great Salt Lake City. The reverse side displayed the "all seeing eye of Jehovah" and the words "Holiness To The Lord." The first coin dies later broke. New ones were obtained from England, and from 1851 to 1860 all coins minted carried the 1851 date. After 1860 the coins were changed to feature a beehive, a Mormon symbol of industry, on one side and a crouched lion on the other. All are rare today, no matter what the date. The 1849 coins are quite crude, while later issues were sharp and clear.

No one knows how many coins were minted, for neither Bullock nor Kay kept accurate records, but entries from their diaries and items from the *Deseret News* indicate the number was large. On October 5th, 1850 the Editor of the *Deseret News* wrote, "We stepped into the mint a few days ago and saw two or three men rolling out the golden bars like wagon tires, all ready for the dies. This is what makes trade brisk!"

Occasionally John Kay made diary entries of the total number of coins minted on a given day, but he seldom mentioned the denominations. In a speech Brigham Young stated that "Old Father Rhoades (of

Lost Rhoades Mine fame) had just brought $17,000 in gold to Salt Lake City." An entry in *The Journal History Of The Church* mentions, "In one box was as much gold dust as a man could carry, and there was a box of silver which required three men to lift it."

Although the coins bore the words "Pure Gold," many were actually bullion for it was soon learned that pure gold didn't wear well. In later mintings silver was added to give the metal hardness, which was looked at with suspician by many traders. In California, Mormon coins were often discounted 10%. By the 1860's Mormon coins were no longer needed, so the Mormon Mint was closed on February 26th, 1862.

The vast majority of Mormon coins remain unaccounted for. But it's a safe bet that many are still buried in post-hole banks or cached in secret places around hundreds of abandoned homesteads like those at Burbank. No doubt many were lost, in the same places coins have always been lost, picnic grounds, rodeo corrals, stores and saloons. Anywhere people lived in pioneer Utah is a good place to search. One was found near Ogden and another in Clearfield during the last year. At $10,000 or more per coin, what are you waiting for?

GARRISON

Close to the Nevada border, just off U-21 in Millard County's Snake Valley, several adobe and log cabins mark the site of an outlaw camp that later became a farm town and still later a ghost town. Garrison had its birth as an outlaw ranch. There, Utah cattle were fattened up before being driven across the Nevada border, where buyers asked no embarrassing questions about the variety of brands in the herd. It remained an outlaw

Garrison had its birth as an outlaw ranch used to fatten stolen Mormon cattle.

hideout until Mormon settlers began moving into Snake Valley and settled nearby Burbank. In time the new arrivals crowded out the criminals. As they left Garrison began looking like a town with a future. A post office was established, named Garrison for one of the settlers, and a general store opened by "James & Clay" became a favorite meeting place for valley farmers.

Garrison was built on farming, but it proved to be a pretty shaky foundation. It didn't take them long to realize that Snake Valley wasn't destined to be the garden spot of Zion, and that its parched acres couldn't support more than a minimum number of livestock. As an outlaw ranch it was ideal, but it was no place for poor dirt farmers. Its farms were gradually abandoned until only a few settlers remained, and they subsisted by ranching. With both outlaws and farmers gone, Garrison became a ghost town.

In 1922 part of the great movie epic, "The Covered Wagon" was filmed at the old town. Nothing so exciting has happened since. Judge Clays, who was one of the original settlers at Burbank, was a prominent man at Garrison, a partner in businesses there and in mines in Nevada. Many people at Garrison were like Judge Clays in that they disliked paper money, always taking gold when they could get it, and Mormon gold in particular. Mormon gold was especially welcome at places like Garrison where any kind of coin was hard to come by. Cache hunters shouldn't overlook places like Garrison where lost Mormon gold and outlaw caches are hidden side by side.

FISH SPRINGS

Perched high on a mountainside at the north end of the Fish Springs Range in Juab County stand the ruins of Fish Springs, one of the state's least known mining camps. It should not be confused with the Fish Springs Overland Stage Station which was 15 miles east on the opposite side of the range. In 1899 silver-lead ore was discovered at what would become the Galena Mine, and within only a year both it and the nearby Utah Mine were paying their stockholders regular dividends.

Charles Van Alstine made the first ore find after countless other prospectors had passed by the desolate mountains, apparently believing its barren flanks were bare of ore as well as water and timber. But Van Alstine's discovery proved to be a rich one, and a Salt Lake City reporter who visited there shortly after its vein was opened told his readers that the newly found mine was rich "beyond human calculation!" Other promising finds made by the rush of miners included the Coronation, Walton, Dream, Vulcan, Mayflower and Cactus lodes.

There were no mills or smelters at Fish Springs since there was no water to operate them with, so ore from the camp was hauled by George Aldridge's 16

The General Store at Fish Springs. Walt Reid, 4th man from the right, was killed in a gunfight soon after this photo was taken.
-Utah Historical Society-

horse teams to smelters at Wyno and the Detroit District. Ore from the mines at Fish Springs was rich, especially that from the Utah Mine, assaying as high as 80% lead and 150 ounces of silver to the ton. The Utah Mine shipped $480,000 worth of silver bullion during its first year of operation. With its mines booming, the new camp grew rapidly, claiming 250 miners, camp followers, several stores and a saloon.

By 1904 Fish Springs was a wild and wooly place, with no law except miners' law. That year E.H. Weeds killed his partner, A.F. White, for singing while he was trying to read! Weeds hauled his partner's body 100 miles across the desert to the Sheriff's office at Eureka, where he told lawmen that he killed White, "because I wanted some peace and quiet, but he wouldn't stop that damn singing!" The Judge listened with sympathy to his story, and recognizing the symptoms of "cabin fever," sentenced Weeds to 10 months of "peace and quiet!" Not long after that store owner Walter Reid killed a Fish Springs miner named Kilkoski in a fight for the affections of Kilkoski's wife. But the prize proved difficult to hold onto. A short time later Reid was killed by another of widow Kilkoski's suitors. According to John Peezley, an old-timer who lived at Fish Springs during its palmy days, Mrs. Kilkoski was later knocked unconscious during a fight at the Utah Mine, and was buried alive by a bunch of drunken miners after an equally drunken doctor pronounced her dead!

But the lawless mining camp's days were numbered, for water was encountered as shafts were sunk below the 800' depth, and the primitive pumps then in use couldn't keep them dry. At the Utah Mine, the camp's richest, water was pumped up to the 400' level where it was backed up in a large underground lake, but the next day the water had seeped back into the lower workings and had to be pumped all over again. The ever worsening water problems combined with the hard times brought on by the panic of 1907 sealed the camp's fate. By 1910 the miners were gone and the tough little town on the rocky slopes of the Fish Springs Range was abandoned to the ghosts of men who had died there.

For nearly 50 years, John Fritch of Park City kept the Utah Mine alive. Almost every year he hired a few men to keep its shaft open and shipped a few cars of high grade, so the old buildings there have not been vandalized like so many mining camps. Today those few old buildings, including the post office and Reed's Store where Kilkoski was killed still stand, and on a bleak, windswept ridge a row of crosses marks the last resting place of those who found violent death there. Ghost-towning is a lonely business.

McCORNICK
&
GOLD LIKE GRAINS OF WHEAT

McCornick was the handiwork of William S. McCornick, a banker who made his fortune in the silver mines at Park City. It was located 23 miles north of Fillmore in Millard County, between Delta and Holden. Banker McCornick established his planned farming community in 1917, and with his money, it soon blossomed into a busy town with all the usual businesses and 40 well built homes. In 1919 it became a station on the Delta & Fillmore Branch Railroad, part of the Union Pacific system. But Banker McCornick was deceived by the only wet years the Black Rock Desert country has ever seen. By the time his town got going, the desert reverted to its normal dry state.

A long canal was dug to bring water to McCornick's thirsty acres, but was never successful. When its sandy banks weren't washing away, flooding farms with mud and silt, it filled up with drifting sand and had to be dug all over again. McCornick's up and down existence continued, with noticeably more downs than ups, until 1929 when the great depression struck. Many of its businesses failed as the discouraged farmers left for more promising places. From a population of 500 it waned until there weren't enough people left to keep its church active.

Many of McCornick's buildings were moved to other towns, including the schoolhouse which was moved to Flowell. During its hard life 95 children were born at McCornick and 10 people died there. Their graves and a few tumble-down houses are all that is left. Banker McCornick wanted a thriving farm town as his memorial, but he got a ghost town instead!

Folks who lived at McCornick told a treasure tale that sounded like something right out of the Arabian Nights, but everyone of them believed it was true, and the facts seem to support them.

In 1888 a young fellow named Herschell Hill was prospecting Cedar Mountain and Pavant Butte, and out into the Black Rock Desert, where McCornick would later be built. He had a dog-eared map he claimed would lead him to an old Spanish Mine. Many people around Fillmore met him, and some saw his map, including a store keeper who grubstaked him. Hill made trip after trip into the desert, criss-crossing the country from the north end of the San Francisco Mountains to the Crickett Hills and the House Range. Every time he returned empty-handed people around Fillmore would shake their heads in pity, all but the store owner, who shared Hill's enthusiasm.

With winter near, Hill made a last trip into the desert, riding westward into the face of an approaching storm. He made camp and was prospecting on foot south of Clear Lake. By late afternoon the wind had risen into a blinding sandstorm, blotting out every landmark. Hill realized he was lost. He staggered around until after dark, hoping to find some sort of shelter in the flat windswept desert. Just when he was about to give up, he came to a low-lying wall-like cliff, and felt his way along it to a narrow slit-like opening. Carefully, Hill inched his way into a room-like chamber. He then collapsed onto what felt like dead animal hides and fell into an exhausted sleep.

When Hill awakened, sunlight was streaming through the entrance of the cave. He took his first look at his surroundings. What he had thought were animal hides were pieces of ancient looking leather pack sacks, rotten and black with age. The sacks were piled on top

of each other. From their shrunken, split sides streams of strange looking yellow grains the size of wheat had spilled, mixing with the sand on the cavern floor. Hill dug his hands into the loose grain-like yellow nuggets and felt their heavy weight. Only then did he realize they were gold.

Hill tried to orient himself, but could only tell that he had wandered far south from his camp near Clear Lake. To the south he recognized the outline of the big black volcano west of Fillmore, near the eastern edge of the desert. After filling his pockets with grain-like gold, Hill began the long hike to Fillmore. Looking back, he was surprised to see how the low line of cliffs blended into the sand dunes. It was long after dark when he reached Fillmore, thoroughly exhausted and half delirious from two days without water. His partner at the store examined the golden grains over and over again, unable to understand their strange shape. They were so soft and so heavy that they had to be nearly pure gold. Later the gold Hill brought with him was sold for $3,000.

Although he was still weak, it was only a few days before he and the store keeper tried to return to the treasure cave. Winter winds had erased all signs of Hill's trail, and they could find nothing that even looked like the cliffs where Hill had taken refuge. When spring came Hill made trip after trip trying to retrace his trail. He searched from Fillmore and from his old camp at Clear Lake, and even climbed the great volcano west of Fillmore which he had seen from the cavern, but could find no trace of the low-lying cliffs. To the northwest he could see the outline of the Black Hills and the Confusion Range beyond, but they were too far away. The only place that answered the description were the Crickett Hills, but he couldn't find them, for every passing storm covered or uncovered them with drifting dunes.

How did the gold grains of wheat become hidden in a cavern somewhere out on the Black Rock Desert? Was it a storage place for Spanish gold mined in the mountains to the north? There is only one place which answers the description Hill gave, and that is the Crickett Hills. Their name is misleading, for they are not really hills at all, but only low lying rocky outcrops and ledges that are buried and uncovered by each passing storm. From them you can see the giant volcanic cone west of Fillmore, but you can't always see the Crickett Hills from the cone.

There's another reason you might want to start your search there. In 1929 a sheepherder, who spent the winter on the Black Rock Desert west of Fillmore, quit his job and was next seen at Ogden. He had a sack full of gold that looked like grains of wheat! He sold part of his gold at pawn shops and bars, then skipped town just ahead of federal officers who wanted to question him about the raw gold he was selling. The rancher he worked for knew him only as Juan, and no one around

Fillmore ever saw him again. The legend of Herschell Hill's golden grains of wheat sounds like fiction, but it is a persistent story that hasn't died easily. People at McCornick believed it years ago, and people in the Black Rock Desert still believe it.

GOLD HILL

The famous mining camp of Gold Hill was located near the Nevada border at the north end of Tooele County's Deep Creek Range, 40 miles south of Wendover. Emigrants enroute to California on the Overland Trail first found gold there in 1858, but Indian troubles prevented settlement of the area until the 1870's when nearby Clifton became a booming gold camp. At first, Gold Hill grew slowly, eclipsed by the brighter light of its wild and wicked sister city. It was hardly more than a tent town until mines like the Copper Queen, Copperopolis and Alvorado were located and began producing millions in copper and gold. By then the mines at Clifton were beginning to fail and it was that camp's turn to play second fiddle.

Gold Hill became famous in mining circles everywhere. Its ore was among the richest then known. Substantial stone business buildings lined its busy streets. One of the miners there later became famous as the heavyweight champion of the world. His name was Jack Dempsey! For a decade Gold Hill boomed, but in time even its rich mines were worked out. Even though the hand had been played out, the game wasn't over, for Gold Hill still had an ace in the hole.

During the first world war, arsenic was badly needed for the manufacture of poison gas, and Gold Hill was just the place to find it. Twenty years earlier miners there had dumped countless tons of worthless arsenic ore in their waste dumps! Gold Hill's mines were reopened, new mills were built, and in 1917 rails of the Deep Creek Railroad were laid into town from Wendover. In its new incarnation Gold Hill soon boasted a population of 1,500 with stores, saloons, pool halls and even a newspaper, the *Gold Hill News*. While the war in Europe raged, Gold Hill prospered, but when the war ended and arsenic was no longer needed, the old town's second boom quickly fizzled out. The Lincoln Highway was rerouted north of town, the last ore train left in 1938 and in 1940 the rails were torn up for scrap.

But there was one "rube" who made money at Gold Hill when everything else was folding up. Loeffler Palmer had a gold mine that he worked long enough each year to make a shipment worth about $10,000. Then he would retire for the rest of the year and not make another shipment until he needed money again. Palmer worked his Rube Mine that way for 10 years. During that time he had many offers for his mine, but he wouldn't sell, which only raised the ante higher. Finally, Loeffler sold out at high price and the new owner moved in, bought new equipment and built

an expensive mill, but when his crew went to work they found the ore vein had pinched out. There was no ore left, none, and the new owner was left holding the bag. Meanwhile the "rube" had taken his money, moved to California, and was living it up, knowing who the real rube was!

During the war years of the 1940's arsenic was needed again, and several of Gold Hill's old mines were reopened. But it was only a temporary respite from ghost town status, for when the war ended, so did the mining. Its schoolhouse was locked for the last time in 1946 and the post office closed in 1949. For the third time Gold Hill was left to the ghosts. After all, three strikes and you're out!

CLIFTON
&
CRAZY JOHN'S CACHE

From Wendover, on the Utah-Nevada border, go south on US-50 for 28 miles to where an unmarked road turns west to Gold Hill and continue past that deserted mining camp for 3 miles to a low divide where the road forks. Eastward 1 mile along the nearly vanished right hand fork is the site of Clifton. During the 1870's Clifton was a really wild gold camp, with an impressive business section boasting many fine stone buildings. Gold had been discovered in the Deep Creek Mountains more than a decade earlier, according to tradition, by Major Howard Egan and employees of the Overland Stage Company, but Indian troubles prohibited working the finds at that time. Clifton's gold was especially high grade, and since it had to be shipped all the way to Salt Lake City, road agents stole many of the shipments

"Crazy John" hid a fortune in gold not far from his cabin. It's yours if you can find it.

An old cabin at Clifton built by Brigham and Oliver Young, still solid a century later.

before they got there. To elude the highwaymen a unique and clever stratagem was devised.

Several large hollow iron balls were manufactured by the Eagle Iron Works at Salt Lake City for Clifton's mine owners. The inch thick iron balls weighed 200 pounds and had a flush fitting locked keyway through which they were filled with nuggets, dust and gold concentrate before being locked. The only key to the lock was at a Salt Lake City bank. The gold laden balls were loaded on a sturdy wagon for the long, hard haul across the desert. One day, just as expected, a holdup attempt was made, but the humiliated outlaws soon found that the gold filled balls were too heavy to move and too strongly made to break open. They managed to roll them off the wagon into the deep sand, but then couldn't move them at all. They worked feverishly under the hot desert sun, pounded on them with rocks, and even tried to shoot holes in them with a rifle, but it was to no avail. Finally they were forced to flee at the approach of a posse. The balls were reloaded and in time arrived safely in Salt Lake City. Sometimes the good guys won!

More than 2,500 mining claims were located at Clifton and many of them became rich mines. Among the early producers were the Coleman, Stonewall, Widow and Young America. The Douglas Mine produced ore valued at $200 per ton in silver and lead. Gold ore at the Black Jack Mine assayed $1,800 to the ton. The Cane Springs Consolidated had a gold vein that widened from 3' on the surface to 50' at the 400' level.

Although Clifton's mines produced high grade, most of the ore bodies were shallow, so when rich strikes were made at nearby Gold Hill, Clifton began to fade.

Long after everyone else had gone, two of Brigham Young's nephews stayed on at the deserted camp. Brigham and Oliver Young kept Clifton from being entirely deserted, waiting for a new boom that never came. When they died Clifton lost its caretakers. Over the years the desert has taken its toll, until little is left except their sturdy old log cabin, occupied by a hopeful prospector the last time I was there, and a few skeletons of empty stone buildings along Main Street, most of them nearly hidden in the head high sagebrush.

No one knows what happened to the great iron balls Clifton mine owners shipped their richest ore in, but the relic value of one of them would be great today. There's a chance you'll find one filled with gold!

Years after Clifton became a ghost town, an old miner remembered only as "Crazy John" lived alone in a clapboard shack between Clifton and Gold Hill. As he grew older he became dangerously violent. Finally, the county sheriff had to place him in a mental institution. During rational periods he insisted he was going to go back to his claim and dig up a large "flask" of gold he had hidden there. No one paid any attention to his wild ramblings, but after he died the sheriff talked to a mine owner at Gold Hill who had an interesting tale to tell.

The mine owner said that before "Crazy John" became hopelessly insane he went over to visit him, and

The boarding house at the Utah Mine, Fish Springs mining camp, Juab County.

saw the old man pouring what looked like gold dust into a rusted iron ball. When "Crazy John" saw him approaching he chased him from his claim, threatening to shoot him if he came back. The mine owner recalled that the odd looking iron ball was in a wheelbarrow and that a deep track in the sand led off into the sagebrush.

Was the iron ball in the wheelbarrow one of those used at early day Clifton? If it was could it still have been filled with gold from Clifton's mines or filled with gold from "Crazy John's" own diggings? Remember, the old man always said he had a "flask" of gold buried on his claim. Although a few people have moved to Gold Hill in recent years, all arrived long after "Crazy John" lived there. Thus, it may be difficult to locate his claim, or the cabin where he lived. If mining records at the county seat pin-point it, his buried "flask" could be an easy find for a metal detector equipped treasure hunter.

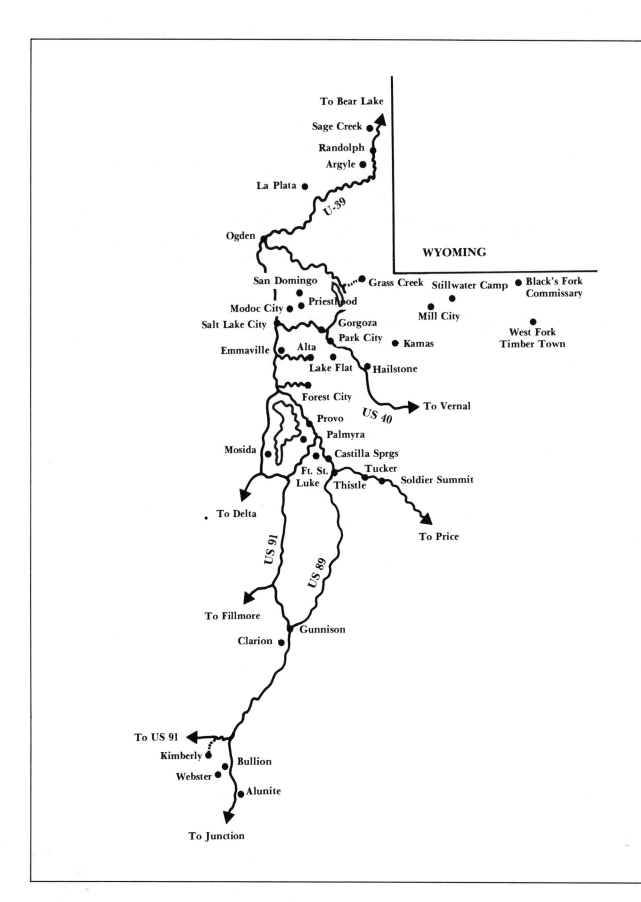

CHAPTER TWELVE

ALONG THE WASATCH

The Wasatch Mountains stretch from the canyonlands country of southern Utah to the Idaho border, and separate the Colorado Plateau on the east from the Great Basin to the west. Along its front in the foothills, and on the other side of its rocky backbone are hidden the towns of yesteryear. Some, like Kimberly and Bullion are abandoned gold mining camps, while others, such as Palmyra and Mosida, were once hopeful farm settlements. At the turn of the century Kimberly's future looked so bright that its citizens had aspirations of becoming the west's leading gold camp, but hard times and poor management reduced it to ruin. While Mosida enjoyed its heyday it was advertised as "Beautiful Mosida By The Lake." It's been a long time since anyone called Mosida "beautiful," but then ghost towns aren't supposed to be beautiful!

The Wasatch also gave birth to Clarion, Utah's only Jewish settlement. They had hoped to build a new Jerusalem in the desert, but neglected tombstones in a forgotten cemetery are all that remain of their dreams. There was also the wild town of Alta where more than one hundred men were killed in gunfights alone! And there are lost mines and treasures galore along the Wasatch, in timber towns and railroad camps. It all adds up to the ghost town bonanza it is today, from its silver, snowcapped peaks to its golden sunsets.

ALTA & EMMAVILLE

Alta, located southeast of Salt Lake City 17 miles above the valley floor at the head of Little Cottonwood Canyon, was one of the west's wildest and most famous mining camps. An unknown rocky basin 8,700 high in the Wasatch Range in 1864 quickly became a rowdy silver camp of 5,000 miners, gamblers, gunfighters and camp followers. From a tent town first called Central City, it mushroomed into a city with more than 200 business buildings, including 6 breweries and 26 saloons, with names like the Bucket Of Blood and Gold Miner's Daughter. It had two newspapers, *The Alta Daily Independent* and *The Cottonwood Observer*, as well as 7 restaurants, dozens of hotels and rooming houses, several billiard halls, a shooting gallery and a boot hill which grew almost as fast as the town did.

S.D. Woodhull, one of the first claim owners, was shot and killed by a claim jumper, and after that no less than 110 men were killed in old-west style shootouts. Even Silver Reef and wicked Frisco paled in comparison to Alta. But twice that number were killed in snowslides. One that occurred in 1874 buried the town's main street in 40' of snow and killed 60 men. In January, 1881 15 men were killed in slides and in Feb-

Pine trees, brush and boulders lined Alta's Main Street when this early photo was taken.

ruary, 1882 a family of seven was lost when a giant slide crushed their home like a matchbox. On March 9th, 1884 another snowslide claimed 10 men and 2 women. Between gunfights and snowslides, the grave digger kept busy.

The silver mines at Alta were among the richest anywhere. The Emma Mine alone produced $37,000,000! The fame of the Emma Mine was so great that it caused a scandal which nearly resulted in war with England! The ore was so rich that it was wrapped in animal hides and dragged down canyon to where it could be loaded on wagons and hauled to San Francisco. There, it was loaded aboard ships and taken to smelters in Wales, half way around the world. When John Woodman located the Emma claim he had only $10 to his name. He lost no time selling out when he was offered $1,500,000 for it! The mine produced millions for its new owners before it was sold to a British syndicate for $5,000,000. Robert Scheuch, United States ambassador to Great Britain, arranged the sale, and included among the purchasers were three members of Parliament. No sooner was the sale completed than the Emma's ore veins were lost in faulted ground and its stock dropped from $150 a share to almost nothing. The British owners screamed fraud, demanded their money back and threatened war! Only last minute diplomatic maneuvering in Washington and London settled the issue.

A satellite town of Alta, called Emmaville, was built by owners of the Emma Mine on Little Willow Creek, 2 miles north of the mouth of Little Cottonwood Canyon. It had been intended as a rest stop between Salt Lake City and Alta. But the trip to the mines by wagon was too long to be made in one day so it grew into a regular town. It also proved to be a convenient place for stonemasons cutting granite blocks for the Mormon Temple to live.

By 1871 Emmaville had a population of 500 and claimed several hotels, two general stores, a blacksmith and livery stable and three saloons. For a half dozen years Emmaville prospered, but in 1874 the Wasatch & Jordan Railroad bypassed it, and chose Granite for its end-of-line. Shortly thereafter several fires wiped out most of Emmaville's business district. After the Emma Mine fiasco and the decline of Alta, there was no more need for the little town, and Emmaville, like ripe fruit on the vine, withered and died.

Besides the Emma, other rich mines at Alta included the Prince Of Wales, Vallejo, Hecla, Cardiff, North Star and Flagstaff. When the Emma Mine failed, its silver veins lost forever in faulted ground, Alta had passed its zenith, and in time its other mines closed. Twice fire visited the town. Its entire business district was wiped out in the great blaze of 1873. The shining city was rebuilt, bigger and better than before, only to be destroyed again on July 11th, 1878. Mine disasters were frequent, and added to the roll call of new graves on boot hill. On September 6th, 1879 six miners lost their lives at the Lovinia Mine while trying to dig out three of their comrades who had been buried in a cave-in.

Shootouts, snowslides, fires and mine disasters hurt Alta, but worked out shafts combined with high costs and low metal prices struck the fatal blow. It's hard to believe a town of 5,000 ever existed where only a few rotting mine buildings and a neglected cemetery remain. But Alta will never be forgotten, for it is now the site of an internationally famous winter sports area where skiers speed down the same trails miners walked a century ago.

PALMYRA & FORT ST. LUKE
&
THE INDIAN MYSTERY MINE

Palmyra was named for the boyhood home of Joseph Smith, the Mormon prophet, and was located near Utah Lake between Spanish Fork and Springville in Utah County. It was established in 1851 when 360 lots were plotted and surveyed. By the following year 75 families were living there and a city charter had been granted. In 1853 the town's population was placed at 412 and a post office had been established, with Charles Davis as postmaster.

From the start Palmyra was a thorn in the side of Chief Wakara's Utes, for it was built in the midst of a choice part of their ancient hunting grounds. Hard feelings festered between the settlers and Indians and lead to the outbreak of the Walker Indian War on July 7th, 1853. Settlers from all over Utah Valley gathered at Palmyra, and for their protection built an adobe wall 10' high and 40 rods square. When the war ended, farmers tried to return to their homes, but the swampy ground at Palmyra proved to be highly alkaline, and many became discouraged. Some moved to the mouth of Spanish Fork Canyon where they established Fort St. Luke.

Because Spanish Fork Canyon had long been the main trail used in earlier times by Spanish miners and slave traders, and later by Ute horse thieves, the settlers were forced to build a high wall around the new townsite to protect their lives and livestock. Only 16 houses had been built when church authorities decided that either a substantial fort would have to be built or that the settlers would have to move back to Palmyra or to Spanish Fork. After several Indian scares the settlers left Fort St. Luke, and most moved to Spanish Fork.

The fort at Spanish Fork was a substantial one, its walls of adobe brick 2′ thick and 20′ high. Its doors were of heavy 4″ planking. There was a well inside its walls to insure an adequate supply when under siege. Brigham Young visited Utah Valley and directed that for the settlers' safety, all must gather at one fort. When he gave his blessing to the new fort at Spanish Fork, the fate of Palmyra was sealed. The few who had stayed were reluctant to leave, but the prophet's order was their command, so Palmyra was abandoned. Its last family left in 1856. Over the years its adobe walls have melted away until hardly a trace remains, and cattle graze where people once lived.

At the edge of the mountains southeast of Fort St. Luke stands the skeleton of Bishop Koyle's Dream Mine. Almost anyone in Spanish Fork can point it out to you. But it won't be easy to find a mysterious ancient Indian (some say Spanish) mine in the canyon beyond the Dream Mine. No one has lately!

Indians told early settlers legends of an ancient mine located in the mountains east of Salem, but no one paid much attention to them until Bishop John H. Koyle located his Dream Mine in 1894. After that prospectors began searching the steep, rocky canyons along the Wasatch Front, and on a cliff not far from Koyle's Dream Mine they discovered ancient petroglyphs.

The petroglyphs seem to show a line of strange animals resembling South American llamas carrying heavy packs, being led by men wearing strange clothing that looks like armor. Excitement reached fever pitch when near the cliff prospectors found the outline of an ancient roadway leading to the ruins of what appeared to be a primitive smelter. One hundred year old trees grew on the slag pile, which contained traces of gold, silver and platinum. But no amount of searching revealed the legendary mine the Indians said white men would never find.

Nearly a half century more passed before a long caved in mine shaft was discovered by hikers. There was no doubt it had been purposely concealed well and only recently reopened by time and weather. Marks around its edge and on its walls indicated it had been chipped out of hard rock with the crudest tools. But it was the 1930's and times were hard, so there was neither money nor interest in opening the ancient looking shaft. A few old-timers in Utah Valley remember when the shaft was found, but none recall where it is. And the Indian legends of the ancient mine are still retold. You can still see the petroglyphs near the Dream Mine, and wih luck you may even find the old smelter site, but it will take more than luck to find the Indian Mystery Mine!

MILL CITY & STILLWATER CAMP
&
THE DEAD MAN MOUNTAIN MINE

As the Union Pacific laid rails westward across southern Wyoming in 1868, an army of lumberjacks moved ahead of them, cutting cross-ties in the high Uintah Mountains south of the Utah border. The ties were stockpiled during the winter then floated down the Bear River on the crest of spring floods. It was a hazardous way to move ties to the end-of-track, and several tie-hacks were drowned. What was worse, from the railroad's point of view, was that the runoff season was too short to insure a steady supply of ties. The answer to their problem arrived in the person of W.K. Sloan, whose genius is remembered by the ruins of a half-dozen ghost towns he fathered.

Sloan proposed building a giant flume from the mountains to the railroad, a huge "V" shaped box built of 3″ planks, a project so vast it was dubbed "Sloan's Folly!" It required 80 tons of square spikes to snake its way down the mountains and through the foothills to the sage covered flats. When it was finished it had cost Sloan $200,000 and was 30 miles long! Known as the Great Hilliard Flume, it originated at a diversion dam high in the Uintahs at Mill City, then followed Mill City Creek to the Bear River. It then crossed miles of sage covered flats, often on high trestles across gulches and canyons to its terminus at Hilliard, Wyoming. Since it worked perfectly no one called it "Sloan's Folly" when it was finished! Of interest to ghost-towners and treasure seekers today is that it left the ghost camps of Mill City, Stillwater Camp, West Fork Timber Town and Black's Fork Commissary in the Uintah Mountains as well as the ghost towns of Hilliard, Piedmont and Sulphur Creek in Wyoming.

Mill City was located high on Gold Mountain, at the headwaters of the Bear River. A short dirt road turns to the west 11½ miles south of the Wyoming border, on State Road 150. You'll have to hike four miles from its end to a row of ancient looking log cabins. When the Union Pacific was laying track they were home to 500 tie-hacks, gamblers and roughnecks. Those sagging old cabins, a rotting wooden diversion dam full of native trout and countless old square spikes used to build the Great Hilliard Flume are all that remain of Mill City's day in the sun. Its ruins should be an excellent place for a cache hunter to spend a few pleasant hours, for men were killed and died there, and without doubt some of them left post-hole caches behind.

Where "Sloan's Folly" crossed the Bear River below Mill City, a feeder flume 6 miles long snaked its way up Stillwater Fork to Stillwater Camp, where a second timber camp was built. Bunk houses and bachelor cabins hidden in the dense pine forest now mark its

Dead Man Mountain. Somewhere on its rocky slopes a gold ledge awaits some lucky searcher.

site. Life wasn't easy at Stillwater Camp's 10,000' elevation. Lumberjacks must have consumed a lot of whiskey to keep warm during the long winters, judging from the hundreds of old bottles that were thrown away 100 years ago! Stillwater Camp was a satellite of Mill City, and so far as can be determined, had no store or commissary of its own. Though small, Stillwater and Mill City are the places to begin your search for the lost Dead Man Mountain Mine.

Any good forest service map of the north slope of the Uintah Mountains will show Dead Man Mountain, 15 miles south of the Wyoming border. It is high country, 13,000' or more, and the Bear and Weber rivers head on its rugged, windswept crags. It is named for a prospector who found a rich gold vein on its north slope and was then murdered for it by his friend.

During the 1920's a sheepherder working for the McKay Ranch near Evanston was herding his woolies in the Uintah Mountains among the snow covered peaks and countless lakes near the headwaters of the Bear River. He became acquainted with a middle-aged, footloose prospector who spent most of his time in the unnamed peaks at the head of the West Fork of the Bear. One day the prospector called excitedly to the herder and ran to meet him. He had a large chunk of white quartz in his hands, all shot througfh with thread-like wires of yellow gold!

The prospector built a cabin, which still stands, at the base of the mountain. But it took so much of his time that it left little to work his find, which was on the mountain somewhere above. Finally, he went into town and acquired a partner, a man he told the sheepherder was an old friend. Apparently they were friends only until the new partner saw the golden vein of quartz. A fight erupted and the partner killed the prospector. There were no witnesses and the partner claimed self-defense. The coroner's jury must have

agreed, because just before winter the partner returned to the prospector's cabin.

The sheepherder had been rounding up the last strays before snow blanketed the high country for six months. As he passed the prospector's cabin he warned the new occupant against staying in the mountains through the winter, He knew that snow drifted 40' deep with temperatures sub-zero for months at a time. But the partner only laughed at his warning. The following spring they found his body in the cabin at the foot of the mountain, frozen solid.

They also found two sacks of heavy gold ore that proved the miner had worked the prospector's ledge for several months before he died. The last page on the wall calendar was February, the coldest month of the year. The days were marked off until the 14th, where a message written in a shaky hand said, "very sick. . .too cold to get out for wood. . ."

Thus two men died for the wire gold, and the secret of its location died with them. The old sheepherder had never known where it was, and no one since has found a trace of a trail leading into the mountains that should start at the prospector's cabin. But the prospector who was murdered by his friend is remembered and has a mountain named after him. Dead Man Mountain!

WEST FORK TIMBER TOWN, BLACK'S FORK COMMISSARY & THE GOPHER HOLE GOLD

West Fork Timber Town isn't an easy place to find, but for a relic hunter it could be worth the time spent. To get there drive 6 miles south of the Wyoming line on SR-150 to where a dirt road leads eastward. Follow it 15½ miles to Lyman Lake (a good place to camp and fish), where an even rougher road turns to the right, and follows the West Fork of the Bear River upstream. After exactly 5½ miles stop and hike into the timber, on the road side of the river, not across it. After less than a half mile you'll see old log cabins green with moss, buried under the pines. There are lone cabins and several in a row that look like a long deserted main street. Rusted cook stoves, broken tools and hundreds of pieces of broken pottery and glass lay hidden under the pines. By searching carefully you might be as lucky as I was, and find an old stone whiskey crock from Evanston's Oak Saloon!

Probably the most impressive of all the timber towns to visit is Black's Fork Commissary. From the fork at Lyman Lake it is 6 miles to the old commissary town, beyond the lake to the northeast, below where the West Fork and Middle Fork of the Bear join. It was an outfitting point for the isolated camps throughout the Uintahs. Black's Fork Commissary was much like a mountain man's fort, with stores, barns, company offices and a post office in a green mountain meadow surrounded by a circle of log cabins. It looks much the same as it did then, except grass now grows on once busy streets while the encroaching pine forest threatens to bury the aged buildings under a canopy of green.

Old-timers say that several men were killed at Black's Fork Commissary and there is a story that a smallpox epidemic claimed many more, but if there's a cemetery there I never found it. Like any isolated mountain camp with hundreds of men, no women, and plenty of whiskey, fights were daily fare among the rough and tumble lumberjacks. Who knows how many forgotten caches and little treasures were hidden there by men who cashed in their chips unexpectedly? But the richest prize of all is still hidden high in the peaks of the Uintahs, where a little known lost gold placer still beckons treasure hunters.

Back in the "old days" a few hardy timber cruisers pushed across the crest of the Uintahs, looking for new and larger stands of timber. Along the way they watched for mineral veins, since they knew that trappers before them had reported seeing ledges of gold and silver in the shining mountains. Later, lumberjacks found flakes of gold in streams rushing down from a mountain later called Gilbert Peak. But nothing was done to trace its source, because during the 1870's and 80's the area was still Indian country, and roving bands of Utes, flushed with victory from the Thornburgh and Meeker massacres, made the mountains an unhealthy place for prospectors.

Only a few timber cutters and wandering prospectors lived at Black's Fork Commissary when an old-timer known as "Hardrock" brought in placer gold which he'd found in a small snow water creek high on the slopes of 13,422' Gilbert Peak. Several lumberjacks repeatedly tried to follow him back to his strike, but he always eluded them by using a different route through the heavy pine forest each time. Many times that summer he returned to Black's Fork Commissary with enough placer gold to buy supplies. And although he was carefully watched, he managed to disappear without leaving a sign or trail.

Finally, the first snows of winter whitened the high peaks, but the old man didn't return. When winter set in with a vengeance, the loggers knew they would never see the old prospector again. The following spring a search began. Everyone expected to find his frozen body in some remote cabin, but instead they found it, mutilated and scalped, where Indians had thrown it into a deep canyon. No trace of his diggings was ever fond. It was speculated that Indians had dragged his body far from his mine to keep other white men from finding it. Gilbert Peak was part of the Ute Reservation at that time, but is now part of the national forest system.

There's not much to go on. About the only clue "Hardrock" ever gave was that his gold came from a snow water creek placer, so during the summer it could be on a dry water course. He also said that he first found the gold when he saw flakes and nuggets shining in the sun on dirt mounds piled up around gopher holes. The old man's gold is still there, somewhere on Gilbert Peak, for no one has found it yet. If you intend to look for it, there's one thing you should know. There are an awful lot of gopher holes in those mountains!

SAN DOMINGO CITY, MODOC CITY & PRIESTHOOD CAMP

Alta may have been Salt Lake County's most famous mining town, but San Domingo City and its satellites, Modoc City and Priesthood Camp, were its strangest. Col. Patrick Connor's soldier-prospectors were probably the first to discover minerals in City Creek Canyon, but the early claims they staked weren't considered to be of sufficient value to mine. The first worthwhile discoveries were made in 1870 when the General Scott and the Magnet claims panned out high values in lead and as much as 25 ounces of silver to the ton. In December of that year the Hot Springs Mining District was organized, and by the time snow left the mountains, some 300 claims had been located.

By 1873 an estimated one thousand men were working in the canyon. A townsite named Modoc City was surveyed 7 miles from Salt Lake City near where the Empire Sawmill was located. 2 miles farther up canyon another group of claims and the cabins the miners built were blossoming into Priesthood Camp, presumably named for the Mormon Priesthood. The name Modoc City remains a mystery. Neither camp had the usual saloons or other diversions designed to separate the miner from his money. Just below Priesthood Camp, where placer diggings had been found, a line of tents and dugouts became knows as Hangtown, named after the famous California camp.

Forgotten lime kilns are sole reminders of San Domingo, Modoc City and Priesthood Camp. -Utah Historical Society-

It wasn't far from the tracks to the Junction House, Thistle's best hotel. -Utah Historical Society-

The richest finds in the canyon were made near the mouth of Cottonwood Fork, where the San Domingo and Treasure Box mines were located. A smelter was built near the Hot Springs north of Salt Lake City which also smelted the low grade ore from the Beacon and Red Bird mines at Priesthood Camp. The smelter was a crude reverberatory type, successful in saving lead from the galena ore but inefficient in recovering silver and gold values.

In September, 1873 the San Domingo City townsite was surveyed. It was thought that a prosperous city would soon blossom forth in City Creek Canyon, but the miners' hopes were in vain. Their crude smelter failed to process the camp's ore profitably, thus miners were forced to leave for the far richer strikes being made near Alta, Park City and in the Oquirrhs. A few diehards returned the following spring, but the days of the would-be boomtowns were numbered.

The district's location was probably its chief handicap, because in 1850 Brigham Young had been granted exclusive rights to City Creek Canyon, including its water, timber and minerals. He built a road into the canyon and exacted a toll on every load of supplies hauled to the diggings and on every load of ore brought out. The expense, added to the poorly designed smelter, put an end to San Domingo City, Modoc City and Priesthood Camp. Only a few caved in shafts and the ruins of a lime kiln in Limekiln Gulch remain of what miners hoped would be another El Dorado.

SOLDIER SUMMIT
TUCKER, THISTLE & CASTILLA

During the winter of 1861 a small group of soldiers left Camp Floyd to join the Confederacy. They crossed

Utah Valley and traveled to the summit of Spanish Fork Canyon where they made camp. That night a blizzard swept into their unprotected camp, freezing two of the soldiers to death. The others buried them the following morning near a small spring on the south side of the pass. Today a tumble-down wooden fence hidden in the mountain sage marks the graves that gave Soldier Summit its name.

When the rails of the Rio Grande Western crossed the pass years later, the railroad town they built there was named Soldier Summit. In 1919 real estate promoter H.C. Mears surveyed a townsite and a rush to purchase building lots began. The population exceeded 1,000 by the time the town was incorporated in 1921, and there were stores, hotels, saloons and restaurants, as well as two churches and a school with 5 teachers and 200 students. The railroad needed Soldier Summit as a place to service the helper engines that were needed to pull freight trains over the steep mountain pass. By the time the helper engines were no longer needed the town had a population of 2,500.

With the appearance of diesel engines Soldier Summit began to slide into oblivion, and remained deserted until 1966 when a cafe for highway tourists was started by Elmer Ebaugh. Since then, several other families have moved to the old town, and provided company for the ghosts that have wandered its streets over the years.

Construction of the D&RGW gave birth to two other railroad towns, both of which are now ghost towns. 7 miles down Spanish Fork Canyon from Soldier Summit the railroad built Tucker. It wasn't a large place, but it did have the usual company store and boarding house, as well as a saloon. It was named for James Tucker and was built to house helper engines that pushed heavy freight trains over Soldier Summit. The same change to modern equipment that killed Soldier Summit dealt the death blow to Tucker as well. Today a roadside rest area covers much of the old townsite.

Tucker was built to house helper engines that pushed the trains over Soldier Summit. -Utah Historical Society-

La Plata, the world's only silver placer camp, now just another lonely ghost town of the Wasatch.

15 miles below Tucker was Thistle, where Thistle Creek empties into Spanish Fork Canyon. Thistle came into being in 1883 when the rails reached there, and soon became an important stop, with several false front business buildings, as well as houses for the railroad workers. In 1890 Thistle became a junction town when the new Sevier Branch Railroad joined the D&RGW with Sanpete County. But after that railroad connected with the Utah Central near Gunnison, a lower, all weather route, Thistle began to fade and it soon became just another station along the way. A few people still call it home, though most live up canyon near Birdseye.

Old-timers who remember Thistle also recall Castilla Hot Springs, a resort built during the 1880's by Sid and Walt Southworth, at a natural hot springs down canyon from Thistle. It was one of the state's most popular resorts, and had a fine three story sandstone hotel, a saloon, a dance pavillion, stores, shops and a restaurant.

The hot springs were discovered in 1776 by Father Escalante, who named the area Rio de Aguas Calientes, River of Hot Waters. Many believed its mineral waters were beneficial to those suffering from rheumatism, but the resort owners got a little carried away when they began advertising the springs as a cure for alcoholism, chain smoking and the tendency to use profane language!

Castilla remained a popular resort until the 1920's. One night after it was closed, a passing hobo built a fire in the grand old hotel to keep warm, and burned it to the ground. The hot springs are still there, and look about the same as they did when Father Escalante first saw them more than 200 years ago. Coin hunters who take the time to trace the outline of the hotel and ballroom could have a field day at old Castilla, for any coins they find were lost long ago, when coins were made of silver and gold, not the funny money we have today.

LA PLATA

In July, 1891 a sheepherder named Johnson was following his sheep in the shadow of James Peak near the head of the Little Bear River in Cache County. He picked up a rock to throw at his dog and noticed that it was unusually heavy. Johnson took the rock to his foreman, W.H. Ney, who recognized it as silver-lead galena and took it to Ogden for assaying. The sample was 45% lead and carried 400 ounces of silver to the ton! Johnson and Ney had no sooner registered their La Plata claim in Logan than the rush was on.

In less than a month more than a thousand miners were on the scene, and newspapers reported 100 men passing through Ogden every day headed for the new diggings. Tents and cabins sprung up as fast as daisies in the spring, while mine machinery and dynamite blasts rocked the mountain's tranquility. Johnson didn't like the new surroundings and sold his half of the La Plata claim for $600, which wasn't the smartest move he ever made.

The new camp, named La Plata, Spanish for silver, was quickly taken over by Salt Lake and Park City mining men, who lost no time turning it into a boom camp. Before the first winter, there were several dry goods stores, grocery and butcher shops, three rooming houses, four restaurants and eight saloons, as well as a post office, a branch of the Thatcher Brothers Bank and a newspaper named the *Special Courier*.

La Plata also boasted a town marshal and a jail, stagecoach lines to both Ogden and Logan and a red-light district. The newspapers warned of the growing number of "vagabonds, rascals, speculators and other loathsome people" arriving daily, while the miners posted warnings that "Chinamen and Dagos are not allowed in town!"

New prospects were located every day, and some of them became good producers of high grade silver and lead. Among the best known were the original La Plata, Sundown, Sunrise, Red Jacket, Yellow Jacket, New State, Lucretta and Mountain Boy mines. Winters were severe at La Plata's 10,000' elevation. Temperatures often dropped to 25 below zero and the snow piled 15' deep. Few women or children remained during the winter, and the miners had to gather at Dan Ensign's bar to fortify themselves with anti-freeze.

When the spring of 1892 arrived an army of prospectors descended upon La Plata, but they found all the best claims already staked. Initially giant boulders of high grade ore could be found almost anywhere. One 15 ton boulder of ore was melted down and produced 12 tons of bullion! There was so much ore on the surface that for a time La Plata was billed as the world's only silver placer camp. But miners soon discovered that La Plata's ore was shallow, with few veins running more than 50' deep. When the easy pickings were gone, little ore was left.

San Domingo and Modoc City were expected to be permanent towns, but they ended up ghost towns.

La Plata might have lasted longer except for the perfidy of man. In 1893 newly elected President Cleveland convinced Congress to repeal the Sherman Silver Purchase Act, which had kept the price of silver high. As a result, the price dropped from $1 an ounce to 25¢. Silver miners all over the west called it the "Crime of '93." Faced with the prospect of digging expensive shafts to mine ore that wasn't worth anything, the mines at La Plata simply gave up and quit.

There were two roads to La Plata, one from Logan via the Little Bear River and the other from Ogden over Wolf Creek. La Plata had three little offshoots. Mineral Point was located high on a pine covered ridge directly above Porcupine Reservoir. Porcupine, or Baxter City, stood where the reservoir is now located and Mound City was just across the Weber County line. Several houses and mine buildings still stand at Mineral Point, but not a trace of Porcupine or Mound City remains. La Plata is surrounded by private land today, which has helped preserve a few of its old cabins. There remain strange looking pieces of rusted mine machinery hidden under the aspen trees, and caving shafts dot the canyon bottom and hillsides. The snows of 80 winters and the fierce winds that howl down from the Monte Cristo Range have taken their toll on the old silver camp, and have left little to show that a booming town once stood there, or that $3,000,000 in galena ore was dug from its mines.

LAKE FLAT
ITS LITTLE TREASURES
&
MANHART'S LOST LEDGE

Lake Flat, in Summit County, was the birthplace of Park City, Utah's most famous and one of the West's richest silver camps. It was built on the shores of a small mountain lake 2 miles southeast of present-day Park City in 1869, around the workings of the Hawkeye, McHenry, Lady Of The Lake and other mines. Most of

Lake Flat's first settlers were Scots and because their little camp with its green meadows and snow fed lake looked like a scene out of Robert Burns, they called it the Robin's Nest Of The Wasatch. There were the usual log cabins and clapboard rooming houses that all mining camps had, as well as a store and saloon. Lake Flat residents visited each other by poling across the little lake in the center of town.

Lake Flat was home of the famous Ontario Mine, producer of more than $50,000,000 in silver, as well as owner of one of the world's largest underground water pumps. The famous "Cornish Pump" was installed to pump water from the mine's 1,000' level, and its size still seems incredible. The huge steam engine which powered the pump was on the surface, while the pump was 1,000' down the shaft. The two were joined by a connecting rod 1,060' long! The engine's flywheel was 35' in diameter and weighed 70 tons! Every stoke of the pump's giant 20" piston pumped 2,560 gallons of water to the surface, over 4,000,000 gallons every day!

Until Park City boomed into a roaring camp of 10,000 miners and prospectors, Lake Flat was the district's main camp. It wasn't long until it was eclipsed by the brighter lights of the new camp down canyon, where winters were easier and mills and smelters could be built. On October 8th, 1878 the Ontario Mine burned to the ground. While it was rebuilt many of Lake Flat's miners moved to Park City, where there was work at other mines. Although several families lived at Lake Flat until the turn of the century, winters at its 8,000' elevation eventually took their toll, and left little but the mine dumps along the lake shore.

For fifty years Lake Flat was a forgotten mountain ghost until Park City became a winter sports center. Now the little snow water lake has been renamed Silver Lake and its pine and aspen slopes will become home to condominiums, built where miners' cabins once stood. The Lady Of The Lake mine dump has disappeared under the bulldozer's might while McHenry Canyon is scarred with ski runs. Whispered stories tell of long buried caches uncovered by construction workers. But not all of Lake Flat's treasures have been found, and the biggest of all, Manhart's Lost Ledge, still awaits some modern argonaut.

A mine foreman at the Ontario named McFadden lived several houses below Grose's Boarding House in Ontario Canyon. Old-timers in Park City may be able to point out the site. He spent most nights gambling in Park City's saloons where he won much more than he lost. It was common knowledge that he hid his winnings near his cabin in the canyon, and that he never banked a cent.

One night, McFadden was shot by a drunken miner in an argument over a card game. Before he died he tried to tell where his money was hidden. His final words were not to build a fire in his stove and an admonition to take care of his well. When his kitchen stove was examined, the pipe was found to be stuffed with paper money! But the investigators knew that most of his money was in gold, and not a coin was found in the house. The well was checked, but was full of icy water. They probed it with hooks in hopes of snagging onto a sack of some kind, but nothing was found in its depths.

Many years have passed since then, and today McFadden's cabin site is only a scar on the mountainside, and the place where his well was dug is a depression hidden in head high sage. When McFadden died no one thought of looking behind the stones in the well, so it might be a good thing to do now, if you can find the well. Maybe I'll check it out myself, if summer ever comes!

Dick Smith was an old-timer in Park City who used to talk about an old Irishman who was killed at the Massachusetts Mine, across the ridge from the Ontario, in Empire Canyon. Before he died, the Irish miner described where he had hidden a can of gold coins that he had saved over the years to buy a ticket back to the old country. It was supposed to be buried under a tree on the mountainside behind the Massachusetts Mine boarding house. No one has found it yet, maybe because there are an awful lot of trees on that mountainside!

Below Lake Flat, at the south end of Deer Valley, beyond where the ski resort has been built, the old road to Heber City crosses a sage covered flat and climbs over the shoulder of Mt. Neff. A fork in the road leads past the old rifle range and over a low pass to Clark's Ranch. Years ago there were a number of powder magazines by the side of that road in Deer Valley, where mine owners stored dynamite far from town, should it explode.

An old bachelor "Cousin Jack" (the common nickname for a Cornishman) miner lived all alone in a one room shack in Deer Valley. He spent his life in the mines and saved his money for a rainy day. He hid his gold in a coffee can, buried by one of those old powder magazines, where he could see it from his cabin. One day, a man I'll call "Bart" passed by the magazine with his wife while riding their horses to Heber City. As they passed the magazine, "Bart" saw the coffee can sticking up out of the ground where rain had washed the top soil away from it. He got off his horse, scraped fresh dirt over the can, and then went on his way.

"Bart" told me about this years after the "Cousin Jack" miner had been killed in a mine accident, and said that as far as he knew the coffee can was still there by the side of the powder magazine, which is only a broken rock foundation in the sage now. When I asked him why he hadn't dug it up, he became indignant and snorted that he hadn't because it wasn't his, that it belonged to "Little Billie!" They don't make men like "Bart" anymore!

In 1893 the editor of the *Park Record* of Park City related as strange a tale as you'll ever hear. Two prospectors examining an abandoned shaft in the hills above Lake Flat found a miner's skeleton. It was sur-

mised that many years before the nameless miner had fallen into the shaft and was so badly injured he couldn't get out. Alongside his skeleton was a rusted lunch pail, and inside, a scrap of yellowed paper so fragile it crumbled when touched. The writing on it said: "Dear God! I am dying . . . I have found wealth at the cost of my life. The samples are . . . from a ledge . . . my hands tremble . . I am . . ." With the note were pieces of white quartz shot through with stringers of yellow gold!

Sam Raddon was the editor, and Sam never lied. It sounds like fiction, but it isn't. Raddon's story made old-timers remember a rich gold find made years before by another prospector who couldn't find his strike again. Although the stories are years apart in time, they are similar in circumstances. But the mystery is becoming clearer all the time.

A few years ago an easterner came to Park City seeking information on a long lost relative who had last written from Lake Flat, almost a half century before. The relative's name was Truelove Manhart, and he had written that he had found a ledge of gold in the mountains beyond Lake Flat, but that he couldn't find it again because a forest fire had changed the appearance of the country. He asked his brothers to come west to help him and guaranteed that they would get rich. But they had no means to travel so far, and never heard from Manhart again.

Not too long ago people laughed at the lost ledge story. But there was a man named Truelove Manhart, named in Salt Lake City police records, who along with a brother named Freelove Manhart, was arrested for stealing horses several years before he was a prospector in Park City. No one knows what became of Freelove Manhart either, or whether he was the brother Truelove wrote to in Pennsylvania. Thus, Truelove Manhart was real. And surely, the existence of the note and the gold in the miner's lunch pail is beyond dispute, because Sam Raddon and others saw it.

There's a ski resort at Lake Flat now, but the mountains beyond, where Manhart prospected, are much the same as they were then. It's rough country, nearly 11,000' high, and snow covers it at least 6 months of the year. But if you want to look for Manhart's Lost Ledge, Lake Flat is the place to start. Good Luck!

GORGOZA

Nearly every road map shows the town of Gorgoza, although it never existed except in a scalawag's imagination. During the 1880's, when Park City was booming, two rival railroads raced each other up steep and narrow Parley's Canyon from Salt Lake City, trying to reach the giant silver bonanza first. The Fort Douglas & Salt Lake Railroad gave up in the depths of the canyon, but John W. Young's Utah Central kept pushing toward the summit at Altus, a small stage stop and roadhouse at the head of the canyon.

Young, a son of Mormon prophet Brigham Young, was desperately in need of funds to complete his railroad. When he couldn't borrow any more from American banks he headed for Europe. In Spain he was introduced to a wealthy nobleman named Rodriquez Velasquez de la Gorgozada. At first the rich Spaniard was reluctant to invest in Young's railroad, but when he was shown plans of a beautiful city to be built at the foot of Parley's Summit, where Kimball Creek flows into East Canyon, and was given a promise that the city would be named in his honor, Gorgozada agreed to invest $1,000,000.

The Utah Central was completed into Park City, with the aid of Gorgozada's money, but the beautiful city described by Young was never built. A random cluster of shacks used by railroad workers located near the site of the bogus city has appeared as Gorgoza on maps ever since. When the railroad was completed, Senor Gorgozada came to America to ride the Utah Central and visit the city named in his honor. When he was shown the miserable collection of shacks which bore his name, he sued Young to get his money back, but as far as anyone knows, he never recovered a dime.

Today Gorgoza has become a beautiful place. The site has become part of the winter sports haven centered in Park City. A beautiful golf course and high-priced homes are being built where laborers' shacks once stood. No expense is being spared to make it the beautiful city John W. Young said it would be, even if it did take a little longer than he planned! Senor Gorgozada would be proud of it.

GRASS CREEK

Coal was first discovered on Grass Creek, a small stream that joins the Weber River just north of Coalville in Summit County, during the 1860's. Miners built cabins and dug the shiny black gold on a small scale for the next few years, but it wasn't until the silver mines at nearby Park City boomed during the 1870's and 80's that Grass Creek really came into its own. R.C. Chambers, Superintendent of the famous Ontario Mine, built the five mile long narrow gauge Summit County Railroad from the rails of the Union Pacific to the coal mines at Grass Creek. Chambers needed coal to fire the giant steam boilers that provided power for the huge Cornish Pump at the Ontario. The railroad he built was different in that it had three rails. It was designed to allow the narrow gauge engines of his Summit County Railroad and those of the standard gauge Union Pacific to use the same grade.

As ever increasing quantities of coal were needed at the Ontario Mine, more and more miners were needed at Grass Creek, and the little settlement grew by leaps and bounds. Substantial stone buildings were erected alongside cabins and false front slab buildings. There was even a Chinatown. Beckwith & Louder's general store supplied most of the miners' needs. The growing

town also boasted a post office, church and saloon. The residential section was located on the north side of the canyon while most of the businesses were on the south side.

At its peak Grass Creek claimed a population of 500. Its coal was of the lignite type, fine for firing boilers but hazardous for use in railroad engines since it produces a fine fly ash which caused many fires along the right-of-way. Coal from Grass Creek was used in large quantities at Park City because of the excessive demand of the mines there. But its coal was bedded in soft clay and that caused many dangerous cave-ins. When better grade coal was discovered where it could be mined cheaper with less risk, Grass Creek's mines closed and its little narrow gauge line was abandoned.

Grass Creek remained deserted until 1893 when the Cullen and Church mines were reopened by local owners and the little town resettled. The mines were worked out by 1912, and Grass Creek faded like a rose in winter's first icy blast. The entire canyon is now private ground, but the owners usually allow visitors on request. A dirt road leaves US-189 at Echo Reservoir and follows Grass Creek for five miles past several deserted ranch buildings to the townsite. Little remains except broken foundations and the shell of one brick building. Grass Creek could be a real sleeper for treasure hunters, since few have heard of it and fewer yet have visited it. There's no telling what you might find there!

HAILSTONE
THE HERMIT'S COIN CACHE
&
THE LOST BOREN & BETHER'S MINE

Midway between Park City and Heber City there was a settlement named Hailstone, known for a while as Elkhorn. It wasn't named for the hail storms that roar down from the mountains there, but for William Hailstone, one of its first settlers. The town was started in 1864 and soon claimed several dozen families. It was a prosperous place; most of its citizens owned large acreages of farm and grazing land.

Hailstone boasted some of the finest homes in Heber Valley, including a red sandstone mansion built by William Moulton in 1877. It contained two master bedrooms, two staircases and two inside bathrooms, real luxuries in 1877, because Moulton had two wives. The old mansion was torn down in 1959, but many still remember it as Lee's Ranch.

Another fine home at Hailstone was built by Bennie Norris under a towering rocky crag alongside the Provo River. No one could miss it because an American flag had been painted on the face of the cliff above his house. It's uncertain how the flag got there. Some say Norris painted it, but others claim that soldiers of the California Volunteers, under the command of Col. Patrick Connor at Fort Douglas, painted it long before

Hailstone was settled. Either way, Norris maintained it and in recent years it has been repainted, and remains a point of pride for area residents.

The Great Lake Timber Company kept the little town alive for many years. When it closed in 1960, there were no jobs around Hailstone, and the town simply died. Although the people moved on, they left many treasure tales for people who take the time to listen.

Sam Lowry lived in the Norris house, beneath the flag, his entire life. He was 29 years old when he was drafted into the army in 1917 and had to sell his cattle with short notice at a loss. He put the $300 in gold coin he received in a quart fruit jar and buried it in a hole at the foot of the ledge below the American flag. Years later he said that he'd dug the hole as deep as he could reach with his arm.

When Sam got out of the army and returned home he searched for his buried money but couldn't find it. He never told anyone about his cache until sixty years later, shortly before he died. He spent those years living alone, knowing his gold was in the cliff face, but so well hidden he couldn't even find it himself.

Sam Lowry's cache isn't large, only $300 in 1917, but it would be worth about $10,000 now, plus the collector value the rare coins might have. And, the site is easy to find; on the cliff directly above it is a huge American flag. It would certainly make a good grubstake for a modern day prospector!

After Bishop Murdock and his Mormon followers settled Heber Valley in 1859, they often heard stories from local Indians of Spanish and Mexican mines in the surrounding mountains that had been worked long before the first mountain man entered the valley.

For several years the new settlers were too busy building homes and trying to grow crops at the valley's 6,000' elevation to spend time looking for old mines, but men cutting timber in the nearby canyons often found evidence of the miners' work. Spanish spurs and metal buckles were found, so old and rusted they fell apart at a touch, and signs unlike Indian petroglyphs were discovered cut into stone ledges, or deep into the bark of ancient pines. Then, in 1896, William Bethers and Henry Boren discovered two ancient mines, two miles from Daniel's Creek.

The mines were driven into solid rock at the head of a slide, where the waste rock wouldn't be noticed. The tunnels were three to four feet wide and five feet high. The portals were covered with rock and brush, as though purposely concealed.

Bethers had discovered a strange "hieroglyphic" rock in the canyon below, which had characters cut into its surface as though with a chisel. He took a man "accustomed to translating such signs" to the rock, but the expert could not decipher their meaning. The characters on the stone were described as "representing the figure of a man with his hands thrown up as if suddenly surprised, another is of a burro or pack animal and

another is of a half moon." Other characters were said to be "perfectly visible but undecipherable." Both Boren and Bethers believed the signs were cut into the ledge as a guide for miners returning to the canyon after a long absence. As a result, they searched the canyon until they were successful.

Before the snow was deep in the mountains, Bethers and Boren had opened one tunnel 75'. Then they encountered a caved-in section too dangerous to dig through. The other was reopened for 25' before winter drove them from the mountains. Both intended to return, but had little time to do so after working their farms. Several years later Bethers moved from the valley and Boren was called on a mission to settle new areas in southern Utah.

There is now a heavily traveled highway through Daniel's Canyon, but only a mile or so from the pavement it isn't much different than it was when Bethers and Boren were there. Somewhere high in the rockslides along its steep sides there are two tunnels, probably caved in again and nearly impossible to see until you're upon them. The "hieroglyphic" stone with the Spanish waybill carved on it might make them easier to find!

KAMAS VALLEY TIMBER CAMPS
&
THE LOST MINES OF RHOADES VALLEY

Mormon explorers pushed eastward across Parley's Park during the early 1850's in search of timber and settlement sites. In a high mountain valley drained by the Weber and Provo rivers a settlement was founded and named Rhoades Valley for Thomas Rhoades, one of their number. Many of his trips to the Lost Rhoades Mine began there.

Those early settlers built a frontier town, long on homemade comforts but short on luxuries. The Indians resented the loss of their beautiful valley with its lush meadows and beaver-filled streams. They remembered the Taos trappers who had been there long before the Mormons who had trapped their wild animals and stolen their children to be used as slaves in New Mexico. And they remembered the miners who forced them to dig yellow rock from deep pits, that they then carried away on their pack trains. To protect themselves, settlers at Rhoades Valley built a fort in 1858 at the east end of the valley.

The fort was 30 rods square with walls 16' high and had gates at its east and west ends. Fifty families lived there in cabins that ringed the fort's interior. As the Indian problem lessened after the Blackhawk War, the fort fell into disuse and was abandoned in 1870. Thomas Rhoades moved away. The new settlement built outside the fort became known as Kamas, named for the chamis root, a food used by both Indians and pioneers.

Because of the valley's high elevation, farming was difficult, but the new town soon found a cash crop in

The mountains above Rhoades Valley hide dozens of old timber camps.

timber. Great pine forests covered every mountain and canyon above town. Timber camps were built near the headwaters of Beaver Creek, the Provo and Weber rivers. The first pioneer timber cruisers came upon long abandoned mines, and discovered the ruins of stone houses. Near the mines they found where timber had been cut so long before that only rotting logs remained.

Later, such well known timber firms as Blazzard's, Grey's River and the Great Lake Timber Company built camps from Poulsen Basin to the Norway Flats and Murdock Mountain. Many of their camps were in use for decades, and today their skeletons can be found in brush-choked canyons and rocky basins all through the mountains. From Kamas follow Beaver Creek along the Mirror Lake highway. Every few miles you will see old side roads leading into the forest. Almost all of them go to timber camps, where relics lost or discarded long ago can be found. Rhoades Fort is now only a memory, while the timber camps of yesterday are hidden in a hundred secret places, but their ghosts still haunt the mountains.

In 1852 Marshal William H. Kimball arrested a party of Mexicans who were taking small Indian children to New Mexico to be sold as slaves. They claimed it was the most profitable business they had had since they'd packed gold ore from the mountains more than 50 years before, thus giving first hand testimony that they had worked mines in the mountains above Rhoades Valley before 1800. When informed that Governor Young had forbidden taking slaves in Utah, the Mexicans agreed never to return, and released the stolen children, who were placed with Mormon families to raise.

The evidence of Spanish and Mexican mining in Utah was strong the day the Mormons arrived. In his journal, Mormon V. Selman recalled pack trains of gold ore being brought down the Provo River from the mountains beyond. "There was a time in those early days when pack trains came down the Provo River, and one camped at my father's place for a few days to rest up their small pack mules. Those mules were loaded with packs which did not appear to be large, but they were all those mules could carry. The Mexicans kept an armed guard at their camp, and no one was allowed near, as if whatever was in those packs was very valuable."

Since then many old mines have been found in the mountains near the head of the Provo River, but none discovered so far could be the one Selman referred to. The first settlers in Rhoades Valley copied maps made by explorers such as Fremont, who in turn had copied even older maps. One spot marked on those ancient maps was atop a 10,000' peak above present-day Hoytsville. It says simply, "Old Spanish Mine." A clue to when that mine was worked might be found in a fascinating discovery made in Rhoades Valley in 1858 when a Spanish cannon was found by General Johnston's army. It was half buried in a sandy wash. When pulled out and cleaned, markings showed it had been cast at Seville, Spain in 1776. How did it get to Rhoades Valley, and why was it abandoned? It must have guarded something very valuable; imagine the labor of hauling it that far, only to abandon it!

Could the cannon have been guarding a discovery made near Kamas in 1870, a discovery described in a pioneer diary? "The Spanish or Mexicans were the first miners in Utah, but the extent of their operations can never be known, for they filled up their excavations after abandoning their mines for the more profitable trade of slavery. These facts are evidenced by a remarkable discovery made on the Kamas Prairie in August (1870). A party of prospectors came upon a sort of hole filled in with loose dirt, and their curiosity aroused, excavated it and opened up an old mine shaft sunk many years before. The vein had been cut by iron tools, and a series of steps led down into the shaft, by which means the ore had been removed. From the bottom of the shaft a tunnel ran a great distance along the vein. Pieces of silver ore were found, but the vein had been worked out."

There have been many such discoveries made around Kamas Valley, some quite recently. There is an old mine in the Silver Meadows which Roy Peterson of Woodland claimed had been long since caved in in 1890. Pioneers found mines in Moon Canyon, several of which can still be seen today. On Beaver Creek, an old codger known as Beaver Creek Charlie located many old diggings, chipped out of the hard mountain rock with iron tools. One of Beaver Creek Charlie's mines can be seen on the mountain just above the ranger station on Beaver Creek. If you don't believe there is gold on Beaver Creek stop at the antique shop at Park City and talk to Ted Grose. He can show you a chunk of gold ore found there only last year. It's like nothing you ever saw before, a dull red colored rock most prospectors wouldn't take a second look at, but is literally filled with gold!

Sid Smith of Park City found old sluice boxes on Currant Creek and others have been found on Hayden's Fork north of Mirror Lake. While prospecting on the upper Weber River, Tom Costas and Joe Peesley nearly fell into an old shaft. It was under an ancient pine which had a stout limb that extended over the shaft. On the limb were marks made when a rope had been pulled over it to hoist an ore bucket out of the shaft. Peezley recalled that the pine was a giant, several hundred years old, but that the marks were nearly grown over.

The list is endless. Every mountain hamlet in the Kamas Valley, from Oakley and Holiday Park to Francis and Woodland, has tales to tell of ancient mines and lost treasure. And they aren't just tall tales; many of the mines marked on ancient maps have been found. To say there are not Spanish mines around Rhoades Valley is to deny empirical evidence.

ARGYLE & SAGE CREEK

The little hamlet of Argyle, originally known as Kennedyville, was located 3 miles southeast of Randolph on Big Creek in Rich County. John Kennedy led a party of Mormon farmers to the area in 1874. A church and schoolhouse were built, but the little town grew slowly because the climate was too cold for farming. For some reason the town was renamed Argyle in 1895, after Kennedy's birthplace in Scotland.

A second room was added to its little one room schoolhouse, but Argyle's growth remained slow. When autos came into general use many people moved to Randolph and commuted to their farms. In 1915 Argyle's schoolhouse doors were closed for the last time. But for a few deserted ranch buildings there's nothing to show it ever existed.

When Argyle began failing some of its citizens settled Sage Creek, 8 miles north of Randolph. Its story is the same as Argyle's with a ten year time lag. As Argyle's church and school lost members, Sage Creek's gained at about the same rate. The mobility afforded by the automobile spelled doom for Sage Creek as well.

There are many abandoned houses at Sage Creek, along with many "no trespassing" signs. If you can obtain the owner's permission, there might be untouched pickings at either settlement. Most of the buildings can be seen (and photographed) without leaving the public roads.

MOSIDA
&
THE LOST ARMY PAYROLL

"Mosida by the lake, a beautiful spot where the land is rich and opportunity beckons!" claimed advertisements by the Mosida Fruit Lands Company in 1910 when they were boasting the advantages of living at Utah County's planned community. Mosida was located on the west shore of Utah Lake, 12½ miles north of Elberta, just west of U-68. It was named for the first two letters of the names of each of its three promoters, MOore, SImpson and DAvis. The community was started on a grand scale. A passenger boat carried prospective buyers across Utah Lake to a pier a few steps from a new $15,000 hotel, and 250 men were hired at the high wage of $4.50 per day to install pumps at the lake's edge, dig irrigation canals and clear land for planting. A series of pumps and canals raised water from the lake onto the parched acres being planted with rows of fruit trees and farm crops.

By 1912, 8,000 acres of desert land had been broken by a giant steam tractor and more than 50,000 fruit trees had been planted. The trees soon died in the salty and heavily mineralized soil, but the same fields would often yield 100 bushels of wheat to the acre. Peanuts also grew well. A school, post office, livery stable and company owned boarding house, which featured two French cooks were built, and the town's population reached 400.

From the beginning pumping water from Utah Lake was too costly, and in 1922 the planned community was taken over by the National Savings & Trust Company for unpaid debts. Operational expenses were far in excess of income and the new owners were on the edge of bankruptcy themselves in 1915 when the lake level dropped during a dry year, leaving the pumps high and dry. Without water, the crops soon died under the desert sun. The company entered receivership in 1917 and left "Beautiful Mosida By The Lake" an empty dream. Today only the foundation of its fine hotel and the empty shells of its pump houses remain to remind visitors of the enterprise.

When the Utah War ended in 1858, it was agreed that General Albert S. Johnston's army would be allowed to build a camp no closer than 40 miles to Salt Lake City. It was built in Cedar Valley and its payroll added considerably to the state's prosperity. One of its first payrolls never helped anyone though, because it was stolen and buried near the site of Mosida.

Old newspaper accounts tell how a lone bandit stole the gold payroll and fled south from Salt Lake City. Soon, an army posse was after him. He would probably have gotten away, though, if his horse hadn't fallen and broken a leg near the south end of Utah Lake. The posse found the crippled horse soon after the bandit left on foot, carrying the heavy saddlebags filled with gold.

The outlaw tried to elude his pursuers by hiding in the head high sagebrush, but at dawn's light he was seen. In a quick gunfight he was killed. He had none of the gold with him, nor was any trace of it ever found. He must have hidden it close to where he died, perhaps in a badger hole, or in the lake. The amount was never announced, but General Johnston had 2,500 troops, so the payroll would have had to have been a large one.

This is a treasure for a metal detector, one with water-proof search coils. What are you waiting for?

FOREST CITY
&
THE INDIAN MINE ON MT. TIMPANOGOS

Silver was first discovered in Utah County's American Fork Canyon in the 1860's. The Miller's Hill, Dutchman, Live Yankee and Sunbeam claims were among the first staked. Later, the Conqueror Mining Company consolidated the Forest, Pilot, Queen Of Sheba and Conqueror properties to become one of the district's leading producers. The richness of the mines soon attracted eastern capital; the Miller's Hill Mine sold for $120,000 in 1872. The new owners built one of the finest boarding houses in the western camps and hired excellent chefs to prepare the miners' meals.

William Vanderbilt, President of the Aspinwall Mining Company of New York spent $400,000 building the 23 mile long American Fork Railroad to join the canyon's mines with the rails of the Utah Central. Vanderbilt's narrow gauge was completed before the Utah Central reached the junction, so in order to get the engine and rolling stock to the canyon they were leap-frogged across the desert on rails laid temporarily in the sand. The American Fork Railroad completed its route on November 26th, 1872 at Deer Creek, four miles below the Sultana Smelter, also built by Vanderbilt. His smelter was a first class plant and kept 20 charcoal kilns busy. Later, a second smelter was built near the mouth of the canyon.

It was near the railroad's end-of-track that the rough and tough mining camp of Forest City bloomed. It was located near the mouth of Mary Ellen Gulch, south of the Dutchman Mine, and west of Graveyard Flat. The famous author, Captain John Codman, visited Forest City while it was still being built and wrote, "Forest City is 4 miles from Miller's Hill Mine, and consists of a smelting works, charcoal furnaces and several shanties." Forest City grew considerably after Captain Codman's visit. Frank Beck ran a saloon, Worthy Nash and C.B. Hawley operated sawmills and near the mouth of the canyon Houtz & Farnsworth opened a shop, where they advertised, "An ample store of provisions for man and beast!"

Among Forest City's mine owners was Jesse Knight of Knightsville fame, who operated the Mineral Hill Tunnel. James Chipman owned the Ontario group of claims, and Matt Cullen, who later built the Cullen Hotel at Salt Lake City, managed the Yankee Mine. The Whirlwind and Silver Bell were also good producers. Ore from Forest City's mines assayed 20 to 30 ounces of silver, 40% lead and $20 in gold, besides having good values in iron and zinc. At one time 40 teams were kept busy hauling ore from its mines.

When Forest City's ore veins began pinching out, new discoveries were made higher in the canyon to take their place. Some upper canyon mines included the Pacific, Pittsburg, Utah Centennial and Belle Orphan. Because the later discoveries were made in country as mountainous and rugged as the Swiss Alps, their development was slow. Forest City couldn't wait for them and eventually went the way of all mining camps. Its narrow gauge railroad was discontinued in 1878 and the Sultana Smelter closed when the Miller's Hill Mine ran out of ore. Over the 100 years since then, Forest City has so completely disappeared that nothing is left but memories and a forgotten little cemetery on Graveyard Flat, where 40 miners and "a few Indians" are buried.

Years later an adventure story began when George Tyng reopened the Old Miller's Hill Mine and uncovered a large body of high grade ore. The winter of 1904 was particularly severe; more than 18' of snow lay on Kalamazoo Flat by December, and slides roared down the steep slopes daily. One tore right through Tyng's office building and killed him instantly. With great effort and at much risk his miner friends slid his frozen body to the canyon bottom and carried it to American Fork. There his will was opened, and in part it read, "If I should be killed in the canyon, make my grave and bury my body on the knoll in front of my cabin on Kalamazoo Flat." It was the spot where he had often sat in perfect contentment, smoking his pipe and watching the sunset.

So beloved and respected was George Tyng that his loyal miner friends strapped his broken body onto a pair of skis and pulled it back up the steep canyon through 20' of snow to Kalamazoo Flat. With snow-slides roaring down on all sides they dug his grave through the deep snow and frozen ground. When it was ready, more than 50 tough, weather-beaten miners, many red-eyed and crying, stood in the freezing cold as their friend was buried on the spot he had loved so well. A broken picket fence marks his grave today. Perhaps he knew that those golden sunsets were the real treasure of Forest City.

At the mouth of American Fork Canyon below Forest City was one of the first settlements in Utah Valley, Mountainville, which is now called Alpine. Early settlers were amazed at the chunks of pure silver Indians brought from the canyons of Mt. Timpanogos to trade for baubles or to make ornaments. But the settlers were too preoccupied to search for the source. Besides, Brigham Young had often said: "There is great mineral wealth in these mountains, I can see all kinds of ores, but the time is not yet here for it to be discovered. In due time the Lord will allow it to be found, but that time is not now!"

By the time of Young's death in 1877 the settlers were more secure on their farms, and some tried to trail the Indians to their mine. None succeeded. One old Indian, who was befriended by a man named Hall, did reveal one meager clue, but it was as much a mystery as the mine's location. The old Indian said, "You will only find it if a big fire comes, or a flood washes out of the canyon!"

Miners at Deer Trail, one of many gold camps in the Tushar Range. -Utah Historical Society-

The mine isn't far from Alpine, because the Indians could be seen entering American Fork Canyon late in the afternoon, probably to avoid being followed after dark, and would return by noon of the following day, with as much rich silver as they could carry.

There is no more likely location for a silver mine than the mountains above Alpine. Forest City boomed in American Fork Canyon during the 1870's and, just across the ridges to the north, Alta became one of the west's leading silver camps. The rich mines of Snake Creek, Brighton and Park City are all on the opposite side of the range. The geological odds of there being silver on Mt. Timpanogos are very good. If the Indians could find it, why can't you?

CLARION

Clarion was a Jewish settlement whose citizens, oddly enough, were called "Gentiles" by their Mormon neighbors. It was 3 miles north of Axtell on the Sevier River in Sanpete County. Clarion had its birth in 1910 when a group of New York and Pennsylvania businessmen, allied as the Jewish Colonial Association, purchased 6,000 acres of land on credit for $11.20 an acre. The purchase was made from the state with the intention of starting a Jewish community. Each of Clarion's citizens received 40 acres of desert wasteland, for which they were assessed $350. Their new community was to be based on farming, despite the fact that most were

merchants or artisans. That was the weak link in their plan.

They were people of means, and thus, built fine homes along wide streets and furnished them tastefully with good furniture and china. They erected a schoolhouse in 1913, a post office in 1915, and soon had 52 families. But as farmers they were failures. They simply couldn't duplicate the system of irrigation practiced by their Mormon neighbors and thus lost many of their badly needed crops. The association soon fell behind in its payments to the state. In 1916, when its debts reached $300,000, its lands were reclaimed.

The discouraged settlers soon moved away and left their homes to the mercy of the desert. Not everyone was lucky enough to start anew, for on a desolate sage covered bluff above the Sevier River two lonely tombstones bearing Hebraic inscriptions mark the last resting place for a man and a child left behind.

To reach Clarion, turn west at the theatre building in Gunnison, 7 miles north of Axtell, and go 5 miles to a dirt road that turns eastward. After 1 mile the road makes a sharp turn to the right and ends at a barbed wire fence. Clarion's cemetery is a short walk across the bare rocky ridge. In 1969, members of the American Legion at Gunnison erected a new fence around the graves. If the road is followed beyond the cemetery turnoff, several old houses can be seen. They are all that is left of Clarion, Utah's Jewish settlement.

BULLION

The Ohio Mining District was organized in 1868 on the eastern slope of Piute County's 12,000' Tushar Range. The district produced gold and silver; its best mines included the Bully Boy, Morning Star, Belcher and Union. Ore at the Copper Belt Mine assayed 13 ounces of gold and 200 ounces of silver to the ton! With such promising finds, it wasn't long before a rough mining camp grew up in Bullion Canyon. By 1872 the Bullion Townsite boasted more than 50 buildings and had. a population in the hundreds. Things looked so promising that the following year it claimed the county seat from Circleville. Every month saw more exciting discoveries made in the wild canyons of the Ohio District. It was one of those discoveries that led to Bullion's early demise.

A new camp named Webster blossomed near the Daniel Webster Mine, and it claimed part of Bullion's miners. Then, a few miles to the southwest a man named Joseph Smith discovered the outcrop which became the famous Deer Trail Mine which he found while trailing a deer. Smith's find proved to be one of the district's richest and soon a new town established there attracted even more of Bullion's citizens. The Tushar Range was a virtual treasure chest of gold lodes. The new finds kept miners busy jumping from one camp to another, rushing to every new strike or rumored bonanza.

One of the new camps was Snyder City which was one of the richest gold camps in the west. Later, it was renamed Kimberly. Bullion became a virtual ghost town, leaving Piute County without a county seat. By the end of the 1870's Bullion was only a memory, its buildings deserted and its miners gone to richer diggings. Marysvale became the new county seat.

Bullion was living proof of the fickleness of the prospector, always hurrying to new diggings that someone claims are better than the ones he's working. The following story could have originated with one of Bullion's founding breed. An old burro prospector died and went to the golden gates where he met Saint Peter. When he tried to enter Saint Peter told him, "Sorry, but our quota of prospectors is filled, you'll have to wait for an opening." The desert-wise old-timer thought it over. Knowing what an itchy-footed lot gold seekers are, he started a rumor that a rich strike had just been made in hell. In the mad rush to the new diggings, heaven was soon deserted. Somewhat amazed Saint Peter told the old prospector to come right in, that there was suddenly plenty of room. The old man hesitated, looked longingly after his partners rushing off to the nether regions, and said, "No thanks your honor. I think I'll just go on down to hell; you know, there might be some truth to that story after all!"

WEBSTER & ALUNITE

Webster was a mining camp which grew up around. the Daniel Webster Mine in Piute County. Among its earliest producers were the Great Western, Homestead, Niagera and Miner's Relief. The Piute Mining Company built one of the camp's first stamp mills. Webster had the stores, saloons, blacksmith shops and other businesses that all mining camps boasted. For awhile it looked like it might become the county seat, but Bullion seized that honor. Over the years, Webster always seemed a little bit behind Bullion.

The ore veins of the Tushar Range were tricky. Overnight a rich pay streak might end at a fault, never to be found again. Several of Webster's best mines ended that way. There was also the competition from Bullion, Deer Trail (for a time quite a promising camp), and a newcomer high in the peaks above called Snyder City. They all claimed some of Webster's roving prospectors and miners.

When Bullion was awarded the county seat and Snyder City boomed into Kimberly, Webster's days became numbered. Water flooded several of its best mines, others lost their ore veins in faulted ground. Like a derelict abandoned by its owner, Webster languished and died. The swinging doors of the honky-tonk saloons were nailed shut and soon cobwebs covered the windows.

Both Bullion and Webster are among the little out of the way places that most treasure hunters have never visited. Their forgotten buildings, now fallen from too many hard winters, are only piles of rotting lumber hidden in brushy canyon bottoms. Relics can be found in every rocky canyon and abandoned waste dump. The road starts at Marysvale and leads straight west into the Tushar Range. Get out your metal detector and get going!

At the mouth of Deer Creek Canyon below Webster City, just off US-89, south of the Big Rock Candy Mountain, are the ruins of a turn of the century mining camp and resort. Around 1900 Alunite was built on the strength of large aluminum deposits found 3 miles up Deer Creek Canyon. The new camp thrived for a short time, but when tariffs were removed from foreign imports the mines were forced to close.

One business in Alunite had a little life left in it. Winklemen's Resort, a good times place featuring a large dance hall, bar room and cabins continued to be a popular get-away long after Alunite folded up. Countless picnics and parties were held there, and coins, watches, rings and who knows what was lost at all of them. The resort came upon hard times when paved highways gave people fast access to larger towns with brighter lights.

KIMBERLY

Kimberly was queen of the Utah gold camps! Unlike many of Utah's mining camps where many basic metals were mined, Kimberly's wealth came

Kimberly, all dolled up for a celebration. -Utah Historical Society-

almost exclusively from gold. It was located near the north end of the Tushar Range in Piute County, in the shadow of 12,000′ Mt. Belknap. When it was first settled Kimberly was known as Snyder City, for William F. Snyder, owner of the pioneer Bald Mountain Mine. Snyder's mine and Charlie Lammerdorf's Sevier Consolidated, both located in the 1890's, were the town's chief producers. The Mammoth and Blue Bird mines were two other good properties. In 1899 Snyder sold the Bald Mountain Mine to Peter L. Kimberly, a wealthy Pennsylvania businessman, for $210,000. Kimberly renamed it the Annie Laurie. When its shafts were sunk into high grade gold ore, Snyder City became Kimberly, Utah's leading gold camp.

Kimberly boomed! It was the richest thing since Frisco and Silver Reef. In less than a season it featured two large hotels, the Southern and Skougaard's, the K&S Store and the Kimberly Mercantile, three saloons, a bakery, dancehall, Shepard Brothers Stage Line and two newspapers, *The Free Lance* and *The Nugget.* Kimberly's peak was in the day of the outlaw. Many a tough nut swilled whiskey over its polished bars, and a few of them spent time in its iron barred jail! That jail is now on display at the Pioneer Village at Lagoon resort, north of Salt Lake City. It was said to be the strongest jail within a hundred miles.

In 1902 the Annie Laurie Mine had 300 miners on its payroll at $3 a day. That same year Mr. Kimberly refused an offer of $5,000,000 for his mine! Gold bars 10″x10″x6″ in size were shipped on the Shepard Stages to the railroad at Sevier. One day the stagecoach overturned on the steep mountain grade and the gold bars were scattered for a half mile down the slope. The stage driver and shotgun guard recovered most of the bars. A

school boy found one the following spring before brush grew over the hillside. The Annie Laurie management did not reveal the amount of the loss, but people couldn't help noticing that their mill bosses spent a lot of time climbing up and down that hillside. There are those who say that some of the bars were never found. It wouldn't be easy, but that rocky hillside might be worth taking a second look at!

In 1905 both the Annie Laurie and the Sevier Consolidated mines were running three shifts a day, seven days a week. But unknown to miners there, Kimberly's day in the sun was coming to an end. That year Mr. Kimberly died and his mine was taken over by a British company that as one old man I talked to said, "Didn't know any more about mining than a hog knows about Sunday School!" The new owners began paying the miners in paper script which could only be redeemed at the company store, instead of the gold coins they were used to, and many of them quit in disgust.

Then, the great panic of 1907 struck. The Sevier Consolidated was deeply in debt for a million dollar mill they'd built. A Salt Lake City hardware firm eventually claimed the Annie Laurie for unpaid debts. Kimberly's mines closed and before another winter set in the once booming camp was deserted. Its deep wet shafts caved and by the time the money panic was over Kimberly was another has-been mining town.

The best way to visit it today is to drive from Sevier on US-89. Turn west 8 miles to where a mountain road forks south. You can follow it to Kimberly, over the crest of the Tushars, down Bullion Canyon past Bullion and Webster, and eventually to the highway again. It comes out just north of the Deer Trail Mine. Stop at all of them, but be sure to include Kimberly.

APPENDIX #1

In researching Utah ghost towns, many names are encountered in published works or observed on old maps which are no longer known or used. The following appendix lists those names most frequently noted, and will hopefully keep treasure hunters from seeking "lost" settlements which still exist, although by another name.

Old/Original Name	Later Name	County Location
Akin	Delta	Millard
Alfalfa	Sugarville	Millard
Allred's Settlement	Spring City	Sanpete
Alma	Flowell	Millard
Alma	Monroe	Sevier
Argenta	Brighton	Salt Lake
Arroepene	Mayfield	Sanpete
Ashley Center	Vernal	Uintah
Ashton	Pintura	Washington
Banner	Mt. Emmons	Duchesne
Ballard	Sego	Grand
Basin	Miner's Basin	Grand
Battle Creek	Pleasant Grove	Utah
Bellview	Pintura	Washington
Bennington	Leeds	Washington
Berryville	Glendale	Kane
Bingham Junction	Midvale	Salt Lake
Blake	Green River	Emery
Blue Valley	Giles	Wayne
Bonanza	Silver Reef	Washington
Bonneville	North Ogden	Weber
Box Elder	Brigham City	Box Elder
Brock	Harper	Emery
Brownsville	Ogden	Weber
Bueno	Plainfield	Grand
Buhl	Bauer	Tooele
Buncetown	Sterling	Sanpete
Burch Creek	South Ogden	Weber
Burtner	Delta	Millard
Butterfield	Herriman	Salt Lake
Buttermilk Fort	Holden	Millard
Cameron	Royal	Carbon
Camp Victory	Rozel	Box Elder
Canal Creek	Chester	Sanpete
Cannon	Cornish	Cache
Carbon	Heiner	Carbon
Carcass Creek	Grover	Wayne
Carson	Elmo	Emery
Cedar Mesa	Coal City	Carbon
Cedar Springs	Holden	Millard
Center Creek	Parowan	Iron
Central City	Alta	Salt Lake
Centre	Ajax	Tooele
Chambers	Manila	Daggett
Chicken Creek	Levan	Juab
Cleveland	Spry	Garfield
Clinton	Birdseye	Utah
Coal Creek	Cedar City	Iron
Coalville	Wales	Sanpete
Cookesville	Grouse Creek	Box Elder
Coonville	Bacchus	Tooele
Connor City	Corinne	Box Elder
Corn Creek	Kanosh	Millard
Cottonwood	Harrisburg	Washington
Coveville	Cove	Cache
Coyote	Antimony	Garfield
Crandall	Rockport	Summit
Crystal	Flowell	Millard
Cuneal	Bennett	Uintah
David City	Lehi	Utah
Deadfall	Blue Creek	Box Elder
Deep Creek	Ibapah	Tooele
Detroit	Joy	Juab
Dobieville	Fairfield	Utah
Draper	Freedom	Sanpete
Drum	Joy	Juab
Dry Creek	Lehi	Utah
East Jordan	Midvale	Salt Lake
Easton/East Weber	Uintah	Weber
Elkhorn	Hailstone	Wasatch
Elk Horn Springs	Enoch	Iron
Enoch City	Rockport	Summit
Evansville	Lehi	Utah
Ewell	Spring Glen	Carbon
Flaxville	Mantua	Box Elder
Floral	Pleasant Dale	Wayne
Fort Bueneventura	Ogden	Weber
Fort Hamilton	Mount Pleasant	Sanpete
Fort Louisa	Parowan	Iron
Fort Sidon	Hamilton Fort	Iron
Fort Utah	Provo	Utah
Franklin	Murray	Salt Lake
Frogtown	Fairfield	Utah
Garland	West Weber	Weber
Geneva	Mantua	Box Elder
George Creek	Yost	Box Elder
Gibson	Consumers	Carbon
Glencove	Veyo	Washington
Gleen's Cove	Glenwood	Sevier
Graball	Scipio	Millard
Graham	Alton	Kane
Grant's Station	Burmeister	Tooele
Grass Valley	Koosharem	Sevier
Grayson	Blanding	San Juan
Great Western	Coal City	Carbon
Hammond	Monticello	San Juan
Hampton	Collinston	Cache
Hay Town	Portage	Box Elder
Henderson	Osiris	Garfield
Hobble Creek	Springville	Utah
Hog Wallow	Gunnison	Sanpete
Houston	Widtsoe	Garfield
Huffdale	Upton	Summit
Indian Creek	Carlisle	San Juan
Inverary	Central	Sevier
Jack Thompson's Settlement	Riverdale	Weber
Johnson's Settlement	Enoch	Iron
Johnson's Settlement	Clover	Tooele
Junction City	Kolmar	Box Elder
Kennedyville	Argyle	Rich
Kingsville	Clawson	Emery
Lake City	American Fork	Utah
Leamington Hill	Lynndyl	Millard
Leesburg	Sterling	Sanpete
Lewis Allen	Manila	Daggett
Lewiston	Mercur	Tooele
Liberty	Latuda	Carbon
Liberty	Tridell	Uintah
Lick Skillet	Tonaquint	Washington
Little Valley	Mantua	Box Elder
Loseeville	New Clifton	Garfield
Lost Creek	Croyden	Morgan
Lower Ferron	Molen	Emery
McArthursville	American Fork	Utah
McPherson's Flat	Anderson	Washington
Meadow Creek	Faust	Tooele
Merrill	Naples	Uintah
Meyo	Moroni	Sanpete
Mill Creek	Slaterville	Weber
Miller's Settlement	Farmington	Davis
Millville	Delta	Millard
Mill Ward	Bennett	Uintah
Moffatt	Gusher	Uintah

APPENDIX

Morrissey	Sulphurdale	Beaver
Morris Town	South Weber	Weber
Mountainville	Alpine	Utah
Mount Nebo	Elberta	Utah
Muddy Creek	Emery	Emery
Muskrat	Hooper	Weber
Neslan	Sego	Grand
Neversweat	Sigurd	Sevier
Neversweat	Tonaquint	Washington
North Bend	Fairview	Sanpete
North Cottonwood	Farmington	Davis
North Willow Creek	Willard	Box Elder
Oak Creek	Springdale	Washington
Oak Springs Bench	Coal City	Carbon
Ogden Center	Home Of Truth	San Juan
Omaha	Sugarville	Millard
Omni	Annabella	Sevier
Orton	Spry	Garfield
Pancake	Greenville	Beaver
Panther	Heiner	Carbon
Parker's Camp	Monument	Box Elder
Pentes	Pinto	Washington
Petersburg	Hatton	Millard
Petty Town	Sterling	Sanpete
Pilot Peak	Lucin	Box Elder
Pine Creek	Ephraim	Sanpete
Pocketville	Virgin	Washington
Pond Town	Salem	Utah
Porter Springs	Perry	Box Elder
Post Of Beaver	Fort Cameron	Beaver
Poverty Flat	Torrey	Wayne
Pratt's Siding	Helper	Carbon
Quincy	Iosepa	Tooele
Rabbit Gulch	Fruitland	Duschesne
Rhoades Valley	Kamas	Summit
Richville	Mills Junction	Tooele
Rochester	Moore	Emery
Rolapp	Royal	Carbon
Round Valley	Heber	Wasatch
Round Valley	Scipio	Millard
Roweville	Bothwell	Box Elder
Ruby Hollow	Eureka	Juab
Sahara	Zane	Iron
Salt Creek	Nephi	Juab
Salt Creek	Warren	Weber
Salt Springs	Henefer	Summit
Sand Ridge	Clearfield	Davis
Sand Town	Goshen	Utah
Seldom Stop	Tonaquint	Washington
Session's Settlement	Bountiful	Davis
Shoebridge	Tintic Mills	Juab
Silver Lake	Brighton	Salt Lake
Slagtown	Martinsville	Tooele
Snyder City	Kimberly	Piute
South Bend	Monroe	Sevier
South Plymouth	Fielding	Box Elder
South Willow Creek	Draper	Salt Lake
Spring Creek	Providence	Cache
Spud Valley	Escalante	Garfield
Squaretown	Plymouth	Box Elder
Summit	Clinton	Davis
Summit Creek	Santaquin	Utah
Taylor's Mill	Riverdale	Weber
Tebbsville	Spry	Garfield
Theodore	Duchesne	Duchesne
Thompson's Springs	Anabella	Sevier
Three Mile Creek	Perry	Box Elder
Twelve Mile Creek	Mayfield	Sanpete
Twenty Wells	Grantsville	Tooele
Uintah Springs	Fountain Green	Juab
Unionville	Hoytsville	Summit
Upper Castle Dale	Orangeville	Emery
Upper Kanab	Alton	Kane
Utah Brewery	Rockwell's Station	Salt Lake
Verdi	Sunnyside	Carbon
Vermillion	Sigurd	Sevier
Wallville	Venice	Sevier
Warm Creek	Fayette	Sanpete
Weber City	Peterson	Morgan
Wheeler	Grafton	Washington
White River	Ignacio	Uintah
Willow Bend	Aurora	Sevier
Willow Creek	Mona	Juab
Willow Springs	Callao	Juab
Wilmoth	Lyman	Wayne
Winder	Widtsoe	Garfield
Winn	Talmage	Duchesne
Winsor	Mount Carmel	Kane

APPENDIX #2

Many old maps of the Utah Territory show counties that no longer exist. To aid the ghost-towner, a list of those counties and their disposition follows.

Carson County	Established in 1854 and transferred to Nevada in 1861. Named for Kit Carson, famed explorer and frontiersman.
Humboldt County	Established in 1856 and transferred to Nevada in 1861. Named for Baron Von Humboldt, a well-known scientist of the day.
St. Marys County	Established in 1856 and transferred to Nevada in 1861. Named for Mary Ogden, Indian wife of Peter Skene Ogden, an early day fur trapper.
Green River County	Established in 1852 and transferred to the Wyoming Territory in 1868. Named for the Green River.
Cedar County	Established in 1856 and absorbed by Utah County in 1862. Named for the abundance of cedar trees found there.
Desert County	Established in 1852 and absorbed by Tooele County in 1862. Named for the Great Salt Lake Desert.
Greasewood County	Established in 1856 and absorbed by Box Elder County in 1862. Named for the greasewood, one of the few shrubs able to grow in its alkali soil.
Little Salt Lake County	Established in 1850 but later renamed Iron County. First named for the Salt Lake and later for the iron ore deposits found there.
Richland County	Established in 1864 but later renamed Rich County, for Charles Rich, an early Mormon leader who settled there.
Rio Virgin County	Established in 1869 and absorbed by Washington County in 1872. Named for Thomas Virgin, an early fur trapper, and the Virgin River.
Shambip County	Established in 1856 and absorbed by Tooele County in 1862. Named for an Indian word meaning rush, for the bulrushes which once thrived around the shores of Rush Lake.

LOST MINES & TREASURES

INDEX